Congress and the Cold War

This book provides the first historical interpretation of the congressional response to the entire Cold War. Using a wide variety of sources, including several manuscript collections opened specifically for this study, the book challenges the popular and scholarly image of a weak Cold War Congress, in which the unbalanced relationship between the legislative and executive branches culminated in the escalation of the U.S. commitment in Vietnam, which in turn paved the way for a congressional resurgence best symbolized by the passage of the War Powers Act in 1973.

Instead, understanding the congressional response to the Cold War requires a more flexible conception of the congressional role in foreign policy, focused on three facets of legislative power: the use of spending measures, the internal workings of a Congress increasingly dominated by subcommittees, and the ability of individual legislators to affect foreign affairs by changing the way that policymakers and the public considered international questions.

Robert David Johnson is a professor of history at Brooklyn College and the Graduate Center of the City University of New York. He has published three books: *The Peace Progressives and American Foreign Policy* (1995); *Ernest Gruening and the American Dissenting Tradition* (1998); and *20 January 1961: The American Dream* (1999). He is the editor of a fourth book: *On Cultural Ground: Essays in International History* (1994). Professor Johnson has published articles or essays in *Diplomatic History, Journal of Cold War Studies, Oxford Companion to American History, International History Review,* and *Political Science Quarterly*, among others.

Congress and the Cold War

ROBERT DAVID JOHNSON
Brooklyn College

CAMBRIDGE
UNIVERSITY PRESS

CAMBRIDGE UNIVERSITY PRESS
Cambridge, New York, Melbourne, Madrid, Cape Town, Singapore, São Paulo

Cambridge University Press
40 West 20th Street, New York, NY 10011-4211, USA

www.cambridge.org
Information on this title: www.cambridge.org/9780521821339

First published 2006

Printed in the United States of America

A catalog record for this publication is available from the British Library.

Library of Congress Cataloging in Publication Data

Johnson, Robert David, 1967–
Congress and the Cold War / Robert David Johnson.
    p.   cm.
Includes bibliographical references and index.
ISBN-13: 978-0-521-82133-9 (hardback)
ISBN-10: 0-521-82133-9 (hardback)
ISBN-13: 978-0-521-52885-6 (pbk.)
ISBN-10: 0-521-52885-2 (pbk.)
1. United States – Foreign relations – 1945–1989.   2. Cold War.
3. United States. Congress – History – 20th century.   4. Legislative oversight –
United States – History – 20th century.   I. Title.
E840.J635   2006
327.73′009′045–dc22   2005008108

ISBN-13   978-0-521-82133-9 hardback
ISBN-10   0-521-82133-9 hardback

ISBN-13   978-0-521-52885-6 paperback
ISBN-10   0-521-52885-2 paperback

Contents

Abbreviations Used in the Text

ABM	Anti-ballistic missile
ACDA	Arms Control and Disarmament Agency
ADA	Americans for Democratic Action
AEC	Atomic Energy Commission
AID	Agency for International Development
AIPAC	America Israel Public Affairs Committee
AWACS	Airborne Warning and Control System
CIA	Central Intelligence Agency
CR	*Congressional Record*
D	Democrat
DCI	Director of Central Intelligence
ESSFRC	*Executive Sessions of the Senate Foreign Relations Committee*
FBI	Federal Bureau of Investigation
FMS	Foreign Military Sales
FNLA	National Front for the Liberation of Angola
FPD	Foreign Policy Defense
FRUS	*Papers Relating to the Foreign Relations of the United States*
HUAC	House Un-American Activities Committee
ICBM	Inter-continental ballistic missile
IPA	International Police Academy
IPR	Institute of Pacific Relations
JCAE	Joint Committee on Atomic Energy
JCS	Joint Chiefs of Staff
JEC	Joint Economic Committee
MAD	Mutually Assured Destruction
MaRV	Maneuverable reentry vehicle
MCPL	Members of Congress for Peace through Law
MIRV	Multiple independently targeted reentry vehicles
MPLA	Popular Movement for the Liberation of Angola

NCPAC	National Conservative Political Action Committee
NLF	National Liberation Front
NSC	National Security Council
PIS	Preparedness Investigating Subcommittee
PRC	People's Republic of China
PSI	Permanent Subcommittee on Investigations
R	Republican
SALT	Strategic Arms Limitation Treaty
SHAFR	Society for Historians of American Foreign Relations
SISS	Senate Internal Security Subcommittee
START	Strategic Arms Reduction Treaty
UN	United Nations
UNITA	National Union for the Total Independence of Angola

Acknowledgments

As with all of my scholarship, my greatest thanks goes to my parents, J. Robert Johnson and Susan McNamara Johnson; my sister, Kathleen Johnson; and my brother-in-law, Mike Sardo, each of whom was involved with this project from its inception and assisted me in countless ways. Kathleen and Mike even undertook research assistance in the Carolinas when I needed it.

My Harvard advisers, Akira Iriye and Ernest R. May, provided the intellectual foundation for my career in academia, Akira with his emphasis on the power of ideas and the varieties of internationalism in understanding U.S. foreign policy, Ernest with his calls for historians to develop a more complex analysis of the American state's inner workings. This project would not have been possible without the personal and intellectual support of Alan Brinkley, Tom Schwartz, Frank Ninkovich, John Milton Cooper, and Lloyd Ambrosius.

Over the past several years, I have benefited from the friendship of Abigail Rosenthal, whose husband, Jerry Martin of the American Council of Trustees and Alumni, has helped me in many important ways. Jerry and ACTA's Anne Neal arranged for a generous grant that covered expenses for research trips to several manuscript collections (those of John Tunney, John Culver, Samuel Stratton, and Thomas Downey) that were specifically opened for me. Congressman Downey not only gave me full access to his papers but also time for a personal interview.

At Cambridge University Press, Lew Bateman has supported my scholarly endeavors for as long as I can remember. I am fortunate to have as an editor someone like him, who has made a reputation as a patron for scholars trained in political and diplomatic history. Ciara McLaughlin offered patient assistance to my questions in preparing this manuscript.

The historical offices of both chambers of Congress are concrete examples of how government funds can improve the study of American political

institutions. Ken Kato of the House Office of History and Preservation provided keen insights on a draft of the manuscript; without his unfailingly
helpful suggestions, I would have missed many necessary political science
works. All historians of Congress, meanwhile, owe an enormous debt to the
Senate Historical Office's Don Ritchie, who has overseen publication of the
invaluable *Executive Sessions of the Senate Foreign Relations Committee*
series as well as the Senate Historical Office's collection of oral histories. As
he had for my previous books, Don critiqued a draft of this manuscript.

As a professor at the City University of New York, I am fortunate to work
at an institution replete with examples of appropriate academic leadership.
Chancellor Matthew Goldstein has fostered a renaissance at the university
with his emphasis on quality and the need for a faculty that values research.
Trustees Jeffrey Wiesenfeld, Randy Mastro, and Kay Pesile have worked
consistently to improve standards at CUNY.

During the writing of this book, I met two people who gave me a crash
course in how lawyers at the top of their profession use government documents, and in the process I dramatically improved my skills as a historian.
Vice Chancellor Rick Schaffer is the model of integrity in the CUNY General
Counsel's office. And I cannot say enough about my attorney, Bob Rosen –
a friend whose remarkable intellect yielded editorial guidance that I often
found myself recalling in writing this book.

At Brooklyn College, I teach a variety of electives in political, legal,
and diplomatic history – what some have called the study of "figures in
power." I have found students strongly receptive to studying this kind of
history, and I have learned a great deal from them in turn. This book
would not have appeared without the efforts of Dan Weininger, Christine
Sciascia, Brad Appell, Isaac Franco, Martine Jean, Yehuda Katz, Ryan Sacks,
Mike Duchaine, Jenna Schlanger, Bobby Hardamon, Samantha Rosenblum,
George Ionnaidis, and John Makaryus. John and Dan also served as my
research assistants – and frequently forced me to redefine how I thought
about the events detailed on the following pages.

This book is dedicated to the nine friends and colleagues who stood by me
through a very difficult period between 2001 and 2003, each at personal –
and, in some cases, professional – cost. As head of the rump lawyers' committee, David Berger offered me his wit, wisdom, and sense of perspective. Andy
Meyer never failed to lift my spirits or remind me of the positive aspects of
academic life. Instead of quietly retiring, Lenny Gordon served as my de facto
protector. Phil Napoli (and Marilyn, Abby, and Adrianna) provided a second
family in New York. Steve Remy greeted me with fairness and then with intellectual companionship. Eric Steinberg helped on a variety of levels, all while
modestly denying that he was doing anything special. The personal, professional, and intellectual integrity of Paula Fichtner never ceases to amaze
me. Finally, two colleagues, Jamie Sanders and Margaret King, endured

especially unfair behavior after they refused to compromise their principles; both, in different ways, displayed remarkable courage in the process.

I would have considered myself lucky if, at some point in my career, I had worked with even one colleague of the intellectual and personal caliber of David, Andy, Lenny, Phil, Steve, Eric, Paula, Jamie, and Margaret. That I can count all as my friends is something for which I am truly grateful.

Prologue

Diego Garcia attracted widespread national attention in 1991, when it served as the only U.S. Navy base from which offensive air operations were launched during Operation Desert Storm. Located 1,000 miles southwest of India, the 17-square-mile atoll described by *Time* as "one of those incongruous specks on the map that once posted the British Empire" passed under U.S. lease in 1966.[1] The island provided strategically placed access to the Indian subcontinent, Central Asia, and the Middle East. After the Iranian Revolution in 1979, Diego Garcia experienced the most dramatic buildup of any U.S. overseas military installation since the Vietnam War, culminating in completion of a $500 million construction project a few years before the Iraqi invasion of Kuwait.[2]

The Gulf War did not represent the first time in which Diego Garcia's fate intersected with momentous national events. In early 1974, ignoring formal protests from the governments of India, New Zealand, Australia, and Sri Lanka, the Navy requested $29 million to expand what was then a limited communications facility into the beginnings of a full-fledged military base. "In terms of political implications and potential for troublemaking," the *Baltimore Sun* noted at the time, "Diego Garcia has dimensions that warrant a full-scale congressional study."[3] A highly charged debate ensued in the House of Representatives: after New York Democrat Bella Abzug came out against the Navy's scheme, Wayne Hays indicated that while he knew little of the issue, he understood that "our presence in the Indian Ocean is going to upset Mrs. [Indira] Gandhi and ... that it upsets the gentlewoman from New York."[4] The notoriously acerbic Ohio Democrat could not "think of two better reasons to be for it."[5]

[1] *Time*, 1 April 1974.
[2] http://www.dg.navy.mil/general_info/frameset.htm, accessed 2 March 2004.
[3] *Baltimore Sun*, 9 March 1974.
[4] 120 *Congressional Record* [hereafter *CR*], 93rd Congress, 2nd session, p. 9843 (4 April 1974).
[5] 120 *CR*, 93rd Congress, 2nd session, p. 9843 (4 April 1974).

The plan's fate remained uncertain throughout the summer of 1974; opponents hoped to use the final House debate on the matter, scheduled for
August 9, to rally support from a public wary of post-Vietnam overseas commitments. This particular discussion, however, received virtually no notice,
either from the media or within the lower chamber itself, since Minority
Leader John Rhodes interrupted consideration of the measure to announce
that Richard Nixon had become the first president to resign, replaced by
Vice President Gerald Ford.[6] Robbed of public attention, the critics' amendment failed overwhelmingly. Opponents of the Navy's plan regrouped in
the Senate, however, and a conference committee between the two branches
agreed to postpone final determination of the matter for a year. Congressional scholar Barry Blechman correctly termed this procedural gambit "a
move typical of legislative decisionmaking."[7]

One of the highest-profile legislators seeking to block the Diego Garcia
expansion, Iowa senator Harold Hughes, described his comrades' philosophy as a "new internationalism," based on the "demilitarization of foreign
policy," with an increased emphasis on cultural and economic factors. This
approach would replace the bankrupt "old internationalism," which had
relied on armed intervention, secret alliances, and military bases. With little
chance that the executive would embrace this approach, the Iowa senator
reasoned, only an empowered Congress could produce a more moral foreign
policy.[8]

The new internationalists were one of two significant factions that
attempted to marshal the institutional powers of Congress to remake Cold
War foreign policy. Congressional power, in this respect, was value-neutral,
since the other bloc to pursue an ambitious legislative foreign policy role
championed a conservative nationalist agenda. In the early 1950s, the "revisionists" (in that they claimed to desire a "revision" of Cold War liberalism)
demanded a more rigorous prosecution of the Cold War at home, a greater
focus on East Asia, and recognition of the ideological dangers of aiding the
social democratic governments of Western Europe.

In the end, both the revisionists and the new internationalists failed in
their efforts, and their leading advocates paid the ultimate political price –
loss of their seats in Congress.

What commentator Walter Lippmann termed the Cold War – the diplomatic,
strategic, and ideological contest between the United States and the Soviet
Union – opened with an institutional memory of an exceptionally active and
powerful legislative branch. In 1919 and 1920, a combination of ideological
disagreements, personal rivalry, and institutional jealousy coalesced in the

---

[6] 120 CR, 93rd Congress, 2nd session, p. 27592 (9 Aug. 1974).

[7] *Washington Post*, 20 July 1975.

[8] 117 CR, 92nd Congress, 1st session, p. 15953 (19 May 1971).

successful campaign to block U.S. membership in the League of Nations, which served only as the most spectacular assertion of congressional power following World War I.[9] Shortly before the Senate considered the Treaty of Versailles, Woodrow Wilson bypassed Congress and sent American troops to revolutionary Russia, and legislators threatened the ultimate sanction: a resolution introduced by California senator Hiram Johnson to cut off funds for the intervention failed by a perilously close tie vote. What Acting Secretary of State Frank Polk termed a demonstration of the "critical spirit of Congress" convinced the administration to withdraw U.S. forces.[10] If anything, Congress assumed a more aggressive posture in the 1920s, attempting to prevent U.S. military intervention in the Caribbean Basin, and in the mid-1930s, especially through the efforts of the Nye Committee, which investigated the U.S. entrance into World War I.[11] Secretary of State Cordell Hull complained that the legislative branch, by approving the Neutrality Acts of 1935 and 1936, had usurped "the constitutional and traditional power of the Executive to conduct the foreign relations of the United States."[12]

Some common patterns guided the interwar congressional approach to foreign relations. A willingness to use roll-call votes on appropriations matters, even on issues such as military spending, enhanced Congress's constitutionally designated abilities to influence international affairs. The prevalence of treaties heightened the importance of the "advise and consent" role that the Constitution assigned to the Senate. Internally, Congress settled into a stable bureaucratic pattern in which the House of Representatives played a minor role and the Foreign Relations Committee reigned supreme in the Senate, producing a relatively small "foreign policy elite" composed of Foreign Relations Committee members and the few other senators who for personal, political, or ideological reasons exhibited intense interest in international affairs.

This structure, however, was unsustainable after World War II. The willingness of the federal government to use its financial might for foreign policy purposes forced Congress to consider the relationship between its appropriations power and international affairs. In addition, a bipartisan consensus came to interpret such undertakings as the Nye Committee and the Neutrality Acts as embodying an excessively aggressive implementation of congressional power. Finally, the advent of nuclear weapons placed the government on what amounted to a permanent war footing, spawning a new

---

[9] Lloyd Ambrosius, *Woodrow Wilson and the American Diplomatic Tradition: The Treaty Fight in Perspective* (New York: Cambridge University Press, 1987).

[10] David Foglesong, *America's Secret War against Bolshevism: U.S. Intervention in the Russian Civil War, 1917–1920* (Chapel Hill: University of North Carolina Press, 1995), pp. 71, 251.

[11] Robert David Johnson, *The Peace Progressives and American Foreign Relations* (Cambridge, MA: Harvard University Press, 1995), chapters 4–5.

[12] Wayne Cole, *Roosevelt and the Isolationists, 1932–1945* (Lincoln: University of Nebraska Press, 1983), pp. 161–178.

interpretation of constitutional theory that redefined the commander-in-chief clause to increase the president's freedom to act unilaterally. The early Cold War, accordingly, is not remembered as a period of intense congressional activism; Michigan senator Arthur Vandenberg complained at the time that issues seemed to reach the legislature only when "they have developed to a point where Congressional discretion is pathetically restricted."[13]

The reality was considerably more complex. In 1947, even as the administration was uniting behind diplomat George Kennan's containment doctrine, three foreign policy alternatives enjoyed strong support in Congress. The most tenacious opposition to the Truman Doctrine came from a small group of liberals, led by Florida senator Claude Pepper, who believed that extending military assistance to the undemocratic regimes in Greece and Turkey would contradict the internationalist ideals for which the United States fought in World War II. To the administration's right, a sizable bloc led by William Knowland in the Senate and Walter Judd in the House demanded that the administration reorient its foreign policy toward East Asia by aiding the nationalists in China's civil war. Finally, nationalists, such as the unscrupulous Pat McCarran, questioned any initiative that would threaten U.S. sovereignty and feared that an activist foreign policy would strengthen the federal government. They instead advocated concentrating on the Cold War at home by cracking down on alleged Communist sympathizers.

Truman spent most of his term addressing the consequences of this shaky base of support. He was hampered further by the era's ineffectual Democratic congressional leadership, few of whose members were entirely convinced by the merits of the containment doctrine. Working with internationalist Republicans was therefore vital: more than flattery was at stake in Dean Acheson's attempts to woo the likes of Vandenberg and his ideological colleagues, Henry Cabot Lodge and Alexander Smith. The trio chastised the administration for conceiving of containment in realpolitik terms and recommended – successfully – framing Cold War foreign policy in a manner more consistent with traditional U.S. ideals of democracy, human rights, and self-determination. The unusual breakdown of Congress thus played an important role in the early stages of the Cold War, but in a different way than has been commonly perceived. The temperaments, ideologies, and inclinations of the internationalist Republicans made them players on virtually every key issue of the day, in a bipartisan foreign policy where formal and informal powers seamlessly intersected.

In 1949 and 1950, however, a combination of events – the Communist triumph in China, the Soviet testing of an atomic bomb, Joseph McCarthy's allegations of Communist penetration of the State Department, passage of the McCarran Internal Security Act, and, most important, the outbreak of

---

[13] William Banks and Peter Raven-Hansen, *National Security Law and the Power of the Purse* (New York: Oxford University Press, 1994), p. 102.

hostilities in Korea – doomed the minimal trust between the parties upon which bipartisan foreign policy rested. The leading GOP internationalists passed from the scene (Vandenberg died in 1951, Lodge lost his seat the following year), and a radically different conception of congressional power emerged. Best captured in the approaches of Pat McCarran, Joe McCarthy, and John Bricker, the revisionists challenged Truman's authority to send troops to Europe, demanded increased legislative control over internal security measures, recommended alliances with right-wing regimes internationally, and championed a constitutional amendment to prevent treaties from superseding domestic legislation.

Eventually the group overreached: the Senate censured McCarthy in December 1954, a few months after it had rejected Bricker's proposed constitutional amendment. McCarran's death the same year removed the bloc's most powerful Democrat. The trio's effects, however, lingered long after their departure from the scene, as their activities linked the idea of enhanced congressional power with a right-wing foreign policy agenda, making liberals skittish about championing a strong Congress in international affairs.

The revisionists' collapse eliminated from the political culture the most formidable critics of what was, in many ways, a postwar constitutional revolution, characterized by the dramatic decline of congressional power over war and treaties. Ambitious members of Congress, however, pursued other avenues to influence affairs. McCarthy, for instance, was the most prominent senator to use a subcommittee to advance his own international agenda, but his activities are best viewed as part of a broader decentralization of power within Congress on national security matters. Overall, the number of foreign policy subcommittees in the Senate alone grew from 7 in 1946 to 31 two decades later, and Dwight Eisenhower's second term witnessed the establishment of 4 important subcommittees, each chaired by a contender for the 1960 Democratic presidential nomination.[14] The quartet's performance highlights the importance of looking beyond the traditional standards of measurement when analyzing the congressional role in the Cold War. The amorphous committee structure gave senators an avenue for direct influence – by facilitating informal ties with members of the national bureaucracy, by using public hearings that sought to shape the course of political debate, and by providing a vehicle for marshaling the appropriations power. In the end, subcommittee government confirmed Dean Acheson's aphorism, "The route from planning to actions leads through the committees to legislation."[15]

While its war-making and treaty-making functions atrophied in the postwar years, Congress displayed a mixed record in its third major constitutional

[14] Robert David Johnson, "Congress and the Cold War: Survey Article," *Journal of Cold War Studies* 3 (2001), pp. 77–101.
[15] Dean Acheson, *A Citizen Looks at Congress* (New York: Harper, 1957), p. 61.

venue relating to foreign policy – the appropriations power. On defense appropriations bills, little initiative appeared until the late 1960s. But congressional involvement with foreign aid was extensive from the program's inception, since overseas assistance so clearly derived from the appropriations power. Foreign aid also allowed the body in which all fiscal matters traditionally originate, the House of Representatives, to play a greater international role than was the case before World War II. Louisiana congressman Otto Passman, chair of the subcommittee with jurisdiction over the program's funding, regularly secured a reduction of 20 to 25 percent of the amount requested by the executive; in 1960, the London *Times* described Passman as "almost a law to himself on foreign aid."[16] Politically, the program's unpopularity provided such a freedom to resist executive branch policies that one Senate aide, noting that political survival dictated his boss becoming "known as an articulate critic of the Administration on at least one issue," observed that foreign aid had "so little public support that it is a tempting choice."[17]

For the early postwar period, foreign aid was primarily targeted by congressional conservatives worried about its excessive cost and the support that it provided for left-of-center regimes. As long as these conservatives remained the only opposition, a bipartisan coalition of northern Democrats and moderate Republicans ensured the program's survival. But beginning in the early 1960s, the program started coming under attack from a group that foreign aid officials labeled the "dissident liberals."[18] Senators such as George McGovern, Albert Gore, Frank Church, Wayne Morse, and Ernest Gruening contended that assistance too often had gone to dictatorial regimes solely because of their anti-Communist credentials. These legislators began offering amendments to deny aid to governments that came to power through undemocratic means, and they gradually expanded their efforts to launch an attack on military aid that veered toward repudiating Cold War liberalism itself.

This opposition occurred at a critical moment, for in the early 1960s foreign aid assumed a new importance. John Kennedy's counterinsurgency theories dictated a considerable expansion in military aid expenditures; the administration also based its boldest new international initiative, the Alliance for Progress, on a multi-year commitment of economic and military assistance to Latin America. Unfortunately for Kennedy, in 1963, Passman's conservatives and the dissident liberals formed an awkward alliance that produced what *U.S. News & World Report* described as the "foreign aid

---

[16] *The Times* (London), 17 Feb. 1960.

[17] Phil to Thomas McIntyre, 6 Oct. 1963, Box 99, Series III, Thomas McIntyre Papers, University of New Hampshire.

[18] Larry O'Brien, "Memorandum for the President," 4 Nov. 1963, Box 53, President's Office File, John Kennedy Presidential Library.

revolt."[19] In the revolt's aftermath, foreign aid bills became a favorite vehicle for policy riders on issues as diverse as human rights, expropriation of U.S.-owned property, and the international policies of recipient regimes. Commentator Robert Pastor correctly termed the annual foreign aid measure "the nearest thing Congress has to a 'State of the World Message.'"[20]

Though he continued to fulminate against the "frustrating, fanatical, frightening, and foolish" program, Passman's power waned after the 1964 death of his mentor, Appropriations Committee chairman Clarence Cannon, but the left-wing critics of foreign aid – the group that Harold Hughes later would describe as the new internationalists – gained strength as the 1960s progressed.[21] In this respect, the tactical and ideological foundation of the congressional dissent against the Vietnam War dated from the late Eisenhower and Kennedy administrations. It unified around three broad principles: first, a concern that in the passion of the Cold War, the United States had too readily endorsed policies, such as aiding dictatorial regimes, that served short-term strategic interests at the expense of traditional American ideals; second, a fear that policymakers relied on military solutions to address fundamentally political problems; and third, a suspicion, best seen in the foreign aid revolt, that the United States had overcommitted itself internationally. Tactically, the period from 1957 through 1963 suggested that Congress could most effectively influence foreign policy through the appropriations power, subcommittee government, and framing how the public considered foreign policy issues.[22]

This dissent, however, emerged when more than 20,000 U.S. troops were already on the ground in Vietnam, with the Johnson administration already well on its way toward Americanizing the conflict. Just as Lyndon Johnson tried and failed to find a middle ground on responding to deteriorating conditions in South Vietnam, so too did most members of Congress. In the process, the Vietnam War polarized the legislature, especially the Senate, while prompting increased emphasis on issues such as European affairs, military aid, and individual weapons systems that had received little legislative attention for the preceding decade.

In the altered environment, the Foreign Relations Committee renewed its influence after a period of decline. Rhode Island senator Claiborne Pell attributed the committee's remarkable power during the Nixon and

---

[19] *U.S. News & World Report*, 25 Nov. 1963.

[20] Robert Pastor, "Coping with Congress' Foreign Policy," *Foreign Service Journal* 52 (1975), pp. 83–104.

[21] Otto Passman, "To the American Taxpayer," 1 July 1971, Box 1920, George McGovern Papers, Princeton University.

[22] For more on this theme, see Michael Kirst, *Government without Passing Laws: Congress' Nonstatutory Techniques for Appropriations Control* (Chapel Hill: University of North Carolina Press, 1979).

Ford administrations to the effect of Stuart Symington, whose presence gave Foreign Relations Committee members the "tremendous advantage of...having knowledge of what was going on in Armed Services."[23] The final senator in American history to sit simultaneously on both national security committees, the Missouri Democrat arrived in the upper chamber after serving as the first secretary of the Air Force; his continued sympathies led critics to label him the "Senator from the Air Force."[24] He achieved national prominence during the Army-McCarthy hearings of 1954, when partisan Democrats hailed his willingness to take on McCarthy, who in turn ridiculed him as "Sanctimonious Stu."[25] A traditional Cold War liberal for his early tenure in the upper chamber, Symington embraced an alternative national security philosophy in the late 1960s, and thereafter developed into the legislature's most effective opponent of military spending. The Missouri senator also chaired the Cold War Congress' most significant subcommittee, the Subcommittee on Security Agreements and Commitments Abroad, which investigated U.S. commitments in Thailand, Spain, and Laos. As Henry Kissinger informed President Nixon at the time, the subcommittee "obtained from DOD, State, and field missions a vast amount of highly sensitive information," mostly of "the type that has never been given to the legislative branch in previous administrations."[26]

In these efforts, Symington transformed the congressional role in Cold War foreign policy. In 1967 hearings on foreign arms sales, he offered a concrete demonstration of the link between military aid and foreign policy. In the 1968–1969 battle against the anti-ballistic missile (ABM), the first full-fledged congressional challenge to a Pentagon weapons system, he showed that dissenters needed detailed technical knowledge of military matters if they hoped to prevail in debates on national security issues. In his inquiry into executive agreements with Spain, he uncovered how overseas bases, frequently obtained without congressional approval, brought with them broader diplomatic requirements. And in the Laotian hearings, he offered a glimpse at how secrecy could obscure not only national security material but also covert wars that were occurring without legislative sanction.

Behind all of these efforts stood a willingness to challenge executive supremacy when considering national security matters, a dramatic shift from the legislative environment of the 1950s and 1960s. The Cold War climate had not only subjected those who voted against defense spending to charges of being soft on Communism, but also the spreading of weapons contracts around the country transformed defense into an economic as well as a

---

[23] U.S. Senate, Rules Committee, *Hearings, Committee System Reorganization Amendments of 1977*, 95th Congress, 1st session, p. 114 (18 Jan. 1977).

[24] *Washington Post*, 3 April 1969.

[25] Flora Lewis, "The Education of a Senator," *Atlantic*, Dec. 1971.

[26] Henry Kissinger to Richard Nixon, 1 Oct. 1969, Box 20, White House Central File, Richard Nixon Presidential Materials Project, National Archives, II.

national security matter. (In 1968, for instance, Lockheed made 88 percent of its sales to the federal government, the comparable figure was 67 percent for General Dynamics, 75 percent for McDonnell-Douglas, 54 percent for Boeing, 62 percent for Martin-Marietta, and 67 percent for Grumman.[27]) As a result, members of Congress rarely endorsed amendments to reduce the Pentagon budget, and even less frequently supported policy riders attached to defense bills, abandoning an interwar custom. The decade between the end of the Korean War and John Kennedy's assassination featured only 22 roll-call votes – in the House and Senate combined – on amendments of any sort to defense appropriations measures. Only by overturning the institutional culture that encouraged deference to the Defense Department could a comprehensive congressional attack on the principles of containment occur.

By the early 1970s, the effects of the conflict in Vietnam, the implications of the Sino-Soviet split, skepticism about the containment theory, and the impact of the Watergate crisis weakened support for unilateral presidential initiatives and many of the anti-Communist assumptions upon which postwar executives had based their policies. In response, the new internationalists fleshed out the ideological alternative that first had appeared in the foreign aid revolt. After the 1973 military coup in Chile, representative Donald Fraser and senator Edward Kennedy opened hearings on Augusto Pinochet's human rights abuses; Congress then enacted a series of measures to end U.S. assistance to the regime. When Turkey invaded Cyprus in 1974, Thomas Eagleton pushed through an amendment cutting off military aid to the Ankara government. The most important such effort occurred in December 1975, when the Senate passed an amendment to the defense appropriations bill introduced by John Tunney terminating covert assistance to anti-Communist forces in Angola; later that winter, an amendment to the foreign aid bill sponsored by Dick Clark extended the ban. The two offerings represented the high point of a congressional revolt against the anti-Communist ethos of the Cold War and executive authority in foreign policy.

Earlier in the Cold War, revisionist aggressiveness triggered a backlash that provoked the group's ideological and political demise; a similar fate befell the new internationalists, but with one important difference. Whereas the revisionists had, by and large, failed to institutionalize their agenda through legislation, the new internationalists passed a host of structural reforms that froze into place elements of their program even after they had lost their political strength. The reaction against new internationalism therefore assumed two dimensions, with opponents seeking to tear down the group's main reforms while also developing a new congressional model for approaching international affairs. Often using tactics pioneered by the new internationalists, in the late 1970s and early 1980s anti-Communist legislators targeted such diverse measures as arms control,

[27] *Congressional Quarterly Weekly Report*, 24 May 1968, 25 March 1972.

the congressional budget process, human rights diplomacy, and intelligence oversight.

The final years of the Cold War also featured a profound shift in the internal balance of power within Congress, as, for the first time, the House emerged as the more powerful branch on international questions. In part, this change flowed from the efforts of the "Watergate class of 1974," which was concentrated in the House and whose influence peaked during the late Carter and Reagan administrations. In the 1980s, the lower chamber featured most of the talented congressional critics of Reagan's foreign policy – figures such as Tom Downey, Les AuCoin, Joseph Addabbo, and Michael Barnes, each of whom actively sought venues for using legislative power to affect U.S. foreign policy. Finally, unlike the situation in the Senate, the House leadership aimed to maximize the lower chamber's international role.

In the end, however, the House proved ill equipped to fashion a sustained alternative on foreign policy and national security issues, although members of the lower chamber put up a good fight. Sometimes they used wit: when the Reagan administration proposed a civil defense plan assuming that Boston residents could escape nuclear war by traversing over the city's always crowded streets en route to New Hampshire, Massachusetts congressman Barney Frank mused that perhaps civil defense planners could lighten traffic by persuading "the Russian military to coordinate their schedule with the Red Sox."[28] Sometimes they used the techniques of subcommittee government, especially after Addabbo assumed the chairmanship of the Defense Appropriations Subcommittee in 1979. And sometimes they used force of intellect: during one arms control debate with Downey, Alabama Republican Jack Edwards conceded that "on the subject of defense, the last thing I want to do is to get into some big debate over what he is very knowledgeable about."[29]

By the end of 1985, however, the most significant ideological and structural reforms of the new internationalists had been scaled back or replaced altogether, culminating in the repeal of the Clark amendment in July 1985. While the old order thus had been swept aside, little time existed for a new consensus to emerge. The sudden end of the Cold War shortly thereafter found the institution adrift on international affairs, poorly situated to assume a prominent position in responding to the post–Cold War world.

In 1990, the late senator Daniel Patrick Moynihan lamented, "The neglect of congressional history is something of a scandal in American scholarship."[30]

---

[28] 128 *CR*, 97th Congress, 2nd session, p. 18580 (29 July 1982).

[29] 129 *CR*, 98th Congress, 1st session, p. 13374 (23 May 1983).

[30] Daniel Patrick Moynihan, *On the Law of Nations* (Cambridge, MA: Harvard University Press, 1990), p. 50.

The ensuing 15 years has featured some progress, especially in the realm of congressional biography. For instance, studies of J. William Fulbright and Frank Church, who between them chaired the Foreign Relations Committee for all but 4 years between 1959 and 1981, impressively place their subjects within the era's broader institutional context.[31] Most other books on Congress during the Cold War focus on the struggle for constitutional supremacy between the legislative and executive branches; with the important exceptions of monographs by James Lindsay and Barry Blechman, they describe a series of events in which Congress either voluntarily yielded its power over foreign policy decisions or stood by while the executive branch usurped it.[32] According to this interpretation, the unbalanced relationship between the Congress and the executive culminated in the escalation of the U.S. commitment in Vietnam, which in turn paved the way for a congressional resurgence best symbolized by the passage of the War Powers Act in 1973.[33]

Understanding the congressional response to the Cold War, however, requires looking beyond instances where Congress did (or did not) declare war or approve treaties to examine three other facets of legislative power: the use of spending measures; the internal workings of a Congress increasingly dominated by subcommittees; and the ability of individual legislators to affect foreign affairs by changing the way that policymakers and the public thought about international questions – qualities inherently more difficult for historians to measure. Even congressional attempts to affect policy through the most tangible of these three elements, the appropriations power, often occurred in indirect ways. To take one example, in the mid-1960s, Frank Church championed ceiling amendments to the military aid program, less from an abstract desire to reduce military assistance expenditures than from a conviction that, due to the fixed nature of NATO assistance, aid to Africa and Latin America, which he considered harmful, would be the first programs cut.

In addition, as Wisconsin congressman Les Aspin once remarked, "Congress loves procedure. It's the next best thing to not having to decide

---

[31] LeRoy Ashby and Roy Gramer, *Fighting the Odds: The Life of Senator Frank Church* (Pullman: Washington State University Press, 1994); Randall Bennett Woods, *Fulbright: A Biography* (New York: Cambridge University Press, 1995).

[32] Barry Blechman, *The Politics of National Security: Congress and U.S. Defense Policy* (New York: Oxford University Press, 1990); James Lindsay, *Congress and the Politics of U.S. Foreign Policy* (Baltimore: Johns Hopkins University Press, 1994).

[33] Louis Fisher, *Presidential War Power* (Lawrence: University of Kansas Press, 1995); John Hart Ely, *War and Responsibility: Constitutional Lessons of Vietnam and Its Aftermath* (Princeton, NJ: Princeton University Press, 1993); Loch Johnson, *The Making of International Agreements: Congress Confronts the Executive* (New York: New York University Press, 1984); Michael Glennon, *Constitutional Diplomacy* (Princeton, NJ: Princeton University Press, 1990).

at all."[34] Only by recognizing the importance of procedural initiatives that superficially seemed devoid of policy content can we appreciate the myriad ways in which the legislature affected the conduct of the Cold War. In addition, as most clearly revealed in Robert Caro's stunning volume on Lyndon Johnson's tenure in the Senate, historians can explicate the role of procedural gambits in Congress only through precise, detailed descriptions of the tactics involved.[35] As with looking beyond the more traditional legislative roles in treaty and war-making, moreover, evaluating the impact of procedural initiatives requires a flexible conception of congressional power, one that focuses on intent and effect. Congressional advocates of enhanced oversight of the CIA, for instance, couched their appeals in the procedural language of fulfilling a basic legislative task, but they expected oversight to make covert operations less likely to occur.

Finally, this preference to address controversial international questions in a back-door fashion resulted in members of Congress often becoming associated with untested policy outcomes that lacked sufficient public support. Ironically, the more powerful that movements such as the new internationalists and the revisionists became, the greater the temptation to use their procedural power in ways that would accelerate their decline. What the *Wall Street Journal* termed "the crippling disease of procedure-itis" occurred when congressional blocs that opposed executive initiatives "for ideological reasons [stuck] to the procedural issues" to hide their agenda's lack of popular support.[36] By removing the built-in check associated with confronting issues openly, this preference for procedure established what amounted to a self-destruction mechanism that prevented the most ambitious of the era's legislative dissenters from achieving their goals. The outcome of the Army-McCarthy hearings provided the most spectacular illustration of how a congressional bloc's procedural success could mask a decline in its popular base, but the new internationalists suffered from a similar problem in the 1970s, when they were slow to realize how much public attitudes about cutting defense spending shifted as the decade progressed.

Iconoclast journalist I. F. Stone once labeled congressional hearings his most valuable source. Since they did not appear in print until several weeks after the event, they were of little use to daily journalists, and therefore did not shape newspaper coverage. But they often contained unexpected insights: hearings are the only forum within the American constitutional

---

[34] James Dillon, "Congressman Aspin and Defense Budget Cuts [sequel]," Kennedy School of Government Harvard University Case C14-75-022S, p. 1.

[35] Robert Caro, *The Years of Lyndon Johnson: Volume 3, Master of the Senate* (New York: Knopf, 2002).

[36] *Wall Street Journal*, 11 Feb. 1985.

structure for extemporaneous, on the record, discussion between members of one branch and policymakers from another. As if to reinforce the point, in 1974 New Jersey senator Clifford Case lectured Secretary of State Henry Kissinger about proper protocol in Foreign Relations Committee hearings, during which "testimony is given on both sides of the bench."[37] To a much greater extent than in a study centered on the executive branch, which rarely made foreign policy in the open, printed documents provide a starting point for any examination of the legislature. The foremost such source, the *Congressional Record*, forms the official record of the proceedings and debates of Congress; while technological and cultural changes have rendered floor proceedings much less substantial since the late 1970s, for most of the period covered in this book, the *Record* is of considerable use, despite members' right to revise their remarks before the document's publication.

Although congressional history involves a branch of the federal government, most archival material falls outside the National Archives system because congressional manuscript collections remain the personal property of the legislator, to deposit wherever desired. This project draws from 107 manuscript collections, of varying quality and status, deposited at 62 different archival sites from Maine to Alaska. This list does not include the collections of several key figures from the early Cold War or from the House, such as Mendel Rivers, Robert Leggett, and Joseph Ball, whose papers were lost or destroyed. Nor does it contain material from relevant current members of Congress, such as Ted Kennedy or Tom Harkin, or from former members such as Charles Percy, Bob Dole, Mark Hatfield, and Jesse Helms, who have not yet opened their papers to scholars. Contemporary journalistic accounts, oral histories, and personal interviews have compensated to the extent possible, but no doubt some aspects of the historical record have fallen through the cracks.

This book also does not claim to examine all aspects of the congressional role in post–World War II foreign policy. Policy toward certain regions, especially the Middle East, largely fell outside of the Cold War framework because of the Arab-Israeli conflict, the role of oil diplomacy, the activities of the Israeli lobby, and the emergence of terrorism in the mid-1970s. Therefore, Middle East questions receive attention only when they involved procedural reforms related to broader themes in the study – such as the legislative reactions to Dwight Eisenhower's Middle East Resolution in 1957 or Ronald Reagan's sale of AWACS planes to Saudi Arabia in 1981. Meanwhile, legislators responded to some types of international issues, notably foreign economic policy and, after 1952, immigration, almost exclusively through

[37] U.S. Senate, Foreign Relations Committee, *Hearings, Foreign Assistance Authorization*, 93rd Congress, 2nd session, p. 30 (7 June 1974).

the lens of domestic political interests, and so the study does not consider these matters.

Dean Acheson once remarked that dealings with members of Congress "follow a distinctly oriental pattern."[38] While recognizing the wisdom of the former secretary of state's comment, this book hopes to remove some of the mystery from the congressional response to the Cold War.

---

[38] Dean Acheson, *Sketches from Life of Men I Have Known* (New York: Harper's, 1961), p. 136.

Archives Consulted

Arizona State University, Tempe, Arizona
    Barry Goldwater Papers

Bates College, Lewiston, Maine
    Edmund Muskie Papers

Boise State University, Boise, Idaho
    Frank Church Papers

Boston College, Chestnut Hill, Massachusetts
    Robert Drinan Papers
    Thomas O'Neill Papers

Bowdoin College, Brunswick, Maine
    Owen Brewster Papers

Bronx Historical Society, The Bronx, New York
    Jonathan Bingham Papers

Central Michigan University, Mt. Pleasant, Michigan
    Robert Griffin Papers

Chicago Historical Society, Chicago, Illinois
    Paul Douglas Papers

Clemson University, Clemson, South Carolina
    Strom Thurmond Papers

Columbia University, New York, New York
    Herbert Lehman Papers

Cornell University, Ithaca, New York
      Thomas Downey Papers

Dakota State University, Madison, South Dakota
      Karl Mundt Papers

Duke University, Durham, North Carolina
      B. Everett Jordan Papers

Dwight Eisenhower Presidential Library, Abilene, Kansas
      Dwight Eisenhower Diaries
      Bryce Harlow Papers
      Legislative Meetings Series

Emory University, Atlanta, Georgia
      Sam Nunn Papers

Gerald Ford Presidential Library, Ann Arbor, Michigan
      Congressional Relations Office Papers
      Counselors to the President – John Marsh Files
      White House Central File

Herbert Hoover Presidential Library, West Branch, Iowa
      Bourke Hickenlooper Papers

Lyndon Johnson Presidential Library, Austin, Texas
      LBJA Papers
      Lyndon Johnson Senate Papers
      Barefoot Sanders Papers
      White House Central File
      White House Confidential File

John Kennedy Presidential Library, Boston, Massachusetts
      Congressional Liaison Office Papers
      President's Official File

Library of Congress, Washington, D.C.
      Joseph and Stewart Alsop Papers
      Edward Brooke Papers
      Tom Connally Papers
      Paul Nitze Papers
      Robert Taft, Sr. Papers
      Robert Taft, Jr. Papers
      William Allen White Papers

Lowell History Center, Lowell, Massachusetts
    Paul Tsongas Papers

Massachusetts Historical Society, Boston, Massachusetts
    Henry Cabot Lodge II Papers
    Leverett Saltonstall Papers

Middle Tennessee State University, Murfreesboro, Tennessee
    Albert Gore, Sr. Papers

Minnesota State Historical Society, St. Paul, Minnesota
    Hubert Humphrey Papers
    Walter Judd Papers
    Eugene McCarthy Papers
    Edward Thye Papers

Mississippi State University, Starkville, Mississippi
    John Stennis Papers

National Archives, Washington, D.C.
    Record Group 46: Senate Armed Services Committee Papers
    Record Group 46: Senate Disarmament Subcommittee Papers
    Record Group 46: Senate Foreign Relations Committee Papers
    Record Group 46: Carl Marcy Chronological Series
    Record Group 46: Subcommittee on Foreign Aid Expenditures Papers
    Record Group 128: Joint Committee on Atomic Energy Papers

National Archives, II, College Park, Maryland
    Record Group 59: Records of the Department of State
    Richard Nixon Presidential Materials Project

Nevada State Historical Society, Reno, Nevada
    Pat McCarran Papers

New York Public Library, New York, New York
    Charles Goodell Papers

Ohio State Historical Society, Columbus, Ohio
    John Bricker Papers
    Frank Lausche Papers

Ohio State University, Columbus, Ohio
    John Glenn Papers

Pennsylvania State Historical Society, Philadelphia, Pennsylvania
    Joseph Clark Papers

Princeton University, Princeton, New Jersey
    George McGovern Papers
    H. Alexander Smith Papers

Rutgers University, New Brunswick, New Jersey
    Clifford Case Papers

Southwestern University, Georgetown, Texas
    John Tower Papers

Swarthmore College Peace Collection, Swarthmore, Pennsylvania
    Committee for a Sane Nuclear Policy (SANE) Papers

Texas Tech University, Lubbock, Texas
    George Mahon Papers

Harry Truman Presidential Library, Independence, Missouri
    Stephen Springarn Papers

United States Senate Historical Office, Washington, DC
    Oral History Collections

University of Alaska-Fairbanks, Fairbanks, Alaska
    Ernest Gruening Papers

University of Arkansas, Fayetteville, Arkansas
    J. William Fulbright Papers

University of California-Berkeley, Berkeley, California
    William Knowland Papers
    Thomas Kuchel Papers
    John Tunney Papers

University of Colorado, Boulder, Colorado
    Gordon Allott Papers
    Gary Hart Papers
    Floyd Haskell Papers

University of Connecticut, Storrs, Connecticut
    Robert Giaimo Papers

University of Delaware, Newark, Delaware
    John Williams Papers

University of Georgia, Athens, Georgia
    Richard Russell Papers

University of Idaho, Moscow, Idaho
    James McClure Papers

University of Iowa, Iowa City, Iowa
    Dick Clark Papers
    John Culver Papers
    Harold Hughes Papers

University of Kentucky, Lexington, Kentucky
    John Sherman Cooper Papers

University of Louisiana-Monroe, Monroe, Louisiana
    Otto Passman Papers

University of Missouri, Columbia, Missouri
    Thomas Eagleton Papers
    Thomas Hennings Papers
    James Kem Papers
    Stuart Symington Papers

University of Nevada, Reno, Nevada
    Eva Adams Papers

University of New Hampshire, Durham, New Hampshire
    Thomas McIntyre Papers

University of North Carolina, Chapel Hill, North Carolina
    Gordon Gray Papers

University of Oregon, Eugene, Oregon
    Maurine Neuberger Papers
    Richard Neuberger Papers
    Wayne Morse Papers

University of Rochester, Rochester, New York
    Samuel Stratton Papers

University of South Dakota, Vermillion, South Dakota
  James Abourezk Papers

University of Stony Brook, Stony Brook, New York
  Jacob Javits Papers

University of Vermont, Burlington, Vermont
  George Aiken Papers

University of Washington, Seattle, Washington
  Brock Adams Papers
  Henry Jackson Papers
  Warren Magnuson Papers

Western Reserve Historical Society, Cleveland, Ohio
  Stephen Young Papers

Wisconsin State Historical Society, Madison, Wisconsin
  Americans for Democratic Action Papers
  Gaylord Nelson Papers
  William Proxmire Papers
  Alexander Wiley Papers

Yale University, New Haven, Connecticut
  Chester Bowles Papers
  Walter Lippmann Papers

Congress and the Cold War

I

Constructing a Bipartisan Foreign Policy

Serious congressional planning for the postwar world dated from Senate consideration of the B_2H_2 resolution in 1943. Named for its original four sponsors – Joseph Ball (R-Minnesota), Harold Burton (R-Ohio), Carl Hatch (D-New Mexico), and Lister Hill (D-Alabama) – the resolution sought to commit the United States to membership in a postwar international organization that included a police power. When Foreign Relations Committee chairman Tom Connally (D-Texas) countered with a vaguely worded offering that urged U.S. membership in a postwar "international authority" of "free and sovereign nations," a Senate debate about how the United States should respond to the postwar environment erupted.

Connally chaired the "Committee of Eight," a special subcommittee created to institutionalize informal cooperation between the administration and the Senate and thereby avoid the institutional tensions that had doomed the Treaty of Versailles in 1919.[1] The thin-skinned Connally, faced with legitimate questions about his resolution's unclear wording, complained about the "debate degenerating into a heckling of the chairman of the committee"; Allen Drury, who covered the wartime Senate for the *New York Times*, perceived that "the gap between the Foreign Relations chairman and the Senate which he must persuade is becoming steadily wider."[2] The Texas senator's political and personal shortcomings highlighted the significance of Michigan senator Arthur Vandenberg, who Francis Wilcox, the Foreign Relations Committee's chief of staff, termed the "indispensable element" in the Senate's response to postwar foreign policy.[3] A newspaperman before his election to the Senate, Vandenberg gradually abandoned his isolationism after

---

[1] Robert Divine, *Second Chance: The Triumph of Internationalism in America during World War II* (New York: Atheneum, 1967), pp. 53–88.
[2] 89 CR, 78th Congress, 1st session, p. 8672 (25 Oct. 1943); Allen Drury, *A Senate Journal, 1943–1945* (New York: McGraw-Hill, 1963), entry for 11 Jan. 1945, p. 337.
[3] Francis Wilcox oral history, U.S. Senate Historical Office.

Pearl Harbor; by 1943, the Michigan Republican reasoned that "detailed specifications" about the U.S. role in the postwar world needed to "await tomorrow's realities," leaving the committee resolution's vagueness "a sense of strength rather than of weakness for the moment."[4]

The B_2H_2 forces, however, dominated Senate debate. Ball, described by Allen Drury as "an effective-looking character," with "his gray hair at 40, his massive size, his rugged face, and his Gary Cooper bashfulness," argued that the constitutionally protected ability of the upper chamber to offer advice on treaties "can have value only to the extent that [the advice] is clear and specific to the greatest degree we can make it so."[5] Addressing the issue from more of an anti-imperialist angle, Claude Pepper (D-Florida) noted that the Connally Resolution's wording could have authorized the Congress of Vienna or a postwar three-power alliance between the United States, the USSR, and Great Britain. Over the initial days of debate, applause frequently greeted addresses by the B_2H_2 senators.[6]

With the B_2H_2 forces envisioning a postwar foreign policy based on a crusading internationalism, conservatives started questioning the basis of any postwar organization. Eugene Millikin (R-Colorado) ridiculed Pepper's advocacy of an "ideological" alliance of democratic states; Harlan Bushfield (R-South Dakota) charged that the B_2H_2 senators "propose to remake the world."[7] The resolution's most powerful opponent was Robert Taft, the Ohio Republican who had led the attack against FDR's prewar foreign policy. The son of former President and Chief Justice William Howard Taft, the Ohio senator critiqued the B_2H_2 advocates' demand that "we should obtain a commitment to the most extreme form of international control before people have thought about the question."[8] Who would control the international police force? Would a postwar international organization be divided into differing branches? How could the great powers achieve the disarmament necessary as a precondition to establishing such a force? Though Ball dismissed such criticisms as obstructionism, Taft veered increasingly toward an attack not only on B_2H_2 but on U.S. participation in a less ambitious international organization.[9]

With debate spinning out of control, the president persuaded Connally to offer a substitute resolution that simply praised the work of Secretary of State Cordell Hull at the 1943 Moscow Conference of foreign ministers. As would occur with similar postwar resolutions, the political and

---

[4] 89 *CR*, 78th Congress, 1st session, pp. 8664–8667 (25 Oct. 1943).

[5] 89 *CR*, 78th Congress, 1st session, p. 8678 (25 Oct. 1943); Drury, *A Senate Journal*, entry for 4 Sept. 1944, p. 259.

[6] *New York Times*, 26 Oct. 1943.

[7] 89 *CR*, 78th Congress, 1st session, pp. 8798 (27 Oct. 1943), 8897 (29 Oct. 1943).

[8] Robert Taft, "Statement on the Ball Resolution," Box 619, Robert Taft, Sr. Papers, Library of Congress.

[9] Joseph Ball to William Allen White, 28 May 1943, Box 77, William Allen White Papers, Library of Congress.

international conditions under which the Senate considered the substitute – after Hull already had completed his work – made it almost impossible to oppose the bill without repudiating executive commitments.[10] But while Roosevelt's gambit temporarily blocked extended discussion about postwar internationalism, the alternatives to mainstream foreign policy would not be so easy to squelch.

Roosevelt's success in preempting congressional debate culminated in the administration's shepherding of the UN treaty through the Senate, but his presidency left unresolved fundamental questions about how Congress would approach the postwar world. Of course, ideological and institutional confusion on foreign policy was not confined to the Congress at the time. The sudden end of the Pacific War left the United States dominant in Japan, but on the Asian continent, matters were considerably less settled – in China, Korea, and Southeast Asia. The Soviets, intransigent regarding Germany's future, consolidated their control over Rumania, Bulgaria, and, ignoring Yalta's requirement of free elections, Poland. In Western Europe, Communist parties scored well in Italian and French elections, while the British Labour government experienced a major financial crisis. Harry Truman's administration struggled to develop a coherent response to this international turbulence, but world events eventually pulled the United States into a more consistent policy. One sign came when Truman warned the Soviets about the need to withdraw from Iran; another came in the administration's decision to extend a government loan to financially strapped Britain in 1946.

The British loan debate demonstrated that the ideological divisions apparent in 1943 persisted, though with some important distinctions. Soviet conduct and growing domestic anti-Communist sentiment eroded internationalist strength.[11] With senators such as Ball and Hatch retreating from their wartime positions, Claude Pepper emerged as the unquestioned internationalist spokesman. The Florida senator remains best known for his House service in the 1980s, as a powerful advocate for the nation's elderly. His political career began, however, in 1936, as the Senate's "boy orator." Before World War II, Pepper sponsored the first Lend-Lease bill; during the conflict, he championed a foreign policy oriented around the principles of the Atlantic Charter. Individual meetings with Soviet premier Josef Stalin and Czech president Eduard Beneš in 1945 convinced him that U.S.-USSR cooperation could continue into the postwar world.[12]

---

[10] Divine, *Second Chance*, pp. 93–113; William Banks and Peter Raven-Hansen, *National Security Law and the Power of the Purse* (New York: Oxford University Press, 1994), p. 102; Philip Briggs, "Congress and Collective Security: The Resolutions of 1943," *World Affairs* 132 (1970), pp. 332–344.

[11] 92 CR, 79th Congress, 2nd session, p. 3088 (4 April 1946).

[12] Claude Pepper, *Pepper: Eyewitness to a Century* (San Diego: Harcourt, Brace, Jovanovich, 1987), p. 83.

In what one colleague termed an "intolerant attack on the British," Pepper critiqued the loan from an anti-imperialist perspective, wondering about the purposes to which London would put the money, given its pattern of "exploitation of little countries."[13] (He cited Jordan, Iraq, Hong Kong, and India as examples.) The Florida senator most worried, however, about the anti-Soviet justifications utilized by colleagues such as Vandenberg. From his perspective, the Soviets keeping troops in Iran was no worse than the British doing likewise in Iraq or the Dutch resisting Indonesian independence. He reminded the Senate that the Soviets had killed more Germans in World War II than the rest of the Allied nations combined, and he speculated that an anti-Soviet foreign policy would transform the United Nations from an agency of peace into a guarantor of the status quo.

Pepper's comments symbolized unease among Senate leftists with the general state of postwar foreign policy. With support from prominent figures outside the administration, such as former First Lady Eleanor Roosevelt and former undersecretary of state Sumner Welles, the internationalists, the London *Times* realized, posed the "one formidable challenge" to Truman's handling of world affairs.[14] Glen Taylor (D-Idaho) criticized the administration for supporting anti-Communist movements in Yugoslavia and Poland; he contended that both included former fascists.[15] Robert La Follette, Jr. (Progressive-Wisconsin) chastised Truman for not disarming quickly enough, thus compounding the "hang-over of war."[16] And Pepper wondered why, if the president wanted to find a foreign nation to demonize, Truman did not focus on Spain, where the ouster of Francisco Franco represented the "hope of democratic-minded people all over the world."[17] Increasingly, the unreconstructed internationalists suffered for their positions: newspapers such as the *Washington Post* cast doubts upon Pepper's loyalty; Taylor's standing deteriorated within the Idaho Democratic Party; and La Follette's anti-militarism played a role in his defeat by a previously little-known World War II veteran, Joseph McCarthy, in the 1946 Republican primary.[18]

With the internationalists on the defensive, the focus of congressional opposition to Truman's foreign policy shifted to the right. A group of conservatives, dubbing themselves "revisionists," claimed that they wanted to revise, rather than reject, the administration's international approach. Owen Brewster (R-Maine) charged that the loan to Britain would subsidize British socialism, a charge echoed by Homer Capehart (R-Indiana) and William

---

[13] 92 *CR*, 79th Congress, 2nd session, p. 3087 (4 April 1946).
[14] *The Times* (London), 11 Nov. 1946.
[15] 92 *CR*, 79th Congress, 2nd session, pp. 4460–4461 (4 May 1946).
[16] 92 *CR*, 79th Congress, 2nd session, p. 6219 (4 June 1946).
[17] 92 *CR*, 79th Congress, 2nd session, p. 6210 (4 June 1946).
[18] *Washington Post*, 3 April 1946.

Knowland (R-California).[19] While revisionist amendments – such as a Knowland offering to release the funds only if the U.S. government was not running a budget deficit or a Capehart proposal to allow the British to use loan funds solely to offset an unfavorable trade balance with the United States – lost overwhelmingly, they did reveal the group's desire to reconcile foreign policy initiatives with their domestic vision. We commonly think of Cold War foreign policy blending the foreign and domestic through liberals' embrace of an anti-Communist foreign policy, which then distorted their domestic viewpoint.[20] Yet the first clear linkage actually occurred through the revisionists' emphasis on constructing anti-Soviet international initiatives in such a way to satisfy their domestic agenda.

British officials, saying that they were not "inclined to risk further debate with Congress," informed the State Department of their willingness to renegotiate the loan.[21] They need not have worried: Vandenberg, embracing the Cold War consensus for which he would become famous, dominated the debate. The Michigan senator saw no choice but to pass the resolution; he cautioned colleagues to learn from the Munich Conference and avoid a foreign policy based on appeasement.[22] The loan sailed through both chambers of Congress.

While the Senate debated internationalism, Congress was also modernizing its internal structure, with a goal of addressing international affairs more effectively. In early 1946, a joint committee co-chaired by La Follette and Representative Mike Monroney (D-Oklahoma) recommended reducing the number of standing committees from 33 to 16 in the Senate and from 48 to 18 in the House, so as to allow more specialization and enhance oversight. The joint committee also called for more clearly delineating committee jurisdiction and providing more money for congressional staff.[23] Translated into law with the Legislative Reorganization Act of 1946, these proposals set the stage for a radically different congressional approach to international affairs. The Military Affairs and Naval Affairs committees, which had rarely focused on policy matters, were consolidated into one committee, Armed Services, which received oversight of the entire defense apparatus. Of the 61 members of the two previous committees, only 35 received slots on Armed Services.[24] The bill also provided the tools – if not, necessarily, the will – for effective

[19] 92 *CR*, 79th Congress, 2nd session, p. 4493 (6 May 1946).
[20] Steven Gillon, *Politics and Vision: The ADA and American Liberalism, 1947–1985* (New York: Oxford University Press, 1987).
[21] John Terrence Rourke, "Congress and the Cold War: Congressional Influence on the Foreign Policy Process" (Ph.D. diss., University of Connecticut, 1974), p. 163.
[22] 92 *CR*, 79th Congress, 2nd session, p. 4080 (22 April 1946).
[23] Roger Davidson, "The Advent of the Modern Congress: The Legislative Reorganization Act of 1946," *Legislative Studies Quarterly* 15 (1990), pp. 357–373.
[24] George Galloway, "The Origins of the Legislative Reorganization Act of 1946," *Political Science Quarterly* 45 (1951), p. 42.

oversight and investigation: before 1946, each member of Congress received funds only for a secretary, most committee staffs consisted of only clerks, and senators and congressmen relied on their own research or material from outside interests when challenging the executive viewpoint on international matters.[25]

Political scientists speak of two types of congressional power brokers – policy entrepreneurs, whose authority comes from mastery of a specific issue; and procedural entrepreneurs, who use bureaucratic minutiae to exert their influence.[26] The fluid atmosphere of the postwar Congress offered fertile ground for procedural entrepreneurs, and no one took better advantage than Connecticut senator Brien McMahon, a freshman senator first elected in 1944. One month after Hiroshima, McMahon introduced a measure to create a federal board consisting mostly of cabinet members to oversee the nation's atomic energy industry, a proposal that suggested less that the Connecticut senator had thought through the issue than that he wanted to be a player. A more comprehensive proposal came from the chairs of the Military Affairs committees, Representative Andrew May (D-Kentucky) and Senator Edwin Johnson (D-Colorado). The May-Johnson bill, which enjoyed the support of the War Department and initially the administration as a whole, called for a nine-member Atomic Energy Commission (AEC), dominated by the armed forces, with full authority over all uses of atomic energy; the measure also mandated stiff penalties – up to $100,000 in fines or 10 years imprisonment – for disclosing any atomic secrets (including in scientific journals).[27]

Initially, it seemed as if the May-Johnson bill would sail through both houses. In a survey of 81 members of Congress conducted in September 1945, only 5 (all Democrats) advocated turning atomic knowledge over to the United Nations; Vandenberg considered "an 'exchange' of scientists and scientific information as sheer appeasement."[28] The nation's atomic scientists, however, opposed the measure, and they searched for a patron to offer an alternative.[29] McMahon was the default choice: he was ambitious, interested, and seemed to have an open mind on the issue of civilian supremacy. In October 1945, a temporary alliance between McMahon and Vandenberg, who wanted to prevent the military committees from getting

---

[25] Robert David Johnson, *The Peace Progressives and American Foreign Relations*, pp. 95–120.

[26] Davidson, "The Advent of the Modern Congress," p. 360.

[27] Steven Del Sisto, *Science, Politics, and Controversy: Civilian Nuclear Power in the United States, 1946–1974* (Boulder: Westview Press, 1979), p. 14; Nelson Polsby, *Political Innovation in America: The Politics of Policy Initiation* (New Haven: Yale University Press, 1984), p. 24.

[28] Barton Bernstein, "The Quest for Secrecy: American Foreign Policy and International Control of Atomic Energy, 1942–1946," *Journal of American History*, 60 (1974), pp. 1020, 1028.

[29] Del Sisto, *Science, Politics, and Controversy*, p. 16.

exclusive jurisdiction, displaced the May-Johnson bill with a measure for a special temporary committee.[30] By Senate custom, the sponsor of a bill calling for a special committee was entitled to the chairmanship, and so the Connecticut senator had his committee, after less than two years of Senate service. "For a freshman senator," the official history of the AEC noted, "this was the opportunity of a lifetime."[31]

The 17 staffers of McMahon's special committee interviewed more than 70 witnesses, producing more than 600,000 words of testimony.[32] Although McMahon possessed only limited knowledge about the specifics of atomic energy, he effectively cultivated the journalistic elite – in early 1946, Joe Alsop, Marquis Childs, Drew Pearson, Walter Lippmann, and Roscoe Drummond all hailed the Connecticut senator's work.[33] Fleshing out his earlier ideas, McMahon proposed a full-time AEC, stressing both the peaceful and military uses of the technology and providing penalties only for acts of espionage. The measure also forbade granting patents for the military use of atomic energy. McMahon conceded that many of the bill's provisions represented a "distinct departure from our usual way of doing things, but we must remember that atomic energy . . . is *sui generis*."[34]

Passing such a measure represented no easy task. The special committee included many of the upper chamber's power barons, figures who owed McMahon no deference. The Connecticut senator adopted a two-pronged strategy, working with administration sympathizers to persuade the president to back his bill while publicly subjecting military witnesses to a "merciless cross-examination" so as to make it appear as if his offering represented the only alternative to a military-dominated atomic energy structure.[35] "If the issue is in doubt," McMahon's chief staffer concluded, "then we've got to make the goddamndest fight we know how to make."[36]

The former effort paid dividends on February 2, 1946, when Truman endorsed the bill. But McMahon struggled to maintain support from other

---

[30] Richard Hewlett and Oscar Anderson, *History of the United States Atomic Energy Commission, volume 1* (State College: Penn State University Press, 1962), p. 424.

[31] Hewlett and Anderson, *History of the United States Atomic Energy Commission, volume 1*, p. 446.

[32] Christopher Bowland to Brien McMahon, "Budget for 1946," n.d., Box 4, Joint Committee on Atomic Energy Papers – Files of Senator McMahon, Record Group 128, National Archives.

[33] Hewlett and Anderson, *History of the United States Atomic Energy Commission, volume 1*, p. 485.

[34] 92 CR, 79th Congress, 2nd session, pp. 6082–6083 (1 June 1946).

[35] Chuck Callins, "The Senate Committee vs. the Army," 14 Jan. 1946, Box 3, Joint Committee on Atomic Energy Papers – Files of Senator McMahon, Record Group 128, National Archives.

[36] Chuck Callins, "The Senate Committee vs. the Army," 14 Jan. 1946, Box 3, Joint Committee on Atomic Energy Papers – Files of Senator McMahon, Record Group 128, National Archives.

committee members, who preferred Vandenberg's approach of establishing an AEC military liaison committee, which could overrule the civilian commissioners on national security issues.[37] The Vandenberg amendment, however, generated strong opposition from scientists and liberals; McMahon privately informed the president that he would oppose any bill that included the Vandenberg offering.[38] The attention generated a public outcry – in less than a month, more than 25,000 people wrote to the special committee denouncing the amendment, prompting Vandenberg to ask McMahon for a compromise.[39] One committee staffer termed it "unprecedented in the history of our Congressional legislation" for a Senate "stalwart" to concede to a freshman who had initially been outvoted 10–1 on his own committee.[40] But McMahon, perhaps better than any member of the immediate postwar Congress, understood how fluid international and institutional conditions could allow even the most junior senator to accrue considerable power.

The most striking aspect of the Atomic Energy Act, however, was its recommendation for a Joint Committee on Atomic Energy (JCAE). The legislation endowed the JCAE, the first regular congressional committee established by statute, with more power than possessed by any congressional committee up to that time.[41] As a joint committee, the JCAE avoided the difficulties associated with House-Senate conference committees, while, unlike other joint committees, it possessed legislative authority, or the status to have bills referred to it for hearings and action.[42] The Atomic Energy Act also required keeping the JCAE "fully and currently informed" of all AEC initiatives, a structure that ensured that on atomic energy matters, the committee's members would be "policy" as well as "procedural" entrepreneurs, almost impossible to challenge on the floor.[43] The McMahon-Vandenberg compromise sailed through the Senate, and strong administration lobbying accounted for House passage by around 50 votes, though with many restrictive amendments. The London *Times* correctly described the bill as

[37] Arthur Vandenberg, Jr., ed., *Private Papers of Senator Vandenberg* (Boston: Houghton Mifflin, 1952), entry for 20 July 1946, p. 253.

[38] Brien McMahon to Harry Truman, 29 March 1946, Box 4, Joint Committee on Atomic Energy Papers – Files of Senator McMahon, Record Group 128, National Archives; *New York Times*, 10 March 1946.

[39] Brien McMahon to John Goldsmith, 24 April 1946, Box 4, Joint Committee on Atomic Energy Papers – Files of Senator McMahon, Record Group 128, National Archives.

[40] Christopher Bowland to Fran, 9 April 1946, Box 4, Joint Committee on Atomic Energy Papers – Files of Senator McMahon, Record Group 128, National Archives.

[41] H. L. Neiburg, "The Eisenhower AEC and Congress: A Study in Executive-Legislative Relations," *Midwest Journal of Political Science* 6 (1962), pp. 120–121.

[42] Harold Green and Alan Rosenthal, *Government of the Atom: An Integration of Powers* (New York: Atherton Press, 1963), pp. 26–27.

[43] Green and Rosenthal, *Government of the Atom*, p. 67.

"in reality a victory of internationalist sentiment over narrow, old-fashioned nationalism."[44]

The conference committee dropped most of the House restrictions, producing a final measure resembling McMahon's initial bill. In this sense, the Atomic Energy Act illustrated the balance of power between the two branches on foreign policy issues. By excluding the House from any role in approving treaties or confirming ambassadors, the Constitution clearly envisioned a more prominent Senate role in international affairs. When Congress challenged executive control of foreign affairs through the major power shared between the branches – the power of the purse – the Senate almost always took the lead, whether in the 1850s disruptions of James Buchanan's Latin American policy, the Johnson amendment of the late 1910s, or in the 1920s, when congressional action checked military interventions in Nicaragua and Haiti. Indeed, with the important exception of tariff legislation, the House played an insignificant foreign policy role in the early twentieth century. During one congressional session in the 1920s, for instance, the Foreign Affairs Committee spent a week debating a $20,000 appropriation for an international poultry show in Tulsa, which one committee member recalled as "the most important issue that came before the Committee in the whole session."[45] The committee's military counterpart, the Military Affairs Committee, went several sessions during the decade without even holding formal hearings.

Then, suddenly, in the late 1930s and early 1940s, the House burst into activity – though through initiatives that did the institution little credit. These undertakings ranged from the quixotic (Indiana congressman Louis Ludlow's attempts to amend the Constitution to require a popular vote before any declaration of war) to the personal (the attacks of New York's Hamilton Fish against the policies of one of his constituents, President Franklin Roosevelt) to the troubling (the institution's decision to renew the Selective Service Act by a scant one vote in the summer of 1941) to the demagogic (the efforts of Texas' Martin Dies and Mississippi's John Rankin to focus the work of the House Un-American Activities Committee [HUAC] against left-wingers). This record produced a backlash after World War II. Allen Drury noticed as early as 1944 that responsible members of the House looked to the other side of Capitol Hill for foreign policy leadership: "They are afraid of the House, of its sudden emotionalism, its tendency to be stampeded by men like John Rankin and Ham Fish."[46] The *New York Times* reporter considered it remarkable that – despite the traditional jealousy between the

---

[44] *The Times* (London), 6 May 1946.
[45] James Sundquist, *The Decline and Resurgence of Congress* (Washington, DC: Brookings Institute, 1981), pp. 94–102.
[46] Drury, *A Senate Journal*, entry for 4 Sept. 1944, p. 259.

branches – House leaders "trust the Senate more than they do themselves."[47]
While, perhaps, few congressmen seemed as eager to dispense with their prerogatives as Kentucky Democrat Elden Spence (who believed that in foreign
policy, the president "ought to have the same powers as the executives or dictators representing the enslaved peoples in the totalitarian governments"),
few imitated the aggressiveness of senators such as McMahon, Pepper, or
Vandenberg.[48]

The McMahon Act and the British loan bill represented the two most
significant international matters to come before Congress in 1946. Unfortunately for the administration, Truman could not match his foreign policy
accomplishments on the domestic front, and the unsettling effects of demo-
bilization combined with a remarkably effective campaign waged by the
Republicans yielded enormous GOP gains in the midterm elections.[49] The
Republicans picked up 13 seats in the Senate and 56 in the House, seizing control of Congress for the first time since 1930. The new class, the
most conservative group of Republican freshmen until the 1994 elections
and Newt Gingrich's "Contract with America," strongly opposed government spending of all sorts, and most also exhibited an antipathy to foreign
entanglements.[50]

The new political alignment seemed to guarantee confrontation between
the GOP-dominated legislature and the Democratic executive. Increased partisan wrangling did occur, most viciously through the efforts of the HUAC,
the body that Truman not incorrectly termed "more un-American than the
activities it is investigating."[51] Working closely with FBI director J. Edgar
Hoover, Chairman J. Parnell Thomas (R-New Jersey) championed legislation to require the registration of Communists; Thomas also oversaw a
high-profile inquiry into Communist influence in the film industry. Cooperative witnesses included Screen Actors Guild president Ronald Reagan
and Walt Disney, who complained that "Commie groups began smear campaigns against me and my pictures" while members of the Cartoonists' Guild
of America wanted to turn Mickey Mouse into a fellow traveler.[52] When ten

---

[47] Drury, *A Senate Journal*, entry for 4 Sept. 1944, p. 259.

[48] Spence quoted in William Long, *U.S. Export Control Policy: Executive Authority Versus Congressional Reform* (New York: Oxford University Press, 1989), p. 22.

[49] James Patterson, *Grand Expectations: The United States, 1945–1974* (New York: Oxford University Press, 1996), pp. 65–104.

[50] Melvyn Leffler, *Preponderance of Power: National Security, the Truman Administration, and the Cold War* (Stanford: Stanford University Press, 1992), pp. 141–145.

[51] Michael Hogan, *Cross of Iron: Harry S. Truman and the Origins of the National Security State* (New York: Cambridge University Press, 1998), p. 256.

[52] U.S. House of Representatives, Un-American Activities Committee, *Hearings, Regarding the Communist Infiltration of the Motion Picture Industry*, 80th Congress, 1st session, pp. 283–284 (24 Oct. 1947).

writers refused to reveal whether they had once belonged to the Communist Party, citing the free speech protections of the First Amendment, the "Hollywood Ten" subsequently were convicted for contempt of Congress.[53] Meanwhile, in a more direct attack on the administration's foreign policy, HUAC freshman Richard Nixon (R-California) leveled spectacular and ultimately convincing allegations that Alger Hiss, a former State Department and UN operative, was a Communist spy.

Despite the activities of HUAC, many key figures also spoke of a bipartisan foreign policy – though they defined the concept in very different ways. (The London *Times* snidely observed that in the Washington of the early Cold War, "'bipartisan' is almost as popular a word as baseball – though its meaning is less well understood."[54]) For Vandenberg, bipartisanship represented an opportunity for the GOP to shed its isolationist legacy and for him to maximize his influence. For New Jersey senator H. Alexander Smith, bipartisanship was a pragmatic approach: the administration, and especially Secretary of State George Marshall, needed "help, not opposition."[55] Congressman George Bender (R-Ohio) complained to GOP colleagues that bipartisanship was a device "to push us into the arms of the Democrats."[56] For Dean Acheson, a bipartisan foreign policy allowed the president to argue that any critic "is a son-of-a-bitch and not a true patriot."[57] Tom Connally considered bipartisanship the opposite of "isolationism."[58] And Truman himself declared that a bipartisan foreign policy "means simply saying that the President can repose confidence in the members of the other party and that in turn the leaders of the party have confidence in the President's conduct of foreign affairs."[59]

In the spirit of this vague bipartisanship, Congress in 1947 considered two of the most important legislative measures of the Cold War – the National Security Act and the administration's proposal to extend military assistance to Greece and Turkey. The bills revealed much about the changing ideological tenor of Congress, the institution's still-fluid internal structure, and the nature of "bipartisan" foreign policy. The early stage of the Cold War, in

53 Walter Goodman, *The Committee: The Extraordinary Career of the House Committee on Un-American Activities* (New York: Farrar, Strauss, and Giroux, 1968), pp. 169–229.
54 *The Times* (London), 21 April 1950.
55 H. Alexander Smith, diary entry, 19 August 1947, Box 281, H. Alexander Smith Papers, Mudd Library, Princeton University.
56 George Bender to Robert Taft, Sr., 14 July 1947, Box 615, Robert Taft, Sr. Papers, Library of Congress.
57 Thomas Paterson, "Presidential Foreign Policy, Public Opinion, and Congress: The Truman Years," *Diplomatic History* 3 (1979), p. 17.
58 Henry Berger, "Bipartisanship, Senator Taft, and the Administration," *Political Science Quarterly* 90 (1975), p. 227.
59 Berger, "Bipartisanship, Senator Taft, and the Truman Administration," p. 225.

this sense, offered a model of an executive-legislative partnership, in which key members of Congress affected foreign policy informally and behind the scenes to an extent that would not reappear again in the Cold War.

The National Security Act originated from wartime proposals for unifying the armed services. On October 23, 1945, Truman called for a single National Military Establishment presided over by a civilian secretary, but the Navy openly opposed the measure. By the middle of 1946, two separate bills were before Congress, one embodying the president's approach, the other mirroring the Navy's preferences. In 1947, the first chair of the Senate Armed Services Committee, Chan Gurney (R-South Dakota), introduced a bill resembling the administration-backed measure of the previous year; Clare Hoffman (R-Michigan) sponsored a companion offering in the House. In contrast to 1946, each service supported the Gurney-Hoffman bill. Navy secretary James Forrestal was the first witness supporting what became the National Security Act, which also created the National Security Council and the Central Intelligence Agency.[60]

Though historian Michael Hogan has argued that consideration of the measure illustrated competing visions of democratization, tradition, and the American identity, that interpretation seems to exaggerate the intellectual significance of the congressional debate.[61] While opponents raised anti-militarist and anti-executive concerns, this rhetoric reflected less heart-felt sentiments than a convenient cover to mask pro-Navy partisanship.[62] Consideration of the National Security Act did, however, reveal two items of long-term significance. The first was the remarkable institutional weakness of the newly created Armed Services Committees in both the House and the Senate, especially given their later emergence as the most powerful congressional committees on national security matters. In the Senate, Gurney barely fended off a parliamentary challenge to refer the bill to the Committee on Expenditures in Executive Departments (later the Government Operations Committee). The argument that the Legislative Reorganization Act gave the latter committee jurisdiction over all matters relating to executive branch reorganizations was overruled by the president pro tempore of the Senate – ironically Vandenberg, who nonetheless used the occasion to offer a limited conception of Armed Services' proper jurisdiction.[63]

The House Armed Services Committee could not even survive a comparable parliamentary challenge, and the bill went to Hoffman's Committee on Expenditures in Executive Departments. This procedural setback

[60] Hogan, *Cross of Iron*, pp. 24–44.
[61] Hogan, *Cross of Iron*, p. 60.
[62] U.S. Senate, Armed Services Committee, *Hearings, National Defense Establishment*, 80th Congress, 1st session, pp. 30 (19 March 1947), 508–510 (30 April 1947); Hogan, *Cross of Iron*, p. 63.
[63] 93 *CR*, 80th Congress, 1st session, pp. 1602–1606 (3 March 1947).

set the tone for the committee's early years; its initial chairman, W. G. Andrews (R-New York), expected Armed Services to deal mostly with "routine, run-of-the-mine affairs, such as easements and obvious little corrections in law."[64] Typical matters addressed by Andrews during his two years as chairman (which he found so unsatisfying that he retired in 1948) included measures to reorganize the Navy's Nurse Corps; to authorize Los Angeles officials to construct a storm drain under land owned by the Navy; to procure doctors in the Army Medical Corps; and to allow 17-year-olds to enlist in the National Guard. In short, it seemed as if the Armed Services Committee, derided by some as a "real estate" committee because of its interest in finding land upon which to construct military bases, would have as little significance as its predecessor bodies from the interwar era.[65]

Committee members also deferred to the military even on those questions over which they clearly did possess jurisdiction. Styles Bridges (R-New Hampshire), for instance, detected "a certain hesitancy of a senator ... in setting his judgment up against that of a man who is clearly devoting his whole time to that job" in the military services.[66] Richard Russell (D-Georgia), who would become the longest-serving chair in the Senate committee's history, agreed that Congress could not possibly "spell out every detail of every component" of national security policy.[67] While the military enjoyed tremendous prestige in the aftermath of World War II, other committees did not share Armed Services' passive attitude. For instance, the House Committee on Expenditures in Executive Departments condemned the Armed Services Committee's reluctance to "legislate tactics"; it did not hesitate to spell out its conception of the proper function of the Army, Navy, Marines, Air Force, and CIA.[68]

Though the authorizing committee, Armed Services, displayed little interest in forceful action on national security matters, the same did not hold for the appropriating committee, especially in the House. Republicans had prevailed in 1946 by promising economy in government, a commitment that the new majority expected to apply to the military budget as well. In early 1947, James Forrestal, now the nation's first secretary of defense, detected the "shadow of Congress" looming over all national security matters, with a

[64] U.S. House of Representatives, Armed Services Committee, *Hearings, Organization of the Committee on Armed Services of the House of Representatives*, 80th Congress, 1st session, p. 6 (28 Jan. 1947).

[65] James Lindsay, *Congress and the Politics of U.S. Defense*, p. 56.

[66] U.S. Senate, Armed Services Committee, *Hearings, National Defense Establishment*, 80th Congress, 1st session, p. 66 (20 March 1947).

[67] U.S. Senate, Armed Services Committee, *Hearings, National Defense Establishment*, 80th Congress, 1st session, p. 98 (25 March 1947).

[68] *CQ Almanac 1947*, p. 460.

legislature determined to enact a "balanced budget and lower taxes" threatening needed defense spending.[69]

Partly due to the growth in the federal budget during World War II, the Appropriations Committee delegated more authority to its subcommittees, which had jurisdiction over individual cabinet agencies. Because of this structure, the National Security Act's most immediate effect on congressional organization came in consolidating the various military spending subcommittees into the Defense Appropriations Subcommittee. And, in sharp contrast to the Armed Services Committee, the subcommittee's first chair, Albert Engel (R-Michigan), intended to examine "the over-all policy of the armed services"; ranking member George Mahon (D-Texas) already had made up his mind on the issue, promising, "This committee is very air-minded."[70]

Samuel Huntington has described how the Cold War politicized the military: each branch wanted more money but vied against the others for funding.[71] The Defense Appropriations Subcommittees provided a central venue for this competition. And, in sharp contrast to virtually every other international issue, the House, as the body in which by tradition appropriations requests originated, possessed leverage over the Senate. The first sessions of the Senate subcommittee featured complaints about House delays, which, as Richard Russell noted, gave "them an unconscionable advantage in power between the two houses" in conference committee.[72]

The ideological foundations for the foreign policy to be executed by the National Security Act dated from 1946. Winston Churchill's Iron Curtain address offered a vivid image of Europe's postwar divisions, while George Kennan's "X" article, published in *Foreign Affairs*, predicted that Stalin would mimic tactics associated with czarist expansionism, probing for signs of Western weakness. Kennan urged containing Soviet strength through deterrence, and Truman implemented this agenda on February 21, 1947, when the British government announced that it no longer could provide financial and military assistance to the right-of-center Greek government. The Truman administration immediately offered financial aid for Greece and also for Turkey, which had recently refused a Soviet demand to cede territory on the nations' joint border and allow Soviet bases in the country. But the State Department anticipated "grave difficulties" in obtaining support

---

[69] Leffler, *Preponderance of Power*, p. 142.

[70] U.S. House of Representatives, Defense Appropriations Subcommittee, *Hearings, Military Functions; National Military Establishment, Appropriation Bill for 1949*, 80th Congress, 2nd session, pp. 14, 28 (16 March 1948).

[71] Samuel Huntington, "Interservice Competition and the Political Roles of the Armed Services," *American Political Science Review* 55 (1961), pp. 40–52.

[72] U.S. Senate, Defense Appropriations Subcommittee, *Hearings, Military Function, Appropriation Bill for 1949*, 80th Congress, 2nd session, p. 33 (14 June 1948).

from the economy-minded Congress.[73] In a famous White House meeting with congressional leaders, Undersecretary of State Dean Acheson delivered an impassioned, dire prediction of Europe's fate should the United States refuse to act.[74] In a similar vein, Truman appeared before Congress to assert that the aid initiative would have "broad implications" for the future U.S. role in the world, implications heightened by his pledge to help free peoples "maintain their free institutions and their natural integrity against aggressive movements that seek to impose upon them totalitarian regimes."[75] To accomplish that goal, the aid package consisted of $150 million in military aid, $50 million in reconstruction assistance, and $100 million in economic aid to Greece; and $100 million in arms for Turkey.

While the reality of a GOP-controlled Congress forced Truman to seek Republican support, this need was intensified by the erratic nature of congressional Democrats, who did not convincingly defend the president's foreign policy. That Truman had served with all prominent Democratic figures in the late 1940s Senate helped him little as president; most of these men had been senior to Truman in the upper chamber and possessed power bases independent of the president. In the Senate, the most tenacious attacks on the Truman Doctrine came from the dwindling group of internationalists, led by Pepper, who opposed extending military aid to undemocratic regimes, but even Democrats critical of Pepper's ideological approach, such as Armed Services Committee ranking member Millard Tydings (D-Maryland), questioned the President's agenda.[76] Tom Connally did as much to injure Truman's cause as assist it: as Acheson tartly observed, the frequently inebriated Texas senator "often does not understand what he is told."[77] (Once, when asked his opinion about Europe, Connally replied, "The plantations over there are very small."[78]) Acheson similarly had a low opinion of the committee's next ranking Democrat, Walter George (D-Georgia), who, the undersecretary of state noted, "contributed very little to political thought and leadership in the United States."[79]

Unlike Connally, George, or Pepper, Vandenberg doubted neither the merits of containment nor the need to aid Greece and Turkey. Acheson later wrote that Vandenberg's mind "was not original, but it was open"; his brilliance

---

[73] Loy Henderson to Dean Acheson, n.d., copy in *Papers Relating to the Foreign Relations of the United States* [hereafter *FRUS*] 1947, vol. 5, p. 52.

[74] Susan Hartmann, *Truman and the 80th Congress* (Columbia: University of Missouri Press, 1971), p. 57.

[75] *New York Times*, 13 March 1947.

[76] U.S. Senate, Committee on Foreign Relations, *Hearings, Military Assistance Program*, 81st Congress, 1st session, p. 55 (9 Aug. 1949).

[77] Henry Cabot Lodge confidential journal, entry for 18 Jan. 1950, Reel 17, Henry Cabot Lodge Papers, Massachusetts Historical Society.

[78] *The Times* (London), 16 April 1952.

[79] Acheson, *Sketches from Life*, pp. 141–142.

lay not in his intellectual insights but in his ability to control the agenda of Senate foreign policy debate.[80] Vandenberg admitted privately that the administration had not consulted him in developing its initiative, but he forgave Truman: "Congress cannot take the lead in foreign relations, because that is the President's job, not only by constitutional requirement but also by practical reality."[81] Nonetheless, to soothe concerns of his colleagues, he invited senators to submit written questions to the State Department, which yielded over 100 responses that Vandenberg then circulated to all members of the Senate, thus fostering a perception that the administration was considering senatorial concerns.[82]

Throughout Senate consideration of the bill, Vandenberg received assistance from two newly named committee Republicans. The first, H. Alexander Smith, was a corporate lawyer, GOP activist, and self-described "strong internationalist."[83] Smith envisioned the Cold War as a contest of ideas between the United States and the USSR; he claimed that resisting Communist expansionism could not occur through an approach dominated by *"balancing of power."*[84] Worried that the administration was too inclined to act unilaterally, Smith opposed intervening in Greek or Turkish internal affairs, lest the United States revive the Pax Britannica of the nineteenth century. He was somewhat less clear on his preferred positive policy, but in general recommended "strong, positive, aggressive" leadership on economic and political issues, increasing emphasis on cultural exchange programs, and acting in the "spirit of collective security" to protect "the little nations of the world."[85]

Smith possessed a sharp mind and was a formidable questioner in committee hearings. But he also was a hypochondriac: in the 80th Congress alone he missed extended periods to what he described as the grippe, insomnia, depression, phlebitis, and viral pneumonia.[86] These illnesses, real and imagined, heightened the importance of Massachusetts senator Henry Cabot Lodge, II. Owner of one of the most famous names in Massachusetts politics, in 1936 Lodge captured the Senate seat once held by his grandfather. Once in the Senate, he generally supported Roosevelt's foreign policy, often

---

[80] Acheson, *Sketches from Life*, p. 130.

[81] Vandenberg, Jr., ed., *Private Papers of Senator Vandenberg*, p. 325.

[82] *CQ Almanac 1947*, p. 247.

[83] H. Alexander Smith to Arthur Vandenberg, Jr., 14 Dec. 1951, Box 104, H. Alexander Smith Papers, Mudd Library, Princeton University.

[84] Smith diary entry, 3 March 1947, Box 281, H. Alexander Smith Papers, Mudd Library, Princeton University.

[85] H. Alexander Smith, "Bipartisan Foreign Policy," NBC, 11 Jan. 1947; H. Alexander Smith to George Marshall, 12 Nov. 1947; both in Box 92, H. Alexander Smith Papers, Mudd Library, Princeton University; H. Alexander Smith to Arthur Vandenberg, 17 March 1947, Box 91, H. Alexander Smith Papers, Mudd Library, Princeton University.

[86] H. Alexander Smith diaries, 1947, H. Alexander Smith Papers, Mudd Library, Princeton University.

backed the president on domestic matters, and sailed to reelection. Shortly thereafter, however, he resigned his position to enter the U.S. Army (the first member of the Senate to do so since the Civil War). Back in the United States after the war, he returned to politics by ousting Democratic senator David Walsh in 1946. Lodge was the only one of the 13 GOP freshmen named to the Foreign Relations Committee – a decision he attributed to "a sort of veteran's preference."[87]

Not an especially probing thinker, Lodge never questioned the basic rationale behind the Cold War. Instead, he focused on legislative politics, international tactics, and public justifications of U.S. actions. To a much greater extent than did the administration, Lodge attempted to reconcile – to his colleagues, the American people, and world public opinion – waging the Cold War with both the internationalist tenets for which the United States fought World War II and the more basic principles, such as anticolonialism, which had long characterized the U.S. approach to world affairs. In this respect, the Massachusetts senator was as much an ideological heir of Woodrow Wilson as of his namesake. Lodge also advocated developing a creative response to the problems of allowing party differences to influence foreign policy, a position that he championed with intensity, cognizant of how the partisanship of the League of Nations fight had besmirched his grandfather's reputation. The Massachusetts senator championed what he deemed an "unpartisan" approach to world affairs, in which the opposition party would function as "the voice of conscience," undertaking "a calm and deliberate reappraisal of the facts" while offering "constructive suggestions."[88] Behind these rather banal suggestions lay an unusual conception of how to make foreign policy in a democracy. Lodge maintained that pressure from Congress and especially the legislative opposition could force "the President to raise his sights" and was the only way to accomplish anything "worth while" internationally.[89]

Partisan and institutional factors gave Vandenberg, Lodge, and Smith disproportionate influence on how Congress responded to Truman's Greek/Turkish proposal.[90] The trio functioned as the administration's congressional watchdogs, warning Truman officials about specifics likely

---

[87] Henry Cabot Lodge, *The Storm Has Many Eyes: A Personal Narrative* (New York: Norton, 1973), p. 61; Anne Blair, *Lodge in Vietnam* (New Haven: Yale University Press, 1995), pp. 1–11.

[88] Lodge to Dwight Eisenhower, 15 June 1950, unprocessed letter, Massachusetts Historical Society.

[89] Lodge, "Lodge Defines Minority Role," *New York Times Magazine*, 17 Sept. 1950. Eventually Smith and Vandenberg joined Lodge in describing their approach as "unpartisan." H. Alexander Smith to Arthur Vandenberg, 14 Dec. 1951, Smith Papers, Box 104, Mudd Library, Princeton University.

[90] Henry Cabot Lodge journal, January 1948, Box 17, Henry Cabot Lodge, II, Papers, Massachusetts State Historical Society.

to arouse Republican opposition and suggesting alternatives that would avoid controversy without altering the administration's intent. The senators displayed their political skills in ensuring that the committee's GOP majority unanimously endorsed the measure, even persuading the likes of Iowa's Bourke Hickenlooper, a Taft-supporting conservative who worried about "the danger of assuming the burdens of keeping the peace of the world."[91]

During debate over the Greek/Turkish aid package, Vandenberg, Smith, and Lodge not only rhetorically challenged administration critics but also undercut the opposition through amendments.[92] Gallup polls taken shortly after Truman's congressional address indicated solid, though not overwhelming, support for the aid package, tempered by criticism of the president's failure to consult the UN. Embracing Smith's suggestion to "wholeheartedly support the spirit of collective security" as a way of bridging the internationalism of World War II and that of the Cold War, Vandenberg amended the bill's preamble to include a statement that the policy would "contribute to the freedom and independence of all Members of the United Nations in conformity with the principles and purposes of the Charter."[93] A second, more significant, Vandenberg amendment required the president to withdraw aid if the UN took action that rendered further U.S. assistance undesirable. Privately, Vandenberg believed that Greece would "collapse fifty times" before the UN addressed the situation.[94] But if such an amendment insulated the bill from criticism, the Michigan senator had no problem with supporting it – and neither did the administration.

The lack of a UN role particularly disturbed the administration's left-wing critics. As had become commonplace, Henry Wallace condemned the president's course of action and urged the public to support the UN rather than "imperialist ventures."[95] (When the former vice president delivered similar remarks during a European tour, Vandenberg lambasted him as the "itinerant saboteur."[96]) Within the Foreign Relations Committee, support for the Wallace viewpoint came from Pepper, who worried about the administration defending the British "lifeline to their Middle Eastern and Indian interests."[97] After the committee reported the bill, the Florida senator

[91] Bourke Hickenlooper to Rollo Bergeson, 24 March 1947, Box 138, Bourke Hickenlooper Papers, Herbert Hoover Presidential Library, West Branch, Iowa.

[92] Justus Doenecke, *Not to the Swift: The Old Isolationists in the Cold War Era* (Lewisburg, PA: Bucknell University Press, 1979), p. 85.

[93] H. Alexander Smith to Arthur Vandenberg, 17 March 1947, Box 91, H. Alexander Smith Papers, Mudd Library, Princeton University.

[94] Vandenberg, Jr., ed., *Private Papers of Senator Vandenberg*, entry for 5 March 1947, p. 340.

[95] *Washington Post*, 20 March 1947.

[96] Vandenberg, Jr., ed. *Private Papers of Senator Vandenberg*, p. 351.

[97] U.S. Senate, Foreign Relations Committee, *Hearings, Assistance to Greece and Turkey*, 80th Congress, 1st session, pp. 37–43 (24 March 1947).

commiserated with UN secretary general Trgvye Lie, who lamented, "One more action like this and the United Nations will be dead."[98]

Pepper substantially expanded upon these sentiments during what his sympathetic colleague, James Murray (D-Montana), termed "one of the most spirited and searching debates I have heard on the floor of the Senate."[99] Fearful of the UN's decay, the Florida senator looked to confine aid to rehabilitation for Greece, with all assistance funneled through the UN; he presciently cautioned that Truman's rhetoric would "be applied alike to all parts of the world where comparable situations exist."[100] Pepper also expressed concern about the nature of the forces that the administration proposed to assist. Greece, he feared, defined as a Communist "every member of a guerrilla band, any agrarian reformer, any democrat who resents the imposition of a royalist dictatorship."[101] If the United States needed a historical primer on the dangers of intervening against nationalist forces, it had only to recall early twentieth century U.S. policies in Caribbean Basin states such as Haiti, the Dominican Republic, and Nicaragua.[102] This rare citation of an event from interwar foreign policy confirmed Pepper's disinclination to accept the emerging consensus of the Cold War as a fundamental break in the U.S. approach to world affairs.

Despite the intensity of Pepper's rhetoric, liberal internationalists struggled to reconcile their worldview with concrete evidence of Soviet intransigence and the growing awareness that the UN could not resolve great-power disputes. Their position, moreover, exposed them to overt Red-baiting. Noting that his Idaho colleague seemed "so much better advised than I am as to what the Communists have in mind," Tom Connally ridiculed Glen Taylor's assertions that the Soviets were interested in peace.[103] *Newsweek* dubbed the Florida senator "Red Pepper," since "when Russia called, he rallied – and rallies again."[104]

With the left on the defensive, the bulk of opposition to the Truman Doctrine came from the revisionist right, whose strength had been fortified by the 1946 Republican sweep, which sent to the Senate Joseph McCarthy (Wisconsin), James Kem (Missouri), Zales Ecton (Montana), Harry Cain (Washington), William Knowland (California), William Jenner (Indiana), John Bricker (Ohio), Chapman Revercomb (West Virginia), and George Malone (Nevada). Like the liberal internationalists, however, this group suffered from an internal contradiction, in their case, reconciling their strident

---

[98] Pepper, *Pepper*, p. 154.

[99] 83 *CR*, 80th Congress, 1st session, p. 3491 (16 April 1947).

[100] 83 *CR*, 80th Congress, 1st session, pp. 3499 (16 April 1947), 3587–3592 (17 April 1947).

[101] 83 *CR*, 80th Congress, 1st session, p. 3394 (15 April 1947).

[102] 83 *CR*, 80th Congress, 1st session, p. 3285 (10 April 1947).

[103] 84 *CR*, 80th Congress, 2nd session, p. 2384 (9 March 1948).

[104] *Newsweek*, 7 April 1947.

anti-leftist rhetoric with a foreign policy position whose possible outcome would be the triumph of Communism in Greece. As noted by Carl Vinson (D-Georgia), the ranking Democrat on the House Armed Services Committee, Truman's policy placed his right-wing critics in an untenable position: "They don't like Russia, they don't like Communism, but they don't want to do anything to stop it."[105]

Perhaps unsurprisingly, then, the revisionists failed to offer a consistent alternative to Vandenberg or the administration. Owen Brewster criticized Truman for following the dictates of the British, Kenneth Wherry (R-Nebraska) contended that the administration had bowed excessively to the French, and George Malone complained that Truman had not sufficiently protested earlier Soviet transgressions. (Such comments left Vandenberg to denounce the group's "persistent drumfire" of misinformation.[106]) Even when the revisionists offered a consistent rationale, their proposals seemed irrelevant to the issue at hand. James Kem, for instance, agreed that the United States needed to "stamp out communism," but urged the president to focus "within our own borders and in our own Government," since the Senate's "first duty is to make democracy work at home."[107] Homer Capehart, Chapman Revercomb, and Wayland Brooks (R-Illinois) endorsed these remarks, but never explained why cracking down on domestic Communism would preclude assisting the Greeks.[108] The final Senate tally on the measure was 67 to 23, after which it went on to the House, which spent a considerable amount of time in debate – four days, longer than any other bill in 1947 – but passed it by a 100-vote margin with few changes.

Debate over the aid package contained numerous paeans to respecting executive authority. Vandenberg said that "noncompliance" with Truman's request would mean that "there would never be another opportunity for us pacifically to impress the next aggressor with any degree of success."[109] Lodge described repudiating Truman as "unthinkable," although he wished the legislature could develop a system that would allow it to consider more alternatives.[110]

Such rhetoric from the Senate's two most important foreign policy players might suggest interpreting the Truman Doctrine as a presidential diktat. In reality, the conventional image of the congressional role in the early Cold War – somewhat condescending nods to Vandenberg's susceptibility to

[105] Chester Pach, *Arming the Free World: The Origins of the United States Military Assistance Program, 1945–1950* (Chapel Hill: University of North Carolina Press, 1991), p. 115.
[106] 83 *CR*, 80th Congress, 1st session, p. 3698 (18 April 1947).
[107] 83 *CR*, 80th Congress, 1st session, p. 3484 (16 April 1947).
[108] 83 *CR*, 80th Congress, 1st session, pp. 3486–3488 (16 April 1947).
[109] 83 *CR*, 80th Congress, 1st session, p. 3473 (16 April 1947).
[110] 83 *CR*, 80th Congress, 1st session, p. 3337 (11 April 1947).

flattery, or what Acheson dubbed the "Vandenberg treatment" – seems well off the mark, since the real practitioners of the "Vandenberg treatment" were Smith, Lodge, and Vandenberg himself. While the trio urged the administration to offer bombastic foreign policy rhetoric, they framed the case exceedingly narrowly when dealing with Republican colleagues, claiming that they had scaled back out-of-control executive requests. The three senators, worried about what they considered the administration's attachment to balance of power politics, also successfully urged the president to justify Cold War foreign policy in a manner more consistent with promoting democracy, human rights, and self-determination.[111] This approach distinguished them from pro-administration Democrats such as Brien McMahon, for whom it made no "particular difference whether Turkey is a democracy, so long as she is resisting aggression."[112]

Senate debate over the Truman Doctrine exposed the weaknesses of the ideological visions competing against containment. Soviet conduct in Poland, Iran, and Hungary, coupled with its UN delegation's regular use of the veto, undermined many assumptions about world politics upon which the liberal internationalists rested their proposals. Meanwhile, the revisionists' hostility to a big federal government – and in particular a strong executive – produced an awkward situation in which they appeared to share Truman's ends while offering less realistic means. (A few years later, Styles Bridges described the Pentagon budget as "the 'Fair Deal' under the guise of defense spending."[113]) When combined with an administration-initiated grassroots lobbying campaign to pressure wavering members of Congress, the congressional debate helped transform public opinion from a UN-first, cost-conscious mentality to a pro-containment viewpoint, providing legitimacy to the executive's preferred policy.[114]

Within Congress, the Greek/Turkish aid debate also had important consequences. Most obviously, it confirmed the preeminence of the Foreign Relations Committee, a body that acted with unusual unity for a Senate committee. Although Vandenberg's bill only set an authorization total for the aid, the Appropriations Committee approved the amount almost without change; the Armed Services Committee did not request jurisdiction on what clearly was a national security matter; and the House displayed such deference that it delayed its floor debate until after the Senate vote. It would be more than a decade before the Foreign Relations Committee's authority to speak for Congress on foreign policy issues would come under serious challenge. Also, self-evidently, once the Greek/Turkish aid bill entered

[111] U.S. Senate, Foreign Relations Committee, *Hearings, Assistance to Greece and Turkey*, 80th Congress, 1st session, p. 22 (24 March 1947).
[112] 95 *CR*, 80th Congress, 1st session, p. 3763 (22 April 1947).
[113] *Congressional Quarterly Weekly Report*, 19 Jan. 1951.
[114] Polsby, *Political Innovation in America*, p. 90.

Congress, it came under the control of Vandenberg and Lodge, to modify as they saw fit. That they essentially accepted the proposal came from their agreement with Truman's policy choices, not a belief in congressional passivity. Indeed, during the debate, *Newsweek* asserted that "where foreign policy is concerned, Vandenberg's influence on Congress is so decisive that it amounts, at the moment, to virtual control."[115]

The general patterns – in terms of ideology, impact on policy, and internal structure – featured in the Greek/Turkish aid bill reappeared after George Marshall informed the 1947 Harvard commencement audience that the United States needed to promote general European economic recovery. This speech formed the genesis of the Marshall Plan, destined to emerge as the most successful foreign aid program undertaken by the United States. In retrospect, passage of the European Recovery Plan (ERP) was never in doubt, even before the March 1948 coup in Czechoslovakia, which toppled the last Eastern European government not under Communist control.[116] In this respect, consideration of the bill offers a glimpse of how Vandenberg and his allies shaped the congressional response to the early Cold War.

By this point, Democratic jealousy of the Vandenberg Republicans' prominence was hard to avoid. Connally, for instance, absented himself from several days of the hearings considering the bill; while present, he sarcastically asked Lodge to "give us a little Harvard language in there."[117] Walter George displayed little more enthusiasm for either the plan or the parliamentary situation. Doubtful "about a good many of the things we are laying down" in the bill, he wanted to make the European nations' renouncing Communism a condition for U.S. aid, a proposal Smith labeled "absurd."[118] George's conduct earned a public rebuke from Marshall, while Acheson detected the hand of Marshall's repudiated predecessor, James Byrnes, in the Georgia senator's attacks.[119]

The anger of Connally and George reflected envy that Vandenberg, Lodge, and Smith were very much in charge. To a much greater extent than had occurred in the Greek/Turkish aid debate, the trio subtly altered the bill to neutralize later opposition. Describing his function as overcoming "the needless and unjustified added public resistance to the bill," Vandenberg changed the authorization request from $6.8 billion over 15 months to $5.3 billion over 12 months, which reduced the overall funding level without actually

[115] *Newsweek*, 7 April 1947.

[116] *Executive Sessions of the Senate Foreign Relations Committee* [hereafter *ESSFRC*], *Foreign Relief Assistance Act of 1948*, p. 373 (29 Feb. 1948).

[117] *ESSFRC, Foreign Relief Assistance Act of 1948*, p. 14 (9 Feb. 1948).

[118] *ESSFRC, Foreign Relief Assistance Act of 1948*, pp. 150–152 (9 Feb. 1948).

[119] Acheson quoted in Walter Millis, ed., *The Forrestal Diaries* (New York: Viking Press, 1951), entry for 4 April 1947, p. 261; U.S. Senate, Foreign Relations Committee, *Hearings, European Recovery Program*, 80th Congress, 2nd session, p. 27 (8 Jan. 1948).

cutting the monthly rate of assistance.[120] This approach, which Lodge considered a "damned good idea," won over the "cut-minded" Appropriations Committee, since it gave Congress a chance to review the program at an earlier date.[121]

Vandenberg and his allies also addressed House concerns by adding a provision to the bill permitting the authority's extension beyond Europe. Lodge was certain that the administration would ignore the rider – as it did – but reasoned that this provision would appease members of the China bloc in the House. Finally, as they had during the Greek/Turkish debate, the moderate Republicans pressed for a foreign policy infused with idealism and internationalism. Along these lines, they beat back George's efforts to authorize assistance to Francisco Franco's fascist government, an outcome that Vandenberg believed would provide a "textual answer to the Henry Wallace's and so-and-sos who say this is a closed corporation."[122] The era's ideological climate led to increased support for initiatives such as the Marshall Plan, and the president might well have succeeded even without support from internationalist Republicans. Nevertheless, the administration understood the importance of figures like Vandenberg, upon whom Truman officials publicly fawned, and Lodge, whose efforts won praise from Acheson, Marshall, and Averell Harriman, ambassador to the Soviet Union during the early stages of the Cold War.[123]

Floor debate on the Marshall Plan (in the Senate alone, 69 of the 96 members participated) featured what H. Alexander Smith termed "real evidence" that the revisionists, in both chambers, were "'ganging up' on us."[124] In a typical attack confirming the connection between the revisionists' domestic and international approaches, Capehart charged that the administration had shirked "before the power of State socialism"; unless the United States compelled recipient nations not to use relief funds in the "typical socialistic method determined by these governments," the Marshall Plan represented the equivalent of a man mortgaging his house to bet on a horserace.[125] Malone dismissed the measure as an "amazingly brazen and preposterous scheme for a world-wide redistribution of wealth"; continued aid to "the socialistic European governments" would undermine American capitalism.[126] While the administrative assistant of Malone's Nevada colleague,

---

[120] *ESSFRC, Foreign Relief Assistance Act of 1948*, pp. 277, 283 (13 Feb. 1948).

[121] *ESSFRC, Foreign Relief Assistance Act of 1948*, pp. 290, 296 (13 Feb. 1948).

[122] *ESSFRC, Foreign Relief Assistance Act of 1948*, p. 182 (12 Feb. 1948).

[123] "Tuesday, August 22, 1950," Conversation with Averell Harriman, Confidential Journal, Reel 17, Henry Cabot Lodge, II Papers, Massachusetts State Historical Society; *Saturday Evening Post*, 31 May 1952.

[124] H. Alexander Smith diary, 5 March 1948, H. Alexander Smith Papers, Mudd Library, Princeton University.

[125] 84 CR, 80th Congress, 2nd session, pp. 2518–2520 (11 March 1948).

[126] 84 CR, 80th Congress, 2nd session, p. 2208 (5 March 1948).

Pat McCarran, ridiculed the Republican's tendency to "talk much and say little," Smith marveled how many of his GOP colleagues "cannot seem to realize that the type of socialism" in Scandinavia or England "is hardly even a distant cousin to Russian communism."[127] The New Jersey senator failed to understand that the revisionists' complaint was primarily domestic, since GOP conservatives recognized that the administration's containment policy, even for a cause with which they sympathized, would strengthen federal power.

The revisionists' ill-concealed contempt for Europe also reflected a fundamentally different conception of U.S. national interests. Capturing the group's thinking on the issue, Owen Brewster argued, "The only thing the Soviet respects and fears is American air power and the atom bomb."[128] Revisionists dismissed the strategic importance of Western Europe, whose socialistic governments, they contended, lacked the will to fight. Funds appropriated for European affairs would therefore be better spent on non-Communist forces in East Asia, where the regimes of Chiang Kai-shek in China, Syngman Rhee in South Korea, and Elpidio Quirino in the Philippines also offered right-wing domestic agendas that appealed to the revisionists. This mindset proved especially powerful in the House, where revisionists successfully included two ideologically acceptable regimes – Nationalist China and Franco's Spain – as among the intended targets of Marshall Plan aid.[129] Though the House-Senate conference committee excised the provision, it symbolized an Asia-first approach that intensified in the years to come. As had occurred with the Greek/Turkish aid package, however, a combination of intellectual and political factors weakened the revisionists' position. Intellectually, the revisionists could never explain why abandoning Europe to its fate would serve American interests.[130] And on this occasion, they also suffered from the defection of Taft, who reasoned that preventing Western Europe from falling to Communism required some aid.

Given the international climate, it is somewhat surprising that foreign policy did not play a greater role in the 1948 presidential election, though two candidates – Henry Wallace, who ran as a Progressive, and Robert Taft, whose bid for the GOP nomination fell short – did attack the administration's international strategy, albeit from differing ideological perspectives. The year's Truman/Dewey contest is best remembered for the president's surprise victory, a result that, in the end, doomed bipartisan foreign policy.

---

[127] Eva Adams to Pat McCarran, November 1947, Box 2, Eva Adams Papers, University of Nevada, Reno; H. Alexander Smith to Wilford Conrow, 9 March 1948, Box 96, H. Alexander Smith Papers, Mudd Library, Princeton University.

[128] Owen Brewster address, 14 April 1948, Speeches File, Box 1, Owen Brewster Papers, Bowdoin College.

[129] Hartmann, *Truman and the 80th Congress*, p. 164.

[130] 84 *CR*, 80th Congress, 2nd session, p. 2209 (5 March 1948).

Embittered Republicans could not resist using international affairs as a venue for partisan attacks, and even some of the administration's most prominent Republican defenders expressed skepticism about the future of the bipartisan approach. Smith was (quite properly) "shocked" after Democrats allotted themselves an 8–5 majority on the Foreign Relations Committee, in contrast to the 7–6 GOP margin in the similarly proportioned 80th Congress.[131] It seemed as if, the New Jersey senator fumed, Democrats thought that bipartisanship meant "presentation of the Administration's program with the suggestion that the minority party sign on the dotted line."[132] J. William Fulbright (D-Arkansas), more optimistic, reminded his Foreign Relations colleagues that "this committee is not like other committees, and it is the only one in the field in which we adopt what is called the bipartisan foreign policy."[133]

Despite the election results, basic trends of postwar relations between Congress and the executive persisted through 1949, completing the foundations of the Atlantic alliance with the ratification of the North Atlantic Treaty and the implementation of a worldwide military aid program. Both initiatives had significant effects within Congress as well – the former by solidifying the right's emerging celebration of congressional power, the latter by confirming the supremacy of the Foreign Relations Committee.

Even in 1948, few in Congress had doubted that a formal political relationship between the United States and Western Europe would complement the economic ties established by the Marshall Plan. That year, the Senate passed a non-binding resolution sponsored by Vandenberg endorsing regional pacts for collective security; the Michigan senator termed Article 51 of the UN Charter, which allowed such arrangements, "the greatest single hope for the United Nations."[134] Eleven months later, on April 4, 1949, the United States joined England, France, Holland, Belgium, Luxembourg, Canada, Portugal, Norway, and Italy in signing the North Atlantic Treaty, a collective security pact deeming an attack against one of the nations an attack against them all. Eight days later, Truman submitted the treaty, which he termed "further evidence of our determination to work for a peaceful world," to the Senate.[135] Unlike earlier Cold War issues, the votes of only 33 senators could prevent approval of the North Atlantic Treaty. And while the Pepper bloc of liberal internationalists continued to weaken, the treaty seemed certain to encounter determined revisionist resistance, since

---

[131] H. Alexander Smith diary, 6 Jan. 1949, Box 282, H. Alexander Smith Papers, Mudd Library, Princeton University.

[132] H. Alexander Smith to Lawrence Fuchs, 28 Nov. 1949, Box 92, H. Alexander Smith Papers, Mudd Library, Princeton University.

[133] *ESSFRC*, vol. 3, p. 230 (1 March 1949).

[134] *ESSFRC, The Vandenberg Resolution and the North Atlantic Treaty*, p. 30 (12 May 1948).

[135] *New York Times,* 13 April 1949.

it involved a binding political commitment to Europe. This need to limit Republican defections meant that the Vandenberg group retained its influence, despite the Democratic majority in the Senate.

So, as had occurred in 1947 and 1948, the Foreign Relations Committee began by considering how best to present the treaty publicly. First, bowing to advice from Lodge and Vandenberg, the administration delayed introducing its military aid bill.[136] Second, to be "extremely careful," Vandenberg and Lodge urged Connally to accommodate demands from ardent revisionists Arthur Watkins (R-Utah) and Forrest Donnell (R-Missouri) to sit with the committee and question witnesses.[137] Connally initially balked (as "one of them wants to be secretary of the committee and the other wants to be chairman"), but he accepted the wisdom of the suggestion: as Lodge noted, "nothing could help the Atlantic Pact more than to have Donnell questioning Acheson, with Acheson making the smart answers that I know he is capable of making."[138]

Lodge, Vandenberg, and Smith viewed the committee's job as not only passing the treaty but reassuring the Senate that joining NATO would not contradict more traditional internationalist principles. As had occurred in previous years, the chief opposition to the administration's foreign policy came from committee Democrats – Pepper, George, and especially Tydings, who had just become the first Democratic chairman of the Armed Services Committee. To an unsympathetic audience, the Maryland senator complained that Armed Services members "feel that they are being bypassed when the security of the United States, with which they are particularly charged, is being considered by the Foreign Relations Committee exclusively."[139]

Sixteen days of public hearings commenced on April 27, with Watkins complaining that he discovered the date the hearings would begin only by reading one of the Salt Lake City newspapers. (To Connally, "All that shows is that the Salt Lake paper is better advised as to what is going on in Washington than the Senator from Utah."[140]) As expected, the revisionists consumed extraordinary amounts of time with hostile questions – Vandenberg "got so sick of that little band of GOP isolationists who are always in the way that I could scream" – but made little headway.[141] Indeed, the

[136] ESSFRC, *The Vandenberg Resolution and the North Atlantic Treaty*, p. 179 (12 April 1949).

[137] ESSFRC, *The Vandenberg Resolution and the North Atlantic Treaty*, p. 196 (12 April 1949).

[138] ESSFRC, *The Vandenberg Resolution and the North Atlantic Treaty*, p. 202 (19 April 1949).

[139] U.S. Senate, Foreign Relations Committee, *Hearings, North Atlantic Treaty*, p. 151 (28 April 1949).

[140] U.S. Senate, Foreign Relations Committee, *Hearings, North Atlantic Treaty*, p. 66 (27 April 1949).

[141] Vandenberg quoted in James Patterson, *Mr. Republican: A Biography of Robert A. Taft* (Boston: Houghton Mifflis, 1972), p. 435.

failure of Donnell and Watkins became apparent as committee members initially somewhat skeptical about the treaty, such as Hickenlooper, changed their minds.[142]

Senate debate nonetheless revealed no great outpouring of emotion for the treaty.[143] With support for NATO so lukewarm, a number of alternatives were floated, but these only highlighted the continued difficulty for Truman's critics to offer a realistic alternative to his Cold War strategy. Guy Gillette (D-Iowa) vaguely envisioned a "positive, affirmative" policy that would reflect America's revolutionary heritage, rather than relying on an "irrelevant" treaty that did "not touch on any of the basic causes which prompt European unrest today."[144] John Sparkman (D-Alabama) called for coupling NATO with comprehensive reform of the UN, to include abolishing the Security Council veto and establishing a "tyranny-proof" international police force.[145] Ralph Flanders (R-Vermont) came up with the most bizarre proposal, urging Truman to use guided missiles and remote-controlled planes to "rain down from the heavens pamphlets and handbills onto the Russian citizens so that those living in Russia may by this means learn why it is that the rest of the world fears Russia and arms against it."[146]

None of these schemes particularly appealed to the revisionists. Taft and Wherry attacked the treaty, though Acheson minimized their influence: "Since they both totally lacked humor and possessed unlimited energy, their opposition was undiscriminating and ubiquitous," making it "dull, scattered, and less effective than it could have been."[147] (Wherry, a former undertaker nicknamed the "merry mortician," was known for his malapropisms, such as terming Vietnam "Indigo China" or Wayne Morse, the junior senator from Oregon, "the senator from junior."[148]) Taft contended that the treaty stripped from Congress its power to declare war; several revisionists protested the exclusion of anti-Communist Spain and asked how the administration could justify its continued opposition to German rearmament.[149] These tenets – a suspicion of the expense of Cold War foreign policy, an emphasis on retaining congressional prerogatives in international affairs, and a call to extend American protection to right-wing

---

[142] Bourke Hickenlooper to Kingsley Clarke, 18 Feb. 1949, Box 82, Bourke Hickenlooper Papers, Herbert Hoover Presidential Library; Bourke Hickenlooper to J. P. Hansen, Box 83, Bourke Hickenlooper Papers, Herbert Hoover Presidential Library.

[143] 95 *CR*, 81st Congress, 1st session, pp. 9198, 9199, 9210–9211 (11 July 1949).

[144] 95 *CR*, 81st Congress, 1st session, p. 9204 (11 July 1949).

[145] 95 *CR*, 81st Congress, 1st session, p. 9118 (8 July 1949).

[146] *CQ Almanac* 1949, p. 346.

[147] Acheson, *Sketches from Life*, p. 133.

[148] David Oshinsky, *A Conspiracy So Immense: The World of Joe McCarthy* (New York: The Free Press, 1985), p. 130.

[149] Robert Taft notes, 29 March 1949, Box 618, Robert Taft, Sr. Papers, Library of Congress; Robert Taft radio address, "Drew Pearson Hour," 24 July 1949, Box 619, Robert Taft, Sr. Papers, Library of Congress.

dictatorships – would form the basis of a powerful revisionist critique of the Cold War consensus over the next several years. This critique, in turn, would have an important effect in shaping attitudes about Congress' proper role in foreign policy.

In a debate dominated by the GOP, Vandenberg, Lodge, Smith, Morse, and the recently appointed John Foster Dulles (R-New York) challenged the revisionists' view, which, "in all frankness," Lodge considered "motivated by a good deal of false logic."[150] Dulles, delivering a passionate maiden address, denounced the "disastrous" ramifications of the Taft/Wherry viewpoint, which he maintained would leave the United States "encircled."[151] When pressed by Watkins, the future secretary of state previewed a GOP split of the 1950s, declining to engage "in a long discourse, a law lecture, so to speak, about the constitutional twilight zone" between Congress and the president in foreign affairs – unlike those on the other side, who harbored a "curious delusion that the whole world is bound by the Constitution of the United States, and that there cannot be war until Congress declares it."[152] Smith, meanwhile, continued his efforts to reconcile the treaty with an earlier brand of internationalism. He described NATO as more than a military alliance; since the organization could focus "on what may be called the social, economic, spiritual values which go into making a real defense against aggression."[153] In the end, only 13 senators cast negative votes against NATO; even Taft, in a last-minute surprise, supported the treaty.

The administration followed up approval of the North Atlantic Treaty by requesting $1.45 billion in military aid for the NATO states, along with Greece, Turkey, Iran, Korea, and the Philippines. The extraordinarily broad bill did not specify the amounts each country would receive and gave the president discretionary power to extend military aid to "any nation," a term the measure curiously defined as "any foreign government or country, or group thereof."[154]

The bill generated two sharp areas of dispute, one entirely predictable, the other more surprising. The immediate controversy concerned executive power. In what he termed "the most vigorously candid speech of my life," Vandenberg contended that the bill's definition of "nation" granted unlimited power to the president to dispense weapons.[155] Privately, he charged that the proposal placed "the old bipartisan business . . . out the window."[156]

---

[150] *95 CR*, 81st Congress, 1st session, p. 9114 (8 July 1949).

[151] *95 CR*, 81st Congress, 1st session, pp. 9275–9278 (12 July 1949).

[152] *95 CR*, 81st Congress, 1st session, p. 9284 (12 July 1949).

[153] *95 CR*, 81st Congress, 1st session, p. 9192 (11 July 1949).

[154] *New York Times*, 26 July 1949.

[155] ESSFRC, *Military Assistance Program: 1949*, 81st Congress, 1st session, p. 22 (2 Aug. 1949); Arthur Vandenberg telegram, 9 Aug. 1949, copy in Vandenberg, ed., *Private Papers of Senator Vandenberg*, p. 508.

[156] Vandenberg, ed., *Private Papers of Senator Vandenberg*, entry for 25 July 1949, p. 503.

But the Michigan senator prematurely fretted. Acheson had not studied the bill before initially testifying in its favor, and upon returning to the State Department, laced into subordinates for their sloppiness in drafting. "Even a child," he maintained, "would have picked up the weakness" in the legislation.[157] When the State Department then scaled back the funding level, delineated the amount of aid each country would receive, and eliminated the "nation" definition, Vandenberg rejoiced that "we have killed the 'war lord bill' which would have made the President the top military dictator of all time."[158] Indeed, the Michigan senator (quite correctly) believed that the administration had "totally surrendered on eighty percent of my criticisms," in the process demonstrating "that the Republican contribution to the so-called 'bipartisan foreign policy' is not on a 'me-too' basis."[159]

Ironically, the most significant dispute about the bill came not between Congress and the executive but within Congress itself. By early 1949, other than the areas over which the JCAE possessed jurisdiction and the national security issues into which the House Appropriations Committee had delved, the Foreign Relations Committee shaped the congressional response to international matters. As a result, Lodge observed, the committee was "regarded with mixed emotions by the rest of the Senate." On the one hand, virtually every senator wanted to serve on a committee of such prestige. On the other, non-members considered it "a sort of vermiform appendix of the State Department." Given these sentiments, Lodge worried that unless the committee aggressively assumed jurisdiction over the military aid bill, the Appropriations Committee, eager to match its House counterpart's international powers, would seize the initiative. Such a development, Lodge understood, would make approval less likely, since Foreign Relations could frame the issue in "a much more sympathetic way," while other committees lacked "understanding" of important international matters.[160]

Though correct in anticipating a jurisdictional fight, the Massachusetts senator misjudged the source. For its first two years of existence, the Armed Services Committee (with Chan Gurney, a South Dakota Republican not known for his political skills, as chair) did little more than re-fight the internal disputes of the three military services and bog itself down in whether the United States should adopt universal military training.[161] The Democratic capture of the Senate in 1948 brought far more effective leadership. Millard

---

[157] Pach, *Arming the Free World*, p. 232.

[158] Vandenberg, ed., *Private Papers of Senator Vandenberg*, entry for 1 Aug. 1949, p. 507.

[159] Vandenberg to Walter Lippmann, 9 Aug. 1949, in Vandenberg, ed., *Private Papers of Senator Vandenberg*, p. 508.

[160] ESSFRC, *The Vandenberg Resolution and the North Atlantic Treaty*, 81st Congress, 1st session, pp. 183, 186 (12 April 1949).

[161] Hogan, *Cross of Iron*, p. 95.

Tydings first won election to the Senate in 1926, and he attracted national attention in 1938, as one of the conservative Democrats to survive FDR's attempted purge in that year's party primaries. By the late 1940s, Tydings was one of the upper chamber's most powerful figures: he was the only member of the 81st Congress to serve on the Appropriations, Armed Services, and Foreign Relations committees. Not only Tydings' ambition predicted a more active role for Armed Services; ideologically, the Maryland senator teamed with George to champion a more nationalistic brand of foreign policy.

Having openly complained about the North Atlantic Treaty hearings excluding his committee, Tydings made his stand on the military aid bill. On July 28, 1949, speaking with the "very highest regard" for his Foreign Relations colleagues, he demanded the bill's referral to Armed Services. The Maryland senator denied that military aid was a foreign policy issue: "the only and single justification for one bullet or one gun that belongs to the American people being given to any other country is the ultimate defense of the United States of America." Since the Legislative Reorganization Act assigned to Armed Services all matters relating to defense – and, he added, since members of Foreign Relations were "not well informed" on the topic – the bill fell within his committee's jurisdiction. A panicked Connally proposed a compromise for joint hearings; an even less enthusiastic endorsement came from Lodge, who considered opposing the unanimous consent request needed for the two committees to sit together, but backed off, since, he claimed, engaging in "a hair-splitting argument on jurisdiction" required "a type of training and of outlook that I do not possess."[162]

By the next morning, Lodge had apparently developed a taste for such jurisdictional disputes. The Massachusetts senator complained that the joint referral posited a false "conflict between defense and foreign policy."[163] Tydings' claim of Armed Services predominance on any measure involving the military would leave Foreign Relations "with world federalism and the Atlantic Union and that's about all."[164] To the Massachusetts senator, both positive and negative reasons dictated Foreign Relations control over military aid. On the positive side, the main effect of European rearmament would be "overwhelmingly political."[165] On the negative, the question was too important to leave "to these fellows in uniform," including the Joint Chiefs of Staff (JCS).[166] Sourly, Tydings expressed his appreciation that Lodge had

---

[162] 95 *CR*, 81st Congress, 1st session, pp. 10327–10330 (28 July 1949).
[163] *ESSFRC, Military Assistance Program: 1949*, p. 2 (29 July 1949).
[164] *ESSFRC, Military Assistance Program: 1949*, p. 2 (29 July 1949).
[165] *ESSFRC, The Vandenberg Resolution and the North Atlantic Treaty*, 81st Congress, 1st session, p. 208 (19 April 1949).
[166] *ESSFRC, The Vandenberg Resolution and the North Atlantic Treaty*, 81st Congress, 1st session, p. 210 (19 April 1949).

not objected to the unanimous consent agreement and instead had confined himself to a "long harangue."[167]

Ironically, after having fought so hard for the right to be heard, Tydings could not persuade his Armed Services colleagues to shake their traditional lethargy and participate actively in the joint hearings. In a way, the Maryland senator was a decade ahead of his time. Only in the late 1950s would the committee as a whole discover what Tydings (and Lodge) had perceived in 1949: that given the growth of the national security state and the Pentagon budget, the Legislative Reorganization Act, by granting the committee jurisdiction over "national defense," made Armed Services potentially the most powerful congressional committee on all international issues.

Congressional deference to the nation's senior military leadership – perhaps understandable, in the aftermath of World War II – in part accounted for Armed Services' reticence. Wherry believed that "when it comes to military matters, a layman must give way to the judgment of military men"; Tydings gave the JCS de facto veto power over the defense authorization bill, since leading generals "know more about such matters than we do."[168] Even the more aggressive Wayne Morse conceded "the delicacy" of speaking on military strategy because he had "not been a member of the armed services in time of war."[169] To avoid such uncomfortable issues, the committee instead spent most of 1949 and early 1950 in a futile quest to resolve intra-service rivalries; its House counterpart divided over whether the Navy or the Air Force deserved more funds.[170] (Vermont's Charles Plumley demanded more generous funding for both services, so the United States could fulfill "the white man's burden."[171]) This congressional pressure frustrated the administration's efforts to hold down Pentagon spending; in March 1949, James Forrestal was "frank to say" about the defense budget "that the tangible evidences of economy are not great as of now."[172]

While the Armed Services Committee spent little time on military aid, Foreign Relations hearings indicated fairly wide disagreement, foreshadowing the breakdown of the bipartisan consensus. As had become the established pattern, Vandenberg, Lodge, Smith, and Dulles chided the administration for not sufficiently reconciling the new program with internationalist tenets. Accordingly, Smith offered amendments to reaffirm the U.S. commitment to the Vandenberg Resolution of 1948 and to have the president report every six months about progress toward international disarmament; Vandenberg

---

[167] ESSFRC, *Military Assistance Program: 1949*, p. 2 (29 July 1949).

[168] 95 CR, 81st Congress, 1st session, pp. 6631, 6635 (23 May 1949).

[169] 95 CR, 81st Congress, 1st session, p. 6708 (24 May 1949).

[170] 95 CR, 81st Congress, 1st session, pp. 4432, 4436 (12 April 1949), 4498, 4500 (13 April 1949).

[171] 95 CR, 81st Congress, 1st session, p. 4432 (12 April 1949).

[172] U.S. Senate, Armed Services Committee, *Hearings, National Security Act of 1949*, 81st Congress, 1st session, p. 12 (24 March 1949).

called for suspending the assistance program once the NATO council had charted out its own military aid scheme.

The committee adopted each of these amendments – the Republicans' political position remained vital – but not without complaint. Connally testily asked Smith how many times the Senate needed to reaffirm the Vandenberg Resolution, and complained that his New Jersey colleague seemed "every 20 minutes to be referring to disarmament when we are arming."[173] As for Vandenberg's amendment, the Texan saw no sense in "just sitting around here twiddling our thumbs for three months," playing "pinochle," while the NATO council determined its objectives.[174] Fulbright urged his Republican colleagues to offer a better word to describe the United States than "peace-loving," since "I am getting sick of that."[175] McMahon said that Smith and Vandenberg could offer all the amendments they wanted, but "that isn't going to change the basic fact that we are in an arms race."[176] Tydings, conceding that his opinion was "emotional rather than logical," indicated that he trusted the military's judgment "upon what is needed a whole lot more than my own."[177]

While most Democrats embraced a more hard-line military role than did either the administration or the Vandenberg Republicans, they applied pressure on other issues as well. George sponsored the most contentious amendment, a measure to reduce the authorization by $300 million, or roughly 25 percent. The Georgia Democrat argued both that war with the Soviet Union was unlikely and, if a conflict occurred, military aid would not improve U.S. security. Implementing the program, he further claimed, would force the U.S. government to increase taxes and embrace socialism, ensuring the nation's long-term decline. To prove his point, he cited events of World War II: France fell because "she had become emaciated through socialistic influences," and England almost lost to the Germans for the same reason.[178] (McMahon wondered how anyone could seriously contend that prewar British prime ministers Stanley Baldwin and Neville Chamberlain harbored secret socialist tendencies.[179]) In an early version of Dwight Eisenhower's famous Farewell Address, George detected the hand of "all international financiers and all manufacturers in this country" behind the bill.[180]

Meanwhile, the committee's newest Republican, William Knowland, described by some as the "senator from Formosa," demanded more support for the Kuomingdang (KMT) forces in China. Knowland's efforts drew

---

[173] *ESSFRC, Military Assistance Program: 1949*, p. 250 (23 Aug. 1949).
[174] *ESSFRC, Military Assistance Program: 1949*, p. 77 (10 Aug. 1949).
[175] *ESSFRC, Military Assistance Program: 1949*, p. 221 (23 Aug. 1949).
[176] *ESSFRC, Military Assistance Program: 1949*, p. 356 (26 Aug. 1949).
[177] *ESSFRC, Military Assistance Program: 1949*, p. 343 (25 Aug. 1949).
[178] *95 CR*, 81st Congress, 1st session, pp. 13082–13084 (21 Sept. 1949).
[179] *95 CR*, 81st Congress, 1st session, p. 13084 (21 Sept. 1949).
[180] *ESSFRC, Military Aid Program: 1949*, p. 402 (29 Aug. 1949).

strong public support from the first grassroots foreign policy movement of the Cold War, the China lobby. A combination of hard-line anti-Communists, supplicants of KMT leader Chiang Kai-shek, and former Christian missionaries and those influenced by the religious portrayal of China centered on the *Time/Life* empire of Henry Luce – himself a missionary's son – the lobby claimed to have one million members behind a policy of massive military and economic assistance to Chaing's beleaguered forces in the Chinese civil war.

The Knowland proposal generated no support in the committee but received praise from revisionists in both chambers. Twenty-one senators issued a public letter to Truman urging military aid to the Chinese; in the House, Washington Democrat Warren Magnuson spoke for a growing bipartisan bloc fearful "that in our concentration on Europe we have overlooked the fact that we are part of a Pacific community and that the independence and stability of the nations of the East are of grave concern to us."[181] James Kem put the Asia-first lobby's case the most bluntly: "We have poured billions of dollars into western Europe to erect a wall against Communism there but we have permitted Communism to run rampant in the Far East."[182] Commenting on the intensity of the China aid effort, pacifist leader A. J. Muste remarked, "For isolationists these Americans do certainly get around."[183]

Lodge provided the most powerful critique of both the George and Knowland viewpoints. He dismissed George's claim that military aid would overtax the U.S. economy. Instead, the Massachusetts senator maintained, the program was "like adding a 12th player to the team," since if a major war came, "it will be absolutely vital to our survival to have friends and allies."[184] The amendment still garnered 33 votes, including the support of 11 Senate Democrats, the highest total for any anti-administration offering on foreign policy between 1946 and 1949. Lodge displayed even less patience for Knowland. Western Europe needed arms as soon as possible; no argument existed "on a comparable scale with regard to the Far East."[185] Vandenberg ultimately defused the Knowland threat with an amendment granting the president discretionary authority to provide $75 million in military aid in the "general area of China." Ironically, this attempt to avoid involvement in

[181] Warren Magnuson to H. B. Hazelton, 19 October 1949, Box 123, 1945–1956 Series, Warren Magnuson Papers, University of Washington.

[182] James Kem to H. Alexander Smith, 15 Dec. 1949, Box 98, H. Alexander Smith Papers, Mudd Library, Princeton University.

[183] Thomas Paterson, "Presidential Foreign Policy, Public Opinion, and Congress: The Truman Years," *Diplomatic History* 3 (1979), p. 5.

[184] U.S. Senate, Foreign Relations Committee, *Hearings, Military Assistance Program*, 81st Congress, 1st session, p. 76 (10 Aug. 1949).

[185] U.S. Senate, Foreign Relations Committee, *Hearings, Military Assistance Program*, 81st Congress, 1st session, p. 76 (10 Aug. 1949).

an Asian civil war provided the opening for the first direct U.S. military aid in Vietnam.

The military aid bill ultimately passed by a 55 to 24 margin, with Vandenberg celebrating the fact that the Senate considered the issue "in comparatively calm, patient peace" as a triumph of bipartisan foreign policy.[186] From an ideological angle, legislative debate in the bipartisan era exposed the weaknesses of the main alternatives to the Cold War consensus – liberal internationalism and revisionism – in part explaining the ease with which Truman's agenda achieved public backing. Meanwhile, Vandenberg, Lodge, and Smith achieved influence, often in subtle ways, contradicting the period's image as one of executive dominance. The particular international and partisan environment, however, that allowed these moderate Republicans to affect policy would prove difficult to replicate over time. Finally, significant innovations occurred in the procedure through which Congress addressed foreign policy issues, whether in specific initiatives such as the JCAE, broader matters such as the Legislative Reorganization Act, or by confirming the pre-existing status quo, as in the continued preeminence of the Foreign Relations Committee. As the bipartisan era came to an end, many of these procedural innovations would be marshaled by a congressional faction that offered a radically different ideological alternative for waging the Cold War.

---

[186] 95 *CR*, 81st Congress, 1st session, p. 13160 (22 Sept. 1949).

Legislative Power and the Congressional Right

Between 1949 and 1954, the revisionists coupled their Asia-first strategy with an increasingly vehement contention that the fundamental threat posed by Communism came on the home front. Though McCarthyism and the HUAC remain the best-known instruments of this effort, the most important legislative player was Pat McCarran, who returned to the chairmanship of the Judiciary Committee after Democrats reclaimed Senate control in 1948. The committee, to which 40 percent of the bills in the 81st Congress were referred and which longtime Lyndon Johnson aide George Reedy described as "an independent empire under McCarran's jurisdiction," provided a perfect forum for a crusade to stifle internal dissent.[1]

In 1950, *Time* labeled "the silver-haired spokesman of the silver bloc" one of the eight worst members of the Senate.[2] With a visceral dislike for the president from their time together as senators and a 26 percent party unity score during the Truman administration – 22 percent lower than the next lowest Senate Democrat – McCarran occupied the fringe of Democratic thought during the late 1940s.[3] (The Nevada senator explained his voting record by asserting, "I never compromise with principle, [and] almost everything is principle to me."[4]) McCarran built his influence by placing supporters in various executive agencies and through the operations of his staff, described by one writer as "the finest intelligence service on Capitol Hill."[5]

---

[1] Alfred Steinberg, "McCarran: Lone Wolf of the Senate," *Harper's*, Nov. 1950; George Reedy, *The U.S. Senate: Paralysis or a Search for Consensus?* (New York: Crown, 1986), p. 135.

[2] *Time*, 20 March 1950; Jerome Edwards, *Pat McCarran: Political Boss of Nevada* (Reno: University of Nevada Press, 1982).

[3] *Congressional Quarterly Weekly Report*, 2 Feb. 1951; Michael Ybarra, *Washington Gone Crazy: Senator Pat McCarran and the Great American Communist Hunt* (Hanover, New Hampshire: Steerforth Press, 2004), pp. 370–372.

[4] Steinberg, "McCarran: Lone Wolf of the Senate," *Harper's*, Nov. 1950.

[5] Steinberg, "McCarran: Lone Wolf of the Senate," *Harper's*, Nov. 1950.

Motivated by a thinly veiled anti-Semitism, McCarran used his committee position to frustrate initial postwar attempts to allow more Holocaust survivors to enter the United States. Instead, in early 1948, Congress passed a measure allowing 100,000 displaced persons in refugee camps as of December 22, 1945 to enter the United States. Since this cutoff date excluded most Jewish refugees, during the 1948 campaign, both Truman and GOP nominee Thomas Dewey promised to support a more humane refugee law if elected.[6]

In the Congress that assembled in 1949, however, such legislation had to proceed through the Judiciary Committee, where McCarran cited concerns about the effects of increased immigration on internal security, to question Truman's proposal. In reality, Majority Leader Scott Lucas (D-Illinois) understood, the chairman wanted "to kill the bill" by "conducting a two-bit Un-American activities committee hearing."[7] McCarran, in turn, claimed that his critics wanted to "have every Communist and undesirable from every country in the world swarming to these shores."[8] Such Red-baiting tactics only inflamed an already highly charged issue; one Judiciary Committee hearing on the matter turned so stormy that the Capitol police had to be summoned to restore order. When all else failed, McCarran beseeched divine intervention, concluding that on immigration policy, the United States needed "God's help to guide us and show us the right way to win over the dark and sinister planning of our enemies."[9]

In the secular world, it was the Nevada senator who possessed the final say. In 1949 and 1950, McCarran successfully weakened the administration's displaced persons bill; at the same time, he also championed legislation to restrict the entry of Communist diplomatic personnel assigned to the UN. (The *Washington Post* scoffed that "the United States can hardly insist that Communist countries choose anti-Communists to fill their diplomatic posts over here without inventing a reciprocal demand that all our emissaries be anti-republicans."[10]) Most important, in 1952, the Nevada Democrat teamed with Representative Francis Walter (D-Pennsylvania) to author the McCarran-Walter Act, the first immigration bill since the Alien Act of the late 1790s to establish an ideological litmus test for admission to the United States. Commentator Drew Pearson lamented that with the measure, which governed immigration policy for the next 13 years and was

---

[6] Ybarra, *Washington Gone Crazy*, pp. 460–465.

[7] U.S. Senate, Immigration and Naturalization Subcommittee, *Hearings, Communist Activities among Aliens and National Groups*, 81st Congress, 1st session, p. 308 (15 July 1949); Ybarra, *Washington Gone Crazy*, p. 460.

[8] Pat McCarran to William Byrne, 16 Feb. 1950, Series IV, Box 51, Pat McCarran Papers, Nevada State Historical Society; *Washington Post*, 17 March 1950.

[9] Pat McCarran to J.C. Rice, 22 Feb. 1950, Series IV, Box 51, Pat McCarran Papers, Nevada State Historical Society.

[10] *Washington Post*, 19 July 1949.

approved over Truman's veto, "We might as well send the Statue of Liberty back to France."[11]

In 1949, Lucas complained that McCarran "has tried to take over foreign relations, the judiciary, and a large field of domestic policy."[12] Offering a strikingly different analysis of the Cold War than that of the administration, the Nevada senator considered internal subversion "the most dangerous thing we have to deal with," since "we can lick an enemy from without, but we can't always find the borers from within."[13] McCarran did not underestimate the difficulty of the task ahead. "The deeper you get into the investigation of communism in this country," he believed, "the more appalling it becomes"; to the senator, whose daughter was a Catholic nun, internal subversion "literally is the anti-Christ."[14]

McCarran's chief effort as the Judiciary Committee chair came in championing comprehensive internal security legislation. To James Eastland (D-Mississippi), the senator's closest ally on the committee, only one explanation existed for the growth in postwar Soviet power: "There is in the city of Washington somebody high in this Government with great power that is aligned with the Communist movement."[15] The Mississippi senator concentrated on exposing the "tremendous Red influence in the city of New York," mostly by badgering witnesses who invoked due process protections and accusing the American Civil Liberties Union (ACLU) of advocating the violent overthrow of the U.S. government.[16]

With Eastland's efforts typifying the hearings' intellectual quality, it came as little surprise that the committee produced a draconian internal security measure, described by its sponsor as "possibly more important to the future of this country than any other single action this Congress can take at this time."[17] Combining the provisions of the 32 internal security bills already before the Congress, the McCarran Internal Security Act required that all Communists within the United States register, after which they could not work in defense or military-related jobs; that groups listed as "Communist front" organizations reveal all sources of their funds and the names of their members; and that all literature published by such groups be labeled

---

[11] *Washington Post*, 23 March 1952.

[12] Ybarra, *Washington Gone Crazy*, p. 433.

[13] Pat McCarran to Philip Harper, 11 July 1950; Pat McCarran to Stephen Chess, 31 July 1950; both in Series IV, Box 51, Pat McCarran Papers, Nevada State Historical Society.

[14] Pat McCarran to Bernard Hartney, 2 March 1950, Series IV, Box 51, Pat McCarran Papers, Nevada State Historical Society.

[15] U.S. Senate, Subcommittee on S. 1194 and S. 1196, *Hearings, Control of Subversive Activities*, 81st Congress, 1st session, p. 53 (4 May 1949).

[16] U.S. Senate, Subcommittee on S. 1194 and S. 1196, *Hearings, Control of Subversive Activities*, 81st Congress, 1st session, pp. 54, 69 (4 May 1949), 104 (6 May 1949).

[17] Pat McCarran to Tom Miller, 13 Sept. 1950, Series IV, Box 51, Pat McCarran Papers, Nevada State Historical Society.

"Communist in origin."[18] Only maverick William Langer (R-North Dakota) filed a minority report, dismissing the measure as "the product of hysteria and frantic, unthinking fear."[19]

Once it reached the floor, the bill passed with only 7 dissenting votes in the Senate and 20 in the House; the revelation of Soviet spy rings in the U.S., Canadian, and British spy programs left few politicians willing to cast a vote that could be construed as countenancing a soft line against Communist infiltration. The bill's effects on civil liberties, nonetheless, were clear. One White House aide counseled that signing the measure "would represent an action of moral appeasement on a matter of highest principle," and Truman vetoed the bill.[20] In the House, Speaker Sam Rayburn had to plead for quiet amidst the tumult that greeted the president's veto, which the lower chamber overwhelmingly overrode.[21] In the Senate, McCarran had more than enough votes to override the veto and pass what the London *Times* termed "one of the most stupid and unworkable laws ever passed by a democratic legislature."[22]

The xenophobia personified by McCarran also stimulated opposition to the Genocide Convention, which reached the Senate in 1950. Initially, the treaty, which made genocide an international crime, seemed certain to pass; its only prominent opposition came from a committee of the American Bar Association. As the Senate examined the convention, however, currents of McCarranism surfaced. Southern senators feared that approving the treaty could prevent the United States from suppressing race riots.[23] From another angle, Alexander Wiley (R-Wisconsin), one of the Foreign Relations Committee's more conservative Republicans, feared allowing an international court composed of "nations who have been indulging for centuries in just that sort of thing" to interpret genocide.[24] Even the normally temperate H. Alexander Smith worried about the ramifications of approving the pact; he expected the Soviets to charge that the United States "genocided the American Indian, and it is pretty nearly true, too."[25] In this political and intellectual climate the treaty stalled.

The shifting ideological currents also affected developments in the JCAE, where the politically sensitive Brien McMahon changed direction on a variety

[18] *New York Times*, 29 Aug. 1950.

[19] 96 *CR*, 81st Congress, 2nd session, pp. 14319–14320 (7 Sept. 1950).

[20] Stephen Springarn, "Memorandum for the Files," 22 July 1950; Stephen Springarn, "Memorandum for the Files," 20 Sept. 1950; both in Box 1, National Defense, Stephen Springarn Papers, Harry Truman Presidential Library.

[21] Oshinsky, *A Conspiracy So Immense*, pp. 173–175.

[22] *The Times* (London), 23 Sept. 1950.

[23] Natalie Kaufman, *Human Rights Treaties and the U.S. Senate: A History of Opposition* (Chapel Hill: University of North Carolina Press, 1990), pp. 41–56.

[24] *ESSFRC*, vol. 2, pp. 385, 395.

[25] *ESSFRC*, vol. 2, p. 399.

of issues in an effort to maximize his personal standing. In 1949 and 1950, the JCAE – suddenly willing, even eager, to antagonize the executive – featured McMahon often adopting positions directly contradicting those that he previously had taken. After returning to the chairmanship in 1949, the Connecticut senator had been wondering how to get the committee (and himself) back into the media's eye; his chief staffer came up with a list of 15 possible issues for hearings, including the CIA's ability to obtain information on foreign atomic programs or how a world with atomic weapons required the JCAE to have input into all matters relating to national defense. Such topics generated little interest or even outright hostility within the committee.[26]

Seemingly blocked, McMahon took advantage when Bourke Hickenlooper publicly charged AEC chairman David Lilienthal with "incredible mismanagement," "misplaced emphasis," and "maladministration."[27] The chair promptly convened hearings on allegations that virtually everyone in Washington considered spurious. The first day's gathering immediately adjourned, after Hickenlooper claimed he had received insufficient notice of the hearing time. At the next meeting six days later, the Iowa senator led off with a series of disjointed questions; when Illinois congressman Melvin Price interrupted, Hickenlooper responded that he needed to proceed as he desired, and only "thereafter" could the committee's other 11 members speak.[28] (Price sarcastically thanked his colleague for conceding "that it is the right of the other members to ask questions."[29]) Hickenlooper then asked Lilienthal to discuss specific individuals – labeled anonymously, by letters – but McMahon cut off this line of questioning on due process grounds, causing another sudden adjournment.[30]

By the late 1940s, Hickenlooper's tendency for making himself look ridiculous produced the phrase "to pull a Hickenlooper."[31] Over a 10-week period, in 45 hearings, 24 of which were public, the joint committee explored a variety of empty allegations emanating from the Iowa senator.[32] Frustrated Democrats urged McMahon to terminate the proceedings: Representative Henry Jackson (D-Washington) noted that Hickenlooper did not even supply

[26] Brien McMahon to Frederic Org, 16 March 1948; Bill Borden to Brien McMahon, 20 Dec. 1948; both in Box 5, JCAE Papers – Files of Senator Brien McMahon, RG 128, National Archives.

[27] Bourke Hickenlooper to Charles Coryell, 16 Aug. 1949, Box 16, JCAE Series, Bourke Hickenlooper Papers, Hoover Presidential Library; *Washington Post*, 3 June 1949.

[28] U.S. Congress, Joint Committee on Atomic Energy, *Hearings, Investigation into the United States Atomic Energy Project*, 81st Congress, 1st session, p. 33 (1 June 1949).

[29] U.S. Congress, Joint Committee on Atomic Energy, *Hearings, Investigation into the United States Atomic Energy Project*, 81st Congress, 1st session, p. 34 (1 June 1949).

[30] U.S. Congress, Joint Committee on Atomic Energy, *Hearings, Investigation into the United States Atomic Energy Project*, 81st Congress, 1st session, p. 109 (3 June 1949).

[31] Robert Griffith, *The Politics of Fear: Joseph R. McCarthy and the Senate* (Lexington: University of Kentucky Press, 1970), p. 66.

[32] Green and Rosenthal, *Government of the Atom*, p. 8.

colleagues with an agenda until the morning of each hearing.[33] McMahon ignored the pleas: the committee was once again front-page news. Lilienthal found the joint committee's atmosphere "angry, scared, ugly," distorted by McMahon's efforts to "increase the prestige and power of his committee and of himself."[34]

While Lilienthal and his staff were spending their days responding to Hickenlooper's latest allegations, the AEC was involved in the single most important decision it made in its three decades of existence. The Soviets' testing their first atomic bomb in October 1949 ended the U.S. atomic monopoly, sparking debate over whether the United States should build a hydrogen bomb – the "super" – even though the weapon could have no conceivable military use. Citing strong opposition from most atomic scientists, led by Robert Oppenheimer, the commission voted against recommending construction. The bomb's advocates, however, sustained the fight, urging the president to overturn the AEC's recommendation.

The debate over the super could not have come at a more propitious time for the figure dubbed "the atomic senator."[35] As Oppenheimer noted in late October 1949, McMahon had "tried to find something tangible" ever since the Soviets atomic test.[36] The cause reinforced the Connecticut Democrat's dramatically more pessimistic view of the Cold War. Lilienthal found private discussions with the JCAE chair "pretty discouraging," since McMahon, convinced of "the inevitability of war with the Russians," championed pre-emptive war.[37] Otherwise, the senator cautioned, once the Soviets obtained a sufficient number of atomic bombs, they "will park them in the harbors of the United States, and will turn this country into a shambles."[38] As a political master himself, Truman recognized the motives of McMahon, who faced re-election in 1950. After Lilienthal recounted one pessimistic meeting with McMahon, the president grinned and replied, "Oh, just wait till Brien is re-elected and he won't think we're going to hell in a hand basket."[39]

McMahon received a summer 1949 briefing from one of the few atomic scientists to favor the H-bomb, Edward Teller; thereafter, this figure who had touted civilian supremacy covertly allied with the military to overturn the AEC's recommendation.[40] The Connecticut senator appointed his closest

[33] U.S. Congress, Joint Committee on Atomic Energy, *Hearings, Investigation into the United States Atomic Energy Project*, 81st Congress, 1st session, p. 231 (4 June 1949).

[34] David Lilienthal, *Journals of David Lilienthal, volume 2: The Atomic Energy Years* (New York: Harper and Row, 1967), entry for 4 June 1949, p. 539; entry for 18 July 1949, p. 545.

[35] William S. White, "McMahon: Senator and Atomic Specialist," *New York Times Magazine*, 12 Feb. 1950.

[36] Green and Rosenthal, *Government of the Atom*, p. 235.

[37] Lilienthal, *Journals of David Lilienthal: volume 2*, entry for 1 Nov. 1949, p. 585.

[38] *ESSFRC, Military Assistance Program: 1949*, p. 406 (29 Aug. 1949).

[39] Lilienthal, *Journals of David Lilienthal: volume 2*, entry for 9 Nov. 1949, p. 595.

[40] Hewlett and Anderson, *History of the AEC, volume 2*, p. 400.

ally on the joint committee, Representative Chet Holifield (D-California), to chair an ad hoc subcommittee to investigate the AEC's handling of the case; unsurprisingly, the subcommittee concluded that the commission had acted improperly.[41] McMahon then proposed that the JCAE formally urge Truman to annul the AEC's decision, an approach even committee Republicans deemed presumptuous.[42] But the chairman ignored the guidance, and, with his staff director, Bill Borden, prepared a 5,000-word document citing "the profundity of the atomic crisis" as justification for building the super.[43]

In February 1950, McMahon launched a speaking tour – which, he boasted, received a "tremendous" reception – to increase national support for the super, as well as for smaller atomic weapons that could be used on the battlefield.[44] He introduced the Senate to the new technology in a speech that, according to *New York Times* correspondent William S. White, "held many of his Senate colleagues in a sort of chilling suspense."[45] And when Truman ultimately proceeded with the super, the JCAE deserved some of the credit (or blame) for the move.[46]

Of course, McMahon was not the only senator to play off increased Cold War tensions and marshal congressional power to serve his political self-interest. Nor was he the most shameless to do so. Until early 1950, Joseph McCarthy had registered almost no impact in the upper chamber, bouncing from issue to issue while siding with the revisionists on foreign policy matters. The outline of McCarthy's anti-Communist crusade is well-known. In a Wheeling, West Virginia, address, the senator claimed to possess a list of 205 known Communists working for the State Department. By the time of a Reno, Nevada, speech two days later, the number had been narrowed to 57 card-carrying Communists, with 205 "bad risks." On February 20, 1950, he repeated many of these charges in Senate remarks, mostly using discredited material from earlier HUAC investigations.[47] Friendly questions from other revisionists made clear the partisan aspect of the matter. Scott Lucas hoped to defuse the issue by cobbling together a resolution referring McCarthy's charges to the Foreign Relations Committee.

The committee struggled to determine how to proceed. Connally delegated the problem to a special subcommittee, with Millard Tydings,

---

[41] Kolyard Dylan and Francis Garron, *Chet Holifield: Master Legislator and Nuclear Statesman* (Lanham, Maryland: University Press of Maryland, 1996), p. 35.

[42] Bourke Hickenlooper to Brien McMahon, 27 Jan. 1950, Box 21, JCAE Series, Bourke Hickenlooper Papers, Hoover Presidential Library.

[43] Hewlett and Anderson, *History of the AEC, volume* 2, p. 393.

[44] Brien McMahon to Frank Folsom, 20 Feb. 1950, Box 6, JCAE Papers – Files of Senator Brien McMahon, Record Group 128, National Archives.

[45] *New York Times*, 3 Feb. 1950.

[46] Barton Bernstein, "Crossing the Rubicon: A Missed Opportunity to Stop the H-bomb?," *International Security* 14 (1989), pp. 146–148.

[47] 96 CR, 81st Congress, 2nd session, pp. 1953–1980 (20 Feb. 1950).

Brien McMahon, and Theodore Francis Green (D-Rhode Island) to represent the majority, Lodge and Hickenlooper the minority. (Lodge agreed to serve only after several other moderate Republicans declined.) The full committee failed to draw up a specific charge, given that, as Tydings observed, "you could drive a horse and wagon through any place in this resolution."[48] The first subcommittee meeting fared little better; Tydings, exasperated, asked, "What are we to do?"[49] McCarthy declined to supply the subcommittee with the names of the alleged Communists in the State Department's ranks, claiming that the administration should instead release to Congress its federal loyalty files, which Truman refused to do. With the impasse, as Tydings understood, "We are all on the spot."[50]

This analysis especially applied to Lodge. Since Hickenlooper would clearly sustain McCarthy's allegations and the three Democrats would deny them, Lodge had to choose between party loyalty and his principles. More so than any member of the Senate minority, even Smith or Vandenberg, Lodge maintained that "elementary prudence" justified the administration's international approach; the case offered by the opposition, he realized, was "very weak."[51] The senator's attitude attracted the attention of Dean Acheson, who became secretary of state in 1949. Sharing comparable backgrounds as well-educated products of the "Eastern Establishment" – Acheson had attended Groton and Yale, Lodge Middlesex and Harvard – the two men had come to Washington endowed with a sense of public service and an internationalist outlook. Personally, as well, they possessed similar traits. In words that could have applied to himself, Lodge once described Acheson "as in some ways a lonely man – not in the family sense or in the sense of lacking personal friends – but in the official sense where his close associates appear to me to be entirely subordinates."[52]

In personal meetings with Lodge that the secretary himself requested, Acheson confided his disappointment in Tom Connally, on matters both of temperament and substance.[53] (During one foreign aid discussion, for instance, the Texas senator claimed that the United States had fought Poland during World War II.[54]) Nor was the secretary more impressed with other committee Democrats, such as the always unreliable Claude Pepper; Watter George, the power baron among committee conservatives; or

---

[48] *ESSFRC*, vol. 2, p. 209 (25 Feb. 1950).

[49] *ESSFRC*, vol. 2, p. 218 (27 Feb. 1950).

[50] *ESSFRC*, vol. 2, p. 238 (27 Feb. 1950).

[51] Henry Cabot Lodge, "Estimate of the Situation," 2 June 1950, in Confidential Journal, Reel 17, Henry Cabot Lodge, II, Papers, Massachusetts State Historical Society.

[52] Lodge Confidential Journal, entry for 18 Jan. 1950, Reel 17, Henry Cabot Lodge, II, Papers, Massachusetts State Historical Society.

[53] Lodge Confidential Journal, entry for 18 Jan. 1950, Reel 17, Henry Cabot Lodge, II, Papers, Massachusetts State Historical Society.

[54] *ESSFRC*, vol. 3, part 2, p. 87 (20 Aug. 1951).

Brien McMahon, "who wants to fight a preventive war."[55] With partisanship increasing on the Republican side and Vandenberg suffering from terminal cancer, the committee system was "unworkable."[56] Acheson therefore searched for a new device of congressional relations, offering to take Lodge into his confidence and have him function as the administration's de facto Senate leader on foreign policy issues.[57] The Massachusetts senator willingly acceded, despite the political risks: as he later admitted, his goal in politics was "to take sides on the big questions of the day and try to be effective with regard to them."[58] Over the next several months, the two men met regularly, cognizant that Connally "would probably have a fit if he discovered."[59] Lodge pressed the secretary to revitalize the Atlantic Alliance through a dramatic gesture, such as appointing Dwight Eisenhower supreme commander of NATO forces. Otherwise, he worried that the revisionists' aggressive recommendations, which were "popular politically," might force the administration into a "showdown" with the Soviets.[60]

By late 1950, William S. White articulated the Washington consensus: Lodge had "become his party's leader on foreign affairs."[61] Ruminating on the state of international relations that June, the Massachusetts senator contended that "elementary prudence indicates that as long as the Western world is in a position of weakness that it runs the risk of being overwhelmed by the Soviets."[62] Accordingly, he favored long-term programs of economic and military assistance to Europe and stationing U.S. troops in Western Europe as part of a NATO force. A few weeks later, H. Alexander Smith concluded similarly: Congress and the administration needed to cooperate to produce a positive foreign policy, "formed on some higher principle than mere negative hostility to Communism" and centered on military aid, international economic planning, and increased attention to the psychological aspects of the Cold War.[63]

---

[55] Lodge Confidential Journal, entry for 18 Jan. 1950, Reel 17, Henry Cabot Lodge, II, Papers, Massachusetts State Historical Society.

[56] Lodge Confidential Journal, entry for 18 Jan. 1950, Reel 17, Henry Cabot Lodge, II, Papers, Massachusetts State Historical Society.

[57] Lodge Confidential Journal, entry for 18 Jan. 1950, Reel 17, Henry Cabot Lodge, II, Papers, Massachusetts State Historical Society.

[58] Lodge to George Cabot Lodge, 31 Dec. 1963, Box 32, Henry Cabot Lodge, II, Papers, Massachusetts State Historical Society.

[59] Henry Cabot Lodge confidential Journal, entry for 18 Jan. 1950, Reel 17, Henry Cabot Lodge, II, Papers, Massachusetts State Historical Society.

[60] "Conversation with Secretary Dean Acheson, Friday, February 17, 1950," Lodge Confidential Journal, Reel 17, Henry Cabot Lodge, II, Papers, Massachusetts State Historical Society.

[61] *New York Times*, 9 Sept. 1950.

[62] Henry Cabot Lodge, "Estimate of the World Situation," 2 June 1950, Reel 17, Henry Cabot Lodge, II, Papers, Massachusetts State Historical Society.

[63] H. Alexander Smith, undelivered speech, 27 June 1950, Box 103, H. Alexander Smith Papers, Mudd Library, Princeton University.

The willingness of Lodge, Smith, and an increasingly ill Vandenberg to work with the administration maintained aspects of the bipartisan structure, at least with regard to international assistance. Reversing previous practice, in 1950 Congress considered all economic aid as part of a single bill, linking Marshall Plan funds, aid to UN programs, assistance to South Korea and other non-Communist forces in Asia, and a new program, Point Four, which provided technical assistance to underdeveloped nations. As occurred with all other packages during the Truman years, the critical battles on Point Four and 1950 foreign aid occurred in the Senate. But, unlike in past years, organized resistance existed: McCarran headed a newly created ad hoc "watchdog" committee of foreign aid critics, which delayed consideration of the bill through parliamentary tactics and issuing hostile reports. The Nevada senator championed cutting European aid appropriations by 50 percent each year – so that "the final shock of cutting it entirely won't be felt."[64]

McCarran's cohort unsurprisingly demanded reductions in funds. But revisionists also offered a positive program by intensifying efforts to extend U.S. aid to Spain. The previous year, the Nevada senator had introduced an amendment to compel the president to extend $50 million to Franco's "democratic" and "God-fearing" government.[65] In remarks that the London *Times* tartly observed "exhausted his vocabulary of praise for the present Spanish regime," McCarran peculiarly interpreted the European strategic balance as based on control of the Iberian Peninsula.[66] To some effect, he personally lobbied conservative colleagues in both parties, but the amendment was ruled out of order.[67]

McCarran was better prepared in 1950, after having joined Owen Brewster in touring Madrid, at Franco's invitation, before the Senate began its debate. (When the senator claimed that he would discuss possible U.S. aid with the Spanish dictator, *Reporter* labeled him the new "Ambassador from Nevada."[68]) If anything, Brewster was even more extreme than his Nevada colleague: the Maine Republican detected much to like about Franco's regime, the only government in the world "thus far that has successfully purged the Communist menace from its midst."[69] Perhaps this was why "our left-wing comrades," citizens whose "sympathies are not always to the best interests of America," so strongly attacked Franco.[70] While administration

---

[64] Steinberg, "McCarran: Lone Wolf of the Senate," *Harper's*, Nov. 1950.

[65] 95 *CR*, 81st Congress, 1st session, p. 5966 (10 May 1949).

[66] *The Times* (London), 14 May 1949.

[67] Richard Russell to Pat McCarran, 25 July 1949, Series IV, Box 49, Pat McCarran Papers, Nevada Historical Society.

[68] *Reporter*, 13 Sept. 1949.

[69] Owen Brewster address, "American Foreign Policy," Bangor, Maine, 27 Nov. 1949, Box 1, Speeches series, Owen Brewster Papers, Bowdoin College.

[70] Owen Brewster to Stuart Gross, 20 Dec. 1950; Owen Brewster to Richard Hess, 25 Sept. 1951; both in Box 2, Foreign Affairs series, Owen Brewster Papers, Bowdoin College.

opposition and memories of Franco's pro-Nazi sympathies during World War II remained strong enough to defeat the McCarran amendment, it lost by only a scant seven votes. The revisionists clearly were getting stronger, as the Nevada senator demonstrated in 1951, when he pushed through an amendment requiring an emergency loan to Franco's regime. Former Secretary of the Interior Harold Ickes fumed that "no one in or out of Spain could work more assiduously for Fascist Dictator Franco" than the man he mockingly termed "Señor Don Dr. Pat de McCarran"; Drew Pearson ridiculed him as the "chief volunteer public relations counsel to Europe's Number One Fascist dictator."[71]

Although they did not press the issue, the revisionists and even some mainstream figures also wanted Spain to join the circle of America's military allies. Tydings, reflecting the majority viewpoint on the Armed Services Committee, termed denying Spain arms a "very, very ridiculous position."[72] Karl Mundt (R-South Dakota) proposed an international non-Communist police force that would include troops from Spain, Turkey, Nationalist China, and Argentina.[73] And Wherry equated keeping Spain out of NATO with appeasing "the Communists, and the left-wingers, and the pinkoes at home and abroad."[74] (Tom Connally thanked his Nebraska colleague for demonstrating a "mastery of the hot air."[75]) Spain, obviously, possessed some marginal military value. But the revisionists' chief interest in the Iberian dictatorship was symbolic: unlike Labour in England or left-wing coalitions in France and Italy, Franco's government reflected principles that the congressional right found worthy of support.

As with the Spanish aid fight, revisionists lacked majority support to kill the Point Four program in a debate notable for its rancor. (Connally remarked that Robert Taft "seems to know more about less than anyone else I know"; James Kem retorted that that Foreign Relations Committee chairman "regards it as an act of supererogation for any other member of the Senate to express an opinion on foreign affairs."[76]) Point Four and the foreign aid bill cleared Congress in early June 1950, the last major foreign policy initiatives approved before the onset of hostilities in Korea.

After several years of increasing tension between the Communist north and non-Communist south, North Korean forces crossed the 38th parallel in a bid to unify the country under the Stalinist rule of Kim Il Sung. With the Soviets boycotting the UN Security Council to demand the seating of

---

[71] Harold Ickes, "Señor Don Pat McCarran," *The New Republic*, 18 June 1951; *Washington Post*, 23 Nov. 1949.
[72] ESSFRC, *Reviews of the World Situation, 1949–1950*, p. 124 (10 Jan. 1950).
[73] 96 CR, 81st Congress, 2nd session, p. 9528 (30 June 1950); CQ *Almanac 1949*, p. 380.
[74] 96 CR, 81st Congress, 2nd session, p. 9538 (30 June 1950).
[75] 97 CR, 82nd Congress, 1st session, p. 3281 (4 April 1951).
[76] 96 CR, 81st Congress, 2nd session, pp. 7497 (23 May 1950), 9228 (27 June 1950).

the Communist regime as the government of China, Truman obtained a Security Council endorsement for a multinational force to protect South Korea. The primarily U.S. force was placed under the leadership of General Douglas MacArthur, then overseeing the U.S. occupation of Japan. Terming the operation a "police action," the president did not request from Congress a declaration of war, which, in the days following the invasion, he surely would have received. Two years later, Truman would be widely excoriated for his decision. At the time, however, the president's choice seemed prudent. Acheson recalled that placing the matter before Congress risked "one more question in [committee] cross-examination which destroys you"; in backhanded testimony to the revisionists' power, the secretary particularly feared the debate spinning out of control and forcing the administration into a conflict against all forms of Asian Communism, including in China.[77]

For Truman's right-wing critics, as Taft privately noted, "there is no alternative but to support the war, but certainly we can point out that it has resulted from a bungling of the Democratic administration."[78] Some Republicans, such as Wherry, openly charged the president with exceeding his constitutional authority, but most focused on attacks they would not have to disavow if the conflict ended well. Edward Thye (R-Minnesota) attributed the invasion to the administration's failure to "create a military strength through the United Nations."[79] Hickenlooper believed that "the whole soft policy over the last five years or more has forced us into this situation"; by late July, the Iowa senator concluded that the State Department, "led by a strong and cohesive group of Red sympathizers," had prevailed upon Truman to withhold military aid to anti-Communist allies in East Asia – South Korea and Nationalist China – thus all but inviting the North Korean intervention.[80]

Two days before Hickenlooper attributed the outbreak of the Korean conflict to State Department Communists, the Tydings subcommittee issued a report accusing McCarthy of perpetrating a "fraud and a hoax" and dismissing his allegations as deliberate falsehoods.[81] Hickenlooper, as expected, dissented. Lodge took a middle course. Despite rumors that the Massachusetts senator would sign on with the majority, he instead issued "individual views," criticizing the investigation's "superficial and inconclusive" nature.[82]

---

[77] Thomas Paterson, "presidential Foreign Policy," *Diplomatic History* 3 (1979), p. 19.

[78] James Patterson, *Mr. Republican*, p. 455.

[79] Edward Thye to Kitty Passard, 18 Sept. 1950, Box 51, Edward Thye Papers, Minnesota State Historical Society.

[80] Bourke Hickenlooper to Philip Duncan, 17 July 1950; Bourke Hickenlooper to R.A. Holmgren, 19 July 1950; both in Box 148, Foreign Relations Committee series, Bourke Hickenlooper Papers, Hoover Presidential Library.

[81] *New York Times*, 18 July 1950.

[82] *New York Times*, 18 July 1950.

When the situation most demanded it, Lodge could not bring himself to practice the "unpartisanship" about which he had spoken so eloquently.

Lodge's decision allowed Senate Republicans to dismiss the report as a whitewash when Tydings presented the document to the Senate. In a debate over whether to accept the report that the Washington staff of *The New Republic* described as "the most spectacular we ever saw" in a quarter century of covering the upper chamber, Tydings several times was ordered to cease speaking for impugning the personal integrity of other members.[83] The Senate accepted the report on a straight party-line vote.[84]

McCarthy's tactics did trouble a few Republicans. Having waited several weeks in vain for more senior colleagues to confront the issue, Margaret Chase Smith (R-Maine) issued the most famous dissent.[85] On June 1, 1950, Smith expressed her sorrow about the Senate's transformation into "a forum of hate and character assassination sheltered by the shield of congressional immunity." The Maine senator feared that the GOP would replace a failed administration with "a Republican regime embracing a philosophy that lacks political integrity or intellectual honesty," which rode "to political victory on the Four Horsemen of Calumny – Fear, Ignorance, Bigotry and Smear."[86]

Six other Republican moderates affixed their signatures to Smith's "Declaration of Conscience," but despite its rhetorical and moral power, Smith's speech failed to persuade. The only woman in the Senate, the Maine senator herself lacked political influence. McCarthy, of course, was beyond the reach of any outside counsel. Taft, on the other hand, seemed a more appropriate target for Smith's words, since the Ohio Republican enjoyed a reputation for political and intellectual integrity.[87] But publicly, Taft – incredibly stating that if one of McCarthy's cases did not work out, "he should proceed with another one" – praised the Wisconsin senator for having exposed the "pro-Communist group in the State Department"; it was of no relevance whether he possessed "legal evidence" for his case.[88]

As the historian Robert Griffith has observed, McCarthy's power derived not from his allegations per se – which, after all, many revisionists had previously made – but from his ability to generate media coverage and the utter recklessness with which he attacked.[89] In the 1950 midterm elections, McCarthy focused his efforts on ousting Tydings. The incumbent was renominated only after a bitter primary campaign in which one foe attacked him

---

[83] *New York Times*, 21 July 1950; *The New Republic*, 31 July 1950.

[84] Oshinsky, *A Conspiracy So Immense*, pp. 168–172.

[85] Margaret Chase Smith oral history, John Stennis Oral History Project, Mississippi State University.

[86] Margaret Chase Smith, "Declaration of Conscience," 1 June 1950, http://www.mcslibrary.org/program/library/declaration.htm, accessed 3 August 2003.

[87] Patterson, *Mr. Republican*, pp. 445–446.

[88] Patterson, *Mr. Republican*, p. 446.

[89] Griffith, *Politics of Fear*, p. 116.

for giving "the green light to Stalin's agents in this country."[90] In the general election, Republican John Marshall Butler, a first-time candidate, received massive financial, political, and administrative assistance from McCarthy. Butler outraised Tydings by a nearly 3-to-1 margin, and benefited from three McCarthy visits to the state, where the Wisconsin senator railed that Tydings had shielded traitors "at the time when the survival of western non-atheistic civilization hangs in the balance."[91] In a major upset, Butler prevailed by 43,000 votes, besting Tydings by seven percentage points. The incumbent, in fact, began the race with a number of weaknesses other than his role in the McCarthy report, but the perception emerged that the Wisconsin senator was solely responsible for Tydings' defeat.

The two 1950 Senate elections in which the Cold War played the greatest role occurred in states where McCarthy himself had little or no direct involvement. In Florida, Representative George Smathers challenged incumbent Claude Pepper for renomination. Smathers bluntly contended that "the leader of the radicals and extremists is now on trial in Florida," and he ruthlessly exploited Pepper's 1946 remark that Americans should pray for Stalin's good health.[92] Support from business interests hostile to Pepper's New Deal philosophy and covert backing from the president, who privately called Pepper a "publicity hound" and recalled the senator's flirtation with the dump-Truman effort in 1948, gave Smathers a 10-to-1 financial advantage.[93] These funds paid for a campaign that asked voters to retire "Red Pepper," so that "Florida will not allow herself to become entangled in the spiraling web of the Red network."[94] Smathers won easily.

The only contest that exceeded Florida's for nastiness and underhanded tactics occurred in California, which matched two members of the House, Republican Richard Nixon and Democrat Helen Gahagan Douglas. Nixon's national reputation came from exposing Alger Hiss, while Douglas, a former actress, was a favorite of liberals nationally. (The London *Times* noted that the congresswoman's vote against the McCarran Act "shows that she has kept her sense of proportion at a time when the country as a whole seems unappreciative of such feats."[95]) Speaker Sam Rayburn (D-Texas) termed Nixon "the most devious face of all those who have served in Congress in all the years I've been here," and Douglas was no match. Nixon dismissed her as "pink down to her underwear" and promised to keep the congresswoman "pinned to her extremist record"; at one campaign rally, he greeted a mother

---

[90] *Baltimore Sun*, 1 Sept. 1950.
[91] Griffith, *Politics of Fear*, pp. 127–129.
[92] Brian Crispwell, *Testing the Limits: George Armistead Sanders and Cold War America* (Athens: University of Georgia Press, 1999), pp. 39, 49.
[93] Crispwell, *Testing the Limits*, p. 40; Pepper, *Eyewitness to a Century*, p. 196.
[94] Pepper, *Eyewitness to a Century*, p. 198.
[95] *The Times* (London), 24 Oct. 1950.

carrying her baby with the remark, "If you vote for Douglas we will still be at war in America when he's old enough to fight."[96] With the Nixon campaign financially flush, Douglas' hope of relying on her personal magnetism fell well short; the Republican prevailed by almost 700,000 votes, receiving 59 percent of the vote.

Although Democrats narrowly retained their majorities in both chambers after the election, the results demoralized the party's caucus: as one Democratic senator told his brethren, "For whom does the bell toll? It tolls for thee."[97] Shortly after the election, Lodge, with a touch of understatement, predicted that activity "in the next Congress would be in the direction of closer and more critical scrutiny of foreign policy."[98] As if to confirm the point, on December 15, the Senate Republican caucus passed a resolution expressing no confidence in Acheson's performance as secretary of state. Lodge boycotted the meeting, at which only five GOP senators opposed the motion.[99]

This Republican offensive coincided with the most serious showdown to occur between Truman and Congress. The uneasy relationship between the president and MacArthur failed to survive MacArthur's erroneous calculation that the Chinese would not enter the war if U.S. troops moved into North Korea. After the war settled into a stalemate, Styles Bridges (R-New Hampshire) charged that Truman's failure to "untie MacArthur's hands" explained the "slaughter of American troops"; McCarran called for $1 billion in military aid to finance a KMT invasion of China.[100]

MacArthur, meanwhile, chafed under the administration's refusal to bomb China; when House Minority Leader Joseph Martin (R-Massachusetts) released a letter by the general complaining about the president's tactics, Truman relieved MacArthur of command. *Life* described MacArthur's return home as "like nothing else in American history" – ticker-tape parades in San Francisco and New York, an emotional address before a joint session of Congress.[101] (Ironically, MacArthur addressed the legislature the day after the death of Vandenberg, the Republican most associated with a different approach to postwar international affairs.) After the speech, one congressman remarked, "We have seen the hand of God in the flesh, and we heard the voice of God."[102] From a more secular angle, Taft rejoiced that

---

[96] Greg Mitchell, *Tricky Dick and the Pink Lady: Richard Nixon vs. Helen Gahagan Douglas – Sexual Politics and the Red Scare, 1950* (New York: Random House, 1998), pp. 129–225.

[97] *New York Times*, 7 Jan. 1951.

[98] Henry Cabot Lodge, "Confidential Memorandum for General Eisenhower," late Nov. 1950, Reel 28, Henry Cabot Lodge, II, Papers, Massachusetts State Historical Society, Boston.

[99] *New York Times*, 16 Dec. 1950.

[100] *Congressional Quarterly Weekly Report*, 19 Jan. 1951, 2 Feb. 1951.

[101] *Life*, 30 April 1951.

[102] Melvin Small, *Democracy and Diplomacy: The Impact of Domestic Politics on U.S. Foreign Policy, 1789–1994* (Baltimore: Johns Hopkins University Press, 1996), p. 95.

the "whole episode was completely to the advantage of the Republicans," while McCarran hailed "the most masterful speech that has been delivered in the Capitol in a century."[103]

Taft and Kenneth Wherry instantly demanded hearings on MacArthur's dismissal; given the outpouring of public support for the general, Democrats acceded. With members of both parties distrustful of Connally, if for different reasons, Richard Russell, the new chairman of the Armed Services Committee, was pressed to preside over joint hearings; Republicans believed that Russell would be fair, while Democrats counted on the Georgia senator's respect for the institution to keep the hearings from descending into farce. MacArthur arrived 20 minutes late for the opening day of hearings (one Democratic senator fumed that apparently the general's aides "couldn't get him down from the Cross"); for three days, he made his case against Truman's foreign policy.[104] The general was overmatched by Russell, who, in the words of William S. White, "set in motion an intellectual counterforce to the emotional adulation that for a time had run so strongly through the country."[105] Under intense, if polite, cross-examination from Russell, Lodge, and McMahon, MacArthur fared poorly; he repeatedly refused to speculate what would happen if his best-case scenario planning did not occur, nor was he interested in commenting how his policies would affect U.S. strategic interests in Europe or the homeland. Further detailed testimony from Marshall, Acheson, and every member of the JCS exposed the flaws in MacArthur's strategy and cooled the passions on display in his initial return to the United States.[106]

Even though MacArthur, much to his dismay, was an old solider who faded away, the environment that his dismissal created was ripe for a major legislative assault on executive authority. The issue that triggered the battle, however, was an awkward vehicle: Truman's decision to station U.S. troops in Europe without requesting advance authority from Congress. What came to be known as the Great Debate was neither great nor a debate. There was little intellectual give-and-take; Leverett Saltonstall (R-Massachusetts) termed the rhetorical exchanges "somewhat of a gabfest."[107] Nonetheless, a substantive debate about both the balance of power between Congress and the executive and the future course of U.S. foreign policy was, as Lodge perceptively understood, "embodied in a procedural matter" – for neither the first time nor the last in the Cold War era.[108]

---

[103] *Congressional Quarterly Weekly* Report, 20 April 1951; Patterson, *Mr. Republican*, p. 488.
[104] Richard Rovere, "Letter from Washington," *New Yorker*, 21 April 1951.
[105] *Time*, 4 June 1951.
[106] U.S. Senate, Armed Services Committee, *Hearings, Military Situation in the Far East*, 82nd Congress, 1st session.
[107] *ESSFRC*, vol. 3, part 1, p. 91 (1 March 1951).
[108] *ESSFRC*, vol. 3, part 1, p. 161 (6 March 1951).

In terms of policy, the Great Debate offered little not previously covered in discussions over approving the North Atlantic Treaty or supporting the 1949 military aid package. Strikingly new, however, was its abstract discussion of constitutional powers. A more limited conception of executive authority, implicit in previous revisionist critiques, developed much more clearly in the Great Debate; and, in response, supporters of Truman's European policy offered much stronger defenses of executive authority. A few senators shied away from the fight, recognizing that the debate actually featured a dispute over policy masquerading as constitutional conflict. Smith, for instance, reasoned that the constitutional battle was not "a question worth wasting time and effort on," since NATO's formation necessitated "plowing a new field in all this procedure"; the Senate therefore should seek collaboration in whatever form the executive branch "considered most appropriate."[109]

The vagaries of the U.S. constitutional system, however, invited struggle between the branches, with policy or even petty political disputes easily framed as grand constitutional squabbles. On the one side, senators such as John Bricker (R-Ohio) contended that Congress was becoming like "the legislature of a totalitarian state," with the people's representatives fooled by the administration's "cunning and cleverness" into sacrificing their power.[110] Senators on the other side countered with sweeping assertions of executive prerogatives. In a remarkable reading of history, Tom Connally pointed to the Founding Fathers' memory of George Washington's performance in the Revolutionary War as proof that the commander-in-chief clause granted the president absolute authority in the international realm.[111]

Two senators pointed out the dangers of these polarizing constitutional interpretations. Beginning by stating the obvious – "it is hard for me to side consistently with any individual or party as regards foreign policy" – Lodge hoped that senators would "realize that we are actually in an undeclared war" for which the constitutional precedents were murky.[112] Meanwhile, Wayne Morse – dean of Oregon Law School before entering the Senate – cautioned against the logical conclusions of both sides' arguments. The revisionists' interpretations would call into question American willingness to fulfill its international commitments, while the administration's philosophy came dangerously close to granting "the military broad discretionary authority to make decisions in the field of foreign affairs."[113] Much more would be heard from Morse on this point before his Senate career ended.

In the end, the Great Debate concluded with a face-saving compromise, a resolution expressing the sense of the Senate that if Truman wanted to

---

[109] 97 *CR*, 82nd Congress, 1st session, pp. 2580–2581 (14 March 1951).
[110] 97 *CR*, 82nd Congress, 1st session, pp. 2967, 2972–2973 (29 March 1951).
[111] 97 *CR*, 82nd Congress, 1st session, pp. 142 (11 Jan. 1951), 3281 (4 April 1951).
[112] 97 *CR*, 82nd Congress, 1st session, pp. 146 (11 Jan. 1951), 3276 (4 April 1951).
[113] 97 *CR*, 82nd Congress, 1st session, p. 3264 (4 April 1951).

send more than the four U.S. divisions he had already proposed, he would need approval from Congress. Since the president had made clear he had no intention of sending additional troops, the measure in no way restrained his freedom of action. The Great Debate polarized the Senate constitutionally, with revisionists seeking to mobilize congressional power and their critics championing executive freedom of action. This split would reappear on virtually all diplomatic issues relating to the Cold War over the next four years. Though the revisionist movement was politically and intellectually spent by the mid-1950s, the constitutional division it had engendered remained firmly in place, with important consequences for the congressional role in international affairs. Many mainstream liberals, equating congressional power with the revisionist agenda, automatically championed an assertive presidential international role for years after the right-wing nationalists had faded from the scene.

With the building of the super temporarily pacifying McMahon, the most active foreign policy players throughout 1951 and early 1952 were McCarran, McCarthy, and Mahon. After passage of the Internal Security Act, the upper chamber established the Senate Internal Security Subcommittee (SISS), endowed with what McCarran, who named himself chair, "candidly" termed "very broad" authority.[114] Ostensibly, the SISS aimed to determine whether the Internal Security Act was functioning as its sponsors intended. In fact, the subcommittee provided its chair with broad leeway to investigate any issue that he desired in a Senate counterpart to HUAC. During the first two years of its existence, the SISS conducted hearings on immigration law, the Institute of Pacific Relations (IPR), Communist propaganda, the activities of UN employees, the Voice of America, and alleged Communist influence in youth organizations, the telegraph industry, the media, the defense industry, and four different unions. Each undertaking looked to produce not legislation but publicity, so that, in McCarran's words, the people could understand "that we have in this country a dangerous movement seeking to soften this country up from within, making it unprepared for an attack from without."[115] In his quest, the Nevada senator gained invaluable assistance from FBI director J. Edgar Hoover, who sent along hundreds of memoranda about issues before the SISS and by the end of 1951 had assigned 20 agents to work on the subcommittee's behalf.[116]

---

[114] U.S. Senate, Internal Security Subcommittee, *Hearings, Communist Domination of Union Officials in Vital Defense Industry*, 82nd Congress, 2nd session, p. 1 (6 Oct. 1952).

[115] U.S. Senate, Internal Security Subcommittee, *Hearings, Communist Domination of Union Officials in Vital Defense Industry*, 82nd Congress, 2nd session, p. 2 (6 Oct. 1952).

[116] Ybarra, *Washington Gone Crazy*, p. 547; Christopher Gerard, "On the Road to Vietnam: 'The Loss of China Syndrome,' Pat McCarran, and J. Edgar Hoover," *Nevada Historical Society Quarterly* 37 (1994), p. 251.

The *New York Times* described the highest profile of these investigations, which involved the IPR, as undermining "the traditional American belief in freedom of thought."[117] Since the tail end of World War II, the organization had attracted the ire of China lobby activists, who complained that Communists published material under IPR auspices to weaken popular support for the KMT. Attention increasingly focused on Johns Hopkins professor Owen Lattimore, the former editor of the IPR's journal, *Pacific Affairs*, who served as Chiang's wartime political adviser and then as a State Department official in the immediate postwar era. In 1950, McCarthy fantastically described Lattimore as the Soviet Union's chief espionage agent in the United States; the professor's ferocious defense of himself before the Tydings Committee made him a marked man among the congressional right.

In July 1951, McCarran opened public hearings that operated under the thesis that the IPR was "used as a façade for Communists operating shrewdly behind the scenes."[118] But "for the machinations of the small group that controlled and activated the Institute of Pacific Relations," the Nevada senator wildly claimed, "China today would be free and a bulwark against a further advance of the Red Hordes into the Far East."[119] The hearings, which occurred two days a week for almost eight months and produced 5,712 pages of transcripts, featured McCarran at his most tyrannical. The Nevada senator's remarkably flexible interpretation of what constituted Communism (at one point equating it with "this thing of 'liberalism' and 'liberals'") coincided with his dismissal of protecting the civil liberties of witnesses – a luxury, given that subversives "don't play a gentleman's game, and if you try fighting them with kid gloves, they'll destroy you."[120]

McCarran reserved his worst for Lattimore, who endured 12 days of what he termed "savage and harassing examination" by the SISS.[121] Unlike most previous witnesses, Lattimore was not intimidated, and his testimony produced what the *Washington Post* termed "one of the most acrimonious exchanges Capitol Hill has ever had."[122] Blasting the "system of multiple jeopardy" created by the SISS, the professor wondered whether he was still a citizen of the United States or "a subject of Czechoslovakia or Franco Spain."[123] Subcommittee members responded with scorn. In his first day of testimony, under constant badgering from McCarran and

[117] *New York Times*, 15 March 1952.
[118] U.S. Senate, Internal Security Subcommittee, *Hearings, Institute of Pacific Relations*, 82nd Congress, 2nd session, p. 5 (25 July 1951).
[119] *New York Times*, 3 July 1952.
[120] Pat McCarran to L. E. McCoy, 29 July 1950, Series IV, Box 51, Pat McCarran Papers, Nevada State Historical Society; *U.S. News & World Report*, 16 Nov. 1951.
[121] *New York Times*, 22 March 1952.
[122] *Washington Post*, 27 Feb. 1952.
[123] U.S. Senate, Internal Security Subcommittee, *Hearings, Institute of Pacific Relations*, 82nd Congress, 2nd session, pp. 2944–2945 (27 Feb. 1952).

Republicans Homer Ferguson, William Jenner, and Arthur Watkins, Lattimore got through only two pages of his prepared statement.[124] The low point came after Ferguson asked the professor about his relationship with a known Communist named Bissell. Lattimore's observing that the man's name was actually Bilson triggered a lecture: "Where the question admits a direct answer, as such a question does, it would expedite matters, we think, if you would answer it directly."[125] After his SISS experience and several years of legal fights, Lattimore resettled to England; the subcommittee, meanwhile, produced a 226-page final report blaming Communist influence in the State Department for the U.S. decision not to fully support the Chinese Nationalists, with the added implication that the issue symbolized an unhealthy congressional deference to the executive.[126]

In summer 1952, the *Washington Post* lamented, "It sums up the character of this Congress to state an unquestionable fact: that its most important members was Patrick A. McCarran."[127] His position in the majority provided McCarran with far greater institutional power than McCarthy, although the latter continued his campaign to ferret out real and imagined Communists in the State Department. In June 1951, a lengthy speech implying traitorous activity by George Marshall fell flat, though McCarthy enjoyed more success in contributing to the effort to block Philip Jessup's confirmation as U.S. delegate to the United Nations, citing Jessup's affiliation with "Communist-front" organizations.[128] Seeking to constrain the Wisconsin senator's power, William Benton (D-Connecticut) filed a complaint against McCarthy for illegal behavior in the 1950 Maryland Senate race, but the investigating subcommittee, eventually chaired by Thomas Hennings (D-Missouri), moved at a glacial pace.

While McCarran badgered and McCarthy bellowed, Mahon quietly exerted influence. In his magnum opus, *Congressional Government*, Woodrow Wilson stated, "The House sits, not for serious discussions, but to sanction the conclusions of its committees as rapidly as possible."[129] When the Korean War began in June 1950, 1.5 million men served in the U.S. armed forces: the Army had 10 divisions, the Navy 618 ships, and the Air Force 42 groups. One year later, 3.2 million men were under arms: the Army had 18 divisions, the Navy 1,000 ships, and the Air Force 72 groups.[130]

[124] U.S. Senate, Internal Security Subcommittee, *Hearings, Institute of Pacific Relations*, 82nd Congress, 2nd session, p. 2909 (26 Feb. 1952).

[125] U.S. Senate, Internal Security Subcommittee, *Hearings, Institute of Pacific Relations*, 82nd Congress, 2nd session, p. 3019 (28 Feb. 1952).

[126] Gerard, "On the Road to Vietnam," p. 252.

[127] *Washington Post*, 10 July 1952.

[128] Griffith, *Politics of Fear*, pp. 145–152.

[129] Woodrow Wilson, *Congressional Government: A Study in American Politics* (Boston: Houghton Maffir, 1885), p. 69.

[130] Hogan, *Cross of Iron*, p. 285.

Funding for this enormous expansion proceeded through Mahon's Defense Appropriations Subcommittee, which handled more funds than the other 12 Appropriations subcommittees combined.[131]

Described in 1952 by former vice president John Nance Garner as "the best man we've elected in Texas in the past 25 years," Mahon, who neither smoke nor drank and who taught Sunday School for much of his congressional career, earned the nickname "the Deacon."[132] The Texas congressman was torn on how to use this newfound power. On the one hand, like most Appropriations Committee members, he favored reducing federal spending, operating under the premise that the committee existed "to veto or diminish the budget requests as often as reasons deemed sufficient to do so could be found."[133] On the other, the Texas congressman wanted more funds for the Air Force.[134] Mahon increasingly demanded reductions in Army funding as a way of influencing internal military debates over which branch would dominate the defense budget in the years following adoption of NSC 68 in 1950, which dramatically expended the conception of The Cold War threat.

The dramatic expansion of the Pentagon budget made Truman's attempts in 1948 and 1949 to hold defense spending to under $10 billion look quaint. In the short term, however, Korea's most immediate impact came in domestic politics: Truman's inability to end the war doomed Democratic chances in the 1952 elections. Taft openly conceded the linkage of politics and policy: "We cannot possibly win the next election," he informed other GOP senators, "unless we point out the utter failure and incapacity of the present Administration to conduct foreign policy."[135] In the House, Walter Judd (R-Minnesota) articulated the GOP consensus when he predicted that the "Korea fiasco will be only the first installment in the costly payments our country will be making for years for the blunders it made in choosing as it did in 1948" in the Chinese civil war.[136]

With Truman's renomination unlikely, Brien McMahon launched a campaign under the slogan of "McMahon Is the Man," seeking to become the first Catholic president. His political maneuvering with the JCAE, however, went for naught. After several weeks on the campaign trail, McMahon fell ill; doctors discovered an aggressive cancer, and the Connecticut senator died before the Democratic convention opened. McMahon's death also ended the JCAE 's prominent foreign policy role. The committee went leaderless for three months into the new congressional session, due to a boycott by

---

[131] *New York Times*, 22 May 1957

[132] *Washington Post*, 11 May 1952; *New York Times*, 22 May 1957.

[133] Richard Fenno, *Congressmen in Committees* (Boston: Little, Brown, 1973), p. 48.

[134] George Mahon, "Dear Colleague," 25 Oct. 1951; Joe Evins to George Mahon, 21 Jan. 1952; both in Box 284, George Mahon Papers, Texas Tech University.

[135] Patterson, *Mr. Republican*, p. 491.

[136] Walter Judd to Roy Bjorkman, 5 June 1951, Box 22, Walter Judd Papers, Minnesota State Historical Society.

House members, who wanted the chair's position to rotate between the two chambers. They won the argument, but at considerable cost. As members of the lower chamber increasingly dominated the joint committee, the JCAE shifted its focus from international affairs to domestic matters, especially atomic energy.[137]

The real contest in 1952 occurred among the Republicans, with the foreign policy split in the GOP caucus reappearing on the national stage. Taft's enemies from previous battles viewed him as unfit for the presidency, and rallied around Dwight Eisenhower, who narrowly captured the nomination. With Republicans railing against KC² (Korea, Communism, and corruption), the fall race was anti-climactic. Two Senate races, in addition, had long-term consequences. In Arizona, Barry Goldwater upset Majority Leader Ernest MacFarland, bringing to the Senate a key voice for a hard-line defense policy but also paving the way for Lyndon Johnson to become Senate Democratic leader. Meanwhile, in Massachusetts, Lodge was ousted by the ambitious congressman from Massachusetts' 8th District, John Kennedy.[138] George Marshall wrote that he was "terribly sorry" at the Bay State voters' "great error."[139]

Despite their loss of the Massachusetts seat, Republicans narrowly captured control of both the House and the Senate. Taft's continuing influence forced Eisenhower's secretary of state, former senator John Foster Dulles, to devote large amounts of time to dealing with Congress, either formally in committee testimony or informally through at least 160 off-the-record meetings.[140] The scope of Eisenhower's difficulties became clear early in 1953, when the president briefed GOP congressional leaders on his new national security policy, the New Look. To meet the dual threat of containing Communism abroad and preventing excessive federal spending at home, the New Look, formalized in NSC 162/2, relied on nuclear weapons and covert operations, thereby reducing appropriations for expensive conventional arms. Though the strategy ultimately allowed Eisenhower to cut Pentagon spending by roughly 25 percent, this amount did not satisfy Taft, who, "with all due respect for the NSC, didn't believe the members knew anything more than he about these problems."[141] (Coming from a figure who had admitted his knowledge on national security matters came from reading the remarks of military critics in the major newspapers, this was quite an assertion.[142]) While Taft criticized the president for spending too much, other key

---

[137] Green and Rosenthal, *Government of the Atom*, pp. 83–167.

[138] Thomas Whalen, *Kennedy versus Lodge: The 1952 Massachusetts Senate Race* (Boston: Northeastern University Press, 2000).

[139] Whalen, *Kennedy versus Lodge*, p. 157.

[140] Anna Nelson, "John Foster Dulles and the Bipartisan Congress," *Political Science Quarterly* 102 (1987), pp. 44–46.

[141] "Notes on Legislative Leadership Meeting," 30 April 1953, Legislative Leaders Series, Dwight Eisenhower Series, Dwight Eisenhower Presidential Library.

[142] Patterson, *Mr. Republican*, p. 342.

Republicans attacked the New Look for devoting insufficient resources to defense. Saltonstall wanted more Air Force funding, while Knowland, more concerned about politics, warned "that the Democrats would hit hard if the Congress cut military appropriations."[143] The discussion previewed the congressional debates over national security policy that would recur throughout the Eisenhower administration.

The two years of GOP congressional control, however, were most notable as the high point of McCarthyism. The election weakened the influence of McCarthy's major rival among Senate Red-baiters, McCarran, who lost his chairmanships when the Republicans gained a Senate majority. The ideologically quirky and politically weak William Langer, the sole member of the 82nd Congress to have opposed U.S. entry into the UN and the only Republican senator to have opposed the McCarran Act, assumed the chairmanship of the Judiciary Committee. Langer's well-deserved reputation for erratic behavior – he regularly filibustered Supreme Court nominations to protest the lack of a North Dakotan on the nation's highest court – made him a less than influential committee chairman.

McCarthy took advantage of Judiciary's decline, using his chairmanship of a heretofore obscure committee, Government Operations, whose broad but vague authority gave it almost unlimited oversight power for an ambitious chair. McCarthy also assumed the chairmanship of the Permanent Subcommittee on Investigations (PSI), the successor body to the World War II Truman Committee, which had investigated waste in defense contracting and brought the Missouri senator to national prominence. Befitting its previously low-profile status, the PSI included only two senators (McCarthy and Arkansas Democrat John McClellan) who were not Senate freshmen.[144]

In 1952, the PSI held six executive sessions; the following year, its first under McCarthy's chairmanship, the subcommittee convened 117 such sessions, during which it heard from 395 witnesses and compiled 8,969 pages of testimony.[145] McCarthy's high-handedness prompted the subcommittee's three Democrats (John McClellan, Stuart Symington, and Henry Jackson) to boycott hearings for most of 1953, an action that William S. White termed "about as grave a step as can be imagined," since "to lose face within the club that is the Senate is, sometimes, actually to lose all."[146] Nonetheless, the Wisconsin senator's ability to set the agenda in Washington prompted

---

[143] "Notes on Legislative Leadership Meeting," 30 April 1953, Legislative Leaders Series, Dwight Eisenhower Series, Dwight Eisenhower presidential Library.

[144] Donald A. Ritchie, "Introduction," *Executive Sessions of the Senate Permanent Subcommittee on Investigations of the Committee on Government Operations*, 83rd Congress, 1st session, pp. xi–xiii.

[145] Ritchie, "Introduction," *Executive Sessions of the Senate Permanent Subcommittee on Investigations of the Committee on Government Operations*, 83rd Congress, 1st session, p. xiii.

[146] *New York Times*, 12 July 1953; Griffith, *Politics of Fear*, p. 213.

former British prime minister Clement Attlee to wonder whether Eisenhower or McCarthy wielded a greater influence on U.S. foreign policy.[147]

In fact, McCarthy's standing outside of Congress started to decline fairly quickly after the new Congress met; public opinion polls by early 1954 showed that his negative ratings outweighed his positives. Within Congress, however, his ability to fall back on procedural norms allowed him to cushion the effects of his growing unpopularity. Though Democratic threats to block the PSI's funding led the chair to concede to the opposition the right to hire a minority counsel, McCarthy's bureaucratic power remained immense – until he overreached himself. Citing the promotion of an Army dentist, Irving Peress, McCarthy claimed that Communists had penetrated the armed forces; in response, the Army accused McCarthy of improperly demanding special treatment for the subcommittee's former consultant and subcommittee counsel Roy Cohn's traveling companion, Private G. David Schine. Two months of nationally televised hearings culminated in Army special counsel Joseph Welch's dramatic denunciation of McCarthy. After initially attempting to appease the Wisconsin senator, the administration eventually forbade the Army leadership from testifying about private discussions within the executive department – so as, the president asserted, "to preclude the exercise of arbitrary power by any branch of Government."[148] Eisenhower also authorized Director of Central Intelligence (DCI) Allen Dulles to invoke executive privilege and withhold documents subpoenaed by McCarthy. Within the Senate, meanwhile, a special committee chaired by Arthur Watkins favorably reported a censure resolution introduced by Vermont's Ralph Flanders; the overwhelming censure vote in December 1954 effectively ended McCarthy's career.

Viewed from an institutional angle, McCarthy's confrontation with the administration, by buttressing the principle of executive privilege, ultimately represented a clear victory for executive power. So too did the fate of the Bricker amendment.[149] The amendment stemmed from revisionists' fear, as expressed by its sponsor, that "American sovereignty and the American Constitution are threatened by treaty law" through documents authored by "reactionary one-worlders trying to vest legislative powers in non-elected officials of the UN."[150] Bricker's cohort specifically worried that the UN Human Rights Covenant could mandate radical social and economic programs; the Ohio senator, for one, detected a "similarity between the Soviet Constitution and the proposed Human Rights covenants."[151] The

---

[147] *Washington Post*, 13 May 1953.
[148] *New York Times*, 18 May 1954.
[149] Reedy, *U.S. Senate*, p. 81.
[150] *Congressional Quarterly Weekly Report*, 15 Jan. 1954.
[151] John Bricker to Edward Fitzpatrick, 25 Sept. 1953, Box 95, John Bricker Papers, Ohio State Historical Society.

amendment passed through several forms, but its central principles remained constant: any treaty or executive agreement conflicting with the Constitution would have no effect; all treaties would not apply as domestic law except through valid legislation by Congress or the states; and all executive agreements would not apply as domestic law except through valid legislation by Congress or the states.[152] In its most basic sense, the Bricker amendment looked to tilt the treaty-making power in the direction of the legislature – first by giving the House a formal role in the process by prohibiting self-enacting treaties, and second by ending the constitutional provision making treaties the supreme law of the land.

A survey by one Washington magazine in the late 1940s listed Bricker as the worst member of the Senate (Taft was rated best, followed by George and Russell); author John Gunther compared the Ohio senator's intellect to "interstellar space – a vast vacuum occasionally crossed by homeless, wandering clichés."[153] One session left Eisenhower amazed that Bricker's "adviser leaned into his ear every five minutes" because the senator seemed incapable of developing thoughts on his own.[154] Nonetheless, Bricker was a dogged fighter for his cause. "If it is true that when you die," the president once told his press secretary, "the things that bothered you most are engraved on your skull, I am sure I'll have there the mud and dirt of France during the invasion and the name of Senator Bricker."[155]

In addressing the amendment's impact, Eisenhower argued that "we cannot hope to achieve and maintain peace if we shackle the Federal Government so that it is no longer sovereign in foreign affairs."[156] A group of senators (though at the time of the amendment's introduction less than the 33 needed to block its approval) wholeheartedly agreed. J. William Fulbright termed the amendment the most "violent attack" on the Constitution since the 1850s, an initiative that "throttles the President of the United States in his conduct of foreign relations."[157] Alexander Wiley argued that passage would prevent ratification of such beneficial efforts as the international narcotics treaty, thereby asking "the parents of our country to allow floods of illegal dope to pour into our land."[158] John Sherman Cooper (R-Kentucky) asked,

[152] John Bricker form letter, 15 March 1954, Box 101, John Bricker Papers, Ohio State Historical Society.

[153] Duane Tananbaum, *The Bricker Amendment Controversy: A test of Eisenhower's Political Leadership* (Ithaca: Cornell University Press, 1988), p. 24.

[154] "Supplementary Notes," 11 Jan. 1954, Box 1, Eisenhower Legislative Meetings Series, Eisenhower Presidential Library.

[155] Stephen Ambrose, *Eisenhower*, vol. 2 (New York: Simon and Schuster, 1984), p. 155.

[156] Dwight Eisenhower to William Knowland, 25 Jan. 1954, Box 6, Dwight Eisenhower Diary, Eisenhower Presidential Library.

[157] Woods, *Fulbright: A Biography*, p. 192.

[158] Alexander Wiley to W. R. Topping, 25 July 1953, Box 46, Alexander Wiley Papers, Wisconsin State Historical Society.

not unreasonably, why anyone would believe that two-thirds of the Senate would approve a treaty that subverted the Constitution.[159]

Negotiations between the administration and Bricker's forces continued into 1954, but in the end neither side was willing to concede: in Bricker's words, while "the science of politics is in large measure the art of compromise . . . there comes a time in the life of every public official when he must stand fast on issues of principle."[160] As had occurred with McCarthy, the Ohio senator's confidence that his appeals to bolstering congressional power would overcome qualms about his amendment's policy-related effects led him to overreach, spurning a compromise when one might have been possible. Warnings from Establishment figures, meanwhile, stiffened Eisenhower's resistance. Acheson asserted that the amendment would produce "Congressional government, which, in turn, results, under twentieth century conditions, in a negative and vacillating foreign policy"; John McCloy predicted that passage would "have a subtle but definite effect" by weakening confidence in Eisenhower, diminishing presidential authority, and providing a "demoralizing blow" for U.S. world leadership.[161]

In early 1954, Eisenhower pronounced himself "unalterably opposed" to the amendment, and started lobbying GOP senators on the issue.[162] Some Republicans quickly changed their minds: New York's Irving Ives, for instance, even claimed to have originally co-sponsored the amendment "by accident."[163] Seeking to profit from this GOP division, Lyndon Johnson persuaded Walter George to offer a compromise, which stated that executive agreements would have no internal effect without congressional legislation and that no treaty that conflicted with the Constitution would take effect. Johnson was serving a number of agendas: he genuinely opposed the Bricker amendment; he had adopted a clever political strategy of positioning congressional Democrats as more favorably inclined to the president's agenda than their GOP counterparts; and he needed political cover for himself as a senator facing re-election from a state that strongly favored the amendment.[164]

Johnson's machinations doomed the Bricker amendment; by the time his offering came to the floor, Bricker could muster only 42 votes. The administration, however, considered the George amendment equally objectionable, since it would restrict executive agreements; the President, seemingly in vain,

[159] John Sherman Cooper to Charles Hook, 12 Aug. 1953, Box 95, John Bricker Papers, Ohio State Historical Society.

[160] John Bricker to William Cook, 30 March 1954, Box 101, John Bricker Papers, Ohio State Historical Society.

[161] John McCloy to Dwight Eisenhower, 18 Jan. 1954, Box 160, John Bricker Papers, Ohio State Historical Society; Dean Acheson, "The Responsibility for Decisions in Foreign Policy," *Yale Review*, Sept. 1954.

[162] *New York Times*, 22 Jan. 1954.

[163] Tananbaum, *The Bricker Amendment Controversy*, p. 141.

[164] Caro, *Master of the Senate*, pp. 527–535.

searched for a way "to keep this thing from complete disaster."[165] Johnson, however, had Democratic votes in reserve, and, with the roll call balanced 60 to 30, managed to get Harley Kilgore to the floor (the West Virginia senator had been in his office in a deep sleep, caused either by alcohol or the flu, depending on the story). When Kilgore voted nay, the George amendment went down to defeat, and with it, the revisionists' best chance to alter the Constitution.[166]

In retrospect, the combination of McCarthy's implosion, the Bricker amendment's defeat, and McCarran's death from heart failure in September 1954 triggered the irreparable decline of revisionist power. Between 1950 and 1954, however, members of the group monopolized the demand for a greater congressional influence in foreign policy. As a result, increased legislative power in foreign affairs became equated with the revisionist policy agenda: focusing on Asia, supporting right-wing governments overseas, questioning the need for formal alliances, and relying heavily on atomic weapons and the Air Force. For neither the first nor the last time, a willingness to champion congressional power would depend on the initiatives for which that power would be put to use. Those critical of these revisionist issues increasingly advocated a robust presidential role on international matters.

Lyndon Johnson correctly took credit for the defeat of the Bricker amendment. The Texas senator's approach hinted at the partisanship never far from the surface in Democratic comments on foreign policy issues – this was a party, after all, that had lost the White House and control of Congress partly because of demagogic Republican attacks on foreign policy matters, and Democrats now eagerly reciprocated.[167] Averill Harriman, in 1954 the New York Democrats' gubernatorial nominee, argued that party leaders should encourage legislators to ask "questions which it will be difficult for the Administration to answer satisfactorily," thus using foreign policy to embarrass Eisenhower.[168] Congressional Democrats also moved to neutralize political attacks. In August 1954, under pressure from labor leaders to sidetrack a Republican bill granting the attorney general unilateral power to declare a union Communist-controlled, Hubert Humphrey (D-Minnesota) introduced the Communist Control Act, which deemed the U.S. Communist Party "the agency of a hostile power."[169] The Minnesota senator freely admitted his political motives, informing the Senate, "I am tired of reading

---

[165] Dwight Eisenhower and Walter Bedell-Smith, telephone call transcript, 28 Jan. 1954, Box 5, Dwight Eisenhower Diary Series, Eisenhower Presidential Library.

[166] Robert Caro, *The Years of Lyndon Johnson; Volume 3, Master of the Senate* (New York: Knopf, 2002), pp. 536–540.

[167] Thomas Hennings to Keith Brownell, 4 Aug. 1954, Folder 2113, Thomas Hennings Papers, Western Historical Collections, University of Missouri.

[168] Gary Reichard, "Divisions and Dissent: Democrats and Foreign Policy, 1952–1956," *Political Science Quarterly* 93 (1978), p. 56.

[169] *Washington Post*, 13 Aug. 1954.

headlines about being soft toward communism."[170] Testifying to the era's extreme anti-Communist attitudes, only Estes Kefauver (D-Tennessee) voted against the bill.

As William Knowland had warned Eisenhower in early 1953, Democrats eager to score partisan points viewed defense spending as a particularly inviting target, especially a proposed $5 billion cut in Air Force appropriations. Stuart Symington, Truman's secretary of the Air Force before ousting revisionist James Kem in Missouri's 1952 Senate race, unsuccessfully pressed Armed Services Committee chairman Leverett Saltonstall to become more involved in defense policy.[171] The Missouri senator later compared his colleague's attitude to "a bank president saying he didn't want to know anything about his deposits"; at the time, the Missouri Democrat blasted Saltonstall's approach as "so calm as to be concerned with events on another planet."[172] He claimed that the administration had "muzzled" the Air Force at the request of "the new group of inexperienced civilians who have come into the Pentagon placing budget priorities ahead of security."[173] John Kennedy and Henry Jackson advanced similar arguments.

Symington, at least, presented a critique consistent with positions he had taken during the Truman administration. Other congressional Democrats offered nothing in the way of an alternative policy while suggesting that the president was willfully harming national security. Jackson, Mike Monroney (elected to the Senate in 1950), and Paul Douglas (D-Illinois) all claimed that the New Look invited Soviet attack. Albert Gore (D-Tennessee), after announcing his intent not "to blast the administration," accused Eisenhower of operating "with dangerous disregard" for security needs – remarks that John Sparkman (D-Alabama), incredibly, hailed as "completely in the spirit of bipartisanship."[174] Eisenhower received little assistance from his GOP allies: Saltonstall seemed loath to discuss specifics, while Senate Policy Committee chair Homer Ferguson (R-Michigan) and House floor leader Errett Scrivner (R-Kansas) recommended only that Congress should rely on Eisenhower's "sound military experience."[175] In the end, the president had the votes, and in 1953 and 1954 Congress passed his military budgets largely as introduced. But Eisenhower's parsimony exacted a political cost.

As the midterm contests drew near, the Democrats' use of international issues for partisan gain grew more intense, briefly turning the party to Indochina, heretofore a region ignored by Congress. Postwar French

[170] Reichard, "Divisions and Dissent: Democrats and Foreign Policy, 1952–1956," p. 57.

[171] Stuart Symington oral history, Lyndon B. Johnson Presidential Library.

[172] Stuart Symington oral history, Lyndon B. Johnson Presidential Library; 100 *CR*, 83rd Congress, 2nd session, p. 14485 (14 Aug. 1954).

[173] 99 *CR*, 83rd Congress, 1st session, p. 9518 (22 July 1953).

[174] 100 *CR*, 83rd Congress, 2nd session, pp. 647–648, 650 (22 Jan. 1954).

[175] 99 *CR*, 83rd Congress, 1st session, pp. 7974–7976 (2 July 1953), 9562–9563 (22 July 1953).

attempts to reestablish control over their colony had encountered determined resistance from the Vietminh, nationalists headed by Ho Chi Minh, an avowed Communist. After the start of the Korean War, the United States expanded military assistance to France, whose performance nonetheless failed to improve. In early 1954, with French forces surrounded at Dienbienphu, in a remote section of northern Vietnam, Paris appealed for U.S. military intervention; JCS chair Arthur Radford recommended use of atomic weapons. Eisenhower said that he would consider involvement only if England supported such an action and congressional leaders gave their approval. Such backing was not forthcoming. Representing differing ideological camps, William Knowland, Mike Mansfield (D-Montana), and John Stennis (D-Mississippi) all expressed skepticism about the idea, Stennis, who predicted that U.S. involvement would produce an "endless war," in especially vehement terms.[176]

France accordingly settled the conflict with the Geneva Accords, which established an independent, Communist North Vietnam and called for all-Vietnam elections to reunify the country by 1956. With a U.S. military action no longer a possibility, Democrats reversed themselves and attacked Eisenhower's performance – getting some payback for GOP charges of "Who lost China?" from the Truman administration. Humphrey charged that it "does not do any good to talk about massive retaliation" after the Geneva Conference, since the administration proved that when pressed, it would back down.[177] Monroney reasoned that the "deteriorating and steadily worsening condition in the Far East" dictated the United States fortifying Southeast Asia itself, so as to produce "a line which can be used as a bulwark to prevent further Communist aggression."[178] Symington even pushed the administration to consider using nuclear weapons to prevent a Communist triumph in the region.[179]

Partisan skill and the traditional midterm downturn for the party in power were just enough for the Democrats in the 1954 midterm elections, which left the Senate with 48 Democrats, 47 Republicans, and 1 independent, Wayne Morse. The Oregon senator thus received the power to decide which party would organize the Senate. The *Washington Post* later wrote that Morse's "sharp tongue, his skill in debate, his astonishing ability to filibuster by himself, and his disposition to speak his mind regardless of what

---

[176] John Stennis to Evelyn Turner, 14 June 1954, Series 33, Box 20, John Stennis Papers, Mississippi State University; 100 *CR*, 83rd Congress, 2nd session, pp. 1503–1506 (9 Feb. 1954).

[177] 100 *CR*, 83rd Congress, 2nd session, p. 8342 (16 June 1954).

[178] 100 *CR*, 83rd Congress, 2nd session, p. 8432 (17 June 1954).

[179] Stuart Symington to Joe Alsop, 29 Jan. 1954, Box 9, Joseph and Stuart Alsop Papers, Library of Congress; *Congressional Quarterly Weekly Report*, 30 April 1954. The administration's policy toward Vietnam attracted some GOP criticism as well; William Knowland termed the Geneva Conference "a Far Eastern Munich." "Legislative briefing session," 23 Jan. 1954, p. 4, Legislative Briefings series, Dwight Eisenhower Presidential Library.

the consequences might be" made the Senate a perfect forum from which to pursue his "highly personalized version of the public interest."[180] Morse left the Republican Party in 1952 to protest Richard Nixon's nomination as vice president, and thereafter he generally voted with the Democrats. (George Smathers recalled that the Oregon senator "would have considered it a lost day if he had ever been on the majority side of anything."[181]) Morse viscerally disliked Lyndon Johnson, whom the Oregon senator described as a figure who, were he ever to "have a liberal idea, he would have a brain hemorrhage."[182] The minority leader reciprocated the ill feeling: that no prominent Texas Democrat accepted Morse's challenge to file against him, Johnson quipped, only "confirms my conviction that the people of Texas did not pay any more attention to the Senator from Oregon than the Senate does."[183]

Since the election results gave Morse the power to make Johnson majority leader, personal feelings were quickly placed aside. The Oregon senator issued one demand: a seat on the Foreign Relations Committee. Johnson made the deal, much to the administration's dismay.[184] At the White House, Morse's assignment "gave rise to a discussion of the degree of candor that would be possible in off-the-record briefings of congressional committees"; Nixon expressed particular concern.[185] Eisenhower reasoned that "much will depend upon the personal touch," one reason why John Foster Dulles pressed Walter George to relinquish his chairmanship of the Finance Committee to assume the helm of Foreign Relations.[186] Otherwise, Rhode Island's octogenarian senator, Theodore Francis Green, would have become chair; in Dulles' mind, "cooperating with Senator Green is impossible."[187]

The Dulles-George relationship received an immediate test. The simmering tension between China and Taiwan intensified in September 1954, when China began shelling several small islands – Quemoy, Matsu, and the Tachens – on which Chiang Kai-shek had stationed troops as he fled the mainland in 1949. Shortly after the start of the Korean War, Truman had issued an executive order sending the Seventh Fleet to the Formosa Straits, thus committing the United States to defend Taiwan and the nearby Pescadores Islands but leaving the status of Quemoy, Matsu, and the Tachens unclear. While

[180] *Washington Post*, 1 Jan. 1969.
[181] George Smathers oral history, Lyndon Johnson Presidential Library.
[182] *Austin American*, 31 Jan. 1954.
[183] Lyndon Johnson to G.R. Hickok, 6 Feb. 1954, Box 50, LBJA Papers, Lyndon Johnson Presidential Library.
[184] Caro, *Master of the Senate*, p. 557.
[185] "Supplementary Notes," 11 Jan. 1955, Box 1, Legislative Meetings series, Eisenhower Presidential Library.
[186] Nelson, "John Foster Dulles and the Bipartisan Congress," p. 49.
[187] John Foster Dulles and President Eisenhower, 4 March 1957, telephone call transcript, Box 22, Eisenhower Diaries, Dwight Eisenhower Presidential Library.

Eisenhower did not consider the "damned little offshore islands" militarily significant, he feared that abandoning them would have a damaging psychological effect on Taiwan, while also incurring the wrath of the China lobby at home.[188]

A crisis situation emerged on January 18, 1955, after Chinese troops captured Ichiang, a small island adjacent to the Tachens, and seemed ready for an assault on the Tachens. An NSC meeting the next day recommended encouraging Taiwan to abandon the Tachens in exchange for a U.S. commitment to defend Quemoy and Matsu, but Eisenhower insisted that "whatever we do must be done in a constitutional manner."[189] Accordingly, Dulles organized a meeting with congressional leaders to reveal the administration's intent to submit a resolution authorizing the president to employ U.S. armed forces "as he deems necessary" to prevent an attack on Taiwan and the Pescadores, as well as to take "other measures" he deemed "required or appropriate" to defend Taiwan.[190] The latter wording deliberately left unclear whether the United States would consider a Chinese attack on Quemoy and Matsu an act of war.

Eisenhower transmitted to Congress what became known as the Formosa Resolution on January 24, 1955. Cooperative House leaders brought the resolution to the floor under a closed rule – preventing amendments – and limited debate; ultimately only three congressmen (two Republicans and a Southern Democrat) voted against the measure.[191] The Senate, however, featured a much more vigorous discussion. Revisionists, who had spent much of the previous decade blanching at increased executive authority, strongly supported the resolution, even though it weakened Congress' constitutional power to declare war, since it benefited Taiwan. On the other side of the ideological divide, a few senators – "holding the fort of constitutional liberalism all alone," Morse claimed – resolutely opposed the measure.[192] Intellectually, Morse's critique was unanswerable: the resolution undeniably proposed transferring the power to declare war from Congress to the executive. Politically, however, most Democrats would not risk appearing soft on the Chinese Communists. Moreover, having spent the previous half-decade advocating, in the face of pressure from revisionist colleagues, maximum international flexibility for the president, Democrats were boxed in. A few advanced torturous arguments to question the resolution on constitutional

---

[188] Robert Accinelli, *Crisis and Commitment: The United States Policy toward Taiwan, 1950–1955* (Chapel Hill: University of North Carolina Press, 1996), p. 185.

[189] Robert Accinelli, "Eisenhower, Congress, and the 1954–55 Offshore Island Crisis," *Presidential Studies Quarterly* 20 (1990), p. 331.

[190] "Meeting of secretary with congressional leaders," 20 Jan. 1955, Box 2, White House memoranda, John Foster Dulles Papers, Eisenhower Presidential Library.

[191] *CQ Almanac 1955*, p. 278.

[192] Wayne Morse to Walter Reuther, 29 Jan. 1955, Box A-45, Wayne Morse Papers, University of Oregon.

grounds while avoiding contradicting their earlier positions. Mike Mansfield, for example, described himself as "somewhat disturbed at the possibility that the President may be abdicating in a sense a power to us which he already has."[193] Perhaps the most restricted conception of congressional power came from Oregon's newly elected Democratic senator, Richard Neuberger, who confessed that, as "responsibility for our foreign and military policies must of necessity remain with the executive branch of the government," he would save his "shots for natural resources, conservation, schools, and on the issues where I really have some knowledge and self-assurance."[194]

This mindset allowed anti-administration Democrats to go no further than attempting to modify the resolution or score political points before passage.[195] Paul Douglas chastised the administration for its inconsistent statements regarding Chiang Kai-shek, and speculated that U.S. unwillingness to intervene at Dienbienphu the previous year had encouraged the Communists to believe the administration would tolerate a Chinese invasion of Taiwan.[196] Humphrey considered it "tragic" that GOP "political divisions" had compelled the administration "to make concessions to the Knowland wing of the party even at the expense of a sensible and practical foreign policy."[197] Warren Magnuson (D-Washington) attributed the crisis to Eisenhower's 1953(!) State of the Union Address, which he considered insufficiently specific about future U.S. policy in East Asia.[198]

In this sense, congressional Democrats offered what Humphrey characterized as a "limited" dissent.[199] Sharing the administration's basic outlook in international affairs, politically fearful of a frontal attack on the President, Democrats confined themselves to nibbling at the edges of Eisenhower's policy, offering partisan attacks, or making vague and often contradictory assertions about the proper constitutional balance between Congress and the executive. Fulbright conceded as much: although many Democrats "resented the way the matter was presented to the Senate," they understood that Eisenhower's position had popular support (73 percent in one poll).[200]

---

[193] *ESSFRC*, vol. 7, p. 126 (24 Jan. 1955).
[194] Richard Neuberger to Mrs. Ivan Kafoury, 23 June 1955; Richard Neuberger to E. J. Griffith, 11 Feb. 1955; both in Box 6, Richard Neuberger Papers, University of Oregon.
[195] 101 *CR*, 84th Congress, 1st session, pp. 974, 982, 984, 986 (28 Jan. 1955).
[196] 101 *CR*, 84th Congress, 1st session, p. 937 (28 Jan. 1955).
[197] Hubert Humphrey to F. W. Conrad, 12 Feb. 1955, Box 119, Hubert Humphrey Papers, Minnesota State Historical Society.
[198] Warren Magnuson to Robert Merchant, 13 April 1955, Box 127, Warren Magnuson Papers, University of Washington.
[199] *ESSFRC*, vol. 7, p. 217.
[200] J. William Fulbright to Harold Gelwicks, 24 Feb. 1955; J. William Fulbright to John Caldwell, 28 Jan. 1955; both in BCN 46, J. William Fulbright Papers, University of Arkansas; Accinelli, *Crisis and Commitment*, p. 195.

Political scientist James Sundquist has argued that over the course of the twentieth century, Congress willingly surrendered much of its authority to the executive.[201] By not opposing the Formosa Resolution more forcefully, Democrats – and, of course, the revisionist Republicans who had talked so much about reviving congressional power during the previous half-decade – established a precedent for significantly eroding the legislative role in international affairs. Events in the Middle East (1957), Cuba (1962), and Vietnam (1964) would prompt presidents to request comparable advance congressional approval to make war, and these legislatures would find it much harder, given the Formosa Resolution precedent, to resist. In combination with the aftereffects of the Army-McCarthy hearings, which upheld the principle of executive authority to withhold information from Congress, and the defeat of the George amendment, which left unlimited the legal force of executive agreements, the Formosa Resolution completed a constitutional revolution of the early 1950s. The two highest profile international powers shared between Congress and the president – treaties and war-making – tilted substantially in the direction of increased executive authority. That said, it was congressional abuse of power that provoked the broadening of executive privilege – and in an administration led by a war hero who credibly could claim greater expertise on defense issues.

In early 1956, the Democrats' partisan agenda received an opening when Dulles, in a *Life* interview, boasted of having successfully practiced "brinkmanship" diplomacy. Fulbright contended that rather than give interviews, Dulles needed to "tell America the truth about our present peril," lest he "lull us to sleep in an hour when the Soviet Union has launched a powerful diplomatic offensive against us."[202] Matthew Neely (D-West Virginia) urged Dulles to publish his recent statements under the title, "How imbecilic can an American Secretary of State be?"[203] The pettiness of such criticism generated a backlash, even from such friendly sources as the *New York Times*, which ridiculed the opposition's preference for "elegant allusion or vituperative phrase," and *The New Republic*, which termed the Democratic approach on foreign policy a "dishonest conglomeration of irrelevancies and inaccuracies."[204] Humphrey denied allegations of "extreme and reckless" partisanship, astonishingly billing his attacks on Dulles as consistent with "the objective of bipartisanship in foreign affairs."[205]

The Democrats' overwhelming defeat in the 1956 presidential election terminated the era of limited dissent while leaving uncertain the future

---

[201] Sundquist, *The Decline and Resurgence of Congress.*
[202] 102 *CR*, 84th Congress, 2nd session, p. 3369 (27 Feb. 1956).
[203] 102 *CR*, 84th Congress, 2nd session, p. 977 (20 Jan. 1956); *New York Times*, 14 Jan. 1956.
[204] Reichard, "Divisions and Dissent," p. 68.
[205] Hubert Humphrey to Sal Hoffman, 3 April 1956, Box 128, Hubert Humphrey Papers, Minnesota State Historical Society.

congressional role in foreign policy. Revisionists were spent as a political
and intellectual force. From the other ideological extreme, it seemed unlikely
that liberal Democrats could – even if they so desired – use the war-making
and treaty-making powers to affect the administration's foreign policy in
any substantial way. Events between 1957 and 1963, however, would see
Congress' role in U.S. foreign policy fundamentally redefined, with the legislature exerting influence through unforeseen avenues, while beginning a
major internal realignment that would persist until the end of the Cold War.

3

Redefining Congressional Power

Shortly after the 1956 elections, Lyndon Johnson warned Secretary of State Dulles, "We might have some troubles with the Democratic side of the Senate Foreign Relations Committee."[1] The Majority Leader had learned of Hubert Humphrey's plans to demand a committee investigation of the administration's foreign policy. "If we Democrats," the Minnesota senator informed colleague Albert Gore, "are not going to think enough of our country – yes, and of our party – to make a careful and intelligent study and investigation of the security needs and foreign policy requirements of this country, then, indeed, we are not performing our public duty."[2]

Walter George's retirement elevated Theodore Francis Green to the committee chairmanship; the Rhode Island senator, according to Humphrey, threw "cold water" on the plan.[3] Foreign Relations' next ranking Democrat, however, responded more approvingly. In early 1957, J. William Fulbright confessed the obvious: on foreign policy issues, "the Democrats did not function as an opposition party should during the past four years."[4] Given Green's position, the Arkansas senator recommended terming the initiative a "study" rather than an inquiry: "After such a study is underway, of course, it progresses as developments dictate."[5] Though the proposed study did not begin until 1958, congressional liaison William Macomber described the

---

[1] Woods, *Fulbright*, p. 218.

[2] Hubert Humphrey to Albert Gore, 17 Dec. 1956, Box 129, Hubert Humphrey Papers, Minnesota State Historical Society.

[3] Hubert Humphrey to Wayne Morse, 18 Dec. 1956, Box 129, Hubert Humphrey Papers, Minnesota State Historical Society.

[4] J. William Fulbright to Farnsworth Fowle, 4 Jan. 1957, BCN 114, J. William Fulbright Papers, University of Arkansas.

[5] J. William Fulbright to Hubert Humphrey, 19 Dec. 1956, BCN 121, J. William Fulbright Papers, University of Arkansas.

story of Eisenhower's second term as the Senate "asserting its role in the foreign policy business."[6]

Within Congress, the late 1950s witnessed the intensification of a power differential between the House and the Senate, usually at the expense of the House. The lower chamber's impact increasingly was confined to appropriations during these years, with a focus on foreign aid and military spending. The Senate, on the other hand, experienced a transformation under Lyndon Johnson, who revolutionized the position of majority leader, using his authority over scheduling legislation (a meaningful power given his de facto control of the Democratic Policy Committee) to affect the content of legislation, regularizing pairs on roll-call votes, successfully challenging the Senate seniority system, and extensively employing unanimous consent agreements. The majority leader shifted the legislative process away from public debates, which tended to stress the articulation of ideals, to backroom deal-making, reflecting Johnson's own conception of how the Senate should function. Legislation, not educating the public, would be his chief mission as leader.[7]

Eisenhower received a taste of the new environment on January 1, 1957, when he invited a bipartisan legislative delegation to the White House. In a four-hour conference, he outlined a draft resolution giving him authority to send troops to any Middle Eastern nation that requested assistance against a Communist threat, on the grounds "that modern war might be a matter of hours only."[8] Under a closed rule, the resolution sailed through the House, whose institutional structure prevented forcefully challenging the executive against the leadership's wishes. In the Senate, the president received overwhelming Republican support: the revisionists no longer posed a threat. A wide array of Democrats, on the other hand, questioned the resolution's constitutional, policy, and pragmatic necessity, but they struggled to reconcile their positions with their previous expansive interpretations of presidential power.

Most Democrats, in the end, did not challenge the administration's policy (Humphrey privately admitted that "the difference between the Administration and me on this issue is one of emphasis rather than one of principles"), but two followed a different path.[9] As he had with the Formosa Resolution, Wayne Morse expressed dismay with the constitutional ramifications of giving "the President unchecked power."[10] (Alexander Wiley, in turn, denounced Morse for excessive literalism: "The Constitution is no

---

[6] William Macomber oral history, Lyndon Johnson Presidential Library.

[7] Caro, *Years of Lyndon Johnson, Volume 3*, pp. 410–650.

[8] "Legislative Meeting, 1/1/1957," Box 2, Legislative Meeting Series, Dwight Eisenhower Presidential Library.

[9] Hubert Humphrey to Robert Staiger, 27 Feb. 1957, Box 137, Hubert Humphrey Papers, Minnesota State Historical Society.

[10] *ESSFRC*, vol. 9, p. 281 (12 Feb. 1957).

fetish . . . we were a government before the Constitution."[11]) An even bolder position came from Estes Kefauver, who asserted that constitutional objections alone would not justify a vote against the measure, but he detected "too much evidence" that the administration's policy was designed to benefit U.S. oil companies.[12]

Such opinions puzzled Eisenhower. "After all," the president told Dulles, "we are seeking peace, and the only way to do it is to show that our hands are not tied."[13] In fact, the resolution's passage owed much more to the revisionists' legacy than to the administration's intent, pacific or otherwise. On issues relating to war and treaties, the revisionists' ideological agenda had become so wedded to increasing congressional power that mainstream members of both parties celebrated a more aggressive executive role – to such an extent that Congress would pass a vaguely worded resolution targeted at a region the administration could not precisely define to meet a threat that the administration could not specifically identify.

Over the next several years, however, various members would discover alternative ways of marshaling the institution's powers: focusing on foreign policy issues related to appropriations, using the proliferation of subcommittees to influence policy, or highlighting issues or areas of the world neglected by the administration. Unlike the revisionists, this expanded congressional role was initially not associated with any specific ideological agenda. But by the time of John Kennedy's death in November 1963, this combination of tactics would establish a potent congressional influence in U.S. international affairs.

The importance of foreign aid made the appropriations power the most straightforward avenue for Congress to influence international developments. Though foreign aid continued to enjoy considerable support among liberals in both chambers, some disquieting signs emerged for the administration's 1957 proposal in the Senate. Southern Democrats generally had supported foreign aid during the Truman administration, but in 1957, only 6 of the region's 26 Democratic senators, according to one administration estimate, were favorably inclined.[14] Allen Ellender typified this new Southern perspective. In the late 1950s, the Louisiana Democrat started making gaffe-filled international inspection trips, which proved, according to the *New York Herald-Tribune*, that "every American possesses among other freedoms the freedom to make a fool of himself."[15] Fulbright not incorrectly

---

[11] *ESSFRC*, vol. 9, p. 348 (13 Feb. 1957).

[12] 103 *CR*, 85th Congress, 1st session, p. 2898 (1 March 1957).

[13] Eisenhower-Dulles telephone call transcript, 12 Jan. 1957, Box 22, Eisenhower Diaries, Dwight Eisenhower Presidential Library.

[14] "United States Senators – Views on Mutual Security," in Bryce Harlow to Sherman Adams, 6 May 1957, Box 16, Bryce Harlow Papers, Dwight Eisenhower Presidential Library.

[15] Jack Anderson and Drew Pearson, *The Case against Congress: A Compelling Indictment of Corruption on Capital Hill* (New York: Simon and Schuster, 1968), p. 215.

dismissed Ellender's "reform" agenda as cover for opposing "any kind of foreign-aid program," but the Louisiana Democrat occasionally offered thoughtful commentary.[16] He worried that the United States was trying "to do too much too fast" by creating economies that Third World nations could not sustain, citing Ngo Dinh Diem's regime in South Vietnam, where it "appears obvious that our aid effort . . . is being used to fill the coffers of the Vietnamese government."[17] This type of argument opened the possibility of a left-right dissent against foreign aid, since Morse harbored similar concerns.[18]

The situation was less welcoming for the administration in the House, where Bryce Harlow was struck by the "zeal to reduce the *size* of the foreign aid program."[19] No congressman better embodied this viewpoint than Otto Passman (D-Louisiana), a fourth-grade dropout who sold appliances before entering politics. Passman closely allied with Appropriations Committee chairman Clarence Cannon, a conservative who in 1955 elevated the Louisianan over several more senior Democrats to chair the Foreign Operations Subcommittee, which possessed jurisdiction over the foreign aid program.[20]

In his first two years as chair, Passman sufficiently irritated the administration so Dulles advocated transferring the military aid budget to the Pentagon – thus removing the program from the Foreign Operations Subcommittee's jurisdiction.[21] Though Passman publicly proclaimed that he "would be the first one to recommend the abolishment of this committee if savings could be realized or a better job done," in reality, he had no intention of sacrificing control.[22] As he told one Eisenhower official: "Son, I don't smoke; I don't drink; my only pleasure in life is to kick the shit out of the foreign aid program of the United States."[23] Shortly thereafter, the president invited Passman to the White House for a briefing, only to have the congressman lecture him that "never in the history of the world has the mind of man conceived such an unreasonable and unworkable program."[24] "Remind

---

[16] 103 *CR*, 85th Congress, 1st session, p. 14507 (13 Aug. 1957).

[17] 103 *CR*, 85th Congress, 1st session, pp. 1703 (7 Feb. 1957), 14508 (13 Aug. 1957).

[18] 103 *CR*, 85th Congress, 1st session, pp. 8963–8970 (13 June 1957).

[19] Bryce Harlow to Sherman Adams, 6 May 1957, Box 16, Bryce Harlow Papers, Dwight Eisenhower Presidential Library.

[20] Field Haviland, "Foreign Aid and the Policy Process: 1957," *American Political Science Review* 52 (1958), p. 709.

[21] U.S. House of Representatives, Foreign Operations Subcommittee, *Hearings, Mutual Security Act for 1957*, 84th Congress, 2nd session, p. 39 (24 May 1956).

[22] U.S. House of Representatives, Foreign Operations Subcommittee, *Hearings, Mutual Security Act for 1958*, 85th Congress, 1st session, p. 84 (9 April 1957).

[23] Chester Pach and Elmo Richardson, *The Presidency of Dwight D. Eisenhower* (Lawrence: University of Kansas Press, 1991), p. 165.

[24] Otto Passman to Amiee Cook, 29 May 1958, Drawer 3, Otto Passman Papers, University of Louisiana-Monroe.

me," Eisenhower nudged an aide, "never to invite that fellow down here again."[25]

Eisenhower's 1957 bill included a number of reforms ostensibly offered in the name of efficiency that ultimately sought to limit congressional oversight, such as allowing multi-year authorizations for some development projects, ending line-item amounts for specific countries, and shifting the authorizations for military aid programs to a continuing basis, thus making them open-ended. In hearings that he promised would be "long and trying," Passman repeated two arguments mercilessly: first, military aid was really economic aid, since any military assistance the United States supplied allowed recipient nations to spend more on wasteful economic programs; and second, the existence of unexpended funds from previous years' appropriations proved that the administration's funding request was excessive.[26] In fact, in 1957, 90 percent of these funds had already been obligated for projects that were then delayed.[27]

A subcommittee ally, J. Vaughan Gary (D-Virginia), recalled that Passman considered the "bitches and bastards" who represented the State Department and foreign aid program "all crooks and liars" who had "to be squelched."[28] The chair, Gary noted, "browbeats the witnesses," whom he would not let "answer the questions. He does all the talking. He wants to be the whole show on his committee and have everyone rubber stamp his ideas."[29]

On August 14, just over two weeks before the scheduled end of the congressional session, Passman reported a bill with a funding level of $2.525 billion, more than 34 percent below the administration's request. The next day, the full committee adopted Passman's report without review; in a political oversight, the White House had not started lobbying Appropriations Committee members until three days earlier.[30] Asked to defend the reduction on the House floor, Passman accused administration officials "of purposely losing sleep working up figures that cannot be justified and asking for more money than they need."[31] The House subsequently passed the committee's bill, without amendment, 252 to 130, leaving Eisenhower "astounded by the apparent ignorance of men of Congress in the general subject of our foreign affairs."[32]

---

[25] Anderson and Pearson, *The Case against Congress*, p. 229.

[26] U.S. House of Representatives, Foreign Operations Subcommittee, *Hearings, Mutual Security Act for 1958*, 85th Congress, 1st session, p. 162 (19 June 1957).

[27] Haviland, "Foreign Aid and the Policy Process: 1957," p. 711.

[28] J. Vaughan Gary oral history, April 1964, Center for Legislative Archives, Washington, D.C.

[29] J. Vaughan Gary oral history, April 1964, Center for Legislative Archives, Washington, D.C.

[30] Haviland, "Foreign Aid and the Policy Process: 1957," p. 712.

[31] 103 *CR*, 85th Congress, 1st session, p. 14920 (15 Aug. 1957).

[32] Chester Pach, "Military Assistance and American Foreign Policy: The Role of Congress," in Michael Barnhart, ed., *Congress and United States Foreign Policy* (Albany: SUNY Press, 1986), p. 143.

Desperate to recover lost ground, the administration undertook a public relations blitz – Eisenhower offered to give up part of his salary to "meet the pressing need of adequate funds for foreign aid."[33] But such efforts came too late. Passman entered the conference dismissing the Senate bill, which recommended over $1 billion more than the House, as the product of "a lot of breakfasts at the White House and a terrific amount of pressure from top echelons."[34] In the conference, he had leverage: while House conferees united behind his position, their Senate counterparts included Southern Democrats hostile to foreign aid. Moreover, Passman's walking out of the conference would force a special session – something all wanted to avoid. In a one-day conference, the committee recommended $2.769 billion in funds, a slight increase over the House total but still the largest percentage reduction in the program's history to that time. Passman privately termed himself the key to the reduction – and "may our Heavenly Father forgive me if I appear to be bragging."[35]

By the late 1950s, the London *Times* termed Passman "almost a law to himself on foreign aid."[36] A similar appraisal applied to George Mahon's power over defense spending. Like Passman, the Texas Democrat dominated proceedings in his Defense Appropriations Subcommittee. (In one hearing, Errett Scrivner meekly requested permission to ask a question – "after having been here for about two days now and having kept pretty quiet."[37]) As he had in earlier years, Mahon in 1957 reiterated his intent to examine "things on a broad policy level" and to conduct a more detailed review of defense policy than did the toothless Armed Services Committee.[38] In this process, the Texas Democrat pursued three main goals: to support the Air Force; to critique the administration's massive retaliation doctrine; and to reduce Pentagon waste through greater inter-service coordination or, if necessary, decreased Army funding.[39] Mahon argued that such cuts (which totaled nearly $1 billion from the administration's request in 1957 alone) would encourage the Army to recognize that "present tensions and rivalries among the services are unwholesome and dangerous" – since they produced "a trend toward a position of military weakness, which would inevitably lead toward

[33] *New York Times*, 20 Aug. 1957.

[34] Haviland, "Foreign Aid and the Policy Process: 1957," p. 712.

[35] Otto Passman to Charles Rogers, 14 Nov. 1957, Drawer 3, Otto Passman Papers, University of Louisiana-Monroe.

[36] *The Times* (London), 17 Feb. 1960.

[37] U.S. House of Representatives, Defense Appropriations Subcommittee, *Hearings, Department of Defense Appropriations for 1958*, 85th Congress, 1st session, p. 124 (31 Jan. 1957).

[38] U.S. House of Representatives, Defense Appropriations Subcommittee, *Hearings, Department of Defense Appropriations for 1958*, 85th Congress, 1st session, pp. 2, 32 (30 Jan. 1957).

[39] U.S. House of Representatives, Defense Appropriations Subcommittee, *Hearings, Department of Defense Appropriations for 1960*, 86th Congress, 1st session, pp. 1–2 (23 Jan. 1959).

a national policy of appeasement."[40] The intersection between congressional appropriations and inter-service rivalry remained alive and well, with the Air Force still occupying a commanding position.

Both the Pentagon and the administration respected Mahon's abilities, if they did not always share his priorities. A Department of Defense official captured the consensus: "If a program can go through the review given by the Mahon Committee, then in all likelihood it is a reasonably good program."[41] The Texas congressman spent most Saturdays golfing at Maryland's Burning Tree Club, where his partners included former JCS chairman Omar Bradley and, occasionally, both the president and vice president.[42] His future colleague, Michigan's Donald Riegle, correctly observed that "Mahon rules much more by persuasion and reason than he does by an arbitrary use of power."[43] This respect, of course, only made it harder to challenge Mahon's judgments on the House floor; in the words of one House member, "Power is interpretation around here; it's all interpretation."[44]

While Mahon and Passman used the House's customary deference to sub-committee chairs to influence foreign policy, the House Foreign Affairs Committee did little.[45] Committee member James Richards (D-Texas) complained that "evidently the State Department thinks we in the House are kids and the Senate is grown up. The Department pitches a crumb over this way only once in a while."[46] The action, as Richards lamented, remained in the Senate, where Mahon's national security philosophy reflected the approach of most Democrats. Henry Jackson, in 1952 elected to the Senate, affirmed his commitment to what he called a bare-bones defense budget, but his definition seemed to entail every weapons system that the Air Force desired – more B-52 and B-58 bombers and increased appropriations for an early warning capability for the Strategic Air Command.[47] Stuart Symington, meanwhile, maintained that Eisenhower's defense theories threatened national security, since the Communists "have every right to believe . . . that figures are more important to this Government than forces."[48]

The appropriations power intersected with military policy in another way, however, since the late 1950s also featured growing doubts about the prominence of military options in U.S. foreign policy. Congressional anti-militarists selected as their outlet the foreign aid program, which a 1957 Brookings

---

[40] 103 *CR*, 85th Congress, 1st session, p. 7606 (24 May 1957).
[41] Bernard Sorton, "The Military Budget: Congressional Phase," *Journal of Politics* 23 (1961), p. 694.
[42] *New York Times*, 22 May 1957.
[43] *Congressional Quarterly Weekly Report*, 20 May 1972.
[44] Fenno, *Congressmen in Committees*, p. 3.
[45] Fenno, *Congressmen in Committees*, p. 69.
[46] *New York Times*, 21 Feb. 1956.
[47] 104 *CR*, 85th Congress, 2nd session, pp. 1343–1345 (30 Jan. 1958).
[48] 103 *CR*, 85th Congress, 1st session, p. 10668 (1 July 1957).

Institute study termed the "stethoscope held to the heart of the United States foreign policy process."[49] On November 24, 1958, in part to neutralize growing legislative criticism, Eisenhower created a special review committee chaired by former undersecretary of the Army William Draper. The committee wound up recommending a $400 million *increase* in arms assistance, along with such structural reforms as a continuing authorization for military assistance and including military aid funds in the defense budget.[50] These procedural changes would have eliminated the bastion of conservative military aid critics (Passman's Foreign Operations Subcommittee) as well as the chief liberal voice (the Foreign Relations Committee, whose role would become moot once authorizations became continuing rather than annual).

The Congress that considered the Draper suggestions differed radically from any of its Cold War predecessors.[51] In the best year for Democratic Senate candidates in the twentieth century, the party gained 12 seats in the Senate, increasing the Democratic majority in the upper chamber to 30 seats. The newly elected Democrats, mostly liberals from the Midwest and West, retired virtually every remaining revisionist – George Malone, John Bricker, Homer Ferguson, William Jenner, and Arthur Watkins all lost their seats. In addition, they shifted the balance of power within the Democratic caucus. A few days after the new congressional session opened, Morse bluntly informed Johnson "that those of us who do not follow you blindly must expect to travel a rocky political road in the Senate, but I wish to assure you it will not only be our tires which get punctured."[52] By reducing the mastery of the Senate that Johnson had displayed during his first four years as majority leader, the results opened up the possibility for committee chairs, such as Richard Russell and J. William Fulbright, to assert themselves. As important, the election brought to the upper chamber liberals prepared to embrace the revisionists' goal of increasing congressional power, only now for the purposes of championing anti-imperialism and anti-militarism.

The clearest example of the new pattern was Alaska senator Ernest Gruening, a Senate freshman at age 71 whose career as an anti-imperialist activist began in the early 1920s.[53] The Alaska Democrat, in an attitude more characteristic of the interwar period than the high Cold War, contended that the "Constitution recognizes and the Senate has traditionally exercised a special role in the conduct of foreign affairs."[54] Gruening especially looked

---

[49] Haviland, "Foreign Aid and the Policy Process: 1957," p. 702.
[50] *New York Times*, 18 March 1959.
[51] Michael Foley, *The New Senate: Liberal Influence on a Conservative Institution* (New Haven: Yale University Press, 1990).
[52] Wayne Morse to Lyndon Johnson, 15 Jan. 1959, Box 50, LBJA Papers, Lyndon Johnson Presidential Library.
[53] Robert David Johnson, *Ernest Gruening and the American Dissenting Tradition* (Cambridge, MA: Harvard University Press, 1998).
[54] 105 *CR*, 86th Congress, 1st session, p. 12679 (6 July 1959).

to use foreign aid to influence policy; he believed that since "this new financial mechanism has come to supersede and outclass all other diplomatic instrumentalities," Congress should "move into the picture, assume a much larger role, and reassume its traditional function" in foreign affairs.[55]

Ohio voters, meanwhile, replaced perhaps the most conservative member of the Senate (Bricker) with one among the most radical, Stephen Young, in the biggest upset of 1958. The 69-year-old had served four non-consecutive terms as a congressman in the 1930s and 1940s; when he returned to Washington in 1959, he considered the increased power of the military a "remarkable change."[56] The Air Force, the Ohio Democrat observed, "seems like the Mexican Army – few privates, plenty of generals."[57]

New senators such as Young and Gruening contributed to the powerful intellectual case against arms assistance led by Morse, who denounced the Draper recommendations as a "propaganda job," and argued that military aid harmed American security by propping up dictatorial regimes.[58] (Bourke Hickenlooper chastised his colleague for not understanding the "psychology and temperament of the Latin Americans"; leaders such as the "Somoza boys" in Nicaragua, the Iowa senator reasoned, "are trying to do a good job."[59]) In response to Fidel Castro's ouster of pro-American dictator Fulgencio Batista, the largest hike in military aid was made for Latin America. Yet the administration classified the individual country total, suggesting the dual problem faced by the program's opponents: they first had to find a way procedurally to discuss the question; and then they had to prevail on the merits.

In the late 1950s, a good deal of the critics' effort, by necessity, was directed toward the first problem. The Foreign Relations Committee's newest member, Frank Church (D-Idaho), wanted the administration to declassify the amount of U.S. military aid to each Latin American country, since publicity was "essential to intelligent and informed debate."[60] Gruening offered a companion amendment to limit the amount of funding that could be transferred from country to country, as a way of remedying "the delegation by the Congress to the Executive of its constitutional prerogatives."[61] The

---

[55] Ernest Gruening to Myron Cohen, 18 April 1960, Box 44, Senate General series, Ernest Gruening Papers, University of Alaska-Fairbanks; 105 *CR*, 86th Congress, 1st session, p. 12679 (6 July 1959).

[56] Stephen Young, "Straight from Washington," volume 1, number 11, April 1959, Box 56, Stephen Young Papers, Western Reserve Historical Society.

[57] Stephen Young, "Straight from Washington," volume 1, number 11, April 1959, Box 56, Stephen Young Papers, Western Reserve Historical Society.

[58] 105 *CR*, 86th Congress, 1st session, pp. 5241 (25 March 1959), 12687 (6 July 1959).

[59] *ESSFRC*, vol. 11, 85th Congress, 1st session, p. 134.

[60] Frank Church to Douglas Dillon, 27 May 1959, Series 2.2, Box 8, Frank Church Papers, Boise State University.

[61] 105 *CR*, 86th Congress, 1st session, p. 12677 (6 July 1959).

administration argued that Gruening's proposal would deprive the president "of that flexibility which he must have to use the Mutual Security program as effectively as possible," and it also strongly opposed the Church amendment.[62] More successfully, Ellender assembled a left-right coalition to pass by 11 votes an amendment to cut the military assistance authorization by $300 million.

Senate critics did not ignore the policy ramifications of military aid. In August 1959, Fulbright admitted that he disliked "having to support" programs like "defense support and special assistance, such as is involved in Viet Nam."[63] Church believed that too many nations received U.S. weapons that "do not need them, cannot make proper use of them, or can afford to increase their own defense spending."[64] A new figure joined the movement in May 1960, when Albert Gore asserted that the United States was providing arms to "just about any dictator, would-be dictator, or authoritarian regime which appeared willing to fight communism" – while not understanding that "the future can only be secure in a democratic world."[65]

Senators who targeted the foreign aid program faced one unavoidable obstacle: they were reliant, to some extent, on the timing of legislation. But the postwar Congress also featured built-in institutional forums for any member politically clever enough to use them. Among the Legislative Reorganization Act's unintended consequences was the proliferation of subcommittees, since the reform measure granted subcommittee chairs the right to hire staffs and diminished the power of committee chairs to control subcommittee agendas. When combined with the Senate's already strong decentralizing tendency, the act produced what one scholar has termed the era of "subcommittee government."[66] Pat McCarran and Joseph McCarthy were the first two senators to recognize how subcommittees could influence foreign policy through high-profile hearings designed to mobilize public pressure on the executive. With McCarran's death and McCarthy's censure, their subcommittees both went into decline – the normal course of events in the institutionally fluid world of the 1950s. Events during Eisenhower's second term suggested that several of their colleagues, from a variety of ideological viewpoints, learned from their example.

In the mid-1950s, the first key foreign policy subcommittees emerged from the Armed Services Committee. A self-made millionaire who made his fortune rehabilitating bankrupt industries, W. Stuart Symington came

[62] "Detailed Budgets for Mutual Security Program," n.d. [1959], Box 80, Foreign Relations Committee series, Bourke Hickenlooper Papers, Herbert Hoover Presidential Library.

[63] J. William Fulbright to Walker Stone, 8 Aug. 1959, BCN 110, J. William Fulbright Papers, University of Arkansas.

[64] Frank Church to Clara Ellis, 28 June 1960, Series 2.2, Box 8, Frank Church Papers, Boise State University.

[65] 106 *CR*, 86th Congress, 2nd session, p. 9007 (2 May 1960).

[66] Roger Davidson, "Subcommittee Government," in Thomas Mann and Norman Ornstein, eds., *The New Congress* (Washington, DC: American Enterprise Institute, 1981), pp. 99–133.

to Washington in 1945 as a protégé of James Forrestal. He soon attracted the eye of his fellow Missourians, Clark Clifford and Harry Truman, and was named Secretary of the Air Force in 1948. In the Truman White House, Symington earned a reputation as an effective administrator who was overly demanding on his staff – underlings referred to him as "W. Stuart God."[67] He easily defeated GOP incumbent James Kem in 1952; Senate Democratic leaders then assigned him to one of the PSI's vacant slots.

Though he bolstered his national prominence in combating McCarthy, critics dismissed Symington as superficial, a reputation reinforced by the Missouri senator's shrill attacks against the New Look. He focused almost all of his attention on the Air Force, overseeing hearings in 1956 through the newly created Air Force Subcommittee that exhibited an almost unquestioned faith in the service. The senator alleged that a "group of inexperienced civilians" motivated by budget priorities had muzzled dissenting officers, notably Air Force chief of staff Curtis LeMay, as part of an effort "to obscure the disparity in combat strength between this country and Russia."[68] But influential Republicans such as Leverett Saltonstall attacked his agenda, and the Missouri senator conceded the widespread "impression" that "political considerations" had motivated his attacks on the New Look.[69]

Since the Air Force inquiry closed shortly before the Soviets launched the *Sputnik* satellite in 1957, the Missouri senator pressed Richard Russell to appoint a special subcommittee to look into the matter – and to name him as chair.[70] Russell demurred, convinced that Symington "would raise a lot of hell, but it would not be in the national interest."[71] Moreover, the Armed Services chair wanted any political benefit that accrued from the inquiry to go to his protégé, Lyndon Johnson. In 1949, the Senate had appropriated $25,000 for a new body called the Preparedness Investigating Subcommittee (PIS), chaired by Johnson, which soon attracted national attention with its inquiry into difficulties in supplying U.S. troops during the Korean War.[72] After 1953, the subcommittee lost its permanent status, but Johnson sustained it on an ad hoc basis, guided, according to aide George Reedy, by "the same instinct that causes people to store obsolete furniture in an attic rather than throw it in the trash."[73] Now, it once again could be of use. The political benefits of tackling the space issue were obvious: as Reedy

---

[67] *Newsweek*, 9 May 1960.

[68] *ESSFRC*, vol. 8, p. 185 (19 Jan. 1955).

[69] Stuart Symington to John Mathers, 25 July 1956, Folder 1819, Stuart Symington Papers, University of Missouri.

[70] Stuart Symington to Richard Russell, 5 Oct. 1957, Box 403, General series, Richard Russell Papers, University of Georgia.

[71] Caro, *Master of the Senate*, p. 1022.

[72] James Kendall, "History of the Preparedness Investigating Subcommittee(s) of the Committee on Armed Services, United States Senate," n.d., Series 43, Box 2, John Stennis Papers, Mississippi State University.

[73] George Reedy, *U.S. Senate*, p. 182.

told Johnson, "The issue is one which, if properly handled, would blast the Republicans out the water, unify the Democratic Party, and elect you President."[74]

Johnson assured the subcommittee's ranking Republican, Styles Bridges, that there would be "no 'guilty party' in this inquiry except Joe Stalin and Nikita Khrushchev"; to Dulles, he confided that had he not agreed to chair the subcommittee, "it would be done by Symington, and that would be much worse."[75] This claim of nonpartisanship maintained the fiction that the Texas senator placed the national good above political self-interest. After a spectacular opening week of hearings, led off by Edward Teller arguing that Soviet advances required more U.S. defense spending, *Life* gushed that Johnson "went a far piece toward seizing, on behalf of the legislative branch, the leadership in reshaping U.S. defense policy."[76]

Symington, who long had complained that too many Democrats "felt there is no mileage in arguing with the current administration over the character and size of our Military Establishment," had been outmaneuvered.[77] After Johnson ignored his suggestions for a more confrontational inquiry, Symington used public testimony to make his points, but only further confirmed his reputation as a publicity-seeking blowhard.[78] He browbeat Secretary of Defense Neil McElroy, frequently asking the subcommittee reporter to repeat his questions when McElroy's responses dissatisfied him. After he tripled his established time limit, the acting chair, John Stennis, tried to cut him off, prompting Symington to complain wildly about a bipartisan alliance determined to silence him. Twenty minutes later, Johnson arrived to move the proceedings along, but again the Missouri senator protested. Noting that he had prepared his line of questioning for "several days," he ostentatiously asserted that his analysis was uniquely "important to national security."[79] By the time the hearing had ended (when McElroy had to leave to attend a diplomatic dinner), Symington had questioned the defense secretary for more time than all the other members of the subcommittee combined. Soon thereafter, he concluded that "I have done so much shouting that many of my colleagues . . . call me the prophet of gloom and doom."[80]

[74] Robert Dallek, *Lone Star Rising: Lyndon Johnson and His Times, 1908–1960* (New York: Oxford University Press, 1991), pp. 529–531.

[75] Caro, *Master of the Senate*, pp. 1022–1023.

[76] *Life*, 20 Jan. 1958.

[77] 103 *CR*, 85th Congress, 1st session, p. 10670 (1 July 1957).

[78] Stuart Symington to Lyndon Johnson, 21 Nov. 1957, Folder 1984, Stuart Symington Papers, University of Missouri.

[79] U.S. Senate, Preparedness Investigating Subcommittee, *Hearings, Inquiry into Satellite and Missile Programs*, 85th Congress, 1st session, pp. 242–259 (27 Nov. 1957).

[80] Stuart Symington to James Barry, 27 Aug. 1958, Folder 4677, Stuart Symington Papers, University of Missouri.

After their high-profile inquiries, the Symington and Johnson subcommittees receded into the background, although the PIS would return to prominence in the early 1960s. After the 1958 elections, attention shifted to a new subcommittee created by Henry Jackson, who, frustrated by his inability to secure a slot on the Foreign Relations Committee, charged his staff with finding an alternative forum from which he could express his views in international affairs. Shortly after Congress convened in 1959, the Washington Democrat introduced a resolution to study the NSC's effectiveness in confronting the "problems for the free world in the contest with world communism."[81] The senator's tactic was clever in two ways. First, the NSC's centrality in Eisenhower's decision-making structure assured that any study of its role would involve the administration's broader foreign policy. Second, by ostensibly seeking to investigate a structural rather than a policy matter, Jackson ensured the resolution's referral to the Government Operations Committee, on which he served.[82]

For different reasons, Eisenhower, Russell, and Johnson all unsuccessfully attempted to squelch the inquiry, but in the process only enhanced the subcommittee's visibility. Years of relentless Democratic attacks on the president's defense parsimony and a (false) post-*Sputnik* sense that the United States was suffering from a "missile gap" vis-à-vis the Soviet Union made the Jackson inquiry particularly timely. International relations theorist Hans Morganthau, who gushed that upon the subcommittee's "success or failure may well depend the fate of this country," joined the *New York Times* in anticipating "refreshingly new" insights on national security policy; columnist Russell Baker termed Jackson's attempt "to fit democratic government for a prolonged competition with totalitarianism" of "immense importance."[83] A once low-profile inquiry conducted by an offshoot of a minor Senate committee suddenly was on the front pages.

Jackson intended to accomplish three goals. First, he hoped to raise his personal visibility on international questions. Second, he sought to frame public discussion on national security issues for the 1960 campaign. Third, and most ambitiously, he wanted to conduct detailed staff studies of national security policy. None of these functions resembled the traditional roles of congressional subcommittees. But the diffusion of power characteristic of the postwar Senate provided Jackson with freedom to maneuver. An unusually thorough procedure of background interviews gave the subcommittee a reputation – as James Reston put it – for a "scholarly, objective, and

---

[81] Henry Jackson, "Memorandum for the Members of the Subcommittee on National Policy Machinery," 2 Feb. 1959, Box 68, Foreign Policy Defense series [hereafter FPD series], Henry Jackson Papers, University of Washington.

[82] Richard Neustadt personal interview with author, 26 November 1996; Robert Tufts personal interview with author, 15 January 1997.

[83] *New York Times*, 19 July 1959, 20 July 1959, 2 August 1959.

non-partisan" approach, just the image Jackson was hoping to create.[84] The *New York Times* columnist termed the subcommittee's inquiry "one of the most significant in many years," the model of a "legislative investigation at its very best."[85]

Jackson opened the hearings with a carefully coordinated list of witnesses headed by Robert Lovett, former undersecretary of state and defense, with whom the Washington senator explored the need "to spend more on defense and other national security programs."[86] Jackson privately gloated that obtaining testimony from "men who have no political or military ax to grind" revealed "that we face an enormous peril, that we are not doing enough, and that we should do more."[87] Calling for the United States to "compete effectively" with the USSR, he demanded expanding defense spending, reforming an overly bureaucratized decision-making structure, and restoring the hard-line principles associated with NSC 68.[88]

Press commentary on the hearings testified to Jackson's ability to position himself as a leading voice on national security matters. Quincy Howe of ABC, for instance, noted the irony of the Republican Lovett giving "the Democrats better political ammunition than most of their own leaders have yet provided." Syndicated columnist Doris Fleeson argued that the witnesses made the "defense case that Democrats have been groping for but have so far failed to define." Commentator Raymond Brandt hailed Jackson for demonstrating "how to plan a congressional committee to get the results desired." The Washington Democrat was among the first to use congressional hearings to satisfy the media's desire for substance in an age when policymakers like Dulles frequently offered simplistic explanations, at least in public, on international questions.[89]

With the subcommittee's "explosive" potential now fulfilled, the body's ranking Republican, Karl Mundt, realized that Jackson "seems to be using the subcommittee as a forum to advance the argument that the United States is lagging in the military preparedness program."[90] The damage, however, was done: the inquiry had developed into what *New York Times* reporter Cabell Phillips termed the Senate's "subtle spectacular," an "implicit invasion

---

[84] *New York Times*, 26 Feb. 1960.

[85] *New York Times*, 26 Feb. 1960.

[86] U.S. Senate, Subcommittee on National Policy Machinery, *Hearings, Organizing for National Security*, 86th Congress, 2nd session, pp. 94–95 (25 Feb. 1960).

[87] Henry Jackson to Mark Chitter, 5 March 1960, Box 256, 1952–1962 series, Henry Jackson Papers, University of Washington.

[88] Henry Jackson to Hubert Humphrey, 17 November 1960, Box 67, FPD series, Henry Jackson Papers, University of Washington.

[89] Ned Pendleton memorandum, "Press Commentary re hearings," 4 March 1960, Record Group III, Box 570, Karl Mundt Papers, Dakota State University.

[90] Karl Mundt to Bryce Harlow, 12 March 1960, Record Group III, Box 570, Karl Mundt Papers, Dakota State University.

by the Legislative branch of the jealously guarded precincts of the Executive."[91] Indeed, the subcommittee, which remained in place through the 1960s, achieved its prominence without reporting a single piece of legislation. And since each congressional session began with a change of the subcommittee's name, the Washington media began referring to the body simply as the "Jackson subcommittee."[92]

Jackson, Symington, and Johnson presented a viewpoint that alarmed some in the party: Joseph Clark (D-Pennsylvania) lamented in 1960 that too many of his colleagues seemed "more concerned with military defense and preparations for war than with positive programs for peace and disarmament."[93] Clark found a fourth foreign policy subcommittee more to his liking.

Beginning with the 81st Congress in 1949, the Foreign Relations Committee formed a special subcommittee to investigate a specific question and issue a report at the session's conclusion, after which the subcommittee passed out of existence. The first two subcommittees performed as expected, issuing perfunctory reports on the Voice of America and the Point Four programs.[94] Hubert Humphrey harbored more ambitious goals. Partly as a result of his close relationship with Johnson, in 1955 Humphrey persuaded Walter George to name him chair of a special subcommittee on disarmament, even though he himself seemed uncertain what he wanted to accomplish. Initially, he suggested staff interviews of the foreign policy elite, to mine for "ideas as to the realities of disarmament and the related questions of a political settlement."[95] After abandoning as impractical the approach that Jackson subsequently would adopt, Humphrey attempted to create a "Senate counterpart of the National Security Council," reasoning that the topic of nuclear disarmament presented the "unique opportunity" of addressing key issues – foreign policy, military policy, and atomic energy – normally handled by three separate committees.[96] But that plan encountered what Humphrey euphemistically termed "considerable conflicting opinion" as to his exceeding his jurisdiction.[97]

The subcommittee was set to expire on June 30, 1957, when – in a supreme irony – Dulles kept it alive by requesting that the Senate monitor

[91] *New York Times*, 29 May 1960.

[92] Francis Bator, personal interview with author, 12 Dec. 1996.

[93] Joseph Clark, "A Disarmament Policy for Democrats," n.d. [1960], Box 22-W(B), Joseph Clark Papers, Pennsylvania Historical Society.

[94] Carl Marcy oral history, U.S. Senate Historical Office.

[95] Hubert Humphrey to Bourke Hickenlooper, 16 Sept. 1955, Box 11, Foreign Relations Committee series, Bourke Hickenlooper Papers, Herbert Hoover Presidential Library.

[96] Hubert Humphrey to Bourke Hickenlooper, 29 Dec. 1955, Box 11, Foreign Relations Committee series, Bourke Hickenlooper Papers, Herbert Hoover Presidential Library.

[97] Hubert Humphrey to Bourke Hickenlooper, 18 July 1956, Box 11, Foreign Relations Committee series, Bourke Hickenlooper Papers, Herbert Hoover Presidential Library.

the administration's recently initiated disarmament negotiations with the USSR.[98] The now-renamed Subcommittee on Arms Control received a one-year lease on life, during which Humphrey chiefly concentrated on ensuring its permanence.[99] His success in that effort, which drew on Lodge's institutional arguments a decade before regarding the appropriateness of Foreign Relations Committee oversight of military aid and harkened back to the interwar era, when the committee possessed jurisdiction over the naval disarmament treaties of 1922 and 1930, won plaudits even from ideological foes such as Hickenlooper, who noted that the creation of the subcommittee meant that the Senate had "concluded that the question of armaments reduction and control is primarily a problem of foreign policy."[100]

As a result, an issue all but ignored by the Senate between 1949 and 1956 became a major subject of discussion as the Eisenhower years drew to a close, even if most remained skeptical about Humphrey's ideas.[101] Meanwhile, another Foreign Relations subcommittee demonstrated how Congress could focus attention on regions as well as issues overlooked by the executive. The Eisenhower years dramatically expanded the U.S. role in the Third World, through military alliances with right-wing governments and covert operations in Iran and Guatemala. In Latin America, CIA efforts to overthrow the left-leaning Guatemalan regime of Jacobo Arbenz succeeded, though with disastrous long-term repercussions.[102] Outside of Guatemala and to a lesser degree Bolivia, the administration promoted development by encouraging Latin American governments to adopt investment- and business-friendly policies, while also seeming to prefer military governments in the region.[103]

Twin jolts of the late 1950s – a crowd in Caracas attacking Vice President Richard Nixon's motorcade and the triumph of Fidel Castro's revolution in Cuba – exposed the shortcomings of this policy. Even before that time, Democrats had criticized Eisenhower for misunderstanding the problems facing Latin America. George Smathers, hardly a radical, spent so much time attacking the administration's approach that one colleague labeled him "the senator from Latin America."[104] Then, after the Caracas riots, the unlikely

---

[98] Hubert Humphrey to Bourke Hickenlooper, 28 June 1957, Box 12, Foreign Relations Committee series, Bourke Hickenlooper Papers, Herbert Hoover Presidential Library.

[99] Summary, "Conference with Senator Hubert Humphrey," 11 Jan. 1958, Box B-11, SANE Papers, Swarthmore College Peace Collection.

[100] Bourke Hickenlooper to Hubert Humphrey, 20 Feb. 1958, Box 12, Foreign Relations Committee series, Bourke Hickenlooper Papers, Herbert Hoover Presidential Library.

[101] Paul Douglas to Mrs. Ronald Steward, 27 April 1962, Box 206, Paul Douglas Papers, Chicago Historical Society; 104 *CR*, 85th Congress, 2nd session, p. 1613 (4 Feb. 1958); 105 *CR*, 86th Congress, 1st session, p. 3131 (2 March 1959).

[102] Piero Gleijeses, *Shattered Hope: The Guatemalan Revolution and the United States, 1944–1954* (Princeton: Princeton University Press, 1991).

[103] Stephen Rabe, *Eisenhower and Latin America: The Foreign Policy of Anti Communism* (Chapel Hill: University of North Carolina Press, 1988).

[104] Crispell, *Testing the Limits*, p. 102.

duo of Morse and Hickenlooper teamed to champion more economic aid to Latin America.

After reclaiming the Foreign Relations chairmanship in 1949, Tom Connally set up consultative subcommittees for Europe, East Asia, Latin America, the Middle East, and Africa. These bodies met no more than a handful of times annually, usually on Friday afternoons, for informal off-the-record briefings from State Department officials.[105] In May 1958, Morse, chair of the Latin American subcommittee, proposed a study of relations with the region, to conclude by offering policy suggestions.[106] Hickenlooper, the ranking member, initially believed that the publicity associated with such a probe could produce an overreaction in Latin America, since "they have an emotional attitude down there which we do not always understand."[107] Morse, however, pressed the point. One committee staffer recalled that, despite his contentious nature, the Oregon senator was "astute as hell as a politician," and he assured the Iowan that he wanted a detailed, bipartisan reevaluation of policy.[108] Hickenlooper relented; several trips to Bolivia in the 1950s had convinced him the United States needed to help stimulate Latin American economic development. "If we had a situation like this in Iowa," he told one staffer, "then goddamnit, we'd have a revolution, too."[109]

Privately, Morse admitted his bias: the "major cause for the trouble we are having with the other republics of the western hemisphere is due to the support we gave for many years to right-wing dictators in those countries."[110] But he appeased Hickenlooper sufficiently that the two published a joint report asserting that "fundamental social, economic, and political structural changes are obviously indicated in many Latin American countries."[111] The two senators predicted that their colleagues would support more aid if the region's governments made the desired pro-modernization reforms. As Humphrey's subcommittee previewed many of the arms control policies followed by John Kennedy's administration, the Morse/Hickenlooper report forecast the basic approach the Kennedy presidency would initially adopt to Latin America.

[105] Carl Marcy oral history, U.S. Senate Historical Office.

[106] Carl Marcy to Bourke Hickenlooper, 28 May 1958, Box 120, Foreign Relations Committee series, Bourke Hickenlooper Papers, Herbert Hoover Presidential Library.

[107] *ESSFRC*, vol. 10, p. 202 (16 May 1958).

[108] Wayne Morse to Bourke Hickenlooper, 29 Aug. 1958, Box 120, Foreign Relations Committee series, Bourke Hickenlooper Papers, Herbert Hoover Presidential Library; Pat Holt oral history, p. 113, U.S. Senate Historical Office.

[109] Pat Holt, personal interview with author, 20 Nov. 1996.

[110] Wayne Morse to Mrs. Donald Knodell, 13 Dec. 1960, Box A-43, Wayne Morse Papers, University of Oregon.

[111] U.S. Senate, Foreign Relations Committee, *Report, The Bogotá Conference: September 1960*, 87th Congress, 1st session, CIS Document #S0477, p. 2 (27 Feb. 1961).

Personnel changes within Congress facilitated its more creative international role. The single most significant development came at the Foreign Relations Committee, where Fulbright replaced Green as chair. Eighty-nine when he assumed the chairmanship in 1957, Green was frail both physically and intellectually, and Chief of Staff Carl Marcy essentially ran the committee.[112] The chairman focused on picayune issues such as grammatical rules ("that" versus "which" clauses), while his poor eyesight rendered him unable to identify colleagues when they did not sit in their assigned seats during committee hearings.[113]

In early 1959, Green's hometown newspaper, the *Providence Journal*, ran an editorial urging him to resign. Johnson saw an opportunity to achieve Green's removal, which would have the added benefit of elevating to the chairmanship Fulbright, whom the Majority Leader later termed "my secretary of state."[114] After privately persuading Green to leave the chairmanship – in the name of his avoiding further press abuse – Johnson convened a special meeting that, in a typical example of his tendency for flattery and exaggeration, featured committee members, one after another, issuing glowing personal tributes; the Texas senator himself called Green "one of the great men of our time."[115] The committee then went through the motions of asking the Rhode Island Democrat to reconsider his decision, after which the chair, to Johnson's astonishment, promised to postpone resigning.[116] The Majority Leader quickly recessed the hearing, instructing Marcy to take Green to the corridor and tell him to stick by his original decision; in the hearing room – after making sure the door was closed – Johnson informed the other committee members that Green had to go.[117] To everyone's relief, Marcy persuaded Green to relent.

After the announcement, an exultant Chester Bowles who later served at John Kennedy's first under secretary of state, wrote Fulbright, "The Senate Foreign Relations Committee under your chairmanship now has an opportunity to serve as a rallying point for critical and constructive opinion in this country."[118] The new chairman believed that Congress could educate the American public about basic foreign policy principles, although "there are limits to what the Senate can do about the general conduct of foreign policy,"

---

[112] Carl Marcy oral history, U.S. Senate Historical Office.

[113] Donald Ritchie, "Making Fulbright Chairman: Or How the 'Johnson Treatment' Nearly Backfired," *Society for Historians of American Foreign Relations* [hereafter SHAFR] *Newsletter* 15 (Sept. 1984), p. 22.

[114] Carl Marcy oral history, U.S. Senate Historical Office.

[115] *ESSFRC*, vol. 11, 85th Congress, 1st session, p. 134.

[116] *ESSFRC*, vol. 11, 85th Congress, 1st session, p. 147.

[117] Carl Marcy oral history, U.S. Senate Historical Office.

[118] Chester Bowles to J. William Fulbright, 7 Feb. 1959, BCN 135, J. William Fulbright Papers, University of Arkansas.

since its constitutional role was primarily a negative one.[119] The return of energetic leadership at Foreign Relations coincided with the long-overdue emergence of the Armed Services Committee. Although Russell reclaimed the chairmanship when Democrats took control of the Senate in 1955, the Georgia Democrat subsequently focused on coordinating Southern efforts to block civil rights legislation. In 1959, however, he signaled his intent to play a greater role on national security measures. The mechanism was procedural: a seemingly innocuous amendment, Section 412(b) of the Military Construction Authorization Act, to require specific Armed Services Committee authorizations for new weapons systems.

Until the late 1950s, both chambers' Armed Services Committees focused on manpower levels and military construction (chiefly the construction of bases). With the former item having little to do with policy and the latter comprising less than 4 percent of the 1959 Pentagon budget, both committees were active only in cases of intense rivalry between the services.[120] On the more substantive issues of new weapons development, the committees issued blank check authorizations such as, "The Secretary of the Army may procure materials and facilities necessary to maintain and support the Army . . . including guided missiles."[121] Committee members themselves recognized their weakness. Representative Paul Kilday (D-Texas), a power on the earlier Military Affairs Committee, admitted in the mid-1950s that while he once felt confident addressing military issues, "we have fallen behind in our knowledge."[122] Carl Vinson, chair of the House Armed Services Committee after 1955, instructed his colleagues to "have faith" in Pentagon experts lest he have to increase the committee's staff to develop alternative sources of information.[123]

In contrast to Vinson, Russell faced a variety of pressures to adopt a more aggressive approach. In 1957, a senior Republican, Ralph Flanders, claimed that the committee was "not informed" on issues relating to weapons development and policy, and thus was failing to perform its authorization responsibilities.[124] As a result, the Vermont senator contended, the Appropriations Committee had to "take little bits and pieces of the appropriations, glue them together with some imagination, and arrive at an overall defense

[119] J. William Fulbright, Our Responsibilities in World Affairs," *Vital Speeches of the Day*, 15 June 1959.

[120] Sorton, "The Military Budget: Congressional Phase," p. 690.

[121] Herbert Stephens, "The Role of Legislative Committees in the Appropriations Process: A Study Focused on the Armed Services Committees," *Western Political Quarterly* 24 (1971), p. 147.

[122] Sorton, "The Military Budget: Congressional Phase," p. 702.

[123] Sorton, "The Military Budget: Congressional Phase," p. 703.

[124] U.S. Senate, Armed Services Committee, *Hearings, Department of Defense Reorganization Act of 1958*, 85th Congress, 2nd session, pp. 31–32 (12 April 1958).

program."[125] Meanwhile, Russell risked being eclipsed by Symington and Johnson, who had used high-profile subcommittees to attract public notice and influence policy. One White House official speculated that the Georgia senator's amendment mostly showed that he desired "to get back into the act in order to counteract these two publicity hounds."[126]

The Russell amendment generated ferocious opposition. Hanson Baldwin, the *New York Times*' widely respected military affairs columnist, argued that "military decisions properly can be made only by the Pentagon and the President"; Congress, he reasoned, would bypass national security concerns to accommodate political and economic needs.[127] One Eisenhower staffer termed the amendment a "hideous error," and both the White House and the Pentagon worked to delete it.[128] Vinson, meanwhile, worried about creating excessive work for his committee and violating his principle that "military men should make military decisions."[129] But Russell rarely lost a battle over procedural matters. In the conference committee, he agreed to delay the amendment for one year, to coincide with the first budget introduced by the new administration. Beyond that, he would not budge. The amendment ended what one observer termed the "relative insignificance of the Armed Services Committees."[130]

At the time, however, more attention went to the Senate's role in the 1960 presidential election: Kennedy, Johnson, and Humphrey actively competed for the Democratic presidential nomination; Jackson and Symington were both considered compromise candidates. Kennedy's first-ballot triumph ended their chances, and the duo's hope for a vice-presidential nomination was dashed when the Massachusetts senator surprisingly selected Johnson. In the closest presidential election of the Cold War, the Kennedy/Johnson ticket narrowly prevailed after running a campaign that, on the foreign policy front, featured demagogic attacks against Republican nominee Richard Nixon from the right.

In 1961, Kennedy recommended increases of around 33 percent in defense spending, targeted toward conventional weapons designed to enhance U.S. ability to fight brushfire wars in the Third World. In this respect, the new President implemented the approach to defense matters offered in the Symington, Johnson, Mahon, and Jackson hearings of the 1950s. Yet Kennedy also made gestures to anti-militarist sentiment; in June 1961, he proposed the creation of a sub-cabinet Arms Control and Disarmament Agency (ACDA)

---

[125] U.S. Senate, Armed Services Committee, *Hearings, Department of Defense Reorganization Act of 1958*, 85th Congress, 2nd session, pp. 31–32 (12 April 1958).

[126] Sorton, "The Military Budget: Congressional Phase," p. 699.

[127] *New York Times*, 28 May 1959.

[128] Sorton, "The Military Budget: Congressional Phase," p. 697.

[129] Dawson, "Congressional Innovation and Intervention in Defense Policy," p. 53.

[130] Sorton, "The Military Budget: Congressional Phase," p. 690.

to coordinate disarmament-related activities, a move that Clark celebrated for recognizing that "planning for peace is every bit as complex as planning for war, and certainly not less crucial."[131]

After reports surfaced that Major General Edwin Walker, commander of an infantry division in Germany, had distributed literature associated with the far-right John Birch Society to troops under his command, the president also sided with anti-militarists in a bitter debate about military officers commenting on political matters.[132] Fulbright urged the new secretary of defense, Robert McNamara, to revoke a 1958 NSC directive that called for using military personnel "to arouse the public to the menace of the cold war."[133] The Fulbright memorandum aroused sharp attacks from conservatives; Barry Goldwater termed it the "most shocking document I have seen since I have been in the Senate."[134] Strom Thurmond (D-South Carolina), charging that the "Fulbright clan" represented an "insidious influence" in the government, burst into his Arkansas colleague's office and demanded to see the document's original version.[135] Fulbright instructed a staffer to "tell him to go to hell."[136]

Refusing to let the controversy rest, Thurmond introduced a resolution authorizing an investigation into the alleged muzzling of top military officials. (Stephen Young retorted that Kennedy could solve the problem by eliminating Pentagon speechwriters, since "without speechwriters, most generals and admirals would be speechless."[137]) The Armed Services Committee approved the Thurmond resolution with only Alaska's Bob Bartlett dissenting, and the full Senate agreed three days later.[138] The inquiry was turned over to the Special Preparedness Investigating Subcommittee, which consisted of the normal subcommittee plus Thurmond.

Periodic hearings over five months in early 1962 revealed the beginnings of an alignment between the PIS and high military officials that solidified in the mid-1960s. In this instance, reasoning that since "the Reds are well aware of the integrity, patriotic motives, and high qualifications of our military," PIS chair John Stennis speculated that preventing "such people from spreading

---

[131] Joseph Clark to Robert Thompson, 5 Aug. 1963, Box 22-W(B), Joseph Clark Papers, Pennsylvania Historical Society, Philadelphia.

[132] *Washington Post*, 18 April 1961.

[133] 107 *CR*, 87th Congress, 1st session, p. 14433 (2 Aug. 1961).

[134] 107 *CR*, 87th Congress, 1st session, p. 16104 (17 Aug. 1961); *New York Times*, 29 July 1961.

[135] Strom Thurmond to George Harter, 16 Sept. 1961, Box 12, Senate files, Strom Thurmond Papers, Clemson University.

[136] Woods, *Fulbright*, p. 284.

[137] Stephen Young, "Straight from Washington," vol. 3, number 5, Feb. 1961, Box 56, Stephen Young Papers, Western Reserve Historical Society.

[138] U.S. Senate, Armed Services Committee, *Hearings, Defense Secretary McNamara on S. Res. 191*, 87th Congress, 1st session, p. 5 (6 Sept. 1961).

the truth about Communist imperialism" would delight Soviet leaders.[139] At the same time, the Mississippi senator struggled to contain Thurmond, who consumed large amounts of time in pointless but inflammatory questioning of witnesses.[140] Despite a hostile report, however, the administration refused to bow to PIS pressure to allow military leaders free reign to comment on foreign policy issues.

While the efforts of Russell and Stennis suggested more aggressive pro-military pressure from the Senate, the most ambitious congressional assault on the Kennedy-era Pentagon actually came from the left. In 1963, George McGovern (D-South Dakota), who won election by less than 1,000 votes the previous year, introduced an amendment to decrease defense spending by about five percent. Though he privately confessed that he could not "match the Department's technical knowledge of the defense budget," the South Dakota senator publicly rejected the belief "that the growing technical complexity of the military art has required leaving the main judgments about security to our military officers."[141] These efforts struck a chord. An alarmed Russell told administration contacts that he "expected approximately 30 Senate votes in favor of drastic cuts in Defense spending as a result of the McGovern crusade"; the South Dakotan's efforts drew praise from Clark, Young, Church, Morse, and newly elected Gaylord Nelson (D-Wisconsin).[142] But once his amendment reached the Senate floor, McGovern discovered that "it is one hell of a tall order to take on the brass hats and their business allies."[143] With the amendment given no chance of passage, potential supporters declined to absorb political attacks; the South Dakota Democrat especially found it "difficult to get people who had a major defense impact in their state to vote to cut back."[144] Strong administration opposition doomed the amendment to less than five votes.

This mixed record on military issues during the early Kennedy years formed the backdrop to Senate consideration of the first Cold War arms control treaty, the Limited Test-Ban Treaty of 1963, which offered a bureaucratic showdown between Foreign Relations and the PIS. The PIS held lengthy, hostile hearings, featuring skeptical witnesses such as Curtis LeMay and

---

[139] U.S. Senate, Special Preparedness Investigating Subcommittee, *Hearings, Military Cold War Education and Speech Review Policies*, 87th Congress, 2nd session, p. 7 (23 Jan. 1962).

[140] Strom Thurmond to John Stennis, 18 Dec. 1961; John Stennis to James Kendall, 7 April 1962; both in Series 43, Box 3, John Stennis Papers, Mississippi State University.

[141] George McGovern to Stuart Symington, 16 Sept. 1963, Folder 4550, Stuart Symington Papers, University of Missouri; 109 *CR*, 88th Congress, 1st session, p. 13987 (2 Aug. 1963).

[142] Larry O'Brien, "Memorandum for the President," 20 Aug. 1963, Box 53, President's Office File, John Kennedy Presidential Library.

[143] George McGovern, personal interview with author, 8 Jan. 1994; George McGovern to L.S. Stavrianos, 27 Aug. 1963, box 66A 841/16, George McGovern Papers, Mudd Library, Princeton University.

[144] George McGovern, personal interview with author, 8 Jan. 1994.

Edward Teller, at which the main event came in the comments of the sub-committee members themselves. Jackson charged the administration with behaving "like Chamberlain, hat in hand, desperate to the world to try to get an agreement"; Goldwater detected a "subversive force in this country" demanding disarmament.[145] The wildest allegations came from Thurmond. The South Carolina senator, who was shortly thereafter ranked the Senate's least effective member in a magazine poll, first claimed that the treaty for-bade the United States from using nuclear weapons in the event of war with the Soviet Union, and then predicted that Moscow would shift its post-treaty testing operations to the People's Republic of China (PRC).[146] Noting the Sino-Soviet split, ACDA director William Foster dryly responded that the latter scenario "seems very unlikely in view of the present situation in the world."[147]

For the Foreign Relations Committee, meanwhile, the treaty represented the logical culmination of the work begun by Humphrey's disarmament sub-committee. Gore and Morse argued that the United States and the Soviet Union had a common interest in arms control, while Morse praised the administration for excluding the JCS from the negotiating team – proof that "we have not established a military government in this country, not yet."[148] Fulbright, who shepherded the treaty from the committee through final approval in the Senate, indicated disappointment only when learning that the Pentagon would not decrease defense spending as a result of the treaty's approval.[149]

While the Test-Ban Treaty represented Kennedy's most significant diplomatic triumph, the Democrat's foreign policy remains best known for efforts in the Third World. Like his predecessors, Kennedy relied primarily on rhetoric and money in his Latin American, East Asian, and African policy. Unfortunately for the president, the increased importance that he attached to foreign aid coincided with rising congressional skepticism about the program's size and direction, producing the most dramatic showdown between Congress and the executive since the Army/McCarthy hearings – and the most clear-cut congressional victory in a foreign policy battle with the president since the start of the Cold War.

---

[145] U.S. Senate, Preparedness Investigating Subcommittee, *Hearings, Military Aspects and Implications of Nuclear Test Ban Proposals and Related Matters*, 88th Congress, 1st session, pp. 20, 23 (7 May 1963), 315, 321 (26 June 1963), 365 (27 June 1963).

[146] *Pageant*, March 1964.

[147] U.S. Senate, Preparedness Investigating Subcommittee, *Hearings, Military Aspects and Implications of Nuclear Test Ban Proposals and Related Matters*, 88th Congress, 1st session, pp. 33, 54 (7 May 1963).

[148] U.S. Senate, Foreign Relations Committee, *Hearings, Nuclear Test Ban Treaty*, 88th Congress, 1st session, p. 58 (12 Aug. 1963).

[149] U.S. Senate, Foreign Relations Committee, *Hearings, Nuclear Test Ban Treaty*, 88th Congress, 1st session, p. 276 (15 Aug. 1963).

"You have a new administration and you are new," Fulbright informed Robert McNamara in June 1961; "it is time to review our policies."[150] On the surface, Kennedy followed that advice, proposing a bill to consolidate all foreign aid programs into the Agency for International Development (AID). In practice, conservatives continued to complain about the program's cost and tendency to assist governments whose domestic policies were not friendly to U.S. business interests. Liberals still attacked military assistance and aid to non-democratic regimes. And Passman, who declined to endorse Kennedy for president in 1960, still was, one Foreign Relations staffer recalled, a "pain in the ass."[151] (The Foreign Operations Subcommittee's newest Republican, Silvio Conte of Massachusetts, considered Passman "a demagogue" who "hates anybody who disagrees with him."[152]) Continuing to abuse his authority as chair, Passman called Peace Corps Director Sargent Shriver to testify for a Saturday night hearing; on another occasion, he summoned Assistant Secretary of State Mennen Williams back from Cyprus for an unscheduled hearing – only to, on both occasions, cancel the session at the last minute.[153] When attacked for such behavior, the congressman lashed out, informing one critic (whom he dismissed as "quite obviously . . . retarded") that he was grateful to God "for giving us such a great country with so very few emotionally disturbed hotheads like you."[154]

Beyond Passman's antics, Kennedy confronted an increasingly unstable congressional situation. By 1961, conservative Democrats followed the lead of figures such as Ellender in their skepticism about the program, while conservative Republicans began linking their support of foreign aid to conditions that would render the program useless, such as demands that recipient nations cease all commerce with the Soviet bloc.[155] Kennedy's last difficulty involved the group that AID officials described as the "dissident liberals."[156] With the exception of Morse and Gruening, in 1961 every Northern or Western Democratic senator supported the foreign aid program.[157] By the end of 1962, however, dissatisfaction with military aid and Kennedy's sustaining assistance to dictatorial regimes such as Franco's Spain caused a

[150] U.S. Senate, Foreign Relations Committee, *Hearings, International Development and Security*, 87th Congress, 1st session, p. 655 (14 June 1961).
[151] Pat Holt, personal interview with author, 20 Nov. 1996.
[152] Silvio Conte oral history, Jan. 1961, Center for Legislative Archives, Washington, D.C.
[153] *Washington Post*, 9 Sept. 1961.
[154] Otto Passman to H. Don McGirr, 11 Sept. 1961, Drawer 12, Otto Passman Papers, University of Louisiana, Monroe.
[155] 107 *CR*, 87th Congress, 1st session, pp. 16363–16365 (18 Aug. 1961).
[156] Larry O'Brien, "Memorandum for the President," 4 Nov. 1963, Box 53, President's Office File, John Kennedy Presidential Library.
[157] Stephen Young to Ronald Whitley, 31 Aug. 1961, Box 38, Stephen Young Papers, Western Reserve Historical Society; Albert Gore to Paul Nolan, 11 Sept. 1961, Legislation/Foreign Aid 1961 file, Albert Gore Papers, Middle Tennessee State University.

number of Senate liberals, such as Gore, Church, and Stephen Young, to reconsider their position.[158]

Kennedy's most important new foreign policy overture was itself a foreign aid program, an ambitious initiative in the Western Hemisphere to respond to the threat posed by Castro's triumph in Cuba. In late 1960, the President-elect appointed a task force chaired by a veteran diplomat, Adolf Berle, to set up the guidelines for what he dubbed the Alliance for Progress. Acknowledging that the earlier efforts of Morse and Hickenlooper "have helped to lay a groundwork for a new concerted effort," the task force aimed to "divorce the inevitable and necessary Latin American social transformation" from "overseas Communist power politics" by championing Latin American democracy and targeting aid to education, social welfare, and economic development.[159] The plan was lunched in August 1961 at Punta del Este, Uruguay, when the United States pledged to provide $20 million in private and government aid to Latin America within the decade.

Although Kennedy began his term with a solid consensus in the Senate behind the Alliance for Progress – critical, since he could not rely on Passman and the House – the first significant defections came in 1962, when Hickenlooper introduced an amendment to end foreign aid for any regime that expropriated U.S.-owned property. The Iowa senator termed the offering "preventive medicine" against leaders who, "pointing to the success of Castro in Cuba in seizing American property," portrayed nationalization as the quickest route to economic growth.[160] Even though the administration had given U.S. corporations a prominent role in devising inter-American policy, an ideological and institutional gulf separated Kennedy officials from Hickenlooper. Most conservative Republicans assumed that foreign aid should be used as a lever to open doors to U.S. capital, but Kennedy's conception of the Alliance, one State Department official explained, was "primarily political in nature, ultimately designed to encourage the growth of reasonably stable governments capable of absorbing reform and change, secure from both extreme Left and extreme Right."[161] Most Senate Democrats agreed, but not enough to prevent Congress from approving the amendment.

---

[158] Stephen Young to Antoni Short, 27 June 1962, Box 39, Stephen Young Papers, Western Reserve Historical Society; *ESSFRC*, vol. 13, part 2, p. 203 (16 June 1961); 108 *CR*, 87th Congress, 2nd session, p. 9661 (5 June 1962); U.S. Senate, Foreign Relations Committee, *Hearings, International Development and Security*, 87th Congress, 1st session, pp. 754, 756 (15 June 1961).

[159] "Report from the Task Force on Immediate Latin American Problems to President-Elect Kennedy," 4 Jan. 1961, *FRUS, 1961–1963*, vol. 12, pp. 2–4.

[160] George Pavlik to Bourke Hickenlooper, 1 Aug. 1962, Box 120, Bourke Hickenlooper Papers, Herbert Hoover Presidential Library; Bourke Hickenlooper to Walter Graham, 18 April 1962, Box 119, Bourke Hickenlooper Papers, Herbert Hoover Presidential Library.

[161] Arthur Schlesinger, Jr., to Ralph Dungan, 15 Oct. 1962, *FRUS, 1961–1963*, vol. 12, pp. 107–109.

Compounding the administration's difficulties, a growing number of Senate liberals, who would become the core of the new internationalist movement, started to question the Alliance's ideological agenda. After a vigorous internal debate, the administration eventually prioritized promoting security and economic development over the nourishing of democracy.[162] The new internationalists, however, resolved the tensions between the security, developmental, and political goals of the Alliance differently. Stephen Young, for instance, criticized aid to Haiti's François Duvalier as "blackmail [paid] to a ruthless dictator and his henchmen" that would tarnish the image of the United States and doom the Alliance.[163] After a coup in mid-1962 toppled the democratically elected government of Peru, Gruening denounced the administration's failure to take "decisive action" sooner against Latin American military takeovers.[164] To prevent the United States from being "dragooned by crisis after crisis into making huge grants of funds on vague promises" of reform, the Alaska senator sponsored an amendment requiring Kennedy to withhold all aid from Latin American military regimes and to terminate all military aid throughout Latin America.[165] McGovern, meanwhile, devoted his initial Senate address to wondering whether a "dangerous fixation with Castro" had caused the administration to lose "sight of the real interests of the nation in the Western Hemisphere," namely "whether or not the people can overturn an unjust social order through a peaceful democratic revolution."[166] The administration understood the significance of countering the liberals' claims. In 1962, Secretary of State Dean Rusk, conceding that "congressional opinion" considered it "extremely unwise" to extend assistance to Latin American military regimes, asked for "thoughtful commentary" from U.S. missions in Latin America on the "validity" of the critique from "influential members [of] Congress."[167]

Three patterns – the solidifying hostility among conservatives toward foreign aid; liberals expanding their opposition to military aid and assistance to dictatorships to a critique of the program as a whole; and the collapse of the congressional coalition that initially supported the Alliance

---

[162] *ESSFRC*, vol. 13, pt. 2, 87th Congress, 1st session, p. 356 (6 July 1961); U.S. Senate, Foreign Relations Committee, *Hearings, International Development and Security*, 87th Congress, 1st session, pp. 618–620 (14 June 1961).

[163] Stephen Young, "Notes, South American visit," Nov.–Dec. 1961, Box 56, Stephen Young Papers, Western Reserve Historical Society.

[164] 108 *CR*, 87th Congress, 2nd session, pp. 14107–14109 (19 July 1962).

[165] Ernest Gruening to Mark Scherer, 19 November 1962, Box 45, General Subjects file 1959–1963, Ernest Gruening Papers, University of Alaska-Fairbanks.

[166] McGovern draft address, n.d. [1963], Speeches and Statements File, 1963, George McGovern Papers, Princeton University.

[167] Dean Rusk to U.S. embassy Lima, 23 Aug. 1962, State Department Central Policy File, 1950–1963, 723.00/8-2362, Record Group 59, National Archives, II; Dean Rusk, "Circular Telegram from the Department of State to Certain Posts in the American Republics," 10 Aug. 1962, *FRUS, 1961–1963*, vol. 12, pp. 227–228.

for Progress – coalesced in what *U.S. News & World Report* termed the "foreign-aid revolt" of 1963.[168] By the end of the year's congressional session, Congress had cut the President's initial request by more than one-third, by far the largest reduction in the program's history, and had attached an unprecedented number of policy-related amendments to the final bill.

Early on, Kennedy anticipated difficulties with the 1963 bill. In November 1962, he replaced AID director Fowler Hamilton with the more experienced Budget Director David Bell. The following month, the President appointed a special committee to review foreign aid headed by former NATO Commander Lucius Clay, but this move backfired: the committee delivered a report arguing that the program required "substantial tightening up and sharpened objectives in terms of our national interests."[169] Trying to make the best of the situation, Kennedy, in an unprecedented action, reduced his own foreign aid request, from $4.9 billion to $4.5 billion. The move failed to stem the negative momentum, especially after Clay informed the Foreign Affairs Committee that "careful analysis would show the possibility of some further savings" above and beyond the President's own $420 million cut.[170] It came as little surprise when the committee subsequently reduced Kennedy's request by an additional $438 million.

More problems emerged when the bill reached the House floor. Just before adoption, E. Ross Adair (R-Indiana) introduced a surprise amendment to recommit the bill with instructions to reduce the authorization level by $585 million more. The offering broke with tradition; normally motions to recommit occurred when the House sat as a Committee of the Whole, where decisions were made by voice vote (where the Speaker could judge whether "yea" or "nay" registered the loudest response), standing vote (where the Speaker counted members standing for or against a bill), or teller vote (where each member voted "yea" or "nay," but individual votes were not recorded). These devices all allowed representatives to vote for a politically unpopular program like foreign aid without leaving a record. Adair's motion required a roll-call vote, placing moderate members on the spot. Ultimately, 35 Republicans and 10 Southern Democrats voted both with Adair and then for the final bill. With this middling group in the House on his side, Adair's motion passed by a 224-to-186 margin. Kennedy denounced the House vote as "shortsighted, irresponsible, and dangerously partisan."[171]

---

[168] *U.S. News & World Report*, 25 Oct. 1963.

[169] Lucius Clay, et. al., "Report to the President of the United States from the Committee to Strengthen the Security of the Free World," 20 March 1963, Box 31, Foreign Relations Committee series, Bourke Hickenlooper Papers, Herbert Hoover Presidential Library.

[170] U.S. House of Representatives, Foreign Affairs Committee, *Hearings, Foreign Assistance Act of 1963*, 88th Congress, 1st session, p. 156 (10 April 1963).

[171] *New York Times*, 24 Aug. 1963.

The President held out hope that the Senate, as had occurred during the previous decade, would restore the House cuts. But Kennedy staffers discovered that Fulbright, "for the first time," seemed "unwilling to fight and die for the Foreign Aid program."[172] Foreign Relations Committee hearings, meanwhile, were dominated by critics of the bill. Morse, as expected, launched a daily attack against the program; with his sharp mind and ability to think extemporaneously, the Oregon senator posed a problem, as McNamara discovered when Morse pressed him on the administration's record of assisting regimes that had overthrown democratically elected governments.[173] "It depends on how you define overthrown, I would think," the Defense Secretary feebly replied.[174]

The administration's situation deteriorated in mid-July, when Gore returned from vacation and expressed strong opposition to the bill. The Tennessee senator's remarks, one Kennedy official noted, encouraged "renewed antagonism for Foreign Aid" by Morse and Church; indeed, reports had come back that Morse was "going crazy" and "running wild" in the committee.[175] After deferring action on the bill to consider the Test-Ban Treaty, the committee resumed consideration of foreign aid matters in early October. Markup sessions proceeded with excruciating slowness: at one, Congressional Liaison Larry O'Brien reported that "nothing whatever was accomplished because of the general attitude of antipathy to AID and frustration over Vietnam, military coups in Latin America, etc."[176] Finally awakening to reality, David Bell in late October foresaw a "real danger" of drastic aid reductions by the Senate.[177] The committee also started considering what the AID administrator termed "restrictive amendments," the most popular of which was a Morse offering to terminate aid to governments that came to power through a military coup.[178] O'Brien reported back that "support continues to build in the Senate for such an amendment"; the only advice he could offer was to accelerate the upper chamber's consideration of the bill as much as possible.[179]

[172] Mike Manatos to Larry O'Brien, 12 July 1963, Box 16, John Kennedy Congressional Liaison Office Papers, John Kennedy Presidential Library.

[173] James Thomson to Roger Hilsman, 26 June 1963, Box 5, James Thomson Papers, John Kennedy Presidential Library.

[174] U.S. Senate, Foreign Relations Committee, *Hearings, Foreign Assistance Act of 1963*, 88th Congress, 1st session, p. 206 (13 June 1963).

[175] Mike Manatos to Larry O'Brien, 23 July 1963, Box 8, Office Files of Mike Manatos, White House Central Files, John Kennedy Presidential Library.

[176] Larry O'Brien, "Memorandum for the President," 7 Oct. 1963, Box 53, President's Office File, John Kennedy Presidential Library.

[177] David Bell, "Memorandum for the President," 21 Oct. 1963, Box 53, President's Office File, John Kennedy Presidential Library.

[178] David Bell, "Memorandum for the President," 21 Oct. 1963, Box 53, President's Office File, John Kennedy Presidential Library.

[179] Larry O'Brien, "Memorandum for the President," 7 Oct. 1963, Box 53, President's Office File, John Kennedy Presidential Library.

Latin American events prevented this strategy. Between late 1961 and 1963, the Alliance showcased the Dominican Republic, with the United States first supporting the ouster of longtime dictator Rafael Trujillo and then showering economic and military assistance on Trujillo's eventual successor, reformist Juan Bosch, who won a January 1963 election. According to U.S. ambassador John Bartlow Martin, the Kennedy administration was "heavily committed to democratic government in this country – perhaps more so than in any other country of Latin America."[180] Such rhetorical and financial support, however, did not prevent a September 1963 military coup that ousted Bosch's regime.

The United States instantly suspended aid and recalled Martin, and Kennedy even considered sending troops to restore Bosch to power.[181] Eventually, however, the administration decided to play the hand it was dealt, as it had in previous instances of Latin American military coups. (Nine occurred during Kennedy's 1,000 days in office.) The White House hoped that Bosch, who had fled to Puerto Rico, would "1. shut up; 2. stay put; [and] 3. stay friendly."[182] Meanwhile, the president developed a policy "that combines some possibility of achievement with a significant impact on the attitude of the Latin American military generally."[183] Kennedy wanted to resume military aid gradually, to encourage the Dominican junta to liberalize its policies and thereby prevent a radicalization of Dominican political culture from which the Communists could benefit. Privately, the president confided that "if it were not for the Congress . . . we ought to recognize [the junta] now."[184]

This concern with the congressional effects of the Dominican coup produced Kennedy's most significant political blunder regarding the Alliance for Progress. With clearance from a president eager to "counteract" legislative criticism, Assistant Secretary of State Edwin Martin issued a statement claiming that the United States was "addressing the problem of military coups in a number of different ways," since not all military regimes necessarily opposed Alliance-backed reforms.[185] Martin then ripped into the "impatient idealists" who measured U.S. policy not against historical reality, but "against somewhat theoretical notions of the manner in which men should and do

---

[180] John Bartlow Martin to State Department, 9 Aug. 1963, Box 3317, State Department Central Policy File, 1963, Record Group 59, National Archives, II.

[181] President Kennedy to Robert McNamara, 4 Oct. 1963, *FRUS, 1961–1963*, vol. 12, p. 739.

[182] John Bartlow Martin, "Talking Paper for Dungan for Bosch," 16 Oct. 1963, Box 6, Records Relating to the Dominican Republic, 1958–1966, Office of Caribbean and Mexican Affairs, Records of the Bureau of Inter-American Affairs, Record Group 59, National Archives, II.

[183] Benjamin Read, "Memo for Bundy," n.d. [1963], Box 6, Records Relating to the Dominican Republic, 1958–1966, Office of Caribbean and Mexican Affairs, Records of the Bureau of Inter-American Affairs, Record Group 59, National Archives, II; President Kennedy to Robert McNamara, 4 Oct. 1963, *FRUS, 1961–1963*, vol. 12, p. 739.

[184] President Kennedy, quoted in Edwin Martin oral history, John Kennedy Presidential Library, p. 109.

[185] *Washington Post*, 6 Oct. 1963.

operate in a complex world."[186] According to presidential assistant Arthur Schlesinger, Jr., Martin hoped that offering a "sober and realistic description" of the difficulties the administration faced would "cool down" those in "Congress who suppose that military coups constitute definitely evidence of the failure of the Alliance."[187]

Martin's statement, however, was perceived less as a "sober and realistic description" of the situation than as an "apologia for coups" – as even its author eventually conceded.[188] In response, Gruening publicly urged that, after "the supine and spineless compromises of the past," Kennedy demonstrate some "courage" and "take whatever steps are necessary" to restore Bosch to power – even by using military force.[189] Gruening's demand reflected a growing disinclination to allow the executive branch to define the parameters of policy and helped change the framework of debate. On September 30, 1963, 22 senators issued a public telegram urging Kennedy to withhold recognition of the new Dominican government indefinitely, a move that Humphrey justified by citing the Senate's "unique responsibility in connection with the development of the foreign policy of this country."[190]

The Dominican issue represented one topic in which the emerging left-right anti-foreign aid coalition collapsed. During his reign, Rafael Trujillo had aggressively courted Congress, sometimes through junkets or outright bribes. Ellender, one member of the "Dominican lobby," chastised Gruening for not understanding that while Trujillo "might have had to kill a few persons to get where he was," the former dictator provided the leadership that his people needed.[191] Frank Lausche (D-Ohio) viewed the question as "whether the United States will be better served in its security by a strong and positive dictatorship ... or whether our interests lie in the direction of a weak and vacillating idealist in a definite democratic form of government."[192] The Ohio senator feared that "we have too many persons in the Senate who are thinking only of constitutional governments regardless of the affiliations and the leanings toward communism of such pseudo-democracies."[193]

---

[186] *Washington Post*, 6 Oct. 1963.
[187] Arthur Schlesinger, Jr., to President Kennedy, 8 Oct. 1963, *FRUS, 1961–1963*, vol. 12, pp. 150–152.
[188] Edwin Martin oral history, John Kennedy Presidential Library, pp. 102, 111.
[189] *ESSFRC*, vol. 15, 88th Congress, 1st session, pp. 611–612 (26 Sept. 1963); 109 *CR*, 88th Congress, 1st session, pp. 18326–18328 (30 Sept. 1963).
[190] Hubert Humphrey to George Grant, 30 Sept. 1963, Box 302, Hubert Humphrey Papers, Minnesota State Historical Society.
[191] 109 *CR*, 88th Congress, 1st session, p. 18485 (1 Oct. 1963).
[192] Frank Lausche to Charles English, 14 Oct. 1963, Box 264, Frank Lausche Papers, Ohio State Historical Society.
[193] Frank Lausche to James Naylor, 16 Oct. 1963, Box 264, Frank Lausche Papers, Ohio State Historical Society.

For Hickenlooper, the issue was simple: Bosch "let all the Commies come back . . . [now] we have a government that keeps them out."[194]

On October 23, as the Dominican debate raged on, the Foreign Relations Committee finally reported a foreign aid bill. The measure contained a higher-than-anticipated funding level, roughly $600 million more than the House authorization, but also a host of policy-related amendments that the administration opposed, such as a mandatory suspension of aid for Latin American governments that overthrew popularly elected regimes, a ban on all aid to "economically developed" countries, a less flexible interpretation of the Hickenlooper amendment, a requirement for congressional approval for individual projects costing more than $100 million, and tightened restrictions on aid to countries that provided assistance to Cuba.[195] Floor debate opened five days later with Fulbright tepidly defending the program and privately reporting that the opposition, "under the leadership of Senator Morse," had undertaken "the most savage attack upon the bill that I have ever seen."[196] Terming the committee's changes to the administration's measure "feeble and inadequate," Morse urged his colleagues to "rewrite the bill in the Chamber."[197]

U.S. News & World Report correctly labeled Morse and Gruening the "spark plugs" of the foreign aid revolt.[198] The day after Morse's speech, the Alaska Democrat, who had privately promised to support every cut in appropriations and every restrictive amendment before voting against the final bill itself, outlined a bold agenda for Senate activism.[199] Before the advent of foreign aid, Gruening reasoned, the role of Congress in foreign policy was "essentially a negative one," with the legislature voting on treaties or various appropriations measures.[200] "But," he noted, "this role of the Senate was not always thus confined or conceived," quoting Rufus King to the effect that the Senate could "at any time call for full and exact information respecting the foreign affairs."[201] As the years passed, the upper chamber's power never reached this potential level. Its breadth and relationship to the appropriations power made foreign aid the vehicle for the Senate to fulfill the Framers' vision. In this sense, the Alaska senator argued that the program "impels each and every Senator to consider the conduct of our foreign

[194] *ESSFRC*, vol. 15, 88th Congress, 1st session, p. 850 (11 Oct. 1963).

[195] *New York Times*, 24 Oct. 1963.

[196] J. William Fulbright to Jim Smith, 29 Oct. 1963, Series 48:8, Box 29, J. William Fulbright Papers, University of Arkansas.

[197] 109 *CR*, 88th Congress, 1st session, pp. 20343, 20345 (28 Oct. 1963).

[198] *U.S. News & World Report*, 25 Nov. 1963.

[199] Ernest Gruening to Gordon Skrede, 4 Sept. 1963, Box 32, General Subjects 1963–1965 series, Ernest Gruening Papers, University of Alaska-Fairbanks.

[200] 109 *CR*, 88th Congress, 1st session, p. 20500 (29 Oct. 1963).

[201] 109 *CR*, 88th Congress, 1st session, p. 20500 (29 Oct. 1963).

policy his business and responsibility."[202] In the world of 1963, Gruening viewed foreign aid votes more important than the Senate's role in approving treaties.

Two days after Gruening's remarks, the Senate leadership, in yet another unprecedented move, looked to appease the critics. Majority Leader Mike Mansfield and Minority Leader Everett Dirksen (R-Illinois) offered an amendment to reduce the authorization by another $385 million, citing the "most thoughtful" criticisms offered by Morse and Gruening.[203] Mansfield noted that only a handful of colleagues were truly interested in the program – Morse, Gruening, Fulbright, Ellender, and New York Republican Jacob Javits – and with three of those five ardently opposed to the bill, he had no choice but to offer concessions. The Montana senator hoped that Gruening and Morse would respond to his gesture by tempering their remarks against the bill and severing their alliance with anti-foreign aid conservatives. AID officials expected the Mansfield offering to confirm their earlier expectations that "a group of friendly-to-moderate Senators" would ensure the bill's passage.[204]

Both Mansfield and AID administrators were naïve. Instead of pacifying the opposition, the leadership's actions emboldened it. The result, as described by the *Washington Post*, was "a wild melee worthy of the Keystone Cops," in which the bill was "carved and recarved on the Senate floor in a string of amendments so confusing that Senators were voting on dollar figures tossed in the air, often with only the most vagrant notion of what was at stake."[205] The traditional critics of foreign aid – on both the left and right – profited from the confusion. Church offered amendments to decrease military aid to Africa and end assistance of all types to wealthier nations.[206] Young, urging his colleagues to "act boldly against dictatorship in any form," produced an amendment to eliminate aid to Spain.[207] Gore and Church agreed that if the United States stopped military aid entirely, "we would be better off."[208] Gruening revived his amendment to terminate assistance to military juntas in Latin America and also proposed an amendment to block aid to nations preparing aggressive actions against their neighbors – targeted at Nasser's regime in Egypt and Sukarno's in Indonesia. The amendment passed by more than 50 votes, prompting the Egyptian ambassador to protest that "by searching consciences in an effort

---

[202] 109 *CR*, 88th Congress, 1st session, p. 20500 (29 Oct. 1963).

[203] 109 *CR*, 88th Congress, 1st session, pp. 20844 (31 Oct. 1963), 20906 (1 Nov. 1963).

[204] Larry O'Brien, "Memorandum for the President," 21 Oct. 1963, Box 53, President's Office File, John Kennedy Presidential Library.

[205] *Washington Post*, 8 Nov. 1963.

[206] 109 *CR*, 88th Congress, 1st session, pp. 21216–21219 (6 Nov. 1963).

[207] 109 *CR*, 88th Congress, 1st session, p. 21840 (14 Nov. 1963).

[208] 109 *CR*, 88th Congress, 1st session, p. 21222 (6 Nov. 1963).

to determine aggressive intent before the fact, Congress is playing the role of God."[209]

With the leadership having lost all control, the bill became a vehicle for any senator to make a foreign policy point. What Russell Long (D-Louisiana) correctly denounced as the proceeding's "most ridiculous" offering came from Thomas Kuchel (R-California), who wanted to sever aid to countries that extended territorial limits on the high seas beyond those recognized by the United States.[210] (Kuchel acted at the behest of the American Tunamen's Association, after Ecuador unilaterally extended its territorial waters to a 200-mile limit and then seized the boats of several U.S. fishermen who harvested in the disputed waters.[211]) With most senators lacking a strong commitment to foreign aid, the amendment sailed through by a 57-to-29 vote. U.S. diplomats reported that the Marxist press in Latin America was "naturally crowing" over the amendment; Rusk denounced "the tendency in Congress to legislate foreign policy."[212] Nonplussed, Nebraska Republican Carl Curtis quipped to Kuchel: "Us fishermen have to stick together."[213]

By this stage, the only "hopeful note" AID could offer was that the Senate debate would eventually end.[214] When the Senate finally passed the authorization bill after three weeks of debate, commentator Mary McGrory described Mansfield as wearing "his habitual expression of martyred resignation," while Fulbright just "appeared grateful to be alive"; Morse, she noted, "left his mark on foreign aid for all the world to see."[215] The House/Senate conference report retained many of the restrictive amendments while forwarding an authorization figure of $3.6 billion, more than 20 percent below Kennedy's initial request. Surveying the results, the *Washington Post* blasted the "new Democratic Know-Nothings" – Morse, his "deputy commander" Gruening, and the "brigade" of Young, Church, and Gore – for producing a "squalid" debate and imposing "a series of dogmatic restrictions on the use of aid."[216] Lyndon Johnson, who had assumed the presidency after

---

[209] Dean Rusk circular telegram, 14 Nov. 1963, Box 3308, State Department Central File, 1960–1963, State Department Records, Record Group 59, National Archives.

[210] 109 *CR*, 88th Congress, 1st session, p. 21335 (7 Nov. 1963).

[211] August Felando to Thomas Kuchel, 15 Nov. 1963, Box 455, Thomas Kuchel Papers, University of California, Berkeley.

[212] American Embassy Santiago to Secretary of State, 19 Nov. 1963, Box 3509, State Department Central File, 1960–1963, State Department Records, Record Group 59, National Archives; "Pertinent Excerpts from Secretary Rusk's Press Conference Nov. 8 on VietNam and Foreign Aid," Box 202, President's National Security File, John Kennedy Presidential Library.

[213] Carl Curtis to Thomas Kuchel, 8 Nov. 1963, Box 455, Thomas Kuchel Papers, University of California, Berkeley.

[214] Larry O'Brien, "Memorandum for the President," 4 Nov. 1963, Box 53, President's Office File, John Kennedy Presidential Library.

[215] *Washington Star*, 17 Nov. 1963.

[216] *Washington Post*, 15 Nov. 1963.

Kennedy's assassination on November 22, signed the bill while protesting "the growing tendency to hamstring Executive flexibility with rigid legislative provisions wholly inappropriate and potentially dangerous in a world of rapid change."[217]

Since these setbacks dealt with the authorization bill, they preceded the work of the Foreign Operations Subcommittee. Bell had initially demurred about becoming AID director because he considered dealing with Passman "almost totally unappealing."[218] (John Kenneth Galbraith had the "sad impression" that most AID staffers "labor under the handicap of a bad prenatal fright from Otto Passman."[219]) In early 1963, the Louisiana congressman confessed his goal for the year: to achieve an "all-time record of percentage-wise cutting of a presidential request for funds."[220] Subcommittee hearings lasted from April 29 until August 14, totaling more than 800 hours; most weeks, Passman spent five days chairing hearings and weekends conducting research.[221] He certainly was better prepared – and even more hostile – in 1963 than ever before. The congressman greeted Rusk, the opening witness, with press reports detailing foreign aid abuses in Vietnam, Congo, and India, and wondered how the administration could claim accomplishments when "you see these leaders of other countries being knocked off overnight."[222] McNamara fared even worse: by the end of the hearings, the Louisianan mocked other administration witnesses for contradicting the defense secretary – probably, Passman speculated, because they were "trying to shore up Secretary McNamara," who must have been "embarrassed by his testimony."[223]

Lyndon Johnson's performance as majority leader had demonstrated his mastery of Congress, and the new president was confident that he could outmaneuver Passman.[224] In a tactic he used with other conservative Southerners, such as Senate Finance Committee chairman Harry Byrd, Johnson invited the Louisanan to the White House and promised to look into foreign aid waste; the congressman, as usual, responded with a harangue against AID,

---

[217] *New York Times*, 17 Dec. 1963.

[218] David Bell oral history, Lyndon Johnson Presidential Library.

[219] John Kenneth Galbraith to Thomas McIntyre, 5 Nov. 1963, Box 99, Series III, Thomas McIntyre Papers, University of New Hampshire.

[220] Otto Passman to A. Willis Robertson, 19 Feb. 1963, Drawer 25, Otto Passman Papers, University of Louisiana, Monroe.

[221] Otto Passman to Gayle Hamilton, 30 July 1963, Drawer 24, Otto Passman Papers, University of Louisiana, Monroe; *CQ Almanac 1963*, p. 291.

[222] U.S. House of Representatives, Foreign Operations Subcommittee, *Hearings, Foreign Operations Appropriations for 1964, part 2*, 88th Congress, 1st session, p. 32 (14 May 1963).

[223] U.S. House of Representatives, Foreign Operations Subcommittee, *Hearings, Foreign Operations Appropriations for 1964, part 3*, 88th Congress, 1st session, pp. 15, 19 (5 June 1963).

[224] President Johnson and John McCormack, 5:50 PM, 10 Dec. 1963, Tape K6312.07, PNO 9, Recordings of Telephone Conversations – White House Series, Recordings and Transcripts of Conversations and Meetings, Lyndon B. Johnson Library.

but the two men parted cordially.[225] A few hours later, however, Passman held a press conference implying that Johnson had pressured him at the meeting. "I'll go to the White House when I'm invited," he announced, "but if the day comes when I have to yield my own convictions, fully supported by the facts, then I'll go home."[226] "Son of a bitch," Johnson fumed, "I wish he had have listened!"[227] With the president privately calling Passman a "caveman" from the "swamps" of Louisiana who had "a real mental problem," little doubt existed which of the two men was prevailing.[228]

In the *New York Times*, Anthony Lewis termed the AID vote Johnson's "first real test in Congress"; State Department sources announced that the president's "prestige is on the line."[229] If so, Johnson suffered his first setback: the House passed the appropriations bill unchanged from the Passman subcommittee's recommendation. To a correspondent who accused him of "practicing a brand of demagoguery that appeals to all those blinded by fear, hatred, and greed," Passman replied that he had never heard comments "that indicated more stupidity."[230] The congressman concluded, in characteristic fashion, "There is a possibility that you are just a child," and, if so, "then may I wish for you a Merry Christmas and I do hope that Santa Claus may be good to you."[231]

Santa was not being particularly generous to Johnson: not only had the House sustained Passman, but it also stunned the Democratic leadership by adopting an amendment sponsored by Paul Findley (R-Illinois), which barred the Export-Import Bank from guaranteeing sales of U.S. commodities to Communist countries. The president now faced a battle on two fronts: achieving adequate funding from the conference committee and ensuring that a restrictive policy rider did not appear in the final version of the bill.

---

[225] President Johnson and Larry O'Brien, 4:01 PM, 12 Dec. 1963, Tape K6312.08, PNO 4, Recordings of Telephone Conversations – White House Series, Recordings and Transcripts of Conversations and Meetings, Lyndon B. Johnson Library.

[226] *Washington Post*, 12 Dec. 1963.

[227] President Johnson and Larry O'Brien, 4:01 PM, 12 Dec. 1963, Tape K6312.08, PNO 4, Recordings of Telephone Conversations – White House Series, Recordings and Transcripts of Conversations and Meetings, Lyndon B. Johnson Library.

[228] President Johnson, John McCormack, and Carl Albert, 6:06 PM, 20 Dec. 1963, Tape K6312.12, PNO 3, Recordings of Telephone Conversations – White House Series, Recordings and Transcripts of Conversations and Meetings, Lyndon B. Johnson Library; President Johnson and John McCormack, Harriet McCormack, Albert Thomas, Carl Albert, Jack Brooks, and Larry O'Brien, 10:36 PM, 20 Dec. 1963, Tape K6312.13, PNO 5, Recordings of Telephone Conversations – White House Series, Recordings and Transcripts of Conversations and Meetings, Lyndon B. Johnson Library.

[229] President Johnson and George Ball, telephone conversation, 9:55 AM, 16 Dec. 1963, Box 3, George Ball Papers, Lyndon B. Johnson Presidential Library.

[230] William Jacobus to Otto Passman, 14 Dec. 1963; Otto Passman to William Jacobus, 17 Dec. 1963; both in Drawer 24, Otto Passman Papers, University of Louisiana, Monroe.

[231] Otto Passman to William Jacobus, 17 Dec. 1963, Drawer 24, Otto Passman Papers, University of Louisiana, Monroe.

The prospects for success seemed dire: Speaker John McCormack dismissed Johnson's preference for a more aggressive approach on the measure as "suicidal."[232]

Forced to salvage something from the battle, Johnson conceded to Passman on the funding level and concentrated on deleting the Findley amendment. He urged Majority Leader Carl Albert (D-Oklahoma) to emphasize the issue's partisan importance by asking colleagues: "Are you a Democrat or a Republican? These guys want to hurt us. They've got an election coming up; they want to play politics with this thing."[233] This appeal worked, and the conferees neutralized the Findley amendment. Meanwhile, Johnson rallied himself. Foreign aid was a complicated issue. If he could not win in the legislative arena, he would prevail before public opinion – and so the President lobbied newspaper columnists to make it appear that he rather than Passman, the congressional Republicans, or the new internationalists had triumphed. A flattering review in *Newsweek* captured the new consensus, arguing that Johnson had triumphed with "the President's discretionary power in foreign affairs on the line."[234]

Despite Johnson's spin, the foreign aid revolt had succeeded beyond anything Passman, Morse, or Gruening could have imagined. In the process, a new era in executive-legislative relations was inaugurated. Reflecting on the foreign aid battle, Hickenlooper perceptively noted "that the major part of the caustic criticism this year seems to be coming from the Democrats, and it takes a variety of directions."[235] Sharp Democratic divisions, with one faction demanding a more assertive legislative role, suggested that Congress had come full circle in a decade. In the early 1950s, virtually all congressional debate about foreign policy occurred among Republicans, with Democrats passive bystanders and one GOP group, the revisionists, advocating a predominant congressional position. By 1963, the situation had reversed itself. It remained unclear, however, whether the foreign aid revolt would produce as full-blown a congressional challenge to executive authority. The U.S. involvement in Vietnam would provide the catalyst.

[232] *New York Times*, 17 Dec. 1963; *Congressional Quarterly Weekly Report*, 27 Dec. 1963, p. 2242.
[233] President Johnson, Carl Albert, and Albert Thomas, 8:01 PM, 20 Dec. 1963, Tape K6312.13, PNO 1, Recordings of Telephone Conversations – White House Series, Recordings and Transcripts of Conversations and Meetings, Lyndon B. Johnson Library.
[234] *Newsweek*, 6 Jan. 1964.
[235] Bourke Hickenlooper to Elaine Schramm, 31 Oct. 1963, Box 36, Foreign Relations Committee series, Bourke Hickenlooper Papers, Herbert Hoover Presidential Library.

4

The Consequences of Vietnam

William Macomber, who served in both the Eisenhower and Johnson White Houses, later commented that U.S. military involvement in Vietnam intensified an already existing congressional rebellion against Cold War foreign policy.[1] The opposition to the Vietnam War originated from the same institutional and ideological environment that produced the foreign aid revolt of 1963. Unclear in the early 1960s, however, was whether these dissenters also would support an aggressive congressional role to implement their agenda, thereby repudiating the lesson from the revisionist era that increasing congressional power would facilitate a reactionary foreign policy.

For several years after Dienbienphu, conditions in Vietnam attracted legislative mention largely as part of the broader concern with the foreign aid program, but more senators noticed Southeast Asia during the early 1960s. In June 1961, for example, Albert Gore informed Robert McNamara that based on past practice of previous military aid to Diem, he wondered what "more of the same thing would accomplish."[2] The next year, Wayne Morse warned Dean Rusk that "the administration's honeymoon in connection with Southeast Asia is about over," and demanded an "answer to the cumulating evidence that the Government of South Vietnam is not a democratic government."[3]

These comments reflected a concern that the Kennedy administration, seeing Vietnam as a testing ground for flexible response, was dangerously expanding its military commitment in Southeast Asia. In fairness to Kennedy, he inherited a fragile situation: U.S. economic and military aid to South Vietnam had mushroomed while Diem's political position grew more precarious, especially after the National Liberation Front (NLF) launched a

---

[1] William Macomber oral history, Lyndon Johnson Presidential Library.
[2] U.S. Senate, Foreign Relations Committee, *Hearings, International Development and Security*, 87th Congress, 1st session, p. 628 (14 June 1961).
[3] *ESSFRC*, vol. 14, 87th Congress, 2nd session, pp. 195, 200, 201.

revolt in 1960. In 1961, Kennedy advisers Walt Rostow and Maxwell Taylor recommended more aid, as well as the dispatch of an 8,000-man "logistic task force" to assist the South Vietnamese army. Kennedy declined the latter suggestion but accepted the first, and even that restriction carried little force: by the end of 1962, 9,000 U.S. "advisers" were stationed in South Vietnam (the Geneva Accords permitted just over 700), and the U.S. Army had assumed responsibility for training the South Vietnamese military. These policies failed to stem South Vietnam's political unrest. On June 11, 1963, after Diem's refusal to implement an agreement ending religious discrimination, a Buddhist monk set himself on fire, receiving extensive coverage in the international media. Kennedy ruled out withdrawal, which he predicted would "mean a collapse not only of South Vietnam, but Southeast Asia," but he also appointed a new ambassador – his old rival, Henry Cabot Lodge. The former senator, who provided political cover in case the U.S. position in South Vietnam collapsed, set about organizing a coup against the Diem regime, which on August 21 declared martial law.[4]

These developments prompted Frank Church, in the midst of the foreign aid fight, to introduce a sense of the Senate resolution declaring that all aid to Diem should cease. Applying the principles of the foreign aid revolt to Southeast Asian matters, the Idaho senator looked to end the "ossification of opinion about our situation in South Vietnam" by inducing public hearings "to determine the real situation in that country in terms of American involvement."[5] Gaylord Nelson (D-Wisconsin) hoped that the resolution would allow for distinguishing "between the popular sentiment of the United States in this matter and the official pronouncements which must be limited by complex political and ideological considerations."[6] Behind the scenes, the White House encouraged Church's resolution, hoping that its offering would make Diem more amenable to U.S. pressure. Administration officials, however, adamantly opposed bringing the resolution to a vote, a position that killed the measure.[7]

Frustrated in this venture, a few dissenters toyed with the ultimate policy option: withdrawal. Gore privately had urged this course immediately following the Buddhist crisis, while press reports of the first U.S. casualties prompted Ernest Gruening to confide that if his son were killed in Vietnam, "I would not feel that he was dying for the defense of my

[4] Fredrick Logevall, *Choosing War: The Lost Chance for Peace and the Escalation of the War in Vietnam* (Berkeley: University of California Press, 1999), pp. 1–40.

[5] Frank Church to Ernest Gruening, 9 Sept. 1963, Box 3, Legislative File – 88th Congress, Senatorial Papers Series, Ernest Gruening Papers, University of Alaska-Fairbanks.

[6] Gaylord Nelson to Paul Stewart, 13 Sept. 1963, Series 74, Box 355, Gaylord Nelson Papers, Wisconsin State Historical Society.

[7] William Conrad Gibbons, *The U.S. Government and the Vietnam War: Executive and Legislative Roles and Relationships, Part II: 1961–1964* (Princeton, NJ: Princeton University Press, 1986), pp. 166–169.

country."[8] After the failure of the Church resolution, George McGovern announced that "the current dilemma in Vietnam is a clear demonstration of the limitations of military power."[9] Congress would not, however, again seriously consider the issue during the Kennedy presidency. While a lively scholarly debate exists over whether Kennedy would have Americanized the conflict in Vietnam, his successor committed himself to victory. Johnson's more belligerent policy prompted an irregular Senate debate – as in the past, the House largely ignored the issue – which came as close to a strictly partisan division over the war as at any point in the two decades that the United States aided the South Vietnamese regime. Almost without exception, during late 1963 and early 1964 Senate Democrats opposed widening the war, while their GOP colleagues, sensing a campaign issue against the popular new president, advocated a more aggressive approach to Vietnam.

Three Democrats – Ernest Gruening, Wayne Morse, and Allen Ellender – unequivocally recommended withdrawing U.S. troops.[10] In a March 1964 Senate address, Gruening described the conflict as a civil war in which the United States backed corrupt military dictatorships; he also denied the applicability of the domino theory to Southeast Asia and criticized the military's overly optimistic reports about the war. Though he admitted that withdrawal would probably yield a Communist victory, he saw no sense "in seeking to prevent what is ultimately inevitable, in impossible terrain, for people who care not."[11] And then, in a line that the *New York Times* noted "surprised colleagues by his choice of strong words," the 77-year-old senator stated publicly what he heretofore had said only privately: that if his son had died in combat in Southeast Asia, he would feel that the boy had been "mistakenly sacrificed in behalf of an inherited folly."[12]

Although among Southern Democrats only Ellender publicly contemplated withdrawal, his general perspective on the war did not differ noticeably from that of many Southern senators. In May, Olin Johnston (D-South Carolina) argued that the United States had mistakenly attempted to solve a political problem through military means.[13] The ultra-conservative James Eastland (D-Mississippi) publicly praised Morse and Gruening for speaking

---

[8] Ernest Gruening to Gordon Skrede, 4 Sept. 1963, Box 3, Legislative File – 88th Congress, Senatorial Papers Series, Ernest Gruening Papers, University of Alaska-Fairbanks.

[9] 109 *CR*, 88th Congress, 1st session, p. 17884 (21 Sept. 1963).

[10] For Morse, see Wayne Morse to Alan Smith, 17 Feb. 1964, Box B-59, Wayne Morse Papers, University of Oregon; Wayne Morse to Chester Bowles, 3 March 1964, Box I-334, Chester Bowles Papers, Yale University; for Ellender, see 110 *CR*, 88th Congress, 2nd session, p. 10832 (13 May 1964).

[11] 110 *CR*, 88th Congress, 2nd session, p. 4835 (10 March 1964).

[12] 110 *CR*, 88th Congress, 2nd session, p. 4835 (10 March 1964); *New York Times*, 21 March 1964.

[13] 110 *CR*, 88th Congress, 2nd session, p. 10834 (13 May 1964).

out; his Mississippi colleague, John Stennis, phoned Gruening to indicate support.[14] The Senate's critical Southern voice on national security matters, Richard Russell, shared with the Alaska Democrat his "misgivings" about Vietnam.[15] More important, Russell communicated this point privately to the president.

These developments prompted the *New York Times* to observe in March 1964 that Vietnam policy was "stirring unusually harsh controversy" among Senate Democrats; the following month, *U.S. News & World Report* recognized that the "debate over U.S. foreign policy, more and more, looks like an intraparty row."[16] Behind the scenes, NSC staffer James Thomson reported that "although Morse and Gruening appear to have made no admitted converts during this period, they have encountered little rebuttal from their colleagues," because, he theorized, "a growing number of Senators are privately sympathetic with the Morse-Gruening position."[17] Continuing a practice that he had begun with Kennedy, Mike Mansfield penned Johnson a series of thoughtful memoranda urging de-escalation, although, in public, the Montana senator defended the president's policy as the "only feasible choice."[18] (This reticence was critical: in National Security Adviser McGeorge Bundy's opinion, the administration needed Mansfield "not to express his own doubts in public."[19]) J. William Fulbright likewise harbored deep misgivings about Vietnam, but, like Mansfield, placed his trust in Johnson: certainly he did not believe that "senators spouting off [would] help the situation."[20] As Frank Church aide Bryce Nelson recalled, other dissenting senators did not "want to be lumped in with people like Morse and Gruening, at least initially," lest they, too, be deemed extremists.[21]

As a more robust Senate debate about the war developed, a handful of Democrats unabashedly defended the administration's approach. Eugene McCarthy, later famous for his antiwar dissent, in 1964 held that as the president possessed responsibility for conducting foreign policy, "impassioned speeches by Senators or Representatives may be good public

---

[14] Ernest Gruening diary, 11 March 1964, Ernest Gruening Papers, University of Alaska-Fairbanks; 110 *CR*, 88th Congress, 2nd session, p. 10828 (13 May 1964).

[15] Richard Russell to Ernest Gruening, 17 March 1964, Vietnam 1964 box, Brown Boxes series, Ernest Gruening Papers, University of Alaska-Fairbanks.

[16] *New York Times*, 21 March 1964; *U.S. News & World Report*, 6 April 1964.

[17] Gibbons, *U.S. Government and the Vietnam War, II*, p. 249.

[18] Mike Mansfield to Lyndon Johnson, 1 February 1964, Box 1, Memos to the President – McGeorge Bundy, National Security File, Lyndon Johnson Presidential Library; 110 *CR*, 88th Congress, 2nd session, p. 3277 (20 Feb. 1964).

[19] McGeorge Bundy, "Memorandum for the President," 10 Feb. 1964, Box 1, Memos to the President – McGeorge Bundy, National Security File, Lyndon Johnson Presidential Library.

[20] *New York Times*, 21 March 1964.

[21] Gibbons, *U.S. Government and the Vietnam War, II*, p. 277.

relations, but they are not good foreign policy."[22] Frank Lausche, Paul Douglas, Russell Long, Thomas Dodd (D-Connecticut), and Gale McGee (D-Wyoming), meanwhile, all considered Vietnam an important Cold War testing ground, and they questioned only Johnson's not sending more troops to the region.

As the Democrats divided, congressional Republicans spoke with one voice. In an early version of a claim that would intensify as the 1960s progressed, Bourke Hickenlooper charged that "our fighting man is fighting in effect with one arm tied behind his back, under artificial restrictions."[23] Convinced from a 1959 trip to South Vietnam that the Saigon government enjoyed wide support in the countryside, the Iowa Republican claimed that reports to the contrary relied "on gossip in the bars."[24] Hickenlooper concluded that "the so-called Buddhist persecution was a politically created fiction"; he attributed the self-immolations to "a type of hypnotic persuasion used on certain gullible Buddhist zealots."[25] Other Senate Republicans were not quite as belligerent – or bizarre – as Hickenlooper, but even most moderates (an exception was Vermont's George Aiken) criticized the administration's policy from the right.[26]

Johnson attempted to balance competing desires: to avoid Harry Truman's mistake in Korea and put Congress on record behind his Vietnam policy and to keep Vietnam out of the headlines until after the November election. For William Bundy, McGeorge's brother and the new assistant secretary of state for East Asian affairs, the question of whether to seek a resolution modeled on Eisenhower's Formosa and Middle East resolutions constituted the "immediate watershed" confronting the administration in the summer of 1964.[27] When Director of Central Intelligence (DCI) John McCone predicted that such a resolution would "easily" pass, McGeorge Bundy responded bluntly: "Convert Morse first."[28] As early as May 20, the president stated his preference for a resolution, only to back off, lest he trigger a public debate.[29] At the time, only 37 percent in a Gallup poll indicated that they

[22] Eugene McCarthy to T.E. Carey, 17 March 1964, Box 120, Eugene McCarthy Papers, Minnesota State Historical Society.

[23] Bourke Hickenlooper to Frances Jones, 19 May 1964, Box 158, Foreign Relations Committee series, Bourke Hickenlooper Papers, Herbert Hoover Presidential Library.

[24] Bourke Hickenlooper to Thomas Dodd, 15 Jan. 1964, Box 158, Foreign Relations Committee series, Bourke Hickenlooper Papers, Herbert Hoover Presidential Library.

[25] Bourke Hickenlooper to Thomas Dodd, 15 Jan. 1964, Box 158, Foreign Relations Committee series, Bourke Hickenlooper Papers, Herbert Hoover Presidential Library.

[26] 110 *CR*, 88th Congress, 2nd session, pp. 3279 (20 Feb. 1964), 11603 (21 May 1964).

[27] William Bundy, "Memorandum for Discussion: Alternative public positions for U.S. on Southeast Asia for the period July 1–November 15," 10 June 1964, Box 5, Country File – Vietnam, National Security File, Lyndon Johnson Presidential Library.

[28] McGeorge Bundy, "Memorandum for the President," 16 May 1964, Box 2, Memos to the President – McGeorge Bundy, National Security File, Lyndon Johnson Presidential Library.

[29] Logevall, *Choosing War*, p. 147.

were following events in Southeast Asia closely; the White House had no desire to see that figure increase.[30]

Such handling of foreign policy issues later prompted Thomas Kuchel to question "whether the President was trying to apply internationally the techniques of power and influence that worked so successfully domestically," failing to understand that international relations was "a different game with different players and different rules."[31] As Kuchel anticipated, a search for consensus, a hallmark of Johnson's performance as Senate majority leader, would hamper his foreign policy performance as president. In 1964, however, that lesson had not yet emerged; indeed, consideration of the year's legislation on foreign aid – the foreign policy issue for which mastery of Congress played the most important role – suggested that Johnson's approach would pay handsome dividends.

For the 1964 session, the president embraced a suggestion from David Bell and submitted what he termed a "bare-bones request" of $3.5 billion.[32] Hickenlooper correctly guessed that Johnson "knew that he could not get more than that," and adopted this strategy so he could portray the result as a political victory.[33]

This approach generated little opposition in the Senate, but it did not pacify Otto Passman in the House. In April, Silvio Conte confessed that "it's gone from bad to worse with Passman," who behaved like "a jackass" to GOP members.[34] The Louisiana Democrat began the year by falling out with a former subcommittee ally, J. Vaughan Gary, after the Virginia Democrat refused to vote with Passman on several 1963 amendments. Gary, in turn, took to describing Passman, "the most biased man I know," as "emotionally unbalanced."[35]

Passman did not need Gary's vote – until, in August 1964, Appropriations Committee chairman Clarence Cannon died. The committee's next-ranking Democrat, George Mahon of Texas, succeeded to the chairmanship, assumed Cannon's ex oficio position on the Foreign Operations Subcommittee (which reduced Passman's subcommittee majority to one), and worked with Johnson to clip Passman's power. Shortly before the session's key subcommittee vote, Johnson persuaded William Natcher (D-Kentucky) to side with the administration. Passman, described by columnists Rowland Evans and Robert Novak as the "shrill-voiced shopkeeper," then stormed into the

[30] George Gallup, *The Gallup Poll, 1935–1971*, vol. 3, poll of May 27, 1964, p. 1881.

[31] Kuchel quoted in Douglas Cater to President Johnson, 24 Feb. 1965, Box 146, White House Confidential File, Lyndon Johnson Presidential Library.

[32] David Bell, "Foreign Aid Program for FY 1965," 15 Dec. 1963, Box 45, White House Confidential File, Lyndon Johnson Presidential Library.

[33] Bourke Hickenlooper to R.N. Hoerner, 10 July 1964, Box 36, Foreign Relations Committee series, Bourke Hickenlooper Papers, Herbert Hoover Presidential Library.

[34] Silvio Conte oral history, May 1964, Center for Legislative Archives, Washington, D.C.

[35] J. Vaughan Gary oral history, April 1964, Center for Legislative Archives, Washington, D.C.

corridor, screaming, "All right, I'm through ... let them run the committee. This is a parody on the democratic process. Why don't they do like the people down in Haiti and elect that fellow down there [Johnson] for life?"[36] The *Washington Post* spoke for the Establishment in rejoicing that, with the vote, "Passmanism has undergone an almost full eclipse on Capitol Hill."[37] After the 1964 election, Mahon, saying that he wanted to "liberalize this Committee to make it more objective," reduced the subcommittee's membership from 11 to 9 and appointed three new liberal Democrats to the panel, permanently robbing Passman of a majority.[38]

While Johnson thus avoided a legislative attack on the foreign aid program, he could do little to suppress congressional discussion of foreign policy. On March 25, reflecting his belief that a senator should educate the public, Fulbright delivered a major address analyzing the "divergence between the realities of foreign policy and our ideas about it," contending that policymakers' attitudes about international affairs were frozen in time, causing the United States to apply solutions of the early Cold War to the more complicated problems of the early 1960s.[39] Though the Arkansas senator avoided the obvious example to illustrate his thesis – the conflict in Vietnam – his address generated passionate commentary. Syndicated columnist Drew Pearson termed it "one of the most important foreign policy statements made by any Senator in this decade"; the London *Times* argued that the speech brought the "Senate back to the centre of power."[40] Conservative Democrats, on the other hand, vehemently objected: Smathers ridiculed Fulbright as "monumentally naïve and unrealistic," while Lausche described his Arkansas colleague as "completely devoid of a realistic evaluation of the problems that confront us."[41]

The limitations of Fulbright's dissent from Cold War norms became clear in early August, when events in the Tonkin Gulf presented Johnson with his opportunity to obtain formal legislative approval for his Vietnam policy. In summer 1964, with CIA assistance, South Vietnamese armed forces initiated a covert operation called OPLAN 34-A, which involved small-scale naval raids on the North Vietnamese coast. On August 2, shortly after one such raid, North Vietnamese forces fired on the U.S.S. *Maddox*, which was inside North Vietnam's 12-mile territorial waters. As Robert McNamara admitted at the time, the combination of the OPLAN 34-A incidents and the location

---

[36] *Washington Post*, 29 June 1964.
[37] *Washington Post*, 6 July 1964.
[38] George Mahon oral history, May 1965, Center for Legislative Archives, Washington, D.C.; Richard Bolling, *House Out of Order* (New York: Dutton, 1965), p. 93.
[39] 110 CR, 88th Congress, 2nd session, p. 6227 (25 March 1964).
[40] *The Times* (London), 2 April 1964.
[41] Frank Lausche to J.C. Kean, Box 264, Frank Lausche Papers, Ohio Historical Society; *U.S. News & World Report*, 6 April 1964.

of the *Maddox* "undoubtedly led them to connect the two events."[42] After confusing reports suggested an attack two nights later, Johnson invited 16 congressional leaders for a White House briefing; of the group, only Mansfield opposed retaliatory raids against North Vietnam. The next day, the administration proposed a measure, which came to be known as the Tonkin Gulf Resolution, authorizing the president to "take all necessary measures to repel any armed attack against the forces of the United States and to prevent further aggression."[43]

As had been the case with both the Formosa and Middle East resolutions, the House leadership manipulated the rules to prevent sustained debate, and the measure unanimously passed. The situation in the Senate was more complicated. There is no doubt that in the long term, the Vietnam War accelerated the dissent that had developed during Kennedy's presidency. But the fact that U.S. troops were already on the ground in Vietnam robbed critics of the opportunity to present a straightforward argument against sending forces to Southeast Asia. Instead, they had to carry through their ideology to its logical conclusion, as Gruening did, and recommend withdrawal – suffering the associated political risks – or finesse the issue by championing de-escalation, negotiation, and internationalization of the conflict, despite the ideological compromises such a course required.

Beyond the problem of not appearing to abandon troops already in the field, events surrounding the Tonkin Gulf Resolution presented three additional reasons for wavering senators to vote aye. First, the president wanted approval for retaliation that had already occurred. Second, precedent weighed in the administration's favor, since the warnings of policy or constitutional calamities offered by opponents of the Middle East and Formosa Resolutions had proven wildly exaggerated.[44] Third, the resolution presented an opportunity for Johnson to neutralize hard-line criticism from Barry Goldwater, who, less than a month before, had captured the GOP presidential nomination.[45] Commentator Richard Rovere, for one, understood "that the rise of Goldwater had been one of the factors – and perhaps the most important one – determining the timing and magnitude" of the Tonkin Gulf response.[46]

Given these issues, it is surprising not that the Tonkin Gulf Resolution overwhelmingly passed, but that debate over it revealed so much disquiet in the Senate. Behind the scenes, Fulbright, who co-managed the resolution

---

[42] President Johnson and Robert McNamara, 10:20 AM, 3 Aug. 1964, Tape WH6408.03, Citation #4633, Recordings of Telephone Conversations – White House Series, Recordings and Transcripts of Conversations and Meetings, Lyndon B. Johnson Library.

[43] *New York Times*, 6 August 1964.

[44] Carl Marcy oral history, U.S. Senate Historical Office.

[45] George McGovern, personal interview with author, 8 Jan. 1994.

[46] Richard Rovere, "Letter from Washington," *The New Yorker*, 22 Aug. 1964.

with Russell, assured skeptics that Johnson would never use the resolution's full authority.[47] When Nelson and Ellender told Fulbright that they still planned to vote no, the Arkansas senator pacified the duo with floor colloquies.[48] The Wisconsin senator reassured his constituents that this anti-interventionist legislative history meant that the resolution only "expresses support for our continuing mission of providing aid and advice to the South Vietnamese."[49] The record was not nearly so clear. In another exchange with Fulbright, John Sherman Cooper asked directly whether the resolution conferred upon the president "advance authority" to commit additional U.S. forces to Vietnam. Fulbright conceded that it could be interpreted that way, since in the modern world, "it is necessary to anticipate what may occur," as the resolution did.[50]

The two members of Congress who voted against the Tonkin Gulf Resolution rejected such a constitutional interpretation. In seeking to expand U.S. involvement in the war, Gruening contended that the administration had overlooked several key facts: the United States was continuing a colonial war waged by the French; Washington was bypassing the UN; peace could not be established through military means; the North Vietnamese attack on the *Maddox* represented an "inevitable development" of previous U.S. escalation; and the "allegation that we are supporting freedom in South Vietnam has a hollow sound."[51] Morse offered an even more ferocious dissent against those he claimed offered an "alibi for avoiding congressional responsibility."[52] To colleagues who denounced his recommendations as overly idealistic, the Oregon senator responded bluntly: "Only ideals are practical."[53] These remarks of senators dismissed by Richard Rovere as "chronic dissenters" changed no votes, and the resolution passed 88 to 2.[54] Still, Johnson wanted unanimity: he privately denounced Gruening as "no good," and termed Morse "just undependable and erratic as he can be."[55]

The Tonkin Gulf Resolution succeeded beyond Johnson's expectations. As many historians have observed, the measure effectively removed Vietnam as a campaign issue – despite contrary predictions at the time.[56] Public support

[47] Woods, *Fulbright*, pp. 348–355.
[48] Allen Ellender oral history, Lyndon Johnson Presidential Library.
[49] Gaylord Nelson newsletter, Sept. 1964, Box 96, 1980 series, Wisconsin State Historical Society.
[50] 110 CR, 88th Congress, 2nd session, p. 18410 (6 Aug. 1964).
[51] 110 CR, 88th Congress, 2nd session, p. 18413 (6 Aug. 1964).
[52] 110 CR, 88th Congress, 2nd session, p. 18136 (5 Aug. 1964).
[53] 110 CR, 88th Congress, 2nd session, p. 18134 (5 Aug. 1964).
[54] Wayne Morse to Ernest Gruening, 18 Sept. 1964, Box B-49, Wayne Morse Papers, University of Oregon; Richard Rovere, "Letter from Washington," *The New Yorker*, 22 Aug. 1964.
[55] President Johnson and John McCormack, 3:01 PM, 7 Aug. 1964, Tape WH6408.11, Citation #4807, Recordings of Telephone Conversations – White House Series, Recordings and Transcripts of Conversations and Meetings, Lyndon B. Johnson Library.
[56] *Washington Star*, 7 Aug. 1964, 10 Aug. 1964, 17 Aug. 1964.

for Johnson's handling of events in Southeast Asia climbed from 42 percent to 72 percent, followed by a sharp decline in interest in Vietnam that persisted for several months.[57] In the short term, Tonkin Gulf thus came across as a prudent use of U.S. deterrent power. Throughout the campaign, the president avoided mentioning Vietnam whenever possible, and he swept to victory in a triumph that produced 2-to-1 Democratic majorities in both houses of Congress.

When conditions in Vietnam continued to deteriorate, however, early 1965 featured sustained Senate discussion of the war, beginning on February 17, when first Frank Church and then George McGovern addressed the upper chamber.[58] Speaking as a "confirmed internationalist," Church argued that "our intensely ideological view of the Cold War" had blinded leaders to the fact that "the policy of intervening too much in the volatile ex-colonial regions of Africa and Asia is backfiring."[59] McGovern followed up by asserting the Senate's "constitutional responsibility for the conduct of foreign policy in a dialog with the President"; he pressed Johnson to renew a commitment to negotiation.[60]

Divisions among the Senate dissenters remained, however. Gruening scoffed that Church and McGovern had acted "so moderately that it means little."[61] Morse suggested entitling Fulbright remarks on Vietnam, "Yes-no-maybe," though, the Oregon senator scoffed, "I have never heard him give a foreign policy speech that couldn't bear that title."[62] The duo persisted in an aggressive dissent, becoming more extreme in their critique and accomplishing little.[63] As McGovern recalled, colleagues regarded Morse as a "firebrand" who overstated his case, while they "were uncomfortable with Ernest Gruening's strategy on the war," which they considered overly harsh.[64]

Also, the dissenters no longer monopolized Senate discussion of the issue – Tom Dodd, Frank Lausche, Everett Dirksen, and Paul Douglas all vigorously defended Johnson's policy. The administration's most persuasive support, however, came from Gale McGee, a history professor before winning election to the Senate in 1958. Befitting his training, the Wyoming Democrat

---

[57] Melvin Small, *Johnson, Nixon, and the Doves* (New Brunswick, NJ: Rutgers University Press, 1988), pp. 47–50; Kathleen Hall Jamieson, *Dirty Politics: Deception, Distraction, and Democracy* (New York: Oxford University Press, 1992), p. 247.

[58] *St. Louis Post-Dispatch*, 30 Dec. 1964.

[59] 111 *CR*, 89th Congress, 1st session, pp. 2869–2872 (17 Feb. 1965).

[60] 111 *CR*, 89th Congress, 1st session, pp. 2878–2879 (17 Feb. 1965).

[61] Ernest Gruening diary, entry for 18 Feb. 1965, Ernest Gruening Papers, University of Alaska-Fairbanks.

[62] Wayne Morse to Herman Berger, 16 Dec. 1964, Box B-48, Wayne Morse Papers, University of Oregon.

[63] 111 *CR*, 89th Congress, 1st session, p. 3803 (1 March 1965).

[64] George McGovern, personal interview with author, 8 Jan. 1994.

cited the Pax Britannica in the nineteenth century, arguing that "the only force which has been able to keep international relationships on a peaceful plane has been that of balance of power."[65] Munich, meanwhile, provided a lesson to avoid appeasing aggressors; if South Vietnam fell to Communism, Thailand and Malaya would surely follow. (The senator later admitted that he was "disposed to see Soviet machinations behind every banana leaf."[66]) McGee possessed another asset for the administration: among the upper chamber's finest extemporaneous speakers, he could, unlike the intellectually plodding Dodd or Lausche, hold his own debating the president's critics.[67]

As had been the case since the late 1950s, congressional Democrats dominated the foreign policy discussion. GOP legislators tried – as McGeorge Bundy recognized – "to have it both ways," criticizing Johnson for his handling of the conflict but rarely offering any alternative policies beyond the unrealistic option of an all-out war.[68] Even so, for the first six months of 1965, Johnson consistently outmaneuvered real and potential congressional critics of his Vietnam policy, displaying the political skills that had made him master of the Senate in the 1950s.

Like McGee, Johnson applied his own lessons of the past to Vietnam, and using historical analogies served the president as poorly as it did the Wyoming senator. Johnson believed that if a congressional challenge emerged to his foreign policy, it would come from the right. His first term in the Senate, after all, included GOP attacks on Truman's China policy, the Great Debate, Pat McCarran's tenure as Judiciary Committee chairman, McCarthyism, and the Bricker amendment controversy. On the other hand, the era's liberals delivered little more than articulate speeches. Johnson retained a contemptuous attitude toward the political skills of the liberal senators who would later become his most effective critics, mockingly suggesting that "a real plan of attack" for liberals would be to "get ten of them out here at a Georgetown house some night with Arthur Schlesinger," since "that's what they do best: talk."[69]

It nonetheless was no secret, columnists Evans and Novak reported, that Democratic attacks on the President's Vietnam policies were "both galling and embarrassing him," and while he regarded Morse and Gruening "as too heathen for missionary work" on the issue, he wooed the others.[70] Flattery

---

[65] 111 *CR*, 89th Congress, 1st session, p. 8977 (29 April 1965).

[66] *Washington Post*, 14 April 1973.

[67] 111 *CR*, 89th Congress, 1st session, p. 12987 (9 June 1965).

[68] McGeorge Bundy, "Memorandum for the President," 9 Dec. 1965, Box 5, McGeorge Bundy – Memos to the President, National Security File, Lyndon Johnson Presidential Library.

[69] President Johnson and Bill Moyers, 10:00 P.M., 21 Aug. 1964, Tape WH6408.32, Citation #5115, Recordings of Telephone Conversations – White House Series, Recordings and Transcripts of Conversations and Meetings, Lyndon B. Johnson Library.

[70] *Washington Post*, 4 May 1965.

represented one option – even Morse was invited to a one-on-one White House conference, at which the president requested a detailed memorandum explaining his and Gruening's position.[71] Johnson showered Fulbright with public praise; for his part, the Arkansas senator publicly supported the president's decision to initiate the air war against North Vietnam in early 1965.[72] When flattery failed, the president resorted to intimidation. At a March 1965 meeting with McGovern (holder of a Ph.D. degree in history from Northwestern), the president snapped, "Goddamn it, George. You and Fulbright and all you history teachers down there – I haven't got time to fuck around with history."[73] An even more tense exchange occurred between Johnson and Church, when the president recalled the story of William Borah, the Idaho senator who had predicted that Germany would not invade Poland in 1939 because he thought he knew more about foreign policy than did the chief executive. The next day, reports circulated that, after Church responded by referencing the arguments of columnist Walter Lippmann, the president had gotten off a good line: "Frank, the next time you need a dam out in Idaho, go see Walter Lippmann about it."[74] (Johnson had said no such thing, but the president frequently reconstructed conversations as he wished they had occurred.) Church refused to back down. A few weeks later, he delivered a moving tribute on the Senate floor to Borah, praising his predecessor's "reluctance to use force as a method of international diplomacy and his refusal to accept any form of imperialism."[75] And the next time he encountered the president, Church joked that Idahoans were planning to build the "Walter Lippmann Dam."[76]

Despite Church's counterpunches, Johnson retained the initiative: in two high-profile actions in April and May 1965, he first pacified his critics, and then again pressured them into endorsing his policy. The first move came at the Johns Hopkins University on April 7, when the president offered his most in-depth remarks to date about U.S. policy in Vietnam. "We fight," Johnson declared, "because we must fight if we are to live in a world where every country can shape its own destiny, and only in such a world will our own freedom be finally secure."[77] That said, he renewed his commitment to a negotiated settlement and promised a postwar program of economic assistance to Southeast Asia.

---

[71] "Memorandum of Senator Morse's Conversation with the President – Thursday, June 17, 11:30," 1965 folder, Carl Marcy chronological series, Foreign Relations Committee Papers, Record Group 46, National Archives.

[72] Woods, *Fulbright*, p. 366.

[73] Woods, *Fulbright*, p. 365.

[74] Ashby and Gramer, *Fighting the Odds*, p. 200.

[75] 111 *CR*, 89th Congress, 1st session, p. 15072 (29 June 1965).

[76] Ashby and Gramer, *Fighting the Odds*, p. 200.

[77] *Washington Post*, 8 April 1965.

The president himself believed that the Johns Hopkins address "effectively throttled . . . the questioning type of dissent – not Morse and Gruening."[78] He was right. Gruening, "deeply disturbed," contended that Johnson's emphasis on an independent South Vietnam doomed negotiations with the North – which was equally insistent on a reunified Vietnam.[79] But most in the Senate focused on the comments about negotiations. McGovern felt that the President had "yielded to the central point that Church and I had been making that he ought to forget about a military decision and offer to negotiate an end to the war."[80] Church even "withheld a rather hard-hitting speech" he was planning, expecting that the address signaled a new direction in Johnson's Vietnam policy.[81]

The administration's next major initiative dashed such a hope. Through the spring of 1965, Johnson had considered introducing another Tonkin Gulf-like resolution, but rejected the move after Attorney General Nicholas Katzenbach cautioned that "any benefit that would be obtained from the passage of a further resolution, even by a near-unanimous margin, would almost certainly be counteracted by the debate," since "most of the opposition is likely to come from members of our own party."[82] With this option foreclosed, the president chose another route – one almost impossible for members of Congress to oppose. On May 4, he requested a $700 million supplemental appropriation for military operations in Vietnam, to communicate "that the Congress and the President stand united before the world in joint determination that the independence of South Vietnam shall be preserved and the Communist attack will not succeed."[83] The legislation was not necessary, since the Pentagon had legal authority to shift unused funds from other programs to cover the war's costs.[84] The House nonetheless passed the measure 408 to 7, with both parties' leadership arguing that the vote endorsed Johnson's Vietnam policy; the White House correctly foresaw "no trouble on the House side from doves."[85]

Church, who supported the bill, admitted privately that he voted as he did because he believed that "we must give our military forces every possible

---

[78] George McGovern, "Notes from Luncheon with Dick Dudman," 28 Dec. 1965, Box 70A2445/11, George McGovern Papers, Princeton University.

[79] 111 CR, 89th Congress, 1st session, p. 7665 (9 April 1965).

[80] George McGovern oral history, Lyndon Johnson Presidential Library.

[81] Frank Church to Eugene Chase, 21 April 1965, Series 2.2, Box 28, Frank Church Papers, Boise State University.

[82] Nicholas Katzenbach, "Memorandum for the President," 11 June 1965, Box 215, National Defense series, White House Central File, Lyndon Johnson Presidential Library.

[83] *New York Times*, 5 May 1965.

[84] Mike Manatos memorandum, 5 May 1965, Box 321, Names series, Lyndon Johnson Presidential Library; *New York Times*, 14 June 1965.

[85] Henry Wilson, "Memorandum for the President," 17 Feb. 1966, Box 219, ND series, White House Central File, Lyndon Johnson Presidential Library.

support."[86] Indeed, by submitting a bill in which a negative vote could be cast as refusing to support troops in the field, Johnson ensured overwhelming backing. Still, the diehard opposition gained one more adherent, as Gaylord Nelson joined Gruening and Morse in voting no. In the debate's most passionate remarks, the Wisconsin senator asserted that the administration needed "my vote less than I need my conscience."[87] Beyond the three negative votes, the remainder of the Senate divided more or less evenly in interpreting the vote's purpose. John Stennis, Leverett Saltonstall, Gordon Allott (R-Colorado), and Jack Miller (R-Iowa) all urged an increased U.S. military presence, while Albert Gore, Jacob Javits, John sherman Cooper, Joseph Clark, George McGovern, Frank Church, and George Aiken (R-Vermont) all asserted that Johnson needed to return to Congress for additional authority before escalating U.S. involvement. Privately, Gruening concluded that even though his side overwhelmingly lost, at least the mixed message from the debate "showed resentment to Johnson's assumptions."[88]

Two decisions set the stage for the more confrontational relationship between Johnson and Congress that developed after 1965. The first came on April 30, when Johnson sent troops to suppress a revolt against the Dominican junta that had succeeded Juan Bosch. Official justifications for the intervention shifted from protecting the lives of U.S. citizens to a contention that "known Communists" (the number varied anywhere from 3 to 54) had assumed control of the rebel movement.[89] Many of Johnson's claims about conditions in the Dominican Republic strained credulity (at one point the president described widespread decapitations in Santo Domingo), but most in Congress, including even many of his critics, gave him the benefit of the doubt.[90] Fulbright, however, scheduled nine days of informational hearings and then delivered a searing speech described by *The New Republic* as "the best on any subject made on the floor of the Senate during this session."[91] The Foreign Relations Committee chair accused the administration of "a lack of candor," and charged the president with "exaggerated estimates of Communist influence in the rebel movement."[92] Unfortunately,

---

[86] Frank Church to Mrs. F. W. Wifter, 11 May 1965, Series 2.2, Box 28, Frank Church Papers, Boise State University.

[87] *Washington Star*, 7 May 1965.

[88] Ernest Gruening diary, entry for 5 May 1965, Ernest Gruening Papers, University of Alaska-Fairbanks.

[89] H. W. Brands, *The Wages of Globalism: Lyndon Johnson and the Limits of American Power* (New York: Oxford University Press, 1995), pp. 15–22.

[90] 111 *CR*, 89th Congress, 2nd session, p. 10313 (12 May 1965).

[91] Carl Marcy oral history, U.S. Senate Historical Office; Andrew Kopkind, "The Speechmaker," *The New Republic*, 2 Oct. 1965.

[92] 111 *CR*, 89th Congress, 1st session, p. 23855 (15 Sept. 1965).

it appeared as if the United States had morphed into a conservative power, with leaders who closed their "minds to the causes and to the essential legitimacy of revolution in a country in which democratic procedures had failed."[93]

Syndicated columnist Joseph Kraft compared the administration's reaction to the speech to "the stoning reserved by the high priests of primitive communities for those who questioned the efficacy of blood sacrifice."[94] Dodd accused Fulbright of having "shut out from his mind all facts which failed to harmonize with the preconceived thesis that the rebels were right and the administration was wrong," because the Arkansas senator was suffering from "an indiscriminating infatuation with revolutions of all kind – national, democratic, or Communist."[95] (Fulbright countered by dismissing his Connecticut colleague as a "sorry, cheap demagogue."[96]) After an initial response from Press Secretary Bill Moyers, the White House refrained from public comment, doubting, Bundy conceded, "if we really help ourselves by showing how mad his speech made us."[97] Johnson exacted his retribution by banning Fulbright from all White House functions for over a year.[98] Meanwhile, the House passed a resolution effectively endorsing unilateral U.S. intervention anywhere in the Western Hemisphere. Stephen Young tartly observed that if the lower chamber could not legislate more constructively, then it should adjourn.[99]

The Dominican intervention shattered the relationship between Fulbright and Johnson. Meanwhile, the president's decision to Americanize the war ended the hope of other dissenters that Johnson would pursue a foreign policy reflecting their principles. On June 7, U.S. military commander William Westmoreland cabled from South Vietnam to ask for 19 more battalions, over and above the 13 already present in Southeast Asia. On July 28, the president approved Westmoreland's request, since "we are all determined to do all that is necessary" to prevail.[100] Trapped, as Walter Lippmann wrote,

---

[93] III *CR*, 89th Congress, 1st session, p. 23856 (15 Sept. 1965).

[94] *Washington Post*, 4 Oct. 1965.

[95] III *CR*, 85th Congress, 1st session, pp. 24170, 24172 (16 Sept. 1965); for administration assistance with Dodd's remarks, see McGeorge Bundy, "Memorandum for the President," 14 Sept. 1965, Box 4, Memos to the President – Bundy, National Security File, Lyndon Johnson Presidential Library.

[96] J. William Fulbright to W. S. Atkins, 13 June 1967, Box 51, Series 48:18, J. William Fulbright Papers, University of Arkansas.

[97] McGeorge Bundy to President Johnson, 18 Sept. 1965, Box 52, Country File series – Dominican Republic, National Security File, Lyndon Johnson Presidential Library; *New York Times*, 16 Sept. 1965.

[98] Woods, *Fulbright*, p. 385.

[99] III *CR*, 85th Congress, 1st session, p. 25142 (24 Sept. 1965).

[100] *New York Times*, 29 July 1965.

"between the devil of unlimited war and the deep blue sea of defeat," Johnson risked the former.[101]

Even if senators could not directly influence the president's actions in Vietnam, Church told Morse, it was "absolutely vital for the Senate to continue to discuss the alternatives to a widening war in Southeast Asia."[102] Fulbright came to agree. In January 1965, he had written that "it is not exactly within my power to influence the course of events in South Vietnam, other than to express a personal opinion, as the matter is run by the Executive Branch."[103] One year later, he decided that he would try to shape U.S. public opinion regarding the war. The Fulbright Hearings resulted.

The Foreign Relations Committee's prestige reached a low point as 1966 began. When George Smathers switched off the committee, taking a seat on the Judiciary Committee, Marquis Childs explained the move by noting that the Florida senator "has a sensitive nose for where power lies" in the Senate.[104] According to Smathers, "Foreign Relations is the biggest fraud in the Senate . . . everything I heard in closed-door briefings was no different than what I read in the papers."[105] Church conceded that internal divisions had immobilized the committee, "leaving the role of dissent as well as the advocacy of alternative courses to individual senators."[106] Gore doubted the efficacy even of this course; just before Christmas 1965, he admitted that nothing any individual senator said or did "seems to halt the constant widening of the war."[107]

Then, suddenly, the committee's standing revived. From January 28 through February 18, the Foreign Relations Committee held six days of what *Newsweek* termed "the most searching public review of U.S. wartime policy" since the MacArthur hearings in 1951. "You know," Everett Dirksen remarked at the time, "Bill Fulbright has a lot of guts to do a thing like this."[108]

Fulbright confessed that he waited too long to act on Vietnam, "but, to be frank about it, I did not realize the seriousness of the situation until recently."[109] George Kennan and General James Gavin, Kennedy's

---

[101] Brian VanDeMark, *Into the Quagmire: Lyndon Johnson and the Escalation of the Vietnam War* (New York: Oxford University Press, 1991), p. 213.

[102] Frank Church to Wayne Morse, 23 June 1965, Box B-53, Wayne Morse Papers, University of Oregon.

[103] J. William Fulbright to J. K. Garner, 21 Jan. 1965, Box 35, Series 48:11, J. William Fulbright Papers, University of Arkansas.

[104] *Washington Post*, 13 Sept. 1965.

[105] *Newsweek*, 10 May 1965.

[106] Frank Church to Robert Farris, 12 Jan. 1966, Series 2.2, Box 9, Frank Church Papers, Boise State University.

[107] Albert Gore to Frank Church, 17 Dec. 1965, Series 2.2, Box 20, Frank Church Papers, Boise State University.

[108] *Newsweek*, 21 Feb. 1966.

[109] J. William Fulbright to Allen Gates, 21 Feb. 1966, Series 48:18, Box 48, J. William Fulbright Papers, University of Arkansas.

ambassador to France, opened the nationally televised hearings, endorsing an enclave strategy, in which the United States would confine its forces to coastal enclaves until a peace settlement could be negotiated. Both men questioned the value of sustained bombing of North Vietnam; Kennan also concluded that "our country should not be asked to shoulder the main burden of determining the political realities of any other country," since "this is not only not our business, but I don't think we can do it successfully."[110]

The administration aggressively deflected attention from the hearings. On February 8, the day of Gavin's testimony, Johnson hastily scheduled a summit conference with South Vietnamese leader Nguyen Cao Ky. Behind the scenes, the president prevailed upon William Paley, president of CBS, to broadcast a rerun of "I Love Lucy" instead of Kennan's appearance. (Fred Friendly, president of CBS News, resigned in protest; Gruening and Gore denounced Paley's action on the Senate floor.[111]) Johnson also ordered J. Edgar Hoover to examine the hearings "with a view toward determining whether Senator Fulbright and the other Senators were receiving information from Communists."[112]

After Kennan's testimony, Bourke Hickenlooper and Stuart Symington urged Johnson to have Rusk and Maxwell Taylor, former JCS chairman and ambassador to South Vietnam, represent the administration in what *Newsweek* termed "two electric days" of hearings, filled with "superb drama."[113] The most charged moment of Taylor's six-hour appearance came when Morse predicted that the American people would "repudiate" Johnson's Vietnam policy and Taylor coolly replied, "That will be good news to Hanoi."[114] The Oregon senator, momentarily taken aback, responded, "That's the kind of smear artist that you militarists give to those of us who have honest differences of opinion with you."[115] Otherwise, Taylor performed as expected, casting doubt on the enclave theory's utility, claiming that current tactics would succeed, and evading repeated questions about how many troops victory would require. In the Oval Office, the president followed the hearing on two television sets, so he could hear press commentary for each network that broadcast the testimony.[116]

The highlight of the Fulbright Hearings, however, came on February 18, in what McGovern recalled as Rusk and Fulbright, "two Rhodes

---

[110] U.S. Senate, Foreign Relations Committee, *Hearings, Supplemental Foreign Assistance Fiscal Year 1966 – Vietnam*, 89th Congress, 2nd session, pp. 45–256 (8 Feb. 1966, 10 Feb. 1966).

[111] 112 *CR*, 89th Congress, 2nd session, pp. 3038–3041 (16 Feb. 1966).

[112] Woods, *Fulbright*, p. 407.

[113] Newsweek, 28 Feb. 1966; Woods, *Fulbright*, p. 406.

[114] *Washington Star*, 17 Feb. 1966.

[115] *Congressional Quarterly Weekly Report*, 25 Feb. 1966.

[116] *Washington Star*, 17 Feb. 1966.

scholars, glowering at each other."[117] Amidst what the *Washington Post*'s Murray Marder termed "four arduous hours" of "broadly critical questions," the secretary of state justified U.S. involvement by citing the lessons of Munich.[118] As had Taylor, Rusk refused to limit the extent of the commitment in Southeast Asia, and he defended the legality of the intervention, in terms of both international and domestic law. The atmosphere, according to *Newsweek*, "turned cracklingly tense" when Fulbright, exasperated, seized the microphone: "Mr. Secretary," the Arkansas senator began, "I wish these things appeared as simple to me as they do to you."[119] The chairman chided Rusk for describing the conflict as aggression by the North Vietnamese and for devoting insufficient effort to finding a diplomatic solution to the war. Rusk claimed that he was doing his best, but that "we can't get anybody into the discussion."[120] If that were the case, Fulbright pointedly noted, "There must be something wrong with our diplomacy."[121] But the secretary got the better of the exchange: "Senator, is it just possible that there is something wrong with them?"[122]

Reaction to the hearings varied according to the respondent's previous viewpoint. McGovern, realistically, confided that they "had a worthwhile impact, but I sometimes wonder if the war has not taken such a momentum that it will be virtually impossible to call a halt."[123] More optimistically, Gore found the hearings "primarily useful in helping to enlighten and formulate public opinion, as well as in helping the Senate to exercise its constitutional function of advising the President on foreign policy matters."[124] Lausche, on the other hand, found it a "painful experience" to observe the performance of "Senator Fulbright and his associates."[125] Recalling the phrase used by Woodrow Wilson to condemn anti-interventionist senators just before the United States entered World War I, columnist William S. White classified Fulbright and Morse as among a "little band of willful men"

[117] George McGovern personal interview with author, 6 Jan. 1994.

[118] *Washington Post*, 29 Jan. 1966.

[119] U.S. Senate, Foreign Relations Committee, *Hearings, Supplemental Foreign Assistance Fiscal Year 1966 – Vietnam*, 89th Congress, 2nd session, p. 582 (18 Feb. 1966); *Newsweek*, 28 Feb. 1966.

[120] U.S. Senate, Foreign Relations Committee, *Hearings, Supplemental Foreign Assistance Fiscal Year 1966 – Vietnam*, 89th Congress, 2nd session, p. 582 (18 Feb. 1966).

[121] U.S. Senate, Foreign Relations Committee, *Hearings, Supplemental Foreign Assistance Fiscal Year 1966 – Vietnam*, 89th Congress, 2nd session, p. 582 (18 Feb. 1966).

[122] *Congressional Quarterly Weekly Report*, 25 Feb. 1966.

[123] George McGovern to L. S. Stavrianos, 21 Feb. 1966, Box 67A802/22, George McGovern Papers, Princeton University.

[124] Albert Gore form letter, file copy, 18 Feb. 1966, Box A44, Issue series, Albert Gore Papers, Middle Tennessee State University.

[125] Frank Lausche to William Northlich, 3 June 1966; Frank Lausche to Earl Hamilton, 7 July 1966; both in Box 264, Frank Lausche Papers, Ohio State Historical Society.

determined to undermine Johnson's foreign policy.[126] And unabashedly pro-war *Time* scoffed that Fulbright's "circumlocutory sentences and strangled syntax . . . scarcely sounded worthy of a onetime Rhodes scholar."[127]

As the historian Randall Bennett Woods has observed, it is easy to over-state the impact of the Fulbright Hearings: a Harris poll taken immediately after Rusk's appearance showed that only 37 percent knew of the event.[128] (The committee did, however, receive 25,000 letters after the hearings, run-ning 6-to-1 in support.[129]) In the long term, the hearings had three important results. First, as Church somewhat melodramatically asserted at the time, "the long slumbering Foreign Relations Committee finally came to life on the subject of Vietnam."[130] Second, the hearings legitimized dissent, present-ing to the American public not only George Kennan, the father of contain-ment, expressing skepticism about the war, but the sight of Rusk and Taylor receiving relentless questioning from senators such as Fulbright, Church, Morse, Gore, and Clark.[131] That the administration supporters on the com-mittee (Long, Symington, Dodd, Sparkman, and Lausche) rarely attended magnified the influence of the antiwar members.[132] Finally, as George Reedy realized, the hearings polarized senators "by the force of debate into cate-gories where they do not belong."[133] Antiwar senators still lacked a majority, but if events such as the Fulbright Hearings could frame the debate about Vietnam, Reedy cautioned, "deep divisions will result."[134]

A pull from the other direction intensified the growing polarization that Reedy feared. On February 17, the same day of Taylor's testimony, Stennis informed the Mississippi state legislature that by the end of 1966, the United States would have between 300,000 and 400,000 soldiers in Vietnam, en route to an ultimate total of 600,000 men – so as "to take the war effectively to the Viet Cong and their allies."[135] Stennis added that if China entered the conflict, the United States should respond with nuclear weapons. Given

[126] "National Educational Television," 23 May 1966, Box 220, ND series, White House Central File, Lyndon Johnson Presidential Library.

[127] *Time*, 25 Feb. 1966.

[128] Woods, *Fulbright*, p. 410.

[129] William Conrad Gibbons, *The U.S. Government and the Vietnam War: Executive and Leg-islative Roles and Relationships, Part IV: July 1965–January 1968* (Princeton, NJ: Princeton University Press, 1995), p. 249.

[130] Frank Church to Ross Woodward, 4 Feb. 1966, Series 2.2, Box 30, Frank Church Papers, Boise State University.

[131] Carl Marcy oral history, U.S. Senate Historical Office; *Washington Star*, 20 Feb. 1966.

[132] *Washington Post*, 16 Feb. 1966; *Washington Star*, 17 Feb. 1966.

[133] George Reedy to President Johnson, 17 Feb. 1966, Box 80, White House Confidential Files, Lyndon Johnson Presidential Library.

[134] George Reedy to President Johnson, 17 Feb. 1966, Box 80, White House Confidential Files, Lyndon Johnson Presidential Library.

[135] *Washington Star*, 17 Feb. 1966.

the Mississippi senator's reputation for extensive Pentagon contacts, Don Oberdorfer of the *New York Times* reported that the remarks "just scared the hell out of the Senators," since they assumed that Stennis possessed the "inside word."[136]

Throughout 1966, the antiwar bloc struggled to use the Senate's power and reverse the administration's Vietnam policy. On February 28, 18 Democratic senators met in Morse's office to discuss strategy.[137] McCarthy, Young, and Gore recommended aggressively challenging the White House; Gore (considered by Oberdorfer the Senate's "most compelling leader against the Administration") expressed his concern that Senate inaction would produce war with China.[138] Before the group could consider future action, however, dissension emerged over pending matters. At the start of the congressional session, reflecting what Church termed the duo's "'never-never-land' of radically ineffectual dissent," Morse introduced an amendment to rescind the Tonkin Gulf Resolution, while Gruening sponsored an offering to require permission from draftees before sending them to Southeast Asia.[139] Both initiatives were so extreme that even most anti-war senators could not support them; Fulbright requested their withdrawal, arguing that their inevitable overwhelming defeat would strengthen Johnson's hand.[140] Gruening, reluctantly, agreed to withhold his amendment provided Morse did the same. But when the Oregon senator refused, both offerings went forward.[141]

The Morse amendment triggered two days of acrimonious debate. Russell termed the amendment's mere offering a "sorry spectacle"; he claimed that "the lives of some American boys in Vietnam could be lost if we keep shilly-shallying around here a great deal longer with this resolution."[142] The Georgia senator also criticized the Fulbright Hearings, contending that the Senate could have obtained any information on Vietnam that it needed from reading PIS transcripts. (Fulbright retorted that "in my committee, we at least try to inform the people of the country what this is about."[143]) In the debate's harshest line, Stennis contended that "every discussion, every expression of

[136] Henry Wilson, "Memorandum for the President," 18 Feb. 1966, Box 146, White House Confidential File, Lyndon Johnson Presidential Library.

[137] Ernest Gruening diary, entry for 28 Feb. 1966, Ernest Gruening Papers, University of Alaska-Fairbanks.

[138] Henry Wilson, "Memorandum for the President," 18 Feb. 1966, Box 146, White House Confidential File, Lyndon Johnson Presidential Library; *Washington Post*, 10 March 1966.

[139] Frank Church to Eli Oboler (confidential), 28 July 1965, Series 2.2, Box, 28, Frank Church Papers, Boise State University.

[140] J. William Fulbright to Arthur Schlesinger, Jr., 15 March 1966, Series 48:18, Box 50, J. William Fulbright Papers, University of Arkansas.

[141] Ernest Gruening diary, entry for 28 Feb. 1966, Ernest Gruening Papers, University of Alaska-Fairbanks.

[142] 112 CR, 89th Congress, 2nd session, pp. 4292, 4295 (28 Feb. 1966).

[143] 112 CR, 89th Congress, 2nd session, p. 4297 (28 Feb. 1966).

doubt, every expression of uncertainty is an encouragement to our adversaries."[144] Five senators withstood the barrage: Fulbright, McCarthy, and Young joined Morse and Gruening in voting to repeal the Tonkin Gulf Resolution. But, as Fulbright had feared, the margin of defeat allowed Russell to describe the outcome as "a reaffirmation of the President's power."[145]

By this point, the political tension had spread beyond the Senate floor. Throughout his career, Lyndon Johnson personalized political disputes, but the vehement attacks on Vietnam hit particularly close to home. As majority leader, he had placed Morse and Church on the Foreign Relations Committee, ensured Fulbright's accession to the committee chairmanship, helped pass the Alaska statehood bill that allowed Gruening to enter the Senate, and funneled campaign funds to the longshot Senate bids of Joe Clark, Stephen Young, and Vance Hartke (D-Indiana). Now, as increasing signs of a Vietnam quagmire caused his polling numbers to drop and all seven emerged as sharp critics of his foreign policy, he lashed out. At the 1966 Gridiron Dinner, the President opened by announcing that he attended only after hearing "that Vance Hartke wasn't going to be here."[146] A few weeks later, at a congressional dinner, Johnson looked directly at Fulbright and announced, "I am delighted to be here tonight with so many of my very old friends as well as some members of the Foreign Relations Committee."[147]

In September 1966, Fulbright admitted that the position of a dissenter constituted "a new role for me, and not a very easy one under our system."[148] He and his colleagues, however, proved more comfortable in dealing with Southeast Asian issues other than Vietnam, since they could avoid the burden of not supporting troops in the field. In early 1966, Hubert Humphrey made his first appearance with the Foreign Relations Committee since becoming vice president. He expected an informal briefing on his recently completed mission to Thailand. Instead, Gore, Church, and Clark pressed him on the administration's Vietnam policy; Fulbright wanted to know whether the vice president had made any secret pledges to the Thai government. When the Minnesotan suddenly became defensive, the chairman blandly responded that Humphrey was receiving so many questions because the administration had declined to inform the Senate about its true intentions in Southeast Asia.[149] Fulbright admitted that he had a particular concern about Thailand because conditions there resembled those in Vietnam in 1964, when his own "lack of foresight and diligence" had prompted him to support the Tonkin

---

[144] 112 *CR*, 89th Congress, 2nd session, p. 4374 (1 March 1966).

[145] 112 *CR*, 89th Congress, 2nd session, p. 4370 (1 March 1966).

[146] *The New Republic*, 28 March 1966.

[147] Woods, *Fulbright*, p. 417.

[148] J. William Fulbright to Barbara Tuchman, 20 Sept. 1966, Series 48:18, Box 50, J. William Fulbright Papers, University of Arkansas.

[149] *ESSFRC*, vol. 18, pp. 454, 459 (2 March 1966).

Gulf Resolution.[150] The experience so unsettled the vice president that at one point in the session, Humphrey broke down into tears.[151]

When Fulbright subsequently announced his desire to convene open hearings on U.S. policy toward Thailand, the Thai foreign minister stated that his country would "rather go down fighting Communism by ourselves than be a pawn for Senator Fulbright."[152] In the aftermath, the new national security adviser, Walt Rostow, reported that "Congressional criticism of our commitment and presence in Thailand has soured our relations to the point where Thai leaders are beginning to question our resolve."[153] To placate the Thais, Rostow recommended boosting military aid to Bangkok by $60 million annually. Such a course, however, had no chance of clearing the Senate; Morse, for one, asserted that "our aid program seems to be laying the foundation for an American military operation in Thailand."[154] More generally, the Oregon senator claimed that "a great many of our troubles in the world stem from our desire to control events in too many countries, and foreign aid is one of the instruments we use in the effort to do this."[155] The previous year, Morse had predicted a Senate foreign policy "revolt" within 24 months, caused by two forces – foreign aid and Vietnam.[156] The rebellion came a year earlier than expected.

Reflecting on the foreign aid bill's path through Congress in autumn 1966, Mike Manatos, the administration's liaison to the Senate, conceded that "it is becoming increasingly difficult to equate Military Assistance to the mutual security of the United States."[157] When even Manatos could not rebut the left-wing critique of foreign aid, the program was in trouble. While the administration staved off most of the attempted funding cuts in 1966, it lost the intellectual contest, paving the way for a full-scale congressional assault on military aid in the years to come.

In addition to the new internationalists' success in framing military aid as useless for American security, debate over the 1966 foreign aid bill featured four other important developments, two on the ideological front, two on the tactical. First, Fulbright hammered home the point that AID commitments foreshadowed subsequent U.S. interventions in the internal affairs of Third

[150] *ESSFRC*, vol. 18, pp. 454, 459 (2 March 1966).
[151] Gibbons, *The U.S. Government and the Vietnam War: Part IV*, p. 237.
[152] *New York Times*, 24 Sept. 1966.
[153] Walt Rostow, "Memorandum for the President," 15 Oct. 1966, Box 283, Country File, National Security File, Lyndon Johnson Presidential Library.
[154] *ESSFRC*, vol. 18, p. 992 (20 Sept. 1966).
[155] Wayne Morse to Randall Cruikshanks, 30 Aug. 1966, Box B-42, Wayne Morse Papers, University of Oregon.
[156] U.S. Senate, Foreign Relations Committee, *Hearings, Foreign Assistance, 1965*, 89th Congress, 1st session, p. 568 (29 March 1965).
[157] Mike Manatos, "Memorandum for the President," 26 Sept. 1966, Box 8, Office Files of Mike Manatos, White House Central Files, Lyndon Johnson Presidential Library.

World countries – Vietnam was the obvious example here, but Thailand also loomed large.[158] Second, Congress as a whole – not just the new internationalists – attacked what the Pentagon politely termed "Presidential power and flexibility in foreign aid."[159] In what he contended was "only a symbolic gesture," Church led the effort, seeking to eliminate the presidential contingency fund (an almost token $100 million).[160] The measure failed, but by only four votes.

On a tactical level, the foreign aid debate confirmed the reversal between the two houses regarding the program. In March, Church realized that the House "is going to rubberstamp what this administration wants" – the days of Passmanism had passed.[161] In the Senate, however, Fulbright posed an obvious problem: David Bell complained that the Foreign Relations Committee chair "would not respond to any arguments on the merits."[162] Gore, meanwhile, was "almost at the point of voting against the entire foreign aid program," and opposed the administration in every way possible.[163] Church and McCarthy were "not going to be much help on the floor," Hartke, "as usual," was "uncooperative," Young was "unpredictable," and Nelson was "shaky."[164] Each of these senators, five years before, had strongly supported foreign aid – unlike Morse and Gruening, whom Bell labeled "the anti-aid fanatics."[165]

The other item of tactical importance came in the first successful floor amendment to slash military aid, a Church offering to reduce the authorization level by $100 million, in the hopes of compelling the administration to eliminate military aid to Latin America and Africa.[166] Morse dismissed attacks on the proposal from McGee and Dirksen as "another example of the desire of the Defense Establishment to free itself from congressional supervision," and, in a major surprise, the amendment prevailed by 18 votes, which AID's congressional liaison attributed to "the combination

[158] J. William Fulbright to A. J. Crabaugh, 5 March 1966, Box 47, Series 48:18, J. William Fulbright Papers, University of Arkansas.

[159] Office of the Secretary of Defense, "Memorandum for Mr. Mike Manatos," n.d. [1966], Box 16, Office Files of Mike Manatos, White House Central Files, Lyndon Johnson Presidential Library.

[160] *ESSFRC*, vol. 18, p. 587 (4 March 1966).

[161] *ESSFRC*, vol. 18, p. 586 (4 March 1966).

[162] David Bell, "Memorandum for the President," 27 May 1966, Box 57, LE series, White House Central File, Lyndon Johnson Presidential Library.

[163] William Conrad Gibbons, "AID and Congress, Week of May 6–May 13," 13 May 1966, Box 16, Office Files of Mike Manatos, White House Central Files, Lyndon Johnson Presidential Library.

[164] "Senate Survey on Foreign Aid Authorization Bill," n.d. [1966], Box 8, Office Files of Mike Manatos, White House Central Files, Lyndon Johnson Presidential Library.

[165] Ed Hamilton to McGeorge Bundy, 30 Jan. 1966, Box 6, Memos to the President – Bundy, National Security File, Lyndon Johnson Presidential Library.

[166] 112 *CR*, 89th Congress, 2nd session, p. 17340 (27 July 1966).

of liberal Democrat losses together with traditional conservative opposition."[167] Underlying the vote was a growing demand "by the Foreign Relations Committee and the Senate for a larger role in foreign policy decisionmaking" – the upper chamber "wants more of a voice, and there is every indication that it will take whatever steps are possible to achieve this end," not only "during the Vietnam crisis but after that crisis has passed."[168] The new internationalists were replicating the 1950s revisionists' efforts to marshal congressional power for their own ends.

Congressional conservatives struck back, in one case seriously, in another far less so. The HUAC, which had toiled in obscurity since McCarthy seized the anti-Communist banner in 1950, returned to the spotlight in 1966, when Joe Pool (D-Texas) introduced an amendment to criminalize collecting money or goods for delivery to any hostile nation while U.S. troops were engaged in international hostilities. Targeting actions of California antiwar protesters, the measure also made illegal acts of civil disobedience that obstructed the shipment of weapons or the transport of troops. Two subpoenaed witnesses filed suit to enjoin the committee from convening the hearings, claiming that HUAC's charge of investigating anti-American "propaganda" violated the First Amendment. In a ruling unprecedented in U.S. history, federal district judge Howard Corcoran agreed. Speaker McCormack attacked the decision – "we might as well not have any Congress at all" – and Pool announced that he would go ahead with the proceedings regardless.[169] Only minutes before the hearings were scheduled to open, a special three-judge panel dissolved the temporary injunction on technical grounds, allowing the Texas Democrat to proceed free from legal harm.[170]

Pool might have been better served obeying the original order. Civil liberties attorneys William Kuntzler and Arthur Kinoy repeatedly demanded that Pool suspend the proceedings; the Texas congressman eventually had federal marshals eject Kinoy. (Kuntzler then chided the chair for behaving in a "wholly un-American" fashion by "dealing discourteously with an attorney."[171]) Another witness was denied permission to enter the hearing room after he refused to remove a lapel button proclaiming "Advance the Cause of Socialism."[172] HUAC chair Edwin Willis (D-Louisiana) dropped

---

[167] William Conrad Gibbons, "AID and Congress, July 22–29," 29 July 1966, Box 16, Office Files of Mike Manatos, White House Central Files, Lyndon Johnson Presidential Library; 112 *CR*, 89th Congress, 2nd session, p. 17346 (27 July 1966).

[168] William Conrad Gibbons, "AID and Congress, July 22–29," 29 July 1966, Box 16, Office Files of Mike Manatos, White House Central Files, Lyndon Johnson Presidential Library.

[169] *New York Times*, 16 Aug. 1966.

[170] *New York Times*, 17 Aug. 1966.

[171] U.S. House of Representatives, Un-American Activities Committee, *Hearings, Bills to Make Punishable Assistance to Enemies of U.S. in Time of Undeclared War*, 89th Congress, 2nd session, p. 1027 (17 Aug. 1966).

[172] *Washington Post*, 19 Aug. 1966.

by to denounce the "yellow-bellied cowards" agitating against the war, while future attorney general Edwin Meese, then deputy county attorney for Alameda County, California, reported on the un-American activities of Berkeley's Vietnam Day Committee.[173] (One of the Berkeley witnesses, after calling Pool "Joe," ranking Democrat Richard Ichord "Richie," and the committee's counsel "Mr. Lackie," was ejected when he refused to answer a question from Pool, "on the grounds that it nauseates me and I am liable to vomit all over the table."[174]) The committee unanimously reported Pool's bill to the House floor, with a report claiming that the hearings uncovered a "widespread and well-organized effort initiated within the United States by Communist groups" to obstruct the war.[175] A few days later, Justice Potter Stewart, in another highly unusual judicial action, denounced the bill as "clearly and obviously" unconstitutional.[176] Nonetheless, the House passed the measure 275 to 64. The vote was symbolic, since the Senate never took up the bill, and even then an unusually large number of members abstained themselves rather than go on record as supporting Pool's performance.

While the Pool hearings descended into farce, those of the Senate Armed Services Committee presented a formidable conservative critique of Johnson's foreign policy. In January, the committee inquired into the state of the war in Vietnam; Symington, recalling his performances of the 1950s, opened with an impassioned five-minute statement urging the bombing of North Vietnamese industrial centers. John McClellan, in equally heated language, contended that Johnson's policy prevented the military from "fighting to destroy the enemy that is really responsible for the war in South Vietnam.[177] Stennis termed the McClellan and Symington critiques "historic"; Robert McNamara, the opening witness, seemed less impressed.[178]

A few months later, the PIS looked into the nation's strategic posture and international commitments. Although Stennis denied an intention to "infringe or intrude" on the "useful and valuable" functions of the Foreign

---

[173] U.S. House of Representatives, Un-American Activities Committee, *Hearings, Bills to Make Punishable Assistance to Enemies of U.S. in Time of Undeclared War*, 89th Congress, 2nd session, p. 1060 (17 Aug. 1966).

[174] U.S. House of Representatives, Un-American Activities Committee, *Hearings, Bills to Make Punishable Assistance to Enemies of U.S. in Time of Undeclared War*, 89th Congress, 2nd session, pp. 1163, 1169 (18 Aug. 1966).

[175] *New York Times*, 22 Aug. 1966.

[176] *Washington Post*, 1 Sept. 1966.

[177] U.S. Senate, Armed Services Committee, *Hearings, Supplemental Military Procurement and Construction Authorization, Fiscal Year 1966*, 89th Congress, 2nd session, p. 114 (21 Jan. 1966).

[178] U.S. Senate, Armed Services Committee, *Hearings, Supplemental Military Procurement and Construction Authorization, Fiscal Year 1966*, 89th Congress, 2nd session, p. 158 (21 Jan. 1966).

Relations Committee, he clearly envisioned a counterpoint to the Fulbright Hearings, with an intent of proving the need for increased military spending.[179] The hearings featured vehement denunciations of the administration, typified by Strom Thurmond's blaming U.S. international difficulties on Johnson's "playing 'footsie' with the Soviets."[180]

The two sets of Vietnam hearings resembled a shadow conflict between Foreign Relations and Armed Services for the right of expressing the congressional viewpoint on Southeast Asian events. Midway through the summer of 1966, the two sides clashed more directly.

The CIA received almost no scrutiny during debate over the National Security Act; the first member of Congress to demand CIA oversight, ironically, was Morse, then a Republican member of the Armed Services Committee. The idea collapsed not because of opposition to oversight per se but due to suspicions of Morse. By tradition, as occurred with McMahon and the JCAE, the sponsor chaired the committee his resolution created, and fears that a Chairman Morse would leak sensitive material to his press contacts, such as Drew Pearson, doomed the resolution.[181] Oversight, therefore, fell by default to the Armed Services Committee and to the Appropriations Committee, which was responsible for funding the CIA. In the Senate, the two committees set up a joint subcommittee, with three members from each parent committee; in the House, the two committees each established a subcommittee. These subcommittees, however, did little: Clark Clifford recalled that in the late 1940s, "Congress chose not to be involved and preferred to be uninformed."[182] The Senate CIA subcommittee earned the nickname BOGSAT ("bunch of guys sitting around a table"), after "oversight" meetings in which the subcommittee members made clear that they did not want to know what the CIA was doing.[183]

The issue briefly reemerged in 1956, when Mansfield introduced a resolution for a joint oversight committee, so as to confront "the trend toward reposing more and more power in the hands of the executive branch of the Government."[184] Despite admitting that the oversight subcommittee rarely met, and kept no records even when it did convene, Russell argued that Congress needed to "take some matters on faith, without a constant examination of its methods and sources."[185] Saltonstall, the subcommittee's

[179] John Stennis press release, 28 April 1966, Folder 1991, Stuart Symington Papers, University of Missouri.

[180] U.S. Senate, Preparedness Investigating Subcommittee, *Hearings, Worldwide Military Commitments*, 89th Congress, 2nd session, pp. 77, 104 (30 Aug. 1966).

[181] Carl Marcy oral history, U.S. Senate Historical Office.

[182] Frank Smist, *Congress Oversees the Intelligence Community, 1947–1994* (Knoxville: University of Tennessee Press, 1994), p. 5.

[183] Smist, *Congress Oversees the Intelligence Community*, p. 11.

[184] 102 CR, 84th Congress, 2nd session, p. 5924 (9 April 1956).

[185] 102 CR, 84th Congress, 2nd session, p. 6048 (11 April 1956).

ranking Republican, echoed the Georgia senator's arguments, and the Mansfield resolution lost by a 59 to 27 tally.

In the early 1960s, another senator began to champion oversight reform. Outraged by the failure of the Bay of Pigs invasion, Eugene McCarthy introduced a resolution in May 1961 to establish an oversight committee.[186] He then rallied opposition to the 1962 nomination of John McCone after the DCI-designate refused to disclose whether he would authorize an unconstitutional covert operation. Fifteen senators ultimately opposed the McCone confirmation, a remarkable total given that the sole issue at play, as the Minnesota senator admitted, was the "serious concern" about insufficient congressional oversight.[187] Encouraged by the outcome, reformers presented a variety of options the following year. McCarthy revived his proposal for a Joint Intelligence Committee, while Morse demanded Foreign Relations Committee supervision of the CIA, as a check on "police state procedures" in the executive branch's foreign policy apparatus; Fulbright and Church sounded sympathetic.[188] Gruening introduced a resolution to create a select intelligence committee consisting of three members each from the Foreign Relations, Armed Services, and Appropriations committees, a proposal the Armed Services Committee staff termed "sheer murder" and Kennedy publicly opposed.[189]

McCarthy revived his initiative in 1966, though some Foreign Relations Committee liberals, such as Joe Clark, urged a less confrontational approach.[190] Recalling his suggestion to Humphrey a decade before, Fulbright raised the idea of a study of the intelligence community, but the word semantics fooled no one. Lausche, terming it "a very innocent approach to tie your argument upon the word 'study' when manifestly it is an investigation," concluded that merely announcing an inquiry "would be telling the world that the accusations made by the communists are prima facie established."[191] The committee instead voted to summon DCI William Raborn, who had succeeded McCone, for a briefing, while authorizing Fulbright to speak informally to Russell about three Foreign Relations members (Fulbright, McCarthy, and Hickenlooper) joining the existing CIA oversightc subcommittee.[192]

---

[186] Eugene McCarthy to Archie Chelseth, 25 May 1961, Box 110, Eugene McCarthy Papers, Minnesota State Historical Society.

[187] Eugene McCarthy to Yanislav Tiajotoff, 2 Feb. 1962, Box 110, Eugene McCarthy Papers, Minnesota State Historical Society.

[188] *ESSFRC*, vol. 15, p. 802 (10 Oct. 1963).

[189] Armed Services Committee staff memorandum, 14 Oct. 1963, Box 21-W(C), Joseph Clark Papers, Pennsylvania State Historical Society; *New York Times*, 10 Oct. 1963.

[190] *ESSFRC*, vol. 18, p. 209 (25 Jan. 1966).

[191] *ESSFRC*, vol. 18, p. 213 (25 Jan. 1966).

[192] Carl Marcy to J. William Fulbright, 15 March 1966, Box 8, Series 48:1, J. William Fulbright Papers, University of Arkansas.

Fulbright's discussions with Russell went nowhere; dismissing claims that the CIA made foreign policy as "sheer poppycock," the Georgia senator bluntly asserted, "There is no justification whatever for any other committee to muscle in on the jurisdiction of the Armed Services Committee."[193] Raborn's repeated claim that he could share such information about CIA activities only with members of the Russell subcommittee similarly failed to soothe Foreign Relations members. Eventually, under repeated badgering, the DCI answered some policy-related questions, although he asked his startled audience to disregard any negative press commentary about him, since, he claimed, the KGB had launched an international plot to discredit him.[194] Based on his performance before the committee, the Soviets need not have put in the effort. Raborn told Gore that the Volta Dam, an issue of controversy between the United States and Ghana for the previous half-decade, was in Rhodesia; when asked by Fulbright about the extent of Communist penetration of the Dominican Republic, the DCI admitted not having "that information on me."[195] Seeking to avoid more damaging factual questions, Hickenlooper complimented Raborn for recognizing the care needed when dealing with overseas reformist movements, since Communists "have been much smarter than some of our actions in a lot of these places."[196] Fulbright quickly agreed: "We couldn't be more stupid than a lot of the things we have done."[197]

With Russell having rejected informal compromise and Raborn having intensified the committee's concern about the CIA's direction, a 14-to-5 majority reported a bill to establish a Committee on Intelligence Operations, to have nine members, three each from the Foreign Relations, Armed Services, and Appropriations committees. (Lausche ostentatiously walked out of the hearing room during the vote; McGee noted that the "time is here when we might worry less about the arrogance of power and more about the arrogance of dissent."[198]) Behind the scenes, the State Department opposed the measure; J. Edgar Hoover believed that Fulbright intended to "disrupt intelligence operations."[199] Publicly, the *St. Louis Post-Dispatch* editorialized that the oversight committee would subject the CIA to the "claws of the militant doves"; William S. White termed the resolution "another manifestation of a growing and all but automatic hostility within the Senatorial Democrats' left wing to any and every agency of

[193] *New York Times*, 17 May 1966.
[194] *ESSFRC*, vol. 18, p. 360 (25 Feb. 1966).
[195] *ESSFRC*, vol. 18, pp. 355, 377 (25 Feb. 1966).
[196] *ESSFRC*, vol. 18, pp. 360, 380 (25 Feb. 1966).
[197] *ESSFRC*, vol. 18, p. 360 (25 Feb. 1966).
[198] *Washington Post*, 16 May 1966, 22 June 1966.
[199] Henry Wilson, "Memorandum for the President," 24 May 1966, Box 57, LE series, White House Central File, Lyndon Johnson Presidential Library; Woods, *Fulbright*, p. 431.

Government which represents actual power and has the hard duty sometimes to use it."[200]

When the measure reached the Senate floor, Russell protested the "extraordinary procedure" that was followed.[201] The Georgia Democrat raised a point of order that the resolution should have been referred to the Armed Services Committee, allowing a procedural battle to mask a profound philosophical debate. Fulbright and his backers contended that regardless of the original intent of the National Security Act, the CIA now played a "major role in the foreign policy decisionmaking process," and often through questionable activities.[202] Russell and his supporters countered by defending the national security state; to dramatize the point, Senate conservatives successfully demanded that the body convene for a highly unusual secret session to discuss the resolution.

That session featured a verbal confrontation between Fulbright and Russell in which the Georgia senator accused his colleague of "muscling in on my committee" by bypassing Senate rules.[203] Apparently, Russell speculated, Fulbright had gathered from the "distinguished newspaper published in New York" that the CIA made foreign policy; the *New York Times* mistakenly assumed that "oversight means that a legislative committee which is oversighting has some control."[204] When Fulbright countered that he would gladly refer the resolution to Armed Services as long as Russell would promise to report it to the Senate floor, the Georgia senator claimed to have "gone the last mile" in attempting to accommodate his colleagues; he compared Fulbright's demand to "a pistol pointed at my head."[205] The Senate then upheld the point of order by a vote of 61 to 28, and the resolution was referred to Armed Services, which buried it.

A sense of Democratic disarray contributed to the party's poor performance in the 1966 midterm elections, when Republicans scored heavy gains in House and Senate races. Unlike the contests of 1950 or 1958, however, in 1966 the relationship between international developments and congressional elections was less clear-cut. The Southeast Asian conflict posed an obvious problem for Democratic candidates. As early as May 1966, White House aide Joseph Califano reported that Senator Jennings Randolph, an administration stalwart, spoke "at some length about how concerned he is that the Vietnam issue is hurting him badly in West Virginia."[206] Alarmingly, Randolph was receiving specific questions on the war from constituents – and

---

[200] *St. Louis Post-Dispatch*, 18 July 1966; *Washington Post*, 21 May 1966.
[201] 112 *CR*, 89th Congress, 2nd session, p. 15674 (14 July 1966).
[202] 112 *CR*, 89th Congress, 2nd session, p. 15673 (14 July 1966).
[203] 112 *CR*, 89th Congress, 2nd session, p. 15677 (14 July 1966).
[204] 112 *CR*, 89th Congress, 2nd session, p. 15676 (14 July 1966).
[205] 112 *CR*, 89th Congress, 2nd session, p. 15696 (14 July 1966).
[206] Joseph Califano to Walt Rostow, 20 May 1966, Box 221, ND series, White House Central Files, Lyndon Johnson Presidential Library.

he had no clear sense of how to respond. According to one poll, the post-election House contained 30 new members who favored a more aggressive prosecution of the war. Even so, shortly before Election Day, journalist Scotty Reston commented that not only were "the moral, political, and economic consequences of the war" not the primary issues in the races for Congress, "these questions are not even being debated by the candidates."[207] More-over, the 1966 election in which foreign policy played the most prominent role produced a victory for anti-war forces.

In June, arguing that his opposition to the war overrode partisan concerns, Morse expressed his hope that a "goodly number" of Democrats would lose, so the party could "cleanse itself in respect to foreign policy."[208] One Democrat that Morse badly wanted to see defeated was Oregon congress-man Robert Duncan, who challenged the state's Republican governor, Mark Hatfield, for the Senate seat left vacant by Democrat Maurine Neuberger. Hatfield, the only governor to oppose the war at the 1965 National Governors' Association conference, began the race with a wide lead; Duncan countered with claims that since Hatfield and Morse sported "indistinguish-able" records on Vietnam, the state needed at least one senator "to speak up for the U.S. Government." After receiving a weaker than expected 75 per-cent vote in the primary, a showing attributed to concern about his anti-war views, Hatfield publicly criticized the "inexcusable excesses of some antiwar demonstrations." The governor then reversed course again and condemned the administration's bombing of oil depots in Hanoi and Haiphong, after which he removed references to Vietnam from his prepared speeches alto-gether. Duncan, on the other hand, sought to transform the contest into a referendum on the administration's Vietnam policy, describing the cen-tral issue for voters as "whether Americans will die in the buffalo grass of Vietnam or the rye grass of Oregon." By October, the two candidates were neck-and-neck. In the end, Hatfield won, but narrowly, with just under 52 percent of the vote.[209]

Despite the partisan turnover, the new Congress resumed the rebellion against foreign aid that Morse had foreseen. Hickenlooper's chief foreign policy aide noticed in early 1967 that even Foreign Relations Committee members "appear bored with foreign assistance," focusing only on amend-ments that addressed policy-related issues.[210] Military aid was one such issue, with criticism spreading even to those long associated with a pro-Pentagon viewpoint. After convening hearings on the effect of U.S. arms sales to the

---

[207] *New York Times*, 30 Oct. 1966.
[208] Wayne Morse to Chester Bowles, 7 June 1966, Box I-334, Chester Bowles Papers, Yale University.
[209] *Congressional Quarterly Weekly Report*, 14 Oct. 1966.
[210] George Pavlik to Bourke Hickenlooper, 10 Jan. 1967, Box 37, Foreign Relations Committee series, Bourke Hickenlooper Papers, Herbert Hoover Presidential Library.

Middle East and South Asia, Symington concluded that "what we are really doing is promoting the arms race with the Russians.[211] Closing down these hidden forms of military assistance triggered the most important foreign policy battle of 1967, one that matched the same factions as on the question of establishing an intelligence oversight committee, but this time with a different result.

The issue first emerged after a Foreign Relations staff study detailed how, after Congress had slashed the military aid budget and placed multiple restrictions on the assistance program in the 1963 foreign aid revolt, arms sales replaced outright assistance as the preferred method of supplying weapons overseas.[212] Nearly half of these sales were financed through credit arranged by the U.S. government through programs such as Country-X loans, under which Washington ensured repayment of loans while not revealing to the Export-Import Bank which country would receive the funds, and the Pentagon's revolving-door fund, which utilized moneys received for previously authorized arms sales (usually to Europe) to guarantee future weapons sales by private companies to nations in Africa, Asia, and Latin America. The Foreign Relations Committee voted 12 to 6 for an amendment sponsored by Church to terminate the revolving-door fund, a maneuver that commentator Joseph Kraft praised as characteristic of the dissenters' tactic of picking "on small, specific issues where they find in little the practices and patterns that worry them so much in general."[213]

The vote produced a furious counterattack from two senior members of the Armed Services Committee, Henry Jackson and John Tower (R-Texas), who sought not only to annul the Church amendment but also to give the Defense Department new authority to purchase promissory notes tendered to arms manufacturers by foreign governments. Terming the issue of "overriding importance," Tower contended that the Church amendment would "effectively emasculate" the Pentagon's ability to influence Third World militaries.[214] Gore responded that the Jackson-Tower amendment would make the Pentagon the "Federal Reserve Bank of arms credit."[215]

Up until the day of the floor vote, Jackson and Tower predicted victory for their initiative, which Stennis audaciously defended for *helping* the world's weaker nations. (Abolishing the revolving-door fund, he claimed, would "leave those little peoples to the wiles, the mercy, and the selfishness of others

[211] U.S. Senate, Subcommittee on Near Eastern and South Asian Affairs, *Hearings, Arms Sales to the Near East and South Asia*, 91st Congress, 1st session, p. 35 (13 April 1967).

[212] *New York Times*, 26 Jan. 1967.

[213] U.S. Senate, Foreign Relations Committee, *Report, Arms Sales and Foreign Policy: Staff Study*, 90th Congress, 1st session, p. iii (25 Jan. 1967); *Washington Post*, 27 March 1967.

[214] John Tower to Bourke Hickenlooper, 11 Aug. 1967, Box 37, Foreign Relations Committee series, Bourke Hickenlooper Papers, Herbert Hoover Presidential Library.

[215] *Washington Post*, 16 Aug. 1967.

who will come in."[216]) Lausche, a strong supporter of the Jackson-Tower amendment, considered it "frightening to see Senator Church arrogate unto himself a wisdom which no man in history has ever had, including Socrates," and dismissed the Foreign Relations majority for advocating "unilateral disarmament of our friends and allies."[217] Tower and Jackson, however, misjudged the tenor of the Senate. Led by McCarthy, critics of the amendment attacked it on procedural grounds, contending that the Armed Services Committee was attempting to sneak in a new Pentagon authority (to purchase promissory notes) without adequate congressional review.[218] This argument appealed to several moderates, and the initial Jackson-Tower amendment failed by a 50–43 vote. Tower then moved to restore the revolving-door fund, but this effort too failed, by a 46–45 margin. Symington, until this point a strong supporter of military aid, provided the decisive vote after bluntly asking his colleagues why the Senate would "want to vote to further the arms race all over the world."[219] Fulbright rejoiced that the vote produced "one of the most important changes made in the foreign aid program" in recent memory; AID officials confessed that the outcome bequeathed a "virtually useless" arms sales program.[220]

Alongside the revolving-door defeat, Johnson also suffered a major setback on Latin American policy. In spring 1967, the president issued a public call for a second conference at Punta del Este, at which the United States would promise increased funding to pay for social and economic reforms. The month before the conference opened, Johnson submitted a resolution requesting advance agreement for any increased aid the U.S. delegation might promise. Indicative of a more skeptical stance toward economic aid, Gore, Fulbright, Church, and Gruening (as the chief invited witness) took part in a three-and-a-half-hour Foreign Relations Committee discussion on subjects such as Gore's contention that the "whole concept" of inducing reform through outside economic aid was "fallacious."[221] But institutional prerogatives remained the dissenters' primary focus. Fulbright justified his decision to hold in-depth hearings on the resolution by attacking the "tendency, not

[216] 113 *CR*, 90th Congress, 1st session, p. 22566 (14 Aug. 1967).

[217] Lausche quoted in Mike Manatos, "Memorandum for the President," 11 Oct. 1967, Box 220, ND series, White House Central File, Lyndon Johnson Presidential Library; 113 *CR*, 90th Congress, 1st session, p. 22657 (15 Aug. 1967).

[218] Eugene McCarthy to George Williams, 9 Aug. 1967, Box 217, Eugene McCarthy Papers, Minnesota State Historical Society.

[219] 113 *CR*, 90th Congress, 1st session, p. 22641 (15 Aug. 1967).

[220] J. William Fulbright to Richard Martin, 23 Aug. 1967, Box 30, Series 48:8, J. William Fulbright Papers, University of Arkansas; William Gaud, "Foreign Relations Committee Action on the Foreign Aid Authorization Bill," 28 July 1967, Box 63, White House Confidential File, Lyndon Johnson Presidential Library.

[221] U.S. Senate, Foreign Relations Committee, *Hearings, Latin American Summit Conference*, 90th Congress, 1st session, p. 138 (21 March 1967).

only in this instance but in others, to supplant the independent judgment of Congress."[222] Church added that "a resolution of this kind, in fact, constitutes a further erosion of congressional prerogatives," and Gruening recommended rejecting the resolution as a way to "generate more respect for our constitutional procedures."[223] The committee then modified the resolution to render it meaningless, deleting any promise of future aid.

While the new internationalists continued attacking Johnson's handling of the Vietnam War, the president confronted congressional opposition from two new sources. Privately, prominent Democratic conservatives had grown skeptical about the administration's Southeast Asian policies. Russell alleged that as the State Department lacked a "real foreign policy," the administration was playing "gladiator, throwing American boys into the pit of battle whenever Communists appear without even making a serious effort to get any help from those are more involved than we are."[224] In public, however, the Senate right held that as long as the war persisted, the United States needed to fight to win. In the summer of 1967, the PIS convened hearings ostensibly on the air conflict against North Vietnam but actually, Stennis admitted, on "the overall policy and public philosophy governing and controlling the conduct of the entire war."[225] One McNamara biographer termed the hearings a "kangaroo court," since the defense secretary was the only civilian witness to appear before a subcommittee that unanimously favored expanding the air war.[226] I. F. Stone hailed McNamara's refusal to give ground to the subcommittee members "the noblest effort of his career."[227]

As with the Fulbright Hearings the year before, the PIS hearings were more noteworthy for the senators' remarks than for the testimony elicited from the witnesses. Stennis contended that even considering a bombing pause would constitute "a tragic and perhaps fatal mistake"; Jackson reasoned that without aggressive bombing, "I just can't see any kind of light at the end of the tunnel."[228] The subcommittee's report announced that "logic and prudence" required the administration to back whatever policy the military proposed,

---

[222] U.S. Senate, Foreign Relations Committee, *Hearings, Latin American Summit Conference*, 90th Congress, 1st session, p. 15 (17 March 1967).

[223] U.S. Senate, Foreign Relations Committee, *Hearings, Latin American Summit Conference*, 90th Congress, 1st session, pp. 139, 143 (21 March 1967).

[224] Gilbert Fite, *Richard B. Russell, Jr.: Senator from Georgia* (Athens: University of Georgia Press, 1991), p. 450.

[225] U.S. Senate, Preparedness Investigating Subcommittee, *Hearings, Air War against North Vietnam*, 90th Congress, 1st session, p. 2 (2 Aug. 1967).

[226] Deborah Shapley, *Promise and Power: The Life and Times of Robert McNamara* (Boston; Little, Brown, 1993), p. 428.

[227] I. F. Stone, "McNamara and the Militarists," *New York Review of Books*, 7 Nov. 1968.

[228] U.S. Senate, Preparedness Investigating Subcommittee, *Hearings, Air War against North Vietnam*, 90th Congress, 1st session, pp. 2 (2 Aug. 1967), 300 (25 Aug. 1967).

including closing Haiphong harbor and undertaking intensified bombing of North Vietnam.[229] The *New York Times* called the report evidence of "generals out of control"; Mansfield faulted his colleagues for challenging "one of the most fundamental principles of our constitutional structure – the civilian direction of the defense establishment."[230] The hearings nonetheless had a dramatic policy effect: in the weeks following the release of the PIS report, Johnson approved strikes against 52 of the 57 previously denied air targets.[231]

A second, just as politically threatening, source of congressional opposition also emerged in 1967. In June 1966, Fulbright told former Minnesota governor and GOP presidential candidate Harold Stassen that "the Republicans should be carrying more of the burden of debate regarding our foreign policy, rather than accepting it so quietly."[232] After the elections, little change occurred in the House, but in the Senate, a group of GOP moderates, including three first elected in 1966 (Mark Hatfield, Charles Percy, and Edward Brooke), questioned the administration's policy. Observing the opposition party with a degree of surprise, Gruening rejoiced that "for the first time their monolithic support of the war is breaking," making possible the bipartisan alliances that had typified the foreign aid fights.[233]

Aiken began the process in May 1967, when he urged GOP senators to realize that the Johnson administration "cannot achieve an honorable peace in Vietnam," because the president and his advisers were "too bound" by the past.[234] The most significant Republican dissent came from a senior moderate, Clifford Case, who delivered remarks about the Tonkin Gulf Resolution in a tone more characteristic of Gruening than of a figure a colleague described as "one of the most earnest and sincere members of our body."[235] The New Jersey senator accused the president of producing a "crisis of confidence" through the "misuse" and "perversion" of the Tonkin Gulf Resolution, guided by Johnson's "complete distortion" of the resolution's legislative intent in passing the resolution.[236]

Case's remarks generated a firestorm of criticism. To Dirksen, the speech essentially called the 97 other senators who favored the Tonkin Gulf Resolution a "bunch of dummies."[237] Quick, as always, to imply that his opponents

---

[229] *New York Times*, 1 Sept. 1967.
[230] *New York Times*, 1 Sept. 1967.
[231] Philip Davidson, *Vietnam at War* (Novato, California: Presidio, 1988), pp. 464–465.
[232] J. William Fulbright to Harold Stassen, 3 June 1966, Box 50, Series 48:18, J. William Fulbright Papers, University of Arkansas.
[233] Ernest Gruening diaries, 4 May 1967, Ernest Gruening Papers, University of Alaska-Fairbanks.
[234] 113 CR, 90th Congress, 1st session, p. 11436 (2 May 1967).
[235] *New York Times*, 27 Sept. 1967.
[236] 113 CR, 90th Congress, 1st session, pp. 26699–26700 (26 Sept. 1967).
[237] 113 CR, 90th Congress, 1st session, p. 26706 (26 Sept. 1967).

were guilty of treasonous beliefs, Stennis asserted that Case "unintention-ally gave comfort, encouragement, and hope to the enemy."[238] Russell Long contended that "partisan politics" explained Case's words, which could only "give comfort to the enemy"; while colleagues danced around the concept, Lausche offered the constitutional definition of treason, remarking that the New Jersey senator's speech represented the "best way to give comfort and aid to our enemy."[239] Even Mansfield, while sympathetic with Case's senti-ments, shied away from the "vehemence" of the remarks.[240] Case refused to back down, however – pacing back and forth across the center aisle during his address, pounding desks in the Senate chamber as he responded to his critics. He gave as good as he got, recommending, for instance, that Lausche take the trouble to read his remarks, which he had sent to colleagues in advance, "before he opens an attack upon the speech."[241]

While events were forcing Republicans to take bolder positions on the conflict, GOP divisions still paled in comparison with Democratic disagree-ments. At one extreme was Lausche, who blasted the "shortsighted, well-intentioned, but misled idealists" who contended "that our country has nothing to fear from the rapid expansion of communism."[242] In the final analysis, the Ohio senator concluded that "Communist China and Hanoi have greatly succeeded in propagandizing the citizen of the United States, making him believe that the presence of our troops in South Vietnam has no relationship to the security of the United States."[243] At the other extreme was Gruening, in 1967 the only senator to advocate immediate, unconditional withdrawal from Vietnam, a position that the Alaska senator coupled with voting against all defense appropriations offered after 1965 and support for draft resisters.[244]

Between these two poles, the new internationalists came close to a major-ity among Senate Democrats, although their point of view remained a small minority in the House. With the exception of Lausche, McGee, Long, Stennis, Dodd, and Russell, most pro-war Democrats toned down their public sup-port for the president; some, looking ahead to 1968, even reconsidered their approach altogether. Maryland Democrat Joseph Tydings told the White House in August 1967 that political pressures required distancing himself from the administration, and that Fred Harris (D-Oklahoma), Birch Bayh

---

[238] 113 *CR*, 90th Congress, 1st session, p. 26707 (26 Sept. 1967).

[239] 113 *CR*, 90th Congress, 1st session, pp. 26718–26721 (26 Sept. 1967).

[240] 113 *CR*, 90th Congress, 1st session, p. 26703 (26 Sept. 1967).

[241] 113 *CR*, 90th Congress, 1st session, p. 26721 (26 Sept. 1967); *New York Times*, 27 Sept. 1967.

[242] Frank Lausche to Edward Baker, 20 Dec. 1967, Box 264, Frank Lausche Papers, Ohio State Historical Society

[243] Frank Lausche to Edward White, 30 June 1967, Box 264, Frank Lausche Papers, Ohio State Historical Society.

[244] Johnson, *Ernest Gruening and the American Dissenting Tradition*, pp. 243–247.

(D-Indiana), Edmund Muskie (D-Maine), and Philip Hart (D-Michigan) would do likewise.[245] That same month, Thomas McIntyre (D-New Hampshire), a member of the Democratic Senate Campaign Committee, revealed that "the feeling on the committee is that of the 23 Democratic senators up for reelection, only 3 are considered safe."[246]

Despite their growing numbers, limits remained as to what anti-war Democrats could accomplish. Their strength remained, as Fulbright admitted, in educating the public, not in employing formal legislative powers.[247] Given this, Hartke detected an increasing sense of "helplessness" about the war, since it seemed as if "people are sick of hearing about it"; privately even some Senate doves were asking, "What is left to be said?"[248] McGovern described the dissenting bloc as "erratic, disorganized – or maybe I should say unorganized."[249] Indeed, despite repeated requests, the Foreign Relations Committee could not even compel Rusk to testify in public about the administration's policies in Vietnam. Compounding this frustration was the older question of how to oppose the war without undermining the troops. As in the past, most new internationalists focused on peripheral issues – limiting the bombing of North Vietnam, supporting reforms of the draft, encouraging the South Vietnamese government to broaden its political base.

Political conditions also constrained the group. After criticism from Democratic parties in their home states, Clark and Hartke issued public statements expressing support for the broad objectives of the administration's Vietnam policies.[250] McGovern candidly admitted to Gruening that he had not supported his Alaska colleague "100% on all your efforts because of the extremely conservative nature of my state and my forthcoming campaign, but my heart is always with you even when I have not been able to vote with you."[251] Conservatives heightened their attacks on the patriotism of anti-war senators: Lausche denounced the group for "wanting to sacrifice the security of our country and gain for themselves political recognition."[252]

[245] Harry McPherson to President Johnson, 25 Aug. 1967, Box 228, ND series, White House Central File, Lyndon Johnson Presidential Library.

[246] McIntyre quoted in Andrew Hickey to Barefoot Sanders, 25 Aug. 1967, Box 12, Barefoot Sanders Papers, Lyndon Johnson Presidential Library.

[247] J. William Fulbright to Tristram Coffin, 24 May 1967, Box 51, Series 48:18, J. William Fulbright Papers, University of Arkansas.

[248] *Courier Journal and Times*, 7 May 1967.

[249] George McGovern oral history, Lyndon Johnson Presidential Library.

[250] "Statement of Senator Joseph S. Clark's Views on Vietnam," 21 June 1967, Box 26-W(C), Pennsylvania Historical Society; Lyndon Johnson to Vance Hartke, Box 140, Names series, White House Central File, Lyndon Johnson Presidential Library.

[251] George McGovern to Ernest Gruening, 18 May 1967, Box 72A3053/11, George McGovern Papers, Princeton University.

[252] Frank Lausche to John Lokar, 27 Nov. 1967, Box 264, Frank Lausche Papers, Ohio Historical Society; *Congressional Quarterly Weekly Report*, 20 Oct. 1967.

The new internationalists struggled most, however, to rebut the allegation that congressional dissent harmed the welfare of the U.S. troops in the field. Seeking to neutralize this problem, in May 1967 Church assembled an impressive list of signatories – including Cooper, McGovern, Fulbright, Hartke, Nelson, Clark, Young, Hatfield, Morse, and Robert Kennedy – for a public letter to North Vietnam. The senators expressed themselves "steadfastly opposed to any unilateral withdrawal of American troops from South Vietnam" – and, the document reminded Hanoi, the anti-war faction represented a minority in the Senate.[253] At a press conference announcing the letter, Church affirmed that the group did not advocate a "repudiation of American commitments already made to South Vietnam."[254] Privately, McGovern conceded that he had signed to neutralize resolutions condemning him passed by the South Dakota Veterans of Foreign Wars and American Legion; Fulbright admitted that he chiefly wanted to help Church in the Idaho Democrat's re-election contest in 1968.[255]

In the short term, the letter served Church's purpose, generating strong editorial praise.[256] In the longer term, however, most of the signatories regretted the move – for reasons the one high-profile Senate dissenter who refused Church's overtures realized at the time. Gruening told Church that the letter "completely endorsed the administration line that Hanoi was the villain and that failure to come to the conference table was Hanoi's."[257] Moreover, the Alaska senator opposed any statement abjuring unilateral withdrawal, an outcome that he considered preferable to other alternatives, such as "keeping on with what we are doing."[258]

Events from early 1968 vindicated Gruening's position. On January 23, 1968, the North Korean military seized a U.S. intelligence ship, the U.S.S. *Pueblo*, which was operating too close to the Democratic People's Republic of Korea's territorial waters. (When an urgent message from Stennis reached the president in the White House Situation Room – "For God's sake, do something" – Johnson looked up and muttered, "Please thank the senator for his helpful advice."[259]) A few days later, a surprise attack by North Vietnamese forces on the Tet holiday resulted in enemy forces

---

[253] 113 *CR*, 90th Congress, 1st session, p. 13011 (17 May 1967).
[254] Frank Church press conference, 17 May 1967, Box 30, Series 2.2, Frank Church Papers, Boise State University.
[255] Ernest Gruening diaries, 16 May 1967, Ernest Gruening Papers, University of Alaska-Fairbanks.
[256] *Cleveland Plain-Dealer*, 18 May 1967; *Chicago Daily News*, 19 May 1967.
[257] Ernest Gruening diaries, 16 May 1967, Ernest Gruening Papers, University of Alaska-Fairbanks.
[258] Ernest Gruening to Glen Becker, 31 May 1967, Soviet Consular Treaty box, Brown Boxes series, Ernest Gruening Papers, University of Alaska-Fairbanks.
[259] Blechman, *The Politics of National Security* (New York: Oxford University Press, 1990), p. 202.

briefly occupying the U.S. embassy in Saigon. Though the U.S. and South Vietnamese forces eventually rebuffed the Tet Offensive, the administration could not overcome the public relations damage. In early March, Johnson almost lost the New Hampshire presidential primary to Eugene McCarthy, after which Robert Kennedy entered the Democratic contest and the president withdrew from the race. Shortly thereafter, Johnson rejected Westmoreland's latest request for more U.S. troops – which by early 1968 had reached 532,000 – and instructed the new secretary of defense, Clark Clifford, to prepare the foundations for ending the war.

Befitting a chief executive weakened on both political and policy fronts, Johnson faced a flurry of congressional challenges in his final year. The Senate's stormy relationship with the Johnson administration closed out with Rusk's first public appearance before the Foreign Relations Committee in over two years, precipitated by an 8–4 committee vote requesting that the secretary testify publicly.[260] Fulbright opened the hearings by giving his history of the previous four years: through the commitment of more than 500,000 men "to bloody and endless combat in these distant jungles, our leaders have converted a struggle between Vietnamese into a struggle between Americans for possession of the American spirit."[261] Fulbright and Case urged the administration to consider the alternatives to victory in South Vietnam, Young demanded that Rusk resign, and Gore faulted U.S. policy as "based upon almost exclusively western values" and thus doomed to fail.[262] Commentator Drew Pearson described the event as the "Senate's reasserting itself after long years of neglect in scrutinizing American foreign policy."[263]

A few senators kept the faith: Lausche predicted that "if the United States pulls out of Vietnam, communists will try to take Australia. By that time, they will be at our shores."[264] The Ohio Democrat, however, shortly would be out of public life, since former congressman John Gilligan upset him in the Democratic primary. By the middle of 1968, a majority of Senate Democrats and a growing number of GOP senators, while not willing to advocate withdrawal from Vietnam, were sufficiently radicalized by the war to reverse their previous support for a weak legislative role in international affairs. In

---

[260] Harry McPherson to President Johnson, 26 Feb. 1968, Box 63, White House Confidential Files, Lyndon Johnson Presidential Library.

[261] U.S. Senate, Foreign Relations Committee, *Hearings, Foreign Assistance Act of 1968, Part 1 – Vietnam*, 90th Congress, 2nd session, p. 9 (11 March 1968).

[262] U.S. Senate, Foreign Relations Committee, *Hearings, Foreign Assistance Act of 1968, Part 1 – Vietnam*, 90th Congress, 2nd session, p. 44 (11 March 1968).

[263] 114 *CR*, 90th Congress, 2nd session, p. 10142 (22 April 1968); *Washington Post*, 17 March 1968.

[264] Frank Lausche to Carl Andrich, 8 Jan. 1968, Box 264, Frank Lausche Papers, Ohio State Historical Society.

this respect, Vietnam set the stage for the first wholehearted congressional challenge to executive authority since the revisionists' efforts of the early 1950s. When combined with the political and institutional effects of Watergate, Congress was situated to assume a degree of control over U.S. foreign policy unmatched since before World War II.

5

The Transformation of Stuart Symington

In April 1969, Ward Just, the perceptive observer of the Washington socio-political scene, penned a lengthy piece in the *Washington Post*. Subtitled the "path of a high-level defector," Just's article traced Stuart Symington's evolution from a vociferous anti-Communist to a passionate critic of Cold War foreign policy. "When a major political figure actually changes his mind and shifts a position," Just realized, "and does so moreover not from outside pressure but from hard thought, it is an event, a high-level defection. A priest leaves the church, and neither is quite the same again."[1]

South Dakota senator James Abourezk remembered his colleague as "tall and distinguished, with a shock of gray hair ... one of the few senators who actually looked like a senator."[2] Testifying to his Establishment credentials, Stuart Symington adorned the walls of his Senate office with photographs of himself and the preceding generation's key figures in world and U.S. history.[3] During the early 1960s, the Missouri Democrat said that he sacrificed "what might be called Senate authority and power and position in order to get knowledge" on international affairs.[4] Retaining his position on the Armed Services Committee, he obtained slots on the Foreign Relations Committee, the JCAE, and the Jackson Subcommittee, while switching off every assignment he held that dealt with domestic matters – the Public Works, Agriculture, Joint Economic, and Appropriations committees (although he

---

[1] Ward Just, "Stu Symington: The Path of a High-Level Defector," *Washington Post*, 7 April 1969.

[2] James Abourezk, *Advise and Dissent: Memoirs of South Dakota and the U.S. Senate* (Chicago: Lawrence Hill Books, 1989), p. 102.

[3] *Washington Star*, 7 Feb. 1976.

[4] Flora Lewis, "The Education of a Senator," *Atlantic Monthly*, Dec. 1971. The committee configuration that Symington secured was impossible after the Senate revised its rules in 1970, limiting service on major committees. The change, however, was grandfathered in, making Symington the last senator in American history to serve on both the Foreign Relations and Armed Services committees.

remained an ex oficio member of the Defense Appropriations Subcommittee). No senator in American history possessed a similar range of committee assignments dealing with foreign policy and national security issues.

Until fairly late in the decade, Symington did little with his new positions. After the first of several visits to Southeast Asia in 1961, he informed President Kennedy that "we ought to try to hold this place. Otherwise this part of the world will go down the drain."[5] He maintained this position through the mid-1960s; a 1966 White House memo gratefully listed Symington as one of the four Foreign Relations Committee members outside of the "Fulbright majority."[6] That document also unintentionally highlighted the decline of the Missouri senator's standing: being mentioned alongside Senate lightweights Frank Lausche, Tom Dodd, and John Sparkman was a long way from being considered presidential material only a few years before.

Despite the White House praise, Symington grew increasingly skeptical about the war as the 1960s progressed. Even during the Fulbright Hearings, he admitted that if the situation in South Vietnam deteriorated, "without question we must take another look" at the basic policy.[7] As one administration staffer privately conceded, Symington was "obviously more interested in plugging for the Air Force than for the Administration generally."[8] In addition, the Missouri senator worried about the long-term economic effects of the war, while criticizing the secrecy behind U.S. policy – something that he encountered first hand in 1965, when the U.S. ambassador to Laos, William Sullivan, blocked his entrance into the country for a fact-finding mission because the ambassador feared that the Missouri senator would demand an escalation of the bombing campaign over the nominally neutral nation.[9]

This unusual combination of positions prompted Symington to oppose an expanded commitment elsewhere in Southeast Asia. In late 1966, Fulbright convened hearings on the U.S. military presence in Thailand, at which the chief witness, William Bundy, received harsh questions from the Missouri senator, to the surprise of all sides. Perhaps, Symington mused, "we are being so secretive about such an obvious operation" because the administration detected the parallels between events in Thailand and the early stages of the Vietnam War.[10] (Bundy countered that "sophisticated" citizens could find all that they needed to know about Thai affairs in the *New York Times*,

---

[5] Stuart Symington to President Kennedy, 21 Oct. 1961, Vietnam General, Country File, Kennedy President's Office File, John Kennedy presidential Library.

[6] Harry McPherson to President Johnson, 2 March 1966, Office Files of Harry McPherson, Lyndon Johnson presidential Library.

[7] *ESSFRC*, vol. 18, p. 221 (25 Jan. 1966).

[8] Henry Wilson, "Memorandum for the President," 18 Feb. 1966, Box 146, White House Confidential File, Lyndon Johnson presidential Library.

[9] Stuart Symington to Walston Cubb, 20 May 1966, Folder 4946, Stuart Symington Papers, University of Missouri; Flora Lewis, "Education of a Senator," *Atlantic Monthly*, Dec. 1971.

[10] *ESSFRC*, vol. 18, p. 983 (20 Sept. 1966).

an argument that Symington dismissed as "ridiculous."[11]) Throughout the hearing, the committee's new internationalists, recognizing the significance of Symington's potential shift, deferred to him; White House sources consoled themselves that at least "no member of the Committee really pursued the question of what the Administration would do if the insurgent threat to Thailand became more intensive."[12]

As 1966 progressed, Symington distanced himself from the intellectual and social environment of the Armed Services Committee, dropping out of regular Wednesday morning Armed Services breakfast meeting discussions of international affairs coordinated by John Stennis. He instead spent more time with his Foreign Relations Committee colleagues, for instance joining Albert Gore, Eugene McCarthy, and Frank Church in an evening of brainstorming about future policy toward China.[13] Symington's social habits foreshadowed a more significant ideological break with Stennis during the 1966 PIS hearings, which the Missouri senator wanted to focus on the "fairyland" belief that the United States could indefinitely afford the costs of containment.[14] Stennis declined the request, and so Symington went public with his concerns. When pressed by Dean Rusk – who received much warmer treatment before the PIS than he had during the Fulbright Hearings – as to where specifically he recommended scaling back, Symington suggested Thailand.[15]

All of a sudden, this formerly predictable senator had become a wild card in the upper chamber's debates. In early 1967, he opened an inquiry on U.S. military aid and arms sales to Iran, Pakistan, and India. Although the senator claimed to question only "whether the governmental machinery is coordinated adequately," his findings sharply critiqued the shortcomings of the military aid program.[16] The inquiry established a pattern to which Symington regularly returned, combining a few spectacular revelations, a crusade for openness, a preference for using case studies to draw broad conclusions about policy, and a willingness to engage in lengthy technical discussions in which his panoramic knowledge of national security issues allowed him to extract information the witnesses wanted to conceal. Denouncing excessive classification in the program in a slip of the tongue that indicated his struggle

[11] *ESSFRC*, vol. 18, pp. 992–998 (20 Sept. 1966).

[12] "SFRC executive session on Thailand," 20 Sept. 1966, Box 283, Country File, National Security File, Lyndon Johnson presidential Library.

[13] Stuart Symington to Albert Gore, 15 Feb. 1966, Folder 4971, Stuart Symington Papers, University of Missouri.

[14] Stuart Symington to John Stennis, 23 Aug. 1966, Folder 1991, Stuart Symington Papers, University of Missouri.

[15] U.S. Senate, Preparedness Investigating Subcommittee, *Hearings, Worldwide Military Commitments*, 89th Congress, 2nd session, pp. 88–95 (30 Aug. 1966).

[16] U.S. Senate, Subcommittee on Near East and South Asian Affairs, *Hearings, Arms Sales to Near East and South Asian Countries*, 90th Congress, 1st session, pp. 4–5 (14 March 1967).

to position himself within Senate culture, the Missouri senator wondered, "What are the members of the Committee on Armed Services [*sic*] supposed to do when we are not even to know of these things?"[17] After the hearings, journalist Chalmers Roberts termed Symington's evolution the year's "most notable shift" in foreign policy.[18]

A few weeks after the arms sales hearings, the normally understated George Aiken remarked that "the manner in which defense orders can be used for political purposes or for the purpose of creating prosperity in one area of the country and administering punishment" to others made it all but impossible for members of Congress to vote against Pentagon appropriations.[19] Statistics confirmed the observation: the 12 years between the end of the Korean War and the Americanization of the Vietnam War in 1965 featured only 22 roll-call votes – in the House and Senate combined – on amendments of any sort to defense appropriations measures.[20] Of these, only three, introduced in the Senate by either George McGovern or William Proxmire (D-Wisconsin), sought to reduce funding. Each attracted fewer than five votes.

Then, suddenly, congressional suspicion about military policy manifested itself in the 1966 amendments to reduce military aid and the 1967 defeat of the Jackson-Tower amendment, and it emerged with full force against the decade's most significant new weapons system – the anti-ballistic missile (ABM). Appeal for the system, which dated from the late 1950s, grew as the United States closed down its nuclear weapon production lines, confident that its triad of 1,054 land-based inter-continental ballistic missiles (ICBMs), 656 sea-based submarine-launched ballistic missiles (SLBMs), and 400 long-range B-52 bombers provided a sufficient second-strike capacity. The Soviets, on the other hand, responded to the Cuban Missile Crisis by expanding their nuclear stockpile, which focused on large land-based missiles and a strategy based on counter-force weapons and missile defense, raising fears that Moscow could be planning for a first strike.[21]

---

[17] U.S. Senate, Subcommittee on Near East and South Asian Affairs, *Hearings, Arms Sales to Near East and South Asian Countries*, 90th Congress, 1st session, p. 79 (25 April 1967).

[18] *Los Angeles Times*, 31 July 1967; *Washington Post*, 17 Dec. 1967.

[19] George Aiken to Betty Lall, 18 Nov. 1967, Crate 39, Box 6, George Aiken Papers, University of Vermont.

[20] For the relevant roll-call votes, see 100 *CR*, 83rd Congress, 2nd session, pp. 8441, 10174, 10177; 101 *CR*, 84th Congress, 1st session, pp. 6247, 8714, 8705; 102 *CR*, 84th Congress, 2nd session, pp. 7982, 10975; 103 *CR*, 85th Congress, 1st session, pp. 10814, 10821, 11246; 104 *CR*, 85th Congress, 2nd session, pp. 10306, 17743; 105 *CR*, 86th Congress, 1st session, pp. 13281, 13316; 107 *CR*, 87th Congress, 1st session, pp. 11508, 14518; 108 *CR*, 87th Congress, 2nd session, pp. 10378, 10381; 109 *CR*, 88th Congress, 1st session, pp. 17813, 17880, 17889.

[21] William Bundy, *Tangled Web: The Making of Foreign Policy in the Nixon Presidency* (New York: Hill and Wang, 1998), p. 84.

A few especially vehement critics of the military, such as Stephen Young and Joseph Clark, questioned the ABM concept as early as 1966, while Robert McNamara's skepticism about the weapon prevented the administration from moving forward. In early 1968, however, pressured by an apocalyptic report from the JCAE about a possible Chinese nuclear threat, Lyndon Johnson requested an appropriation of $1.2 billion for a missile, dubbed the Sentinel, stressing that Beijing would be its prime target.[22] Within the Senate, opponents rallied around an amendment introduced by John Sherman Cooper and Philip Hart to delay the program for a year, in the hopes that the new administration would reconsider Johnson's decision. The duo came upon the issue accidentally: after hearing from a scientist involved in the project that the ABM probably would not work, Cooper's defense policy assistant, William Miller, persuaded the senator that "the Vietnam experience shows that a 'commitment' to a massive ABM system will involve a further draining of energy both intellectual and physical."[23]

The Cooper-Hart amendment produced the first sustained congressional debate about a weapons system since before World War II. With Symington on their side, a congressional attack on the Pentagon featured a figure who all senators considered knowledgeable about defense details – for the first time in the Cold War. The Missouri senator reasoned that deploying the ABM would threaten any chance at détente with the USSR and create a Maginot Line philosophy among Americans. Most dramatically, Symington took on the military itself. "Somewhere, some day, some time," the former Air Force secretary asserted, "the gigantic cost of this Military Establishment has to be reduced."[24] He challenged ABM supporters "to say we have had a proper return on our gigantic research and development [appropriations] in the military field."[25] (The Armed Services Committee had declined to call any witnesses other than Pentagon supporters of the program.) Symington concluded with the obvious, "for the record": that "what I believed in the past, as compared to what I believe today, are two different matters."[26]

The Senate rejected the Cooper-Hart amendment by a deceptively wide 52–34 margin. Johnson had secured the votes of eight Democrats only by promising that he would never deploy the ABM, and instead that he desired the program as a bargaining chip in arms control negotiations with the USSR.[27]

[22] John Finney, "Winds of Change in the Senate," *The New Republic*, 5 April 1969.
[23] William Miller to John Sherman Cooper, 7 Aug. 1967, Box 615, John Sherman Cooper Papers, University of Kentucky.
[24] 114 *CR*, 90th Congress, 2nd session, p. 18210 (21 June 1968).
[25] 114 *CR*, 90th Congress, 2nd session, p. 18214 (21 June 1968).
[26] 114 *CR*, 90th Congress, 2nd session, p. 18400 (24 June 1968).
[27] Mike Manatos oral history, Lyndon Johnson presidential Library.

The combination of Vietnam and the growing disagreements about defense policy explained why 1968 marked the first year since 1950 in which international affairs played a prominent role in numerous congressional contests. Seven leading anti-war senators faced re-election, and in three of these races – Pennsylvania, Oregon, and Alaska – national security issues contributed to the incumbent's defeat. The political climate still was not ready to tolerate a full-blown congressional assault on the basic assumptions of Cold War foreign policy.

In Pennsylvania, the upper chamber's foremost advocate of arms control negotiations, Joseph Clark, stood for a third term. Clark obtained a slot on the Foreign Relations Committee in the mid-1960s to champion Pentagon budget reductions, fearful that "Johnson has no real understanding of general and complete disarmament under enforceable world law."[28] The Pennsylvania senator grew alienated from mainstream foreign policy as the decade progressed; McGeorge Bundy in 1965 speculated that Clark believed that "the Cold War is more our fault than that of the Communists" – but also that he was "in the very uncomfortable position of a man who has plenty of convictions, but not quite enough courage to give them full expression."[29] Perhaps stung by this reputation, Clark displayed more aggressiveness after the Fulbright Hearings, and in 1968, he voted against the Pentagon budget, contending that the more funds the military received, "the better they think they can do the job of acting as the world's policeman."[30]

Coupled with his support for gun control, this record generated strong passions in Pennsylvania. Representative John Dent, a conservative Democrat from suburban Pittsburgh, challenged Clark in the primary, attacking the incumbent for having "been a constant and torturous critic" of the president, an approach that "has unquestionably given aid and comfort to the enemy."[31] Most observers doubted that the congressman, who simultaneously filed for re-election and stopped campaigning a month before the primary, would receive more than 30 percent. That Dent tallied 47 percent foreshadowed problems for Clark in the fall contest against Representative Richard Schweiker, who – reflecting Aiken's observation on the matter – described the Democrat's hostility to military spending as not only a national security matter but also an important economic issue for a state reliant upon heavy industry. Three weeks before the election, when Clark affirmed that he would support reductions in Pennsylvania defense contracts

---

[28] Joseph Clark to Grenville Clark, 4 Sept. 1964, Box 21-W(C), Joseph Clark Papers, Pennsylvania Historical Society.

[29] McGeorge Bundy, "Memorandum for the president," 5 May 1965, Box 3, Memos to the President – Bundy, National Security File, Lyndon Johnson Presidential Library.

[30] 113 *CR*, 90th Congress, 1st session, pp. 20415–20416 (27 July 1967); 114 *CR*, 90th Congress, 2nd session, pp. 9932, 28946 (18 April 1968, 1 Oct. 1968).

[31] *Congressional Quarterly Weekly Report*, 23 Feb. 1968.

as part of a broader decrease in Pentagon spending, several unions rescinded their endorsement. The labor defections gave Schweiker momentum, and he registered a six-point victory.[32]

In Oregon, Wayne Morse also faced primary opposition, from 1966 Senate nominee Robert Duncan, who ran a one-issue campaign focused on Vietnam. Throughout 1967, Duncan led by more than 20 points in surveys, bolstered by enthusiastic backing from organized labor, traditionally a bedrock Morse constituency.[33] The senator fought back, however, and captured a narrow 49–47 victory in the primary. (The remaining 4 percent of the vote went to a candidate whose views on the war were even more hard-line than Duncan's.) In the fall campaign, Morse faced a young state senator, Bob Packwood, who focused less on the incumbent's policies than on his image. "A senator," Packwood declared, "can't be a leader by impugning the motives of others and by assuming he is never wrong"; the Republican suggested that "vilifying people shouldn't be confused with leadership."[34] In the year's closest Senate election, Packwood edged Morse by 6,000 votes, less than one percentage point.

A combination of his opposition to the Vietnam War and his sharp criticisms of military spending also undid Ernest Gruening. The senator appeared to have escaped a serious primary challenge when a probable opponent, Governor William Egan, lost a 1966 re-election bid. Then, days before the filing deadline, the 38-year-old former state house speaker, Mike Gravel, declared his candidacy, with the theme of "contemporary times require contemporary men." In one advertisement, Gravel promised to work for Alaska first, inviting those who preferred to elect a senator who would focus on Laos or Thailand to support Gruening. On primary night Gravel prevailed by six points, and he cited Gruening's "extreme" foreign policy positions to explain the outcome. The incumbent ran as a write-in candidate for the general election, but his 17 percent of the vote was not nearly enough to return him for a third term.[35]

Nationally, the war had a less predictable effect; Church, McGovern, J. William Fulbright, and Gaylord Nelson all won re-election with comparative ease, and their anti-war stances probably helped Church and McGovern in traditionally Republican but generally dovish Idaho and South Dakota. In the presidential contest, meanwhile, both major candidates profited by distancing themselves from Johnson's handling of the conflict: Richard Nixon's claim to possess a "secret plan" to end the war helped him seize a sizable early lead, while Hubert Humphrey's break from the president by endorsing

[32] Robert Sherrill, "SCRAM, SCAD, ULMS, and Other Aspects of the $89.5 billion Defense Budget," *New York Times Magazine*, 19 Oct. 1972.
[33] *Congressional Quarterly Weekly Report*, 27 Feb. 1968.
[34] *Congressional Quarterly Weekly Report*, 18 Oct. 1968.
[35] Johnson, *Ernest Gruening and the American Dissenting Tradition*, pp. 288–300.

a negotiated settlement helped the vice president launch a furious comeback that fell just short on Election Day.

Nixon's election temporarily stifled congressional activism on Vietnam policy, since most critics of the war granted the new president a grace period to implement his "secret plan." Ironically, the decreased attention to Vietnam heightened the spotlight on the ABM. Syndicated columnist Joseph Kraft considered the "central but unnoticed fact" of early 1969 that "the defense establishment . . . is everywhere on the defensive."[36] By the year's end, the Senate had witnessed the most exhaustive attack in U.S. history against a weapons system, and one of the longest debates on any issue in the postwar era.[37]

On March 14, 1969, Nixon proposed a "substantially modified" ABM system, which he dubbed Safeguard.[38] In contrast to Johnson's Sentinel project, Safeguard intended to shield not population centers but ICBM bases, thus protecting America's second-strike capability. Arlen Large of the *Wall Street Journal* correctly predicted that Nixon's decision would produce "one of the great Congressional battles of the century," since critics would use the issue "as a springboard to attack all they see as wrong with the U.S. military establishment."[39]

Both sides were well prepared when the Senate took up what Nixon's legislative liaison, Bryce Harlow, termed the *"Big Issue."*[40] In early March 1969, head counts suggested that 45 senators would oppose the ABM, with only 25 definitely in support; Harlow informed Nixon that victory required "maximum effort, including all-out Presidential participation."[41] Nixon replied bluntly: "Don't let any of our guys go to the bathroom until it's all over."[42] William Saxbe (R-Ohio) claimed that an administration official threatened to withhold patronage from him after he opposed the ABM, while Charles Mathias (R-Maryland) reported that when he called the White House about a regulatory problem, he was told that the administration's attitude would depend on his ABM vote.[43] The White House undertook

---

[36] *Washington Post*, 28 Jan. 1969.

[37] Alan Platt, "Congress and Arms Control: A Historical Perspective, 1969–1976," in Alan Platt and Laurence Weller, eds., *Congress and Arms Control* (Boulder: Westview Press, 1978), p. 1.

[38] *Washington Post*, 15 March 1969.

[39] *Wall Street Journal*, 6 March 1969.

[40] Bryce Harlow, "Memorandum for the President," 3 March 1969, Box 1, Executive Federal Government [hereafter EXFG] series 30 to 31, White House Central File, Nixon Presidential Materials Project, National Archives, II.

[41] Bryce Harlow, "Memorandum for the President," 10 March 1969, Box 1, EXFG series 30 to 31, White House Central File, Nixon Presidential Materials Project, National Archives, II.

[42] Bryce Harlow, "Memorandum for the President," 10 March 1969, Box 1, EXFG series 30 to 31, White House Central File, Nixon Presidential Materials Project, National Archives, II.

[43] Nathan Miller, "The Senate and the ABM: The Making of a Majority," *Washington Monthly*, Nov. 1969.

what one critic termed "one of the most sophisticated and professional jobs of lobbying we've ever seen."[44] The Citizens Committee for Peace and Security, headed by future DCI William Casey, and the Committee to Maintain a Prudent Defense Policy, chaired by Dean Acheson, made the public case for an ABM.[45] With 22 companies in 16 states having a financial stake in the project, major corporations such as Motorola, General Electric, and Lockheed needed little incentive to lobby members of Congress.

The administration counted on one other factor: the institutional strength of the presidency vis-à-vis the Senate. William Miller, coordinating Cooper's anti-ABM effort, reported in February that White House sources did "not seriously consider that the Senate will be able to sustain its present level of opposition activity." Critics faced a "serious dilemma": the upper chamber would not deal with the issue until the Armed Services Committee reported an authorization for the ABM, yet the opposition could sustain itself only through consistent public debates.[46]

Ironically, a procedural skirmish resolved Miller's problem: for neither the first nor the last time in the Cold War, the politics of procedure had broad policy implications. Because of illness, Richard Russell relinquished the Armed Services chairmanship at the opening of the 1969 congressional session, assuming the helm of the Appropriations Committee; Stennis took over as Armed Services chair. Outlining his conception of the position, the Mississippi senator argued that the Pentagon deserved "a chairman who understands their problems and is highly considerate of those problems."[47] In an early assertion of his authority, Stennis scheduled hearings on the military implications of the recently negotiated Non-Proliferation Treaty. Fulbright quickly countered that since Armed Services felt free to trespass on his committee's jurisdiction, Gore's Disarmament Subcommittee would explore the foreign policy implications of the ABM.[48] This move, as journalist John Finney noted, transformed the ABM contest into a "bristling power struggle . . . between two prideful fiefdoms of the Senate."[49]

The Gore subcommittee's membership consisted solely of critics of the ABM; to stack the deck even further, Gore invited both Symington and Fulbright to attend the hearings. The lead witness, before a national television audience, was Defense Secretary Melvin Laird. Laird held his own for the

---

44 Nathan Miller, "The Senate and the ABM: The Making of a Majority," *Washington Monthly*, Nov. 1969.

45 *Congressional Quarterly Weekly Report*, 30 May 1969.

46 William Miller to John Sherman Cooper, 8 Feb. 1969, Box 615, John Sherman Cooper Papers, University of Kentucky.

47 James Batten, "Why the Pentagon Pays Homage to John Cornelius Stennis," *New York Times Magazine*, 23 Nov. 1969.

48 William Miller to John Sherman Cooper, 12 Feb. 1969, Box 615, John Sherman Cooper Papers, University of Kentucky.

49 *New York Times*, 30 March 1969.

hearing's opening portion. Possessed of what one observer described as a talent for "saying nothing, or saying something that isn't responsive to the question," the Defense Secretary created what *The New Republic* termed a "Twilight Zone of confusion."[50]

Then came a cross-examination from Symington that the *Washington Post*'s George Wilson described as having "stabbed at the heart" of Laird's argument.[51] The Missouri senator asked the defense secretary to explain precisely the need for the ABM. Could not the United States launch Minuteman missiles anyway as part of a second strike? The administration seemed to be saying that U.S. nuclear weapons were defenseless without the ABM, contradicting the principles of Mutually Assured Destruction (MAD) and casting doubt upon the entire doctrine of deterrence. (The *New York Times* agreed that Laird offered a "shocking assessment" of U.S. nuclear capacity.[52]) Laird attempted to parry the point, which heretofore had not been raised in any Senate hearings, but Symington's questioning changed the course of the debate. Instantly, Gore, Church, and Clifford Case followed up, with each hailing their colleague's expertise before exploring what Church described as the "terribly important" contradiction Symington had exposed.[53] Laird, whose appearance went several hours beyond schedule, was forced to claim that rebuffing the Missouri Democrat's argument would require him to reveal classified information. As one who had "been around...for some time in this defense field," Symington was not surprised by Laird's response.[54]

After the hearings, the Pentagon launched what the *Kansas City Star* termed "a whispering campaign" against Symington.[55] But public discussion, reversing the customary practice on defense issues, seemed to strengthen the opposition. In the closest vote in the history of the committee to that time, only 10 of Armed Services' 17 members voted to report the ABM favorably to the Senate floor; 3 of the 7 dissenters – Symington, Stephen Young, and Daniel Inouye (D-Hawaii) – also filed a minority report.[56] As the *Washington Star*'s Mary McGrory noted, the "great tide of anti-military, anti-war sentiment that has swept through the country" startled both the

---

[50] *The New Republic*, 18 July 1969; Robert Sherrill, "SCRAM, SCAD, ULMS, and Other Aspects of the $89.5 Billion Defense Budget," *New York Times Magazine*, 19 Oct. 1972.

[51] *Washington Post*, 28 Feb. 1969.

[52] *New York Times*, 14 March 1969.

[53] U.S. Senate, Subcommittee on International Organizations and Disarmament Affairs, Committee on Foreign Relations, *Hearings, Strategic and Foreign Policy Implications of ABM Systems*, 91st Congress, 1st session, pp. 208–213, 242 (13 March 1969).

[54] U.S. Senate, Subcommittee on International Organizations and Disarmament Affairs, Committee on Foreign Relations, *Hearings, Strategic and Foreign Policy Implications of ABM Systems*, 91st Congress, 1st session, pp. 204–208 (13 March 1969).

[55] *Kansas City Star*, 28 June 1969.

[56] *New York Times*, 8 July 1969; *Congressional Quarterly Weekly Report*, 4 July 1969.

administration and defenders of the Cold War culture in Congress.[57] One long-time defense lobbyist confessed, "It feels like 1929 must have felt to Wall Streeters."[58]

William Miller's White House contacts conceded that the Senate pressure had "opened up the issue again," leaving the president "frantically searching for new justifications."[59] Quickly, the administration changed gears, arguing that the ABM would express confidence in Nixon's abilities as commander in chief while providing a needed bargaining chip in arms control negotiations with the USSR.[60] The program's critics also altered course, to counter what they conceded was a "major problem" posed by the bargaining chip argument, which had, after all, swayed a number of undecided senators in 1968.[61] Dissenters framed the issue as one of – in Gaylord Nelson's words – Congress repudiating past practices of "blindly following the recommendations of our military experts."[62] This strategy shifted the focus away from the diplomatic consequences of a negative vote and onto a more procedurally oriented ground of upholding the Senate's institutional prerogatives.

The debate's highlight came on July 17, when 92 senators attended a six-hour secret session dominated by the Jackson-Symington rivalry. Public debate was raw enough: Fulbright referred to ABM supporters as "stooges of the military"; Stennis, after remarking that "I feel like I'm going off to war," shouted at Margaret Chase Smith on the Senate floor; and George Murphy (R-California) compared Cooper to Neville Chamberlain.[63] Behind closed doors, Symington and Henry Jackson traded charts, arguments, and personal insults. (The so-called "Symington Chart," which the Pentagon refused to declassify, showed that even a functional ABM would not provide enough interceptors to counter a full-fledged Soviet attack; humorist Art Buchwald wondered if the administration therefore would decry the existence of a "chart gap."[64]) Jackson countered that the issue was not the ABM's technical feasibility but the intentions of the Soviet leadership. He, for one, understood that the Kremlin's occupants were a "hard-boiled,

[57] *Washington Star*, 15 July 1969.

[58] *Newsweek*, 6 June 1969.

[59] William Miller to John Sherman Cooper, 12 March 1969, Box 615, John Sherman Cooper Papers, University of Kentucky.

[60] 115 *CR*, 91st Congress, 1st session, pp. 20753 (24 July 1969), 21147 (29 July 1969), 22479 (6 Aug. 1969).

[61] William Miller to John Sherman Cooper, 19 March 1969, Box 615, John Sherman Cooper Papers, University of Kentucky.

[62] Gaylord Nelson press release, 28 March 1969, Box 591, Series 1980, Gaylord Nelson Papers, Wisconsin State Historical Society.

[63] 115 *CR*, 91st Congress, 1st session, pp. 20521–20522 (23 July 1969), 20827–20828 (25 July 1969); Margaret Chase Smith oral history, John Stennis Oral History Collection, Mississippi State University; *Newsweek*, 21 July 1969.

[64] *The New Republic*, 18 July 1969; *Washington Post*, 2 April 1969.

unpredictable bunch, knowing little of foreign reality" and desirous of a first-strike capability.[65] Russell concluded the debate: "If we have to start over again with another Adam and Eve, then I want them to be Americans and not Russians."[66]

While in public the Senate revealed its changing attitudes toward the defense budget, behind the scenes occurred some of the fiercest political fighting associated with any national security issue during the Cold War. At the start of April, Cooper's staffers privately predicted victory by a 53–47 margin, although the positions of 12 senators (7 opposed to the ABM, 5 supportive) were considered soft.[67] In "Operation We Shall Overcome," Symington teamed with former defense secretary Clark Clifford to woo wavering senators. (His new colleague, Thomas Eagleton, raved that Symington "perhaps knows more about military matters than any man" alive.[68]) Cooper, meanwhile, preserved the bipartisan veneer of the anti-ABM crusade by lobbying undecided Republicans.[69]

John Kenneth Galbraith rejoiced that the dissenters' momentum proved that "the military suffers from the same mortal weakness of all bureaucracies – the inability to respond effectively to attack."[70] By June, confidence among ABM opponents was so great that Senate staffers chiefly worried that the administration would find a procedural gambit to prevent "a clear-cut defeat for the Pentagon and a clear-cut victory for the anti-ABM people."[71] Fulbright predicted that "if we can succeed in defeating the military forces in the Congress in one instance, it will greatly encourage Congress to proceed in others"; an anonymous Armed Services Committee member asserted, "Congress is ready to kick the weapons habit."[72]

Momentum shifted, however, in early July. Winston Prouty (R-Vermont) had opposed the ABM in 1968 and again in public remarks in May 1969; with his senior colleague, George Aiken, strongly against the missile, ABM opponents counted Prouty as a certain negative vote.[73] But Prouty faced

[65] 115 *CR*, 91st Congress, 1st session, pp. 19859, 19862 (17 July 1969).

[66] Seymour Hersh, "The Military Committees," *Washington Monthly*, Nov. 1969.

[67] "ABM Vote Estimate 4/1/69," Box 615, John Sherman Cooper Papers, University of Kentucky.

[68] 115 *CR*, 91st Congress, 1st session, p. 23044 (8 Aug. 1969).

[69] "Operation We Shall Overcome" memorandum, n.d., Box 615, John Sherman Cooper Papers, University of Kentucky.

[70] National Committee for an Effective Congress press release, 18 June 1969, Box 3, Crate 22, George Aiken Papers, University of Vermont.

[71] Douglas Bennett to William Miller, 9 June 1969, Box 615, John Sherman Cooper Papers, University of Kentucky.

[72] J. William Fulbright to Harold Willens, 17 May 1969, Series 48:18, Box 57, J. William Fulbright Papers, University of Arkansas; National Committee for an Effective Congress press release, 18 June 1969, Box 3, Crate 22, George Aiken Papers, University of Vermont.

[73] "ABM Vote Estimate 4/1/69," Box 615, John Sherman Cooper Papers, University of Kentucky; *Newsweek*, 28 July 1969.

re-election in 1970 against the state's popular former governor, Philip Hoff; White House operatives made clear that financial support depended on the senator's siding with them on the ABM.[74] Privately complaining about his burdens, the Vermont Republican unexpectedly came out in support of the ABM, citing his disgust with the anti-military rhetoric exhibited in Senate debate.[75] On July 19, a few days after Prouty's reversal, Ted Kennedy, who had played a key role in coordinating scientific opposition to the ABM, was involved in an automobile accident at Chappaquiddick. The Massachusetts senator delayed calling the police for several hours; divers subsequently discovered the body of the car's passenger, a 29-year-old secretary named Mary Jo Kopechne. The incident, which crippled Kennedy's national ambitions, left him absent from the Senate for the concluding weeks of the ABM debate.[76]

After Chappaquiddick, Mansfield conceded that the "odds slightly favor the Administration."[77] When Hart described a close vote either way as a moral victory for ABM critics, John Tower gloated, "We don't count moral victories around here. It's the final vote that counts."[78] The Texas senator, who served as the administration's floor leader on the issue, rejected all compromises, arguing that anything short of Nixon's proposal would "materially weaken our defense posture."[79]

By the last week of July, only five senators remained undecided: Democrats Thomas McIntyre, Mike Gravel, Warren Magnuson, and Clinton Anderson; and Republican John Williams. With vote counts showing 48 senators favoring the ABM and 47 opposed, ABM critics needed to secure the votes of 4 of the 5, and it seemed likely that they would receive none.[80] Then, in the days before the vote, everything started going the opponents' way. McIntyre asked both sides to compromise, proposing an amendment to permit construction of ABM radar facilities in Montana and North Dakota while indefinitely delaying deployment of weapons. When Tower refused, the New Hampshire senator came out against the ABM, basing his decision on the "principle of Congressional control of the decision to deploy."[81] Gravel was the

---

[74] *Congressional Quarterly Weekly Report*, 18 July 1969.

[75] Winston Prouty to Gordon Allott, 16 July 1969, Series 7, Box 93, Gordon Allott Papers, University of Colorado; *Washington Star*, 15 July 1969.

[76] *Washington Post*, 22 July 1969.

[77] *New York Times*, 25 July 1969.

[78] Nathan Miller, "The Senate and the ABM: The Making of a Majority," *Washington Monthly*, Nov. 1969.

[79] *CQ Almanac 1969*, p. 270.

[80] Thomas McIntyre to Walter Dunfey, 29 May 1969, Box 11, Series III, Thomas McIntyre Papers, University of New Hampshire; *New York Times*, 16 July 1969; *Seattle Post-Intelligencer*, 18 July 1969; *Wall Street Journal*, 30 July 1969; *Congressional Quarterly Weekly Report*, 8 Aug. 1969.

[81] Thomas McIntyre robo letter, 26 July 1969, Box 11, Series III, Thomas McIntyre Papers, University of New Hampshire; 115 *CR*, 91st Congress, 1st session, p. 20948 (28 July 1969).

next to side with the critics, after a bitter cloakroom conversation in which Jackson informed him, "If you vote against the ABM, it's going to cause you problems around here."[82] (One witness to the discussion remarked, "That's about as strong as one senator ever gets with another senator – maybe stronger."[83]) When Magnuson joined Gravel in opposing the ABM, opponents needed only one more vote to reach the 51 necessary to kill the program.

Through it all, though, Tower remained confident, even hinting that he had one vote in reserve if necessary. Speculation centered on Massachusetts Republican Edward Brooke or Nevada Democrat Howard Cannon, but the day before the final vote, the identity of Tower's secret weapon emerged. The fifth of August opened unusually in the upper chamber, with a figure described by the *Washington Star* as "an attractive woman in a black outfit resembling a nun's habit" disrupting Senate proceedings by proclaiming, "I, Queen Esther, prophesy in the name of Jesus Christ against the ABM."[84] After security removed the queen, Margaret Chase Smith, who had opposed the ABM in 1968 and again in the committee in 1969, asked to speak. "Not since Cleopatra," an observer noted, "have so many Senators listened to one woman's proposition with such interest."[85] Admitting that she found it "neither pleasant nor easy" to criticize a Pentagon project, Smith criticized the "lack of credibility and consistency" behind the rationale for the ABM.[86] This position, however, required her also to oppose Cooper-Hart, since the amendment allowed research on the ABM to continue.[87] Accordingly, she would vote only for her own amendment, a substitute to strip all funds for Safeguard, which attracted just 11 votes.

Smith's announcement sealed the fate of Cooper-Hart. Any chance the ABM's critics had of victory ended when, just as the roll call started, Anderson confided that "Scoop Jackson's presentation was excellent."[88] In the final tally of 51 to 49 against Cooper-Hart, eight supporters of the ABM switched to oppose it in 1969, while four 1968 opponents, all Republicans, reversed their positions in 1969. After the vote, Smith cryptically remarked, "I'm very pleased. I have always been against the ABM."[89]

---

[82] Nathan Miller, "The Senate and the ABM: The Making of a Majority," *Washington Monthly*, Nov. 1969.

[83] Nathan Miller, "The Senate and the ABM: The Making of a Majority," *Washington Monthly*, Nov. 1969.

[84] *Washington Star*, 6 Aug. 1969.

[85] Nathan Miller, "The Senate and the ABM: The Making of a Majority," *Washington Monthly*, Nov. 1969.

[86] 115 *CR*, 91st Congress, 1st session, p. 22643 (6 Aug. 1969).

[87] Margaret Chase Smith to George Aiken, 6 Aug. 1969, Crate 22, Box 3, George Aiken Papers, University of Vermont.

[88] *Congressional Quarterly Weekly Report*, 8 Aug. 1969.

[89] *Washington Star*, 7 Aug. 1969.

A few days later, Cooper and Hart asserted that, despite the outcome, their sustaining an informed debate confirmed "that important issues of security should come before the Congress, as well as the Executive, for decision."[90] From the other side, George Mahon remarked that defense critics "did their homework as they have not heretofore"; Barry Goldwater admitted surprise "at the depth of their penetration."[91] The *New York Times'* Warren Weaver reported that the debate shook "the Congressional military establishment as it had never done before"; Orr Kelly of the *Washington Star* predicted that the fight would "be seen in the future as the beginning rather than the end of a great debate over American defense policy."[92] Senate opposition forced the administration to change its stated rationale for the missile, thus bequeathing Nixon a Phyrric victory that set the stage for the Strategic Arms Limitation Treaty (SALT) I, which curtailed both sides' ABM systems. More important, the new internationalists' ability to dominate the technical aspects of the debate emboldened them to attack other weapons systems. The legislative effects of this change were dramatic: the upper chamber experienced more than 100 roll-call votes on defense appropriations bills between 1970 and 1975.[93] As Bernard Nossiter of the *Washington Post* realized, "a rigorous and critical scrutiny of military spending, conducted outside of the committees charged with this responsibility, now appears to have become a continuing feature of congressional life."[94]

In theory, the Senate vote was not determinative, since the House still had to approve the system. But no one doubted the outcome in the lower chamber. Armed Services Committee chair Mendel Rivers (D-South Carolina) promised that "it is not going to take me $2\frac{1}{2}$ months" to present the bill, since the House would not feature the "anti-militarism gone beserk" of the Senate debate.[95] Under a restrictive rule that limited debate to four hours—confining some speakers to 45 seconds and prompting cries of "shame" and "gag rule" from the House floor – Rivers further manipulated House rules to deny critics of the system an opportunity to introduce a companion measure to Cooper-Hart.[96] The chamber's leading opponent of the ABM, Robert Leggett (D-California), bitterly remarked after the debate, "If the President of the United States is dumb enough to make anything out of this dumb vote, I say God save the United States."[97]

[90] John Sherman Cooper and Philip Hart to George Aiken, 13 Aug. 1969, Crate 22, Box 3, George Aiken Papers, University of Vermont.

[91] *Washington Post*, 19 Oct. 1969.

[92] *New York Times*, 10 Aug. 1969; *Washington Star*, 5 Aug. 1969.

[93] Robert David Johnson, "The Unintended Consequences of Congressional Activism: The Clark and Tunney Amendments," *Diplomatic History* 27 (2003), p. 232.

[94] *Washington Post*, 19 Oct. 1969.

[95] 115 CR, 91st Congress, 1st session, pp. 27960–27961 (1 Oct. 1969).

[96] *CQ Almanac 1969*, p. 286.

[97] 115 CR, 91st Congress, 1st session, p. 28456 (3 Oct. 1969).

The dramatic difference between the House and Senate debates in part reflected the power of Mendel Rivers. The Charleston representative was a caricature of a traditional Southern congressman – tall and lean, with rolling, silver hair, a tendency to employ flowery rhetoric in debate, and a well-known drinking habit.[98] During the 1950s, he shamelessly cultivated his predecessor as chair, Georgia's Carl Vinson; in one speech, Rivers favorably compared Vinson to John C. Calhoun, Henry Clay, George Washington, Robert E. Lee, Stonewall Jackson, Abraham Lincoln, Daniel Webster, John Paul Jones, Jefferson Davis, Thomas Edison, George Marshall, and Sam Rayburn, before concluding, "As St. Paul sat at the feet of our master, it has been my privilege to sit at the feet of Mr. Vinson."[99] (Neutral observers considered Vinson a tyrant; during one hearing, when then-congressman Lyndon Johnson queried, "Mr. Chairman, when can I ask a question?," Vinson snapped, "You just have."[100]) Upon succeeding Vinson in 1965, Rivers maintained his predecessor's autocratic, bullying approach: Seymour Hersh described the South Carolina congressman as "an extremist in tone and style...an avowed and abusive advocate of the military."[101]

Rivers himself admitted that "the lightning of intellect" had not struck "the taproot of my family tree."[102] He was reflexively anti-Communist and pro-military: at various stages in his career, he advocated using atomic bombs against North Korea, invading Cuba, and blowing up Chinese nuclear laboratories. One GOP colleague remarked that "if Mendel was running things, we'd be in World War V."[103] Rivers was most concerned, however, with representing the military before Congress – and receiving tangible rewards for himself and his district in return. His colleague Robert Sikes (D-Florida) once quipped, "If he puts anything else in Charleston, the whole place will sink completely from sight from the sheer weight of the military installations."[104] (Rivers' own version of this joke was, "I don't believe the Yankees will ever pick a fight with us again, because when we get through, there'll be precious few installations left north of the Mason-Dixon Line."[105]) The congressman traveled home on military aircraft, departing from the airport down Mendel Rivers Highway, traveling past a Navy housing project called Men-Riv Park and a seven-foot granite shaft holding aloft a bust of himself (financed by defense contractors). His district, described by one observer as a "microcosm of the military-industrial complex," included the Charleston

[98] *New York Times*, 29 Dec. 1970; Anderson and Pearson, *The Case against Congress*, p. 275.

[99] Anderson and Pearson, *The Case against Congress*, p. 273.

[100] Smist, *Congress Oversees the Intelligence Community*, p. 7.

[101] Seymour Hersh, "The Military Committees," *Washington Monthly*, Nov. 1969.

[102] Anderson and Pearson, *The Case against Congress*, p. 272.

[103] *New York Times*, 29 Dec. 1970.

[104] Anderson and Pearson, *The Case against Congress*, p. 272.

[105] James Batten, "Why the Pentagon Pays Homage to John Cornelius Stennis," *New York Times Magazine*, 23 Nov. 1969.

Navy Yard and Marine boot camp at Paris Island, both of which predated his arrival in Congress, and also a naval hospital, an Air Force base, a degassing station, an Air Force tank farm, a Marine Corps air station, an Air Force recreation center, two Polaris missile facilities, a Marine Corps recruiting depot, a Navy supply center, an Air Force unarmed radar site, and three Army National Guard offices, all of which came to South Carolina after his congressional service began.[106]

For the first four years of his chairmanship, Rivers ran the committee through six like-minded senior colleagues known as "The Junta" – who had, collectively, 43 military bases or plants in their home districts.[107] (For 25 of the Armed Services Committee's 39 members, Defense Department outlays represented the largest source of federal spending in their district.[108]) In 1969, however, the "Fearless Five" – Democrats Lucien Nedzi of Michigan, Robert Leggett of California, and Otis Pike of New York, and Republicans Charles Whalen of Ohio and Robert Stafford of Vermont – conducted an independent investigation of the Pentagon budget, voted against the authorization bill in committee, and then filed a piercing minority report. When the five carried their fight to the House floor, they produced the lower chamber's first dissension on the Pentagon authorization bill since before the Korean War.

Rivers and his allies did all that they could give the Fearless Five an unpleasant experience. The chairman denounced the "Johnny-come-lately military experts" who advanced "their own political ambitions at the expense of our country's international status."[109] Junta member Samuel Stratton (D-New York) attacked the "anti-military hysteria sweeping" the House, while the committee's second-ranking Democrat, Philip Philbin (D-Massachusetts), accused critics of placing the United States "at the mercy of ruthless, reckless, irresponsible leaders" of the Communist world.[110] John Hunt (R-New Jersey), heretofore best known as the only member of Congress to eject a delegation of anti-war students from his office, spoke for committee Republicans in ridiculing the "bleeding hearts who now resemble the babbling of inbred parrots."[111]

On the House floor, the Fearless Five and their followers offered specific, documented criticisms while advocates of military spending countered with personal attacks or absurd arguments. Nedzi introduced an amendment to prohibit the development of chemical and biological weapons and to require the Pentagon to inform Congress of all shipments of existing weapons;

[106] *Congressional Quarterly Weekly Report*, 24 May 1968.
[107] Seymour Hersh, "The Military Committees," *Washington Monthly*, Nov. 1969.
[108] *Congressional Quarterly Weekly Report*, 24 May 1968, 25 March 1972.
[109] 115 *CR*, 91st Congress, 1st session, p. 28465 (3 Oct. 1969).
[110] 115 *CR*, 91st Congress, 1st session, pp. 28439–28440 (3 Oct. 1969).
[111] *Congressional Quarterly Weekly Report*, 8 Aug. 1969.

Stratton dismissed the offering as "demagoguery and headline-hunting."[112] Leggett, meanwhile, introduced an amendment to reduce funding for the proposed B-1A bomber. The bomber, making its first appearance before Congress, was developed in response to fears that the B-52 would soon become obsolete. With a range of 6,000 miles, the B-1 was a technological marvel, but it had serious drawbacks, namely its cost (over $200 million per plane), its necessity (refurbished B-52s could perform many of the B-1's missions), and concern about its long-term utility (a few years after the B-1's scheduled deployment, the Air Force was expecting a "stealth" bomber, which promised to be nearly invisible to enemy radar). Rivers refused even to debate, announcing that, despite extensive Senate discussion of the issue, confidentiality concerns prevented him from explaining how he knew that the B-1 was in the national interest. The House, therefore, would simply have to take his word.[113] It did: the Leggett amendment lost on a voice vote.

The Leggett amendment's fate reinforced the House's reputation as a "haven for hawks." Cold War critics used the Senate's tradition of disorderly procedures and institutional freedom to dominate debate, an invaluable asset in their campaign to build public support. But, as Norman Miller of the *Wall Street Journal* noted, "the institutional controls of the House, commanded by aged men holding politically safe seats, are used repeatedly to block or hamper rank-and-file efforts to attack hawkish positions." This problem created a dual difficulty for House dissenters, who had to confront the leadership as well as the president when challenging mainstream foreign policy.[114]

That said, neither branch of Congress displayed an aggressive attitude on the Vietnam War for most of 1969, frustrated, as Carl Marcy noted in late December, by "the adeptness of the Administration."[115] Opposition members continued to more effectively marshal congressional power against other aspects of the administration's Southeast Asian agenda.[116] Fulbright convened hearings on Thailand in August, worried about the parallels with early stages of the involvement in Vietnam.[117] When the Defense Department withheld details of the U.S.-Thai military agreement of 1962 (because of a clever bureaucratic maneuver by then-ambassador U. Alexis Johnson, the Kennedy administration had given Bangkok an unconditional security guarantee), even the normally taciturn Aiken was enraged: "If we

[112] 115 *CR*, 91st Congress, 1st session, p. 28432 (3 Oct. 1969).

[113] 115 *CR*, 91st Congress, 1st session, p. 28409 (3 Oct. 1969).

[114] *Wall Street Journal*, 10 June 1970.

[115] Carl Marcy to J. William Fulbright, 17 Dec. 1969, Box 9, Carl Marcy Chronological Series, Foreign Relations Committee Papers, RG 46, National Archives.

[116] Ashby and Gramer, *Fighting the Odds*, p. 293.

[117] U.S. Senate, Foreign Relations Committee, *Hearings, Foreign Assistance Act, 1969*, 91st Congress, 1st session, pp. 292, 294, 300, 302 (6 Aug. 1969).

are becoming a military government, and the military is superseding the State Department, or even Congress, then it is high time we found out about it."[118]

As he had in the ABM debate, Symington played a critical role in creating a more aggressive Senate attitude on Southeast Asian matters. As the only Foreign Relations member with extensive Pentagon contacts, the Missouri senator was the obvious selection to chair a new subcommittee to investigate U.S. commitments overseas, a post he used to explore how commitments initially made on narrow grounds expanded into diplomatic obligations despite a lack of congressional approval. This approach allowed him to investigate a host of issues he had raised in other forums: the need for greater foreign policy openness; the obligation of Congress to oversee all aspects of national security policy; the danger that foreign commitments would run up unanticipated costs, thus threatening U.S. financial stability; and the frequently reckless decisions associated with overseas military activities.[119] Symington concentrated on a few countries: Thailand; Spain, a desirable topic not only because of the nature of the Franco regime but because Congress had never approved U.S. military bases in the country; and Laos, where Symington remembered his exclusion by William Sullivan in 1965.[120] With its agenda decided, the subcommittee looked to demonstrate "a slightly different, responsible means for implementing the new Congressional look at defense/foreign relations as against the . . . harangue approach" common among Pentagon critics earlier in the 1960s.[121]

As events developed, Fulbright's hearings subsumed the Thai inquiry, but the other two cases were well chosen. Subcommittee staffers Walter Pincus and Ronald Paul discovered that the United States had stationed nuclear weapons in Spain; moreover, they revealed contingency plans for a joint U.S.-Spanish military operation in the event of an internal threat to Franco's regime.[122] Six months of contentious negotiations between the subcommittee staff, the State Department, and the Pentagon preceded publication of the subcommittee's transcripts on the Spanish base agreement. Symington and his staff also discovered that in 1968 the Defense Department had provided Congress with incomplete documents on the renewal terms; most damaging, however, was an admission by former JCS chairman Earle Wheeler that "by

[118] 115 *CR*, 91st Congress, 1st session, p. 23081 (8 Aug. 1969).

[119] Carl Marcy to Stuart Symington, 2 May 1969; Carl Marcy to J. William Fulbright, 17 Nov. 1969; "Background and Suggestions for Organization of Ad Hoc Subcommittee on U.S. Security Agreements and Commitments Abroad," 24 Feb. 1969; all in Box 9, Carl Marcy Chronological Files, Senate Foreign Relations Committee Papers, Record Group 46, National Archives.

[120] Walter Pincus to Stuart Symington, 6 June 1969, Folder 2197, Stuart Symington Papers, University of Missouri.

[121] Walter Pincus to Stuart Symington, 18 Aug. 1969, Folder 2197, Stuart Symington Papers, University of Missouri.

[122] Woods, *Fulbright*, p. 511.

the presence of U.S. forces in Spain, the United States gives Spain a far more visible and credible security guarantee than any written document."[123] To Symington, the ties with Spain provided a "good example of a commitment which has not only creeped but which has also in the process generated new justifications as old ones became obsolete."[124] Wheeler's revelation triggered a sense of the Senate resolution, which easily passed, denying a U.S. commitment to Spain. Symington noted that the inquiry showed the "simple theory behind the subcommittee's approach: in order to discuss the substance of foreign policy with the men who have developed that policy, a senator – or anyone for that matter – must first make an effort to obtain the facts."[125]

Even more explosive were the subcommittee's findings on Laos. It took over 100 negotiating sessions and five months for the hearing transcripts to be released, and then only with substantial redactions, including frequent deletions of senators' critical statements that did not involve classified material.[126] The subcommittee nonetheless produced the first detailed official account of the secret war in the Southeast Asian nation. As with the Spanish hearings, Symington obtained his share of damaging admissions: that the United States had spent at least $350 million annually in aid to Laos, after having publicly acknowledged only $12 million; and that for nearly 10 years, U.S. planes based in Thailand had been assisting anti-Communist forces in northern Laos, not, as claimed, bombing North Vietnamese infiltration routes.[127] In response, the State Department, for the first time, publicly stated that the United States was assisting "ethnic Laotians" from Thailand and some Thai "volunteers" fighting in Laos.[128]

Though Henry Kissinger privately raged against what William Bundy later denounced as a "politically motivated investigation," at the time, the *New York Times* hailed the senator for developing into a "legislative haymaker."[129] Speaking, he (as always) reminded his listeners, from "the unique

[123] U.S. Senate, Subcommittee on Security Agreements and Commitments Abroad, Committee on Foreign Relations, *Hearings: Spanish Bases*, 91st Congress, 1st session, p. 145 (2 Oct. 1969).

[124] *Congressional Quarterly Almanac 1970*, p. 1013.

[125] Stuart Symington to editor, *Washington Post*, 28 April 1970, Folder 3874, Stuart Symington Papers, University of Missouri.

[126] Walter Pincus to Stuart Symington, 2 Jan. 1970, Folder 2199, Stuart Symington Papers, University of Missouri; U.S. Senate, Subcommittee on Security Agreements and Commitments Abroad, Committee on Foreign Relations, *Hearings: Kingdom of Laos*, 91st Congress, 1st session, p. 366 (20 Oct. 1969).

[127] All military assistance to Southeast Asia was funneled through the Pentagon, placing it the jurisdiction of the Armed Services Committee.

[128] U.S. Senate, Subcommittee on Security Agreements and Commitments Abroad, Committee on Foreign Relations, *Hearings: Kingdom of Laos*, 91st Congress, 1st session, pp. 436–452 (20 Oct. 1969).

[129] *New York Times*, 13 June 1971; Bundy, *Tangled Web*, p. 69.

vantage point of having been a Pentagon official and now being the only member of either branch of Congress to sit on both the Foreign Relations and Armed Services committees," the Missouri Democrat alleged that excessive secrecy had "developed to a point where military authorities often first create and then dominate foreign policy responses."[130] Regarding Laos specifically, Symington considered congressional oversight the only alternative to an executive-dominated approach that had produced a "varied, oftentimes inaccurate and misleading picture" of policy.[131] Columnists Rowland Evans and Robert Novak scoffed that the Missouri senator's preference for transparency would produce "kiss-and-tell diplomacy."[132]

In response to the concerns raised by the subcommittee, Cooper and Church sponsored an amendment prohibiting the introduction of U.S. combat troops or advisors into either Thailand or Laos. In considering the measure, the Senate went into secret session – for the third time in two years, after doing so only twice previously in the twentieth century. With critics clearly better informed than administration supporters, Gale McGee moved to table the amendment (and keep the vote secret). The motion failed by seven votes, ensuring final passage; the Senate ultimately approved the amendment by a 78–11 vote, with 30 senators who had voted for the McGee motion turning around and backing Cooper-Church in public. In a bid to gain the maximum possible support, the sponsors excluded air operations over Laos from the offering, a concession that allowed the White House to save face.[133] Nonetheless, the vote marked the first occasion since before World War II in which Congress had controlled military operations through the appropriations power, and the initiative provided a model for further legislative actions regarding Southeast Asia.[134]

Cooper and Church would soon team on another ambivalent amendment dealing with the periphery of the Vietnam War. In perhaps the most controversial international move of his presidency, on April 30, 1970, Nixon, without seeking congressional authorization, ordered U.S. combat troops to enter neutral Cambodia, in order to "clean out" Communist sanctuaries on the porous border.[135] A few days later, as campuses around the country erupted in protest, members of the Ohio National Guard shot and killed four anti-war students at Kent State University. On May 11, the Foreign Relations Committee opened hearings to consider a Cooper-Church amendment to cut off funds for the Cambodian incursion; Fulbright claimed that

---

[130] Stuart Symington to William Rogers, 3 Feb. 1970, Folder 2216, Stuart Symington Papers, University of Missouri.

[131] Stuart Symington, "Congress's Right to Know," *New York Times Magazine*, 9 Aug. 1970.

[132] *Washington Post*, 25 June 1970.

[133] *Washington Post*, 16 Dec. 1969.

[134] Bundy, *Tangled Web*, p. 70.

[135] *New York Times*, 1 May 1970.

"next to the civil war, this is the most serious constitutional crisis we've ever faced."[136] At the hearings, both Thomas Pickering, deputy director of the Bureau of Politico-Military Affairs, and Benjamin Foreman, assistant general counsel of the Defense Department, implied that Congress could not prevent the president from supplying Cambodia with military equipment.[137] Mansfield interpreted matters differently, arguing that the American people had appealed to Congress for withdrawing U.S. troops, and "their only hope, I think, is the Senate."[138]

Since a May UPI poll showed 50 senators opposed to Nixon's action, with only 21 (and just 3 Democrats) in support, it appeared as if Cooper-Church would pass with ease.[139] Supporters therefore framed their case broadly, citing what Church termed the "basic constitutional questions" at issue, quiet beyond the specifics of Cambodia.[140] Nixon and his aides responded with a two-track strategy, questioning the patriotism of Cooper-Church supporters while engaging in a de facto filibuster to delay a vote until after the operation's scheduled conclusion. White House chief of staff H. R. Haldeman searched for "inflammatory types to attack Senate doves – for knife in back disloyalty– lack of patriotism."[141] He quickly settled on Barry Goldwater and Bob Dole (R-Kansas) as "gut fighters" who "will really ram them" and would willingly "use the stab in the back line."[142] From another corner of the White House, Pat Buchanan recommended employing Vice President Spiro Agnew in "partisan, iron-booted, hob-nailed assaults on the Congress," looking to "see how much blood we can spill."[143] Nixon approved the strategy: "Don't worry about divisiveness . . . hit 'em in the gut."[144]

Both the vice president and GOP senators responded as desired. Agnew blasted the "Fulbright-crats, the McGovern-crats, and other kind of 'crats' " whose "stock in trade [is] to downgrade patriotism."[145] A few weeks later, at an Air Force Association address honoring Mendel Rivers, the vice president praised the Armed Services chair's efforts "to get communism out of Southeast Asia, to get Russia out of the Middle East, and to get Senator

[136] *Newsweek*, 18 May 1970.
[137] U.S. Senate, Foreign Relations Committee, *Hearings, Foreign Military Sales Act and Amendment: 1970, 1971*, 91st Congress, 2nd session, p. 77 (11 May 1970); *CQ Almanac 1970*, pp. 932–933.
[138] Don Oberforfer, *Senator Mansfield* (Washington, D.C.: Smithsonian Books, 2003), p. 380.
[139] *Washington Star*, 8 May 1970.
[140] 116 *CR*, 91st Congress, 2nd session, pp. 15560 (14 May 1970), 15725 (15 May 1970).
[141] H. R. Haldeman handwritten note, 2 May 1970, Box 41, White House Staff Files – Haldeman, Nixon Presidential Materials Project, National Archives, II.
[142] H. R. Haldeman handwritten note, 16 May 1970, Box 41, White House Staff Files – Haldeman, Nixon Presidential Materials Project, National Archives, II.
[143] Pat Buchanan, "Memorandum to the President," 17 June 1970, Box 139, WHSF – Haldeman, Nixon presidential Materials Project, National Archives, II.
[144] Ashby and Gramer, *Fighting the Odds*, p. 309.
[145] Woods, *Fulbright*, p. 531.

Fulbright out of Washington."[146] In the Senate, Goldwater blasted the "the-oretical foreign policy" articulated by organizations "financed by wealthy groups who do nothing but figure out ways to undercut the United States."[147] The most inflammatory remarks came from Hiram Fong (R-Hawaii), who wildly claimed that "under the Cooper-Church theory, allied forces should never have invaded occupied France to get at the German Nazis in World War II."[148] The attacks served their purpose: as the *New York Times*' John Finney noticed in late May, "what had been cast as a historic constitutional debate was alternately lackadaisical and emotional," polarizing the Senate, often along partisan lines.[149]

When not questioning Democrats' patriotism, Republican senators embraced delaying tactics. Throughout late May, the Senate debated a Dole offering to allow the president to override Cooper-Church if he deemed doing so in the national interest. When, on June 3, the upper chamber defeated the amendment, critics quickly introduced another amendment, this one spon-sored by Robert Byrd (D-West Virginia), denying that Cooper-Church would preclude the president from taking all actions necessary to protect U.S. troops in South Vietnam, Nixon's stated justification for the incursion into Cambo-dia. Contrary to his later image as a senatorial baron, Byrd in the early 1970s possessed a reputation, according to one Senate staffer, as a "king's man" who believed "that the President should not be restrained by legislative action in matters of foreign affairs and national security."[150] The Byrd amendment consumed a week of debate before narrowly losing, 47–52. (When Senate galleries broke into applause after the vote, Agnew threatened to toss the spectators out of the chamber.[151]) Commentator Spencer Rich termed the result a "stunning defeat for President Nixon," since the last four sena-tors to make up their minds – Republicans Margaret Chase Smith and Bob Packwood, Democrats William Spong and Jennings Randolph – all voted against the amendment.[152]

A Church staffer considered the outcome "the *key* to the whole Cambo-dia debate" – prematurely, as it turned out.[153] After the Byrd amendment's defeat, conservatives quickly rallied around a new offering, sponsored by Robert Griffin (R-Michigan), to allow the United States to enter into con-tracts with other nations, such as Thailand, to have their troops fight in

---

[146] 116 CR, 91st Congress, 2nd session, p. 28476 (31 Aug. 1970).

[147] 116 CR, 91st Congress, 2nd session, p. S10283 (30 June 1970).

[148] 116 CR, 91st Congress, 2nd session, p. 16378 (20 May 1970).

[149] *New York Times*, 27 May 1970.

[150] William Miller to John Sherman Cooper, 17 May 1972, Box 642, John Sherman Cooper Papers, University of Kentucky.

[151] *Washington Star*, 13 June 1970.

[152] *Washington Post*, 13 June 1970.

[153] Tom Dine to William Miller, 7 June 1970, Box 632, John Sherman Cooper Papers, University of Kentucky.

Cambodia. (Jackson approvingly quoted Machiavelli to rationalize what opponents denounced as the "mercenary amendment."[154]) In the closest vote of the Cooper-Church struggle, Griffin's proposal initially passed, 47–46. But upon reconsideration, Walter Mondale (D-Minnesota), who had missed the first tally, arrived in the Senate chamber, while Allen Ellender, who privately opposed much of Nixon's foreign policy, conveniently absented himself after having initially favored the amendment.[155]

As it became increasingly clear that administration supporters would continue to offer delaying amendments, Cooper-Church supporters attempted to appease the critics – but only wound up weakening the amendment. In mid-May, Mansfield introduced a preamble deeming the amendment "in concert" with the president's Southeast Asian policies.[156] Then, a few weeks later, the Majority Leader negotiated a compromise that led to the overwhelming passage of a second Byrd amendment, which reaffirmed the president's power as commander in chief, and which William Miller feared "could be regarded by many, and particularly the youth, as a sell-out."[157] Privately, Church admitted that the modifications met Nixon's constitutional interpretations and timetable (the president had promised to withdraw from Cambodia, regardless of congressional action, by July 1), but nonetheless maintained that passage "would establish the properly shared responsibility between the Congress and the President."[158] Others were not as sure. I. F. Stone lamented that by being "too busy splitting ... constitutional hairs," Cooper-Church advocates had ignored the key issues: "the nature of our foreign policy and the size of the military establishment."[159]

By the end of the debate, Cooper – suffering from what one observer described as a "noticeably quizzical strain" in his voice – admitted, "I'm tired. I don't know what it is, the pressure of the last few weeks or what."[160] Even when the Senate passed his handiwork by an impressive margin of 58–32, Cooper's staffers realized that the action was "of symbolic value"; as expected, the House rejected the amendment by 84 votes.[161] When the leadership closed off debate with a parliamentary maneuver, an exasperated Abner Mikva (D-Illinois) wondered, "How do you go to college commencements

---

[154] 116 *CR*, 91st Congress, 2nd session, p. S10259 (30 June 1970).

[155] *New York Times*, 1 July 1970.

[156] Ashby and Gramer, *Fighting the Odds*, p. 304.

[157] William Miller to John Sherman Cooper, n.d., Box 615, John Sherman Cooper Papers, University of Kentucky.

[158] Frank Church to Harold Hughes, 22 May 1970, Box S212, Harold Hughes Papers, University of Iowa.

[159] I. F. Stone, *Polemics and Prophesies, 1967–1970* (New York: Random House, 1970), pp. 138–141.

[160] *Louisville Courier*, 4 July 1970.

[161] William Miller to John Sherman Cooper, 3 July 1970, Box 615, John Sherman Cooper Papers, University of Kentucky.

and tell of the importance of working within the system?"[162] For six months, a conference committee deadlocked, until finally the Senate conceded to the amendment's withdrawal.

Though Senate new internationalists possessed a majority to restrict funding for operations in Laos, Cambodia, and Thailand, they still lacked the votes on Vietnam itself. Employing the same tactic as Cooper and Church, in early 1970 George McGovern and Mark Hatfield offered an amendment to cut off appropriations for all military operations in Vietnam except those related to the pullout of U.S. troops, with a full withdrawal required by June 30, 1971. Both senators framed their dissent in almost exclusively moralistic terms. "What kind of men have we at the helm of government," Hatfield wondered, who "would deliberately coerce the public into accepting their policies on the threat of being branded traitors," a tactic perfected by Nazi Germany and Czechoslovakia after the Prague Spring.[163] McGovern, meanwhile, chastised Americans for obscuring "the impact of death and destruction on the other side"; to the South Dakota senator, "the case might be made" that U.S. policy in Vietnam was "protecting the profits of the warlord manufacturers of destruction who are so given to toying with the lives of our youth by taking out advertisements in the newspapers dismaying the spread of communism."[164]

With little chance that such rhetoric would woo moderate senators, McGovern, Hatfield, and their allies returned to the Vietnam strategy employed by Morse and Gruening – rallying public opinion to pressure wavering senators. That this tactic – almost wholly ineffective in the mid-1960s – had some chance of success signified the major shift in public attitudes on the war. The new internationalists' most innovative effort came in purchasing 30 minutes of television time on NBC (at a cost of $70,000), during which Church, McGovern, Hatfield, Harold Hughes, and Charles Goodell (R-New York) made their case.[165] Senate discussion of the amendment lasted throughout the summer of 1970; on September 1, McGovern closed off debate with an emotionally charged speech claiming that as "every senator in this chamber is partly responsible for sending 50,000 young Americans to an early grave, . . . this chamber reeks of blood."[166] Administration backers unsurprisingly attacked the motives of the amendment's backers, but, more important, two key Republicans – Cooper and Aiken – believed that the offering went too far. When the amendment lost, 55–39, Press Secretary Ron Ziegler hailed the "overwhelming victory" as a "solid vote of

[162] *CQ Almanac 1970*, p. 946.
[163] Mark Hatfield press release, 18 Aug. 1970, Box 1552, George McGovern Papers, Princeton University.
[164] George McGovern to Leo Miller, 7 Nov. 1979, Box 1437, George McGovern Papers, Princeton University; George McGovern to Robert Anson, 2 Nov. 1970, Box 1552, George McGovern Papers, Princeton University.
[165] *New York Times*, 13 May 1970.
[166] 116 CR, 91st Congress, 2nd session, p. 32195 (1 Sept. 1970).

confidence" in Nixon's policy; Agnew praised the Senate for rejecting a "blueprint for the first defeat in the history of the United States."[167]

As had been the case in 1969, however, Nixon's congressional critics performed more impressively on issues beyond Southeast Asia. For instance, Congress strongly challenged the national security state during debates over the Foreign Military Sales (FMS) program, what one Pentagon official termed "a deliberate and comprehensive attempt" to neutralize congressional criticisms of military assistance.[168] Convinced that "the only thing we can do is to cut the funds," Fulbright led a successful effort to scale back and to place policy-related restrictions on the program.[169] The only major defeat for FMS critics provided a moral victory, when a Hartke amendment to exclude the Greek military government from the program fell short by only two votes. Strom Thurmond admitted that "the narrow margin of victory on the Hartke amendment and other similar legislation is not too encouraging for those of us who seek to maintain a strong America and secure America in a leadership role for the Free World."[170]

A similar pattern of congressional assertiveness appeared on other 1970 military-related measures. At the start of the session, John Finney reported that "the loose, bipartisan confederation of Pentagon critics in the Senate enters this year's battle over the defense bill convinced that it is better prepared than last year."[171] The movement's newest asset was a group launched in 1967, Members of Congress for Peace through Law (MCPL), which Representative Paul McCloskey (R-California) described as a "rebel organization" against "the close tie between the administration and committee chairmen who have a monopoly on information."[172] By 1970, MCPL claimed a membership of 28 senators and 70 representatives, one-third of whom were Republican.

In an effort that involved 60 congressional offices, MCPL produced a 200-page report on the 1970 defense bill and staff studies on individual weapons systems.[173] According to Hatfield, the group wanted to undertake a "broad overview of our defense posture," rather than to focus solely on individual weapons systems, as critics had done in 1969.[174] In this sense, the Oregon senator maintained, the dissenters' activity reflected

[167] *Washington Post*, 2 Sept. 1970; *Congressional Quarterly Weekly Report*, 21 Aug. 1970.
[168] Henry Kuss, Jr. to John Tower, 4 Sept. 1968, Box 909, John Tower Papers, Southwestern University; Garrett, "Arms Transfers...," p. 193.
[169] U.S. Senate, Foreign Relations Committee, *Hearings, Foreign Military Sales Act Amendment: 1970, 1971*, 91st Congress, 2nd session, p. 127 (11 May 1970).
[170] Strom Thurmond to Chris Levintis, 7 July 1970, Box 26, Military Assistant Series, Strom Thurmond Papers, Clemson University.
[171] *New York Times*, 16 April 1970.
[172] *Congressional Quarterly Weekly Report*, 31 July 1970.
[173] *National Journal*, 16 May 1970.
[174] Mark Hatfield to Thomas Foley, 17 Feb. 1970, Box 53, FPD Series, Henry Jackson Papers, University of Washington.

the belief that "the constitutional responsibility for making judgment about national security matters was shared, at least to some extent, by all members of Congress."[175] Along with the emergence of more pragmatic anti-military groups, such as the Council for a Livable World (headed by Thomas Halstead, a former ACDA official), MCPL allowed Pentagon critics to match the strength of the pro-defense lobby for the first time.[176]

Amendments introduced by new internationalists consumed most of the month-long debate on the defense measure. Fulbright sought to limit funding for the Pentagon's public relations office, which he considered guilty of the "worst kind of deception" during the ABM debate.[177] Brooke proposed an amendment to block deployment of multiple independently targeted reentry vehicles (MIRV), which he considered an impediment to arms control, since they would render numerical missile restrictions meaningless by expanding the number of warheads individual missiles could carry.[178] The Senate had every right, the Massachusetts Republican asserted, to "tender its advice concerning the larger problems of the arms race."[179] Clifford Case sponsored an amendment to strike funding for the CVAN-70 aircraft carrier, contending that such a vessel would have use only as "a major instrument of intervention," and therefore "must be considered within the larger context of our national interests abroad."[180] Harold Hughes called for eliminating all funds for the ABM – and received 33 votes, triple the total of Margaret Chase Smith's amendment of 1969. Nelson sponsored an amendment to prohibit funds for the military application of defoliant chemicals, while Gravel proposed a more ambitious amendment to eliminate funding for chemical or biological weapons.[181] Proxmire and Mathias co-sponsored an amendment to reduce $5 billion from the administration's proposed $71 billion authorization.[182]

While each of these amendments failed, they nonetheless demonstrated a willingness more characteristic of the interwar era than the Cold War to use amendments to military appropriations bills to affect broad policy issues. The offerings also allowed defense critics to control the framework of the debate. Stennis privately complained that floor debate left "all of these

[175] Mark Hatfield to Strom Thurmond, 7 April 1970, Box 2, Military Assistant Series, Strom Thurmond Papers, Clemson University.
[176] Edward Lawrence, "The Changing Role of Congress in Defense Policymaking," *Journal of Conflict Resolution* 20 (1976), p. 222.
[177] 116 CR, 91st Congress, 2nd session, p. 25938 (29 July 1970).
[178] 116 CR, 91st Congress, 2nd session, p. 10304 (3 April 1970).
[179] Edward Brooke to George McGovern, n.d. [1969], Box 657, George McGovern Papers, Princeton University.
[180] U.S. Senate, Joint Subcommittee on the CVAN-70 Aircraft Carrier, *Hearings, CVAN-70 Aircraft Carrier*, 91st Congress, 2nd session, p. 178 (8 April 1970).
[181] 116 CR, 91st Congress, 2nd session, p. 22018 (29 June 1970).
[182] *CQ Almanac 1970*, p. 406.

items – major items – under the control of the Senators who are really attacking them."[183] Searching for an explanation, some conservatives faulted the military itself. Both Thurmond and Peter Dominick (R-Colorado) demanded a more resourceful Pentagon public relations office: Thurmond cited the need "to mold public opinion in favor of the military," while Dominick wanted to target "the group of [age] 30 and below."[184] Stennis, meanwhile, complained that Pentagon witnesses too often emphasized "the military strength of the Soviets," thereby "downgrading our own forces" and unintentionally making it seem as if the Defense Department had wasted previous military appropriations.[185]

Given public sentiment, Pentagon supporters tried to appease defense critics. John Finney reported that for Stennis, the 1969 ABM fight "left an indelible impression on him and in many ways changed his perspective and political way of life."[186] The Mississippi senator certainly was better prepared in 1970: he demanded "all of these facts and points in advance of the beginning of this bill," and in a jargon-free format, since "I cannot use a memorandum where I have to stop and figure out what abbreviations may mean."[187] The Armed Services Committee chair nonetheless made an enormous concession before the debate even started, supporting a nearly $2 billion cut in the committee authorization level. Conservatives did not attempt to hide their displeasure of the move: Thurmond announced that he would support the measure only with "misgivings and reservations," while former JCS chairman Earle Wheeler warned that the congressional cuts fell "at the borderline of acceptable military risk."[188]

Defense critics' relentless pressure also had an unexpected effect in the House. One staffer in the lower chamber noted that "it may be that what we are doing here is helping create a climate in which [George] Mahon can make the cuts he knows have to be made."[189] The Defense Appropriations chairman, less active in the 1960s than in his first decade as chair, responded. Not only did the Mahon subcommittee slash the authorization request, but the Texas congressman – in what *Newsweek* deemed the most

[183] John Stennis to Edward Braswell, 21 April 1970, Series 43, Box 5, John Stennis Papers, Mississippi State University.

[184] U.S. Senate, Armed Services Committee, *Hearings, Fiscal Year 1972 Authorization for Military Procurement, Research and Development, Construction and Real Estate Acquisition for the Safeguard, ABM, and Reserve Strengths*, 92nd Congress, 1st session, pp. 219 (15 March 1971), 285 (16 March 1971).

[185] John Stennis to James Kendall, 11 Dec. 1971, Series 43, Box 5, John Stennis Papers, Mississippi State University.

[186] *New York Times*, 20 March 1970.

[187] John Stennis to Edward Braswell, 21 April 1970, Series 43, Box 5, John Stennis Papers, Mississippi State University.

[188] 116 CR, 91st Congress, 2nd session, pp. 25757–25758 (24 July 1970); *CQ Almanac 1970*, p. 382.

[189] *National Journal*, 16 May 1970.

spectacular example of "Congress' anti-military complex" – claimed on the House floor that the military's "many mistakes" had impaired public confidence in national security policy.[190] Mendel Rivers, visibly angry, denounced Mahon for "playing into the hands of the enemies of the military, and the other body [the Senate] is full of them"; "keep on saying it," the Armed Services Committee chairman fumed, "and the enemies of the military will love you for saying it."[191] Rivers charged that Mahon's subcommittee lacked "the guts to stand up here and stop some of these crazy programs that we have, for instance, the Job Corps ... But they will go to the military and cut them to smithereens."[192] A public confrontation between Rivers and Mahon, John Finney realized, "illustrated how the changing Congressional climate toward the Pentagon had thrown the military establishment in Congress on the defensive."[193]

Analyzing the defense bill in retrospect, Arlen Large of the *Wall Street Journal* observed that the "frontal assaults" by congressional critics on Pentagon programs usually failed, but "flanking attacks often succeed."[194] Large detected a pattern of "little constrictions, often imposed silently in committee rooms, while the Administration was winning the limelight fights on the Senate floor," with the result that "priorities are slowly being reordered."[195] Congress – especially the Senate – was "asserting a new countervailing force against the vast national security bureaucracy that prospered in the 1960s."[196] In 1969, legislators cut the administration's requested defense budget by more than $8 billion, the largest such reduction, in percentage terms, since the first post-Korean War budget.[197] In 1970, the pattern continued, with Congress ultimately appropriating $66.6 billion in defense funds, 6.3 percent below the administration's request.[198]

The results of the 1970 midterm elections intensified congressional assertiveness. While four strong Senate critics of Nixon's foreign policy failed to win re-election, three (Ralph Yarborough in Texas, Joseph Tydings in Maryland, and Charles Goodell in New York) lost mostly because of intra-party disputes.[199] Only in Tennessee did voters deliver a clear-cut rebuke to the new congressional consensus; GOP nominee William Brock, an

[190] *Newsweek*, 2 June 1970.
[191] *New York Times*, 21 May 1970. That evening, Rivers, as was his prerogative, revised his statement for the *Congressional Record* to eliminate these remarks.
[192] *Newsweek*, 2 June 1970.
[193] *New York Times*, 21 May 1970.
[194] *Wall Street Journal*, 3 Sept. 1970.
[195] *Wall Street Journal*, 3 Sept. 1970.
[196] *Wall Street Journal*, 3 Sept. 1970.
[197] *CQ Almanac 1969*, p. 454.
[198] *CQ Almanac 1970*, p. 415.
[199] Michael Barone and Grant Ujifusa, *The Almanac of American Politics 1972* (Boston: Gambit, 1972), pp. 345, 562.

articulate if uninspiring conservative congressman, complained that "our college campuses are infested with drug peddlers," charged that incumbent Albert Gore's votes against defense programs had betrayed the men in Vietnam, and dismissed the incumbent as "the third senator from Massachusetts."[200] The Nixon administration considered defeating Gore its highest priority in the elections; Agnew visited the state several times, telling voters that Gore should be "removed to some sinecure where he can simply affect those within the sound of his own voice," perhaps with the "radical-liberal friends he hobnobs with up in Manhattan and Georgetown."[201] The incumbent, who trailed in every poll taken, lost by a six-point margin.

While Gore failed to survive his transformation into a high-profile foreign policy critic, Symington overcame the burden of being a self-declared national security specialist who admitted having misjudged the most pressing national security matter of the day, the Vietnam War. Symington's criticism of defense programs also eroded his support among Missouri's business community: the co-chairman of McDonnell-Douglas, Missouri's largest employer and a company that received three-quarters of its funds from the federal government, chaired the finance committee of Republican challenger John Danforth, the state's attorney general.[202] A former divinity school student and heir to the Ralston-Purina fortune, the 34-year-old Danforth had a temperate personality and moderate image, allowing him to run a campaign that simultaneously criticized Symington for having supported a war gone bad and having sided with radical anti-war demonstrators. (A Nixon endorsement hailed Danforth as an example of the next generation of Republicans, a group that compared favorably with young Democrats, who uttered "smutty four-letter words."[203]) In the final weeks, sensing an upset possibility, the Republican flooded the state with advertisements denouncing Symington as suffering from "Senate senility," terming the incumbent a "disgrace."[204] The incumbent, taken by surprise ("I thought this fellow was a gentleman"), slipped in the polls, but he recovered by attacking Nixon's foreign policy and noting that Danforth, who had started the campaign as a dove, welcomed campaign appearances from John Tower.[205] This response reversed the momentum, and Symington prevailed with 51 percent of the vote.

Symington's victory was more typical of the 1970 elections than Gore's loss. (Winston Prouty, however, did prevail, even though the Council for a Livable World made him the sole senator that the group targeted for

---

[200] *New York Times*, 13 October 1970; *Wall Street Journal*, 20 October 1970.
[201] *Congressional Quarterly Weekly Report*, 24 July 1970; *New York Times*, 23 Sept. 1970.
[202] *Washington Post*, 31 August 1970.
[203] *Washington Post*, 31 August 1970; *New York Times*, 20 October 1970.
[204] *Washington Post*, 31 August 1970; *New York Times*, 20 October 1970.
[205] *Washington Post*, 27 July 1970.

defeat, because of his ABM switch.[206]) In House contests, the results trended clearly in one direction, especially in high-profile primaries. In California's 7th District (Berkeley and parts of Oakland), Ron Dellums unseated Democratic incumbent Jeffrey Cohelan after a campaign that faulted the incumbent for his insufficiently vigorous opposition to Nixon's foreign policy. In Colorado's 1st District (Denver), 30-year-old lawyer Craig Barnes, propelled by a grassroots effort staffed by anti-war students, finished 30 votes ahead of longtime incumbent Byron Rogers. And in New York's 19th District (parts of Manhattan), Bella Abzug, assisted by appearances from singer Barbra Streisand, bested Congressman Leonard Farbstein in a campaign where foreign policy played a critical role. As syndicated columnist Joseph Kraft recognized, in 1970 House races presented "the best chance of truly transforming national politics."[207]

The year's most significant House contest occurred in Massachusetts' sprawling 3rd District, which began in the Boston suburbs of Newton and Brookline, with their sizeable Jewish and anti-war constituencies, spread west on Route 2 to wealthy, traditionally Republican Concord, Lincoln, and Lexington, moved even further west to the mill towns of Fitchburg, Leominster, and Gardner, peopled mostly by conservative ethnic Democrats who one commentator described as still having "a 19th-century flavor to their politics," and ended near the New Hampshire line in tiny Winchendon, which billed itself the "toy town."[208] The district's incumbent, 72-year-old Philip Philbin, a onetime protégé of the state's first Irish-American senator, David Walsh, was the caricature of a party hack. Though old-timers still fondly recalled him as "Fighting Phil Philbin," the center on the only Harvard football team to play in the Rose Bowl, a typical day in the House found the congressman arriving early, chatting with friends such as Speaker McCormack, taking a seat near the Speaker's platform, and then falling asleep. The workings of the seniority system, however, gave Philbin positions of power. In both the Armed Services Committee and the CIA oversight subcommittee, he ranked second behind Rivers, whom he regularly supported. Beyond supplying his vote, Philbin contributed little: according to one Democrat, "Phil does nothing on the committee. He has absolutely no interest in the issues."[209]

Philbin was, however, expert at constituent service. Returning home every weekend, he received a steady stream of visitors requesting assistance with federal problems. He regularly attended social gatherings around the district; a piano player during the silent movie days, Philbin often entertained (one

[206] Council for a Livable World, "The Senate Elections of 1970," Box 53, FPD Series, Henry Jackson Papers, University of Washington.
[207] *Washington Post*, 10 June 1970.
[208] William Kennedy, "Father Runs for Congress," *Look*, 22 Sept. 1970.
[209] *Wall Street Journal*, 20 July 1970.

friend described him as "terrific on Gilbert and Sullivan tunes"), and his ability to deliver pork for the district earned him passionate labor support. The incumbent's backing crossed partisan lines: the GOP mayor of Leominster switched party registration to vote for Philbin in the primary, and speculated that 80 percent of his city's Republicans had done likewise. In addition, unlike Rivers, Philbin cultivated his foes. Despite supporting both the Vietnam War and every major weapons system of the 1960s, Philbin's campaign literature described him as a "zealous, untiring worker for the cause of world peace." The leader of one local anti-war group admitted that the congressman "almost sounds like a pacifist" on the campaign trail.[210]

In 1970, anti-war activist and war hero John Kerry hoped to unite the anti-Philbin constituency, but local liberals preferred Robert Drinan, dean of the Boston College Law School. Drinan, a Jesuit priest, campaigned as an unabashed dove; he advocated immediate withdrawal from Southeast Asia and condemned the "merchants of death" of the defense industry.[211] The candidate who syndicated columnist Jack Anderson described as the "fiery Jesuit peace advocate" did not mince words about Philbin, whom he termed "an unthinking rubber stamp" for Rivers.[212] This approach generated strong opposition from party regulars – Philbin's campaign manager dismissed Drinan as "one of those intellectuals, [who] looks down on the mob."[213] But the challenger also assembled an extraordinary base of support: by one estimate, almost 70 percent of the district's households (41,000 voters) received a visit from one of Drinan's 3,000 volunteers.[214]

Drinan had a number of obstacles to overcome: in a district where 70 percent of the voters were Catholic, one poll showed that 35 percent of the district's Catholics considered it improper for a priest to run for political office.[215] Moreover, a third candidate, State Representative Charles Ohanian, jumped into the race at the last minute, splitting the anti-Philbin vote. The incumbent campaigned as usual, in low-key, apolitical sessions; he refused to debate Drinan – citing the press of his duties in the Capitol – and coasted on early summer polls showing him ahead by a 2–1 margin. Even Drinan's own internal polling gave Philbin a 48–16 lead in the early summer, due to the incumbent's overwhelming support among Catholics.[216] But Drinan's effort surged in the final weeks, with the insurgent's campaign telling voters that the primary provided "a chance to vote

[210] *Wall Street Journal*, 20 July 1970.
[211] *New York Times*, 16 June 1970.
[212] *Washington Post*, 10 Sept. 1970; *New York Times*, 16 June 1970.
[213] *Boston Globe*, 30 Aug. 1970.
[214] *New York Times*, 17 Sept. 1970.
[215] *Boston Globe*, 27 April 1970.
[216] Oliver Quayle campaign survey, May 1970, Box 1, Campaign series, Robert Drinan Papers, Boston College.

on the Vietnam War."[217] On a rainy primary day, his volunteers, using computers to identify likely anti-war voters, got their supporters to the polls. In what the *New York Times* termed "one of the notable upsets of the year," Drinan bested the incumbent 49 to 38 percent, with Ohanian trailing at 13 percent.[218]

Philbin refused to accept defeat, and launched a write-in bid. Reversing the passive approach he had exhibited in the primary, he lashed out at Drinan's supporters for seeking to "undermine the foundations of this nation, to promote a bloody revolution and topple us into a totalitarian state"; the priest's mostly young volunteers, he claimed, were "spreading unrest, hatred, violence, and radical ideas" at the behest of "outsiders working to 'liquidate' " the congressman.[219] (One local newspaper termed Philbin's campaign "one of the most scurrilous in the history of the Commonwealth."[220]) Ohanian, meanwhile, denounced Drinan as a radical and endorsed Republican nominee John McGlendon, who positioned himself ideologically between Philbin and Drinan and implied that the priest was emotionally unstable.[221] With Drinan strong in the Boston suburbs, especially Newton, McGlendon and Philbin wooed the mostly ethnic voters in the district's western section; the editor of Leominster's newspaper described that city's Philbin and McGlendon campaigns as "an affront to the intelligence of man."[222] The attacks, nonetheless, had some effect, as most undecided voters broke for McGlendon – but not enough.[223] In a tight, three-way race, Drinan edged McGlendon by two points, with Philbin receiving 27 percent as a write-in; a hand-made sign at the victory celebration proclaimed, "Our Father Who Art in Congress."[224] One Armed Services Committee member recognized the significance of Drinan's victory: "The lesson may sink in, and some votes may change."[225]

Drinan's triumph symbolized a broader realignment in how Congress approached international affairs. In the Senate, the rivalry between the Foreign Relations and Armed Services committees intensified, with Foreign Relations increasingly on the offensive. The Symington subcommittee altered the balance of power between the two: one observer nicknamed it "the Foreign Relations Subcommittee for the Legislative Oversight of the Armed Services

[217] Drinan campaign brochure, n.d. [1970], Box 1, Campaign series, Robert Drinan Papers, Boston College.
[218] *New York Times*, 17 Sept. 1970, 18 Sept. 1970.
[219] *Boston Globe*, 21 Oct. 1970; *Worcester Telegram*, 26 Oct. 1970.
[220] *Hudson News-Enterprise*, 14 Oct. 1970.
[221] *Washington Post*, 2 October 1970.
[222] *Leominster Enterprise*, 27 Oct. 1970.
[223] *Boston Globe*, 29 Oct. 1970.
[224] *Newsweek*, 16 Nov. 1970.
[225] *New York Times*, 29 Dec. 1970.

Committee."[226] In an institution where knowledge was power, Symington repeatedly embarrassed both Stennis and Russell's successor as Appropriations chairman, Allen Ellender, by revealing information, such as details about the U.S. operation in Laos, which Stennis and Ellender should have known but did not.[227] Further confirming the extent of his transformation, Symington tweaked Stennis that "it has never been clear to some of us just what is the relationship, committee-wise, between the CIA and the Senate," and he urged his onetime ally to support establishment of an independent intelligence oversight committee.[228]

By 1970, as commentator Robert Sherrill noted, the Foreign Relations Committee was dealing "with the Pentagon and the State Department almost as one country with another."[229] Articulating an extremely broad conception of its role, Fulbright envisioned the committee as a "forum of free and wide-ranging discussion," thereby providing an "institutional forum" for dissenters who lacked institutional power.[230] As part of this process, the committee trespassed on areas traditionally under the jurisdiction of Armed Services Committee, from weapons systems such as the ABM to the new FMS program. To his dismay, Stennis discovered he lacked a formal recourse; his own top staffer conceded that under the Legislative Reorganization Acts of 1946 and 1970, the Foreign Relations Committee's jurisdiction was "broad enough to justify inquiries and studies...of defense agencies and defense programs."[231]

Meanwhile, the ABM debate shattered the culture of deference to senior Armed Services Committee members. "By developing a competence on the ABM," one commentator observed, "members and their staffs saw that the issue of arms wasn't that complicated...One of the things that had held members back was the fact that they had not wanted to be made a fool of by Stennis."[232] As John Holum, hired by McGovern as a staff assistant on arms control, noted, "The major decisions are made by members of the Armed Services Committee whose only expertise is they've been doing it a few years. Any intelligent person can do the same thing."[233]

---

[226] James Batten, "Why the Pentagon Pays Homage to John Cornelius Stennis," *New York Times Magazine*, 23 Nov. 1969.

[227] 117 *CR*, 92nd Congress, 1st session, pp. 18412–18429 (7 June 1971).

[228] Stuart Symington to John Stennis, 7 July 1971, Folder 2217, Stuart Symington Papers, University of Missouri.

[229] Robert Sherrill, "Who Runs Congress?," *New York Times Magazine*, 22 Nov. 1970.

[230] U.S. Senate, Committee on the Judiciary, *Hearings: War Powers of Congress and the President*, 92nd Congress, 1st session, p.52 (12 March 1971).

[231] James Kendall to John Stennis, 26 Jan. 1971, Series 43, Box 49, John Stennis Papers, Mississippi State University.

[232] Robert Sherrill, "Who Runs Congress?," *New York Times Magazine*, 22 Nov. 1970.

[233] Robert Sherrill, "SCRAM, SCAD, ULMS, and Other Aspects of the $89.5 Billion Defense Budget," *New York Times Magazine*, 19 Oct. 1972.

After Proxmire assumed its chairmanship in 1969, the Armed Services Committee also received an unexpected challenge from the Joint Economic Committee. Noted, according to the *New York Times*, "for long, boring speeches, not much sense of humor, fierce independence, and a knack for remaining in the minority," the Wisconsin senator was listed as the institution's fourth-worst senator in a mid-1960s poll.[234] But as his longtime aide, Howard Shuman, recalled, Proxmire also "knew more about what Woodrow Wilson called the 'informing function' than almost any other senator."[235] The senator put that knowledge to good use in Joint Economic Committee (JEC) investigations about Pentagon budget overruns – inquiries always held when Congress was out of session, when the Washington press corps wanted fresh copy.[236] More broadly, Proxmire recognized that targeting cost overruns could overcome the traditional argument that "senators do not have enough information and are not expert enough to second guess the military."[237] It was not long before the Armed Services Committee elite tried to neutralize or sidetrack Proxmire. Tower advocated encouraging the Wisconsin senator to focus on contracting procedures rather than weapons systems, while Stennis pressed his staff to find "some way to beat Senator Proxmire to the punch."[238]

Finally, Symington's path helped trigger a subtle but significant change in the Armed Services Committee itself. Even before the Missouri Democrat's defection, the committee contained one outspoken critic of the Cold War consensus, Stephen Young. Joining the Symington/Young axis were two Republicans elected in 1968, Ohio's William Saxbe and Pennsylvania's Richard Schweiker. When Young retired in 1970, he was replaced on the committee by a very different type of personality, Iowa senator Harold Hughes. A recovered alcoholic and trucker before entering politics, Hughes thrice won election as Iowa's governor, where he attracted national attention for his religious fervor and his public doubts about Johnson's policy in Vietnam. His victory in 1968 made him Iowa's first Democratic senator in a generation, and also, one commentator observed, "the emerging New Darling of the New Left."[239] Convinced of the "obsolescence of traditional foreign policy in a dramatically changing world," Hughes promised to "have the courage

[234] John Herbers, "What Makes Proxmire Run," *New York Times Magazine*, 10 April 1971.
[235] Howard Shuman oral history, U.S. Senate Historical Office.
[236] Howard Shuman oral history, U.S. Senate Historical Office; *Congressional Quarterly Weekly report*, 2 Jan. 1970.
[237] 116 *CR*, 91st Congress, 2nd session, p. 30275 (27 Aug. 1970).
[238] John Tower to E. L. Hicks, Box 54, John Tower Papers, Southwestern University; John Stennis to Edward Braswell, 8 Nov. 1969, Series 43, Box 97, John Stennis Papers, Mississippi State University; John Stennis to Edward Braswell, 21 April 1970, Series 43, Box 5, John Stennis Papers, Mississippi State University.
[239] James Deakin, "1972?," *Esquire*, Feb. 1970.

to take the steps for peace."[240] He joined the Armed Services Committee because "the committee was unbalanced: there were too few liberals."[241]

Once on the committee, Hughes worked closely with Symington, whom he termed "a firm supporter and advisor" of his crusade against the "monumental defense establishment."[242] The Iowa senator conceded the unusual nature of his political situation – in that "since Iowa receives only a tiny portion of the huge defense budget," efforts to trim Pentagon spending "have not generated much local opposition."[243] With this free pass on Pentagon matters, he could vote his conscience. Some found that conscience grating – one colleague, anonymously, termed Hughes a "fanatic" – but most in Washington viewed him as a "cornfield Bobby Kennedy."[244] Commentator Mary McGrory gushed that Hughes was a "horizon-filling figure" who "looks though he stepped down from Mount Rushmore and who talks about love and forgiveness."[245]

By the early 1970s, then, while Armed Services remained more pro-Pentagon than the Senate as a whole, its members no longer monolithically supported the military. This change reflected a broader shift on national security matters in the upper chamber. In 1967, only seven senators cast anti-military votes on 80 percent or more of national security roll calls. Between 1969 and 1972, however, that number fluctuated anywhere from a low of 20 to a high of 32 (in 1972). Such roll calls, moreover, were occurring with increasing frequency. Between 1957 and 1967, the Senate featured an average of one roll-call vote on defense bills every two years. Between 1968 and 1971, the annual average totaled 20.7 votes.[246]

While committee struggles symbolized the Senate splits on foreign policy issues, the divide in the House fell more along generational lines. Pennsylvanian Thomas ("Doc") Morgan chaired the Foreign Affairs Committee, a body described by one observer as "a cushy berth for hack politicians" that "dawdles endlessly over foreign aid bills."[247] (The *Washington Post* remarked in 1970 that the committee "has been a rubber stamp for the

---

[240] Harold Hughes to Doug Schroeder, 3 Nov. 1969, Box S6, Harold Hughes Papers, University of Iowa.

[241] Harold Hughes to Janis Kapler, 17 April 1974, Box S81, Harold Hughes Papers, University of Iowa.

[242] Harold Hughes to Gerald Goddard, 1 June 1972, Box S207, Harold Hughes Papers, University of Iowa; Harold Hughes to Mr. And Mrs. Kenneth Webber, 8 Sept. 1971, Box S32, Harold Hughes Papers, University of Iowa.

[243] Harold Hughes to Janis Kapler, 17 April 1974, Box S81, Harold Hughes Papers, University of Iowa.

[244] *Congressional Quarterly Weekly Report*, 7 May 1971.

[245] *Congressional Quarterly Weekly Report*, 7 May 1971.

[246] Edward Lawrence, "The Changing Role of Congress in Defense Policymaking," *Journal of Conflict Resolution* 20 (1976), pp. 244–247.

[247] *Wall Street Journal*, 10 June 1970.

executive branch for so long that many people are not aware that it exists."[248]) Morgan himself displayed almost no interest in international affairs; most weekends, he returned home to his suburban Pittsburgh congressional district, where he tended to his medical clinic.[249] He considered the committee a subordinate partner to the executive branch, a view reinforced by his limited work ethic: from 1965 through 1971, he repeatedly resisted calls from younger colleagues to investigate U.S. policy in Vietnam. Such an inquiry, Morgan claimed, would require independently verifying information coming from the executive branch, causing excessive work – a special "concern of the Members who have acquired seniority after years of service."[250]

The seniority system that he so celebrated, however, eventually weakened Morgan's power. In 1971, four relatively junior Democrats – Iowa's John Culver, Indiana's Lee Hamilton, New York's Benjamin Rosenthal, and Minnesota's Donald Fraser – assumed subcommittee chairmanships. The quartet hired new staff consultants, many veterans of the peace movement, who distanced themselves from senior staffers close to Morgan. The result, according to the *National Journal*, was a "more critical appraisal of U.S. foreign policy from the House than anyone on Capitol Hill can recall."[251]

Changes also were occurring, though much more slowly, on the Armed Services Committee. On December 28, 1970, Rivers died of complications from heart surgery, and was succeeded as chair by Louisiana Democrat F. Edward Hébert. (Had Drinan not ousted him, Philbin would have become the new chairman.) Hébert shared his predecessor's ideological inclinations – he once remarked that "the military-industrial complex is a part of us, a necessary part" – but he brought a different temperament to the chairmanship.[252] As Charles Bennett (D-Florida) recalled about Rivers, "If you opposed him, he took it as a personal insult, and while he didn't come out and say it, you got the distinct impression he was questioning your patriotism."[253] The new chairman, on the other hand, initially presented the appearance of fairness: he kept a small cooking timer – an old gift from his wife – to enforce a five-minute rule for questioning, thus ensuring that younger members would have a chance to ask questions.[254]

Hébert, however, lacked his predecessor's institutional clout; within weeks of assuming the chairmanship, he lost a major battle to keep off the

[248] *Washington Post*, 20 July 1970.
[249] *National Journal*, 19 June 1971.
[250] *National Journal*, 19 June 1971.
[251] *National Journal*, 19 June 1971.
[252] *New York Times*, 29 Dec. 1970.
[253] *New York Times*, 10 April 1971.
[254] *New York Times*, 10 April 1971.

committee two anti-war congressmen, Les Aspin (D-Wisconsin) and Michael Harrington (D-Massachusetts). One of Robert McNamara's "whiz kids" before unseating a GOP incumbent in 1970, Aspin had obvious qualifications and strong labor support for the slot; Harrington, on the other hand, the chairman considered completely unacceptable. After capturing a 1969 special election from a traditionally Republican district, the Massachusetts congressman earned a reputation as an outspoken liberal who failed to respect House customs. (He once noted that the Armed Services Committee, "which is supposed to be a watchdog, is really the Pentagon's lap dog."[255]) Since Philbin's defeat entitled New England to a seat on the committee, Hébert recommended Louise Day Hicks, the Boston anti-busing leader who in 1970 won her first and only term in the House.[256] After the New England Democratic caucus, by a 9–6 vote, endorsed Harrington, Hébert unsuccessfully lobbied to reduce the number of vacant committee seats to deny Harrington a position.[257]

In 1971, Congress made its most serious effort yet to end funding for the Vietnam War. In the House, Charles Whalen and Lucien Nedzi offered an amendment to cut off funding, which, though rejected 158–254, marked the first time in which a majority of House Democrats (135–106) supported an end-the-war amendment.[258] In the Senate, McGovern and Hatfield revived their efforts to terminate appropriations for the conflict. To Bob Dole, the ranks of McGovern-Hatfield's supporters "read like a Who's Who of has-beens, would-be's, professional second-guessers, and apologists for the policies which led us into this tragic conflict in the first place"; Stennis scowled that passing the amendment would "be tantamount to the desertion of our American boys on the battlefield."[259] Consideration of the measure followed upon William Calley's conviction on murder charges for the My Lai massacre, but McGovern still could not get sufficient support. And so, 90 minutes before the vote, the South Dakota senator consented to a compromise sponsored by newly elected Lawton Chiles (D-Florida) to cut

[255] Robert Sherrill, "SCRAM, SCAD, ULMS, and Other Aspects of the $89.5 Billion Defense Budget," *New York Times Magazine*, 19 Oct. 1972.

[256] *New York Times*, 1 Feb. 1971.

[257] Such membership turnover slightly changed the ideological tenor of the committee. In the 91st Congress (1969–1970), the average national security index (a rating system developed by the pro-military American Security Council) of an Armed Services Committee member was 86.4 percent, as opposed to a 75.1 percent House average. For the 92nd Congress (1971–1972), the totals dropped to 82.4 percent and 68.1 percent, respectively. Bruce Ray, "The Responsiveness of the U.S. Armed Services Committees to Their Parent Bodies," *Legislative Studies Quarterly* 5 (1980), p. 505.

[258] *CQ Almanac 1971*, p. 310.

[259] John Stennis to Sally Martin, 4 June 1971, Series 33, Box 86, John Stennis Papers, Mississippi State University; *CQ Almanac 1971*, p. 283.

off funds as of June 1, 1972, provided that North Vietnam had released all American POWs. Stennis denounced the offering as a "will-o-the-wisp that is thrown out at the last minute as a lifeguard throws a rope to a drowning man."[260] The gambit drew the votes of four McGovern-Hatfield opponents (Democrat Everett Jordan and Republicans Ted Stevens, Milton Young, and Charles Percy), but the Chiles substitute nonetheless failed, 52–44.

From the White House, Henry Kissinger detected a "clear" pattern: Senate opponents of the war "would introduce one amendment after another, forcing the Administration into unending rearguard actions."[261] Shortly after the defeat of McGovern-Hatfield, Cooper and Church presented their newest offering, to terminate funds for U.S. forces anywhere in Southeast Asia except to the extent necessary to withdraw and protect troops already on the ground, while Mansfield introduced an amendment declaring it national policy that the United States would pull out its troops from Southeast Asia within nine months. The well-timed amendment, introduced shortly after the release of the *Pentagon Papers*, the top-secret study that suggested duplicity in the Kennedy and Johnson administrations' handling of the war, passed 61 to 38, winning support from 10 conservative Democrats and four moderate Republicans who had voted against McGovern-Hatfield.[262] Joe Alsop fumed that the Majority Leader, acting not unlike "a very good, religious man who believes that the earth is flat as a matter of faith," proved that he was "actively, unashamedly eager to see the United States defeated in war."[263]

Fresh off such results, Symington penned a letter to Fulbright speculating that 1972 "could be the 'year of decision,'" in which "we either do or do not establish a position for the Senate with respect to the formulation and conduct of foreign policy."[264] Events failed to fulfill these expectations. McGovern's unexpected capture of the Democratic presidential nomination meant that partisanship would affect all issues associated with his candidacy, even among Republicans heretofore critical of Nixon's foreign policy. In April 1972 hearings on Vietnam policy, Cooper, Jacob Javits, and Case all defended the administration's handling of de-escalation, while exchanges between Fulbright and administration witnesses seemed even testier than usual.[265] Aiken, who exhibited the most dramatic shift, charged that "uncontrollable political ambitions are causing inevitable damage to our reputation

---

[260] *Congressional Quarterly Weekly Report*, 18 June 1971.
[261] Henry Kissinger, *White House Years* (Boston: Little Brown, 1979), p. 513.
[262] *CQ Almanac 1971*, p. 287.
[263] *Washington Post*, 5 Nov. 1971.
[264] Stuart Symington to J. William Fulbright, 6 Dec. 1971, Folder 2159, Stuart Symington Papers, University of Missouri.
[265] U.S. Senate, Foreign Relations Committee, *Hearings, Foreign Assistance Act of 1972*, 92nd Congress, 2nd session, pp. 35, 47 (17 April 1972), 134 (18 April 1972).

throughout the world," to such an extent that North Vietnam was deliberately prolonging the war out of a belief that a Democratic administration would present a more favorable peace settlement.[266]

With the McGovern campaign changing the political equilibrium, the *New York Times'* John Finney sensed that "much of the energy and organization had gone out of the anti-war effort in the Senate."[267] Confusion filled the vacuum. The chief legislative vehicle for anti-war activism in 1972 came in an amendment co-sponsored by Church and Case to cut off funds for the war as of December 31, 1972, assuming a release of all POWs before that date. In response, Robert Byrd – the administration's "friendly neighborhood Democrat," according to commentator Tom Wicker – introduced an amendment to make an internationally supervised cease-fire (which Hanoi was certain to reject) a precondition of cutting off appropriations.[268] When Byrd's offering passed by four votes, congressional efforts to end the war seemed over for the year.

The administration's victory was short-lived. Cooper unexpectedly offered an amendment to cut off all funds for the war by the end of 1972, regardless of the disposition of the POW issue.[269] ("Good God!," Henry Kissinger exclaimed from the White House. "What does this do?"[270]) Brooke and Alan Cranston (D-California) then offered the milder Case-Church amendment as a substitute, after which the Senate experienced a dizzying array of roll-call votes – 11 in one afternoon – that culminated in a vote on a Mansfield motion to table (kill) a Pastore motion to reconsider the vote by which the Cranston amendment, as changed by the Brooke substitute, was adopted. (Nixon denounced Mansfield's act as a "horrible, irresponsible thing."[271]) The success of this complicated maneuver inserted the Case-Church amendment into the final military aid bill, thus establishing, for the first time, a mandatory cutoff of all funds for Southeast Asian operations. In this case, however, the critics' victory was short-lived: Senate conservatives, joined by 13 longtime liberal opponents of military aid, voted against the final bill, which lost by a 48–42 margin, thereby killing the Case-Church amendment.[272]

This legislative disarray suggested the difficulty of Congress micromanaging an ongoing conflict. Beyond the specifics of military appropriations, the

---

[266] George Aiken, *Aiken: Senate Diary, January 1972–January 1975* (Brattleboro, VT: Stephen Greene Press, 1976), entry for week ending 29 July 1972, p. 79; Ashby and Gramer, *Fighting the Odds*, p. 387.

[267] Ashby and Gramer, *Fighting the Odds*, p. 389.

[268] Hubert Humphrey to David Ekvall, 11 Jan. 1972, Box 7, Legislation 1972 series, Hubert Humphrey Papers, Minnesota State Historical Society; *New York Times*, 13 May 1972.

[269] 118 *CR*, 92nd Congress, 2nd session, p. 26384 (2 Aug. 1972).

[270] Ashby and Gramer, *Fighting the Odds*, p. 388.

[271] Oberforfer, *Senator Mansfield*, p. 410.

[272] *Washington Post*, 3 Aug. 1972.

year's major foreign policy developments – Nixon's mission to China, the Paris peace talks on Vietnam – involved matters solely within the purview of the executive branch, with one exception. In a preview of future events, congressional conservatives finally adapted to the new legislative climate and imitated some of the tactics pioneered by their ideological foes.

As Nixon had promised when the Senate approved the ABM, he opened negotiations with the Soviet Union on the issue. Formalized in the SALT I treaty, which restricted each country's total of ABM sites, these negotiations also produced a five-year interim agreement limiting each side's number of ICBMs.[273] Kissinger kept ranking Foreign Relations Committee members informed as the negotiations proceeded, but neither he nor the president consulted their key allies from the ABM fight, most notably Henry Jackson, assuming that as the Washington senator had so consistently supported the administration's national security policies to date, he would back the interim agreement as well.[274]

This decision proved ill-considered. Jackson long since had developed a reputation as an unusually ferocious advocate of increased defense spending, and for reasons not wholly related to national security. Robert McNamara, among others, labeled the Washington Democrat the "Senator from Boeing"; Aiken caustically remarked that "other areas benefit from government contracts, too, but not all their elected members of Congress are as ardent in their endeavors as Scoop Jackson is."[275] In Armed Services Committee hearings, Jackson criticized the loosely negotiated interim agreement, focusing on the numerical advantages that the Soviets received (a necessary part of the bargain because of U.S. technological superiority). Yet with the administration firmly behind both SALT and the interim agreement, passage seemed assured.

William Bundy remembered Jackson as "a man of principle but also of consuming ambition, tinged with jealousy of others whom he considered to have risen beyond their desserts. Exceptionally sure of where he stood, he was courageous and forthright, and at the same time tended to see opponents as foolish, lazy, or even malevolent."[276] Realizing that he could not kill SALT, he decided to use it as a vehicle for ensuring future support for his national security priorities by introducing an amendment demanding numerical equality in any subsequent strategic arms treaty. In seeking co-sponsors, he disingenuously told colleagues that he was only asking for "equality";

---

[273] U.S. Senate, Armed Services Committee, *Hearings, Military Implications of the Treaty on the Limitations of Anti-Ballistic Missile Systems and the Interim Agreement on Limitation of Strategic Offensive Arms*, 92nd Congress, 2nd session, pp. 27, 47 (6 June 1972), 165 (20 June 1972).

[274] Bundy, *Tangled Web*, p. 343.

[275] Aiken, *Senate Diary*, entry for week ending 12 Aug. 1972, p. 89.

[276] Bundy, *Tangled Web*, p. 344.

other senators signed on chiefly as a favor to Jackson.[277] With nearly 30 senators having endorsed the amendment, the Washington Democrat approached the State Department, which, fearful of alienating him, went along.[278] Jackson then presented the State Department's concession as an agreement to support a host of new weapons systems, such as the B-1 bomber and Trident submarine.[279]

As Aiken realized, "Jackson's crowd does not want an effective interim arms control agreement."[280] Ron Ziegler subsequently issued a confusing statement reiterating Nixon's support for the Jackson amendment while disputing "separate elaborations" from senators such as Gordon Allott (R-Colorado), who claimed that the amendment represented a "clear determination not to allow the ongoing SALT talks to be a reason for tolerating developments in which the survivability of the United States deterrent forces is endangered."[281] Understandably not reassured by Ziegler's remarks, the Foreign Relations Committee unanimously voted against the Jackson amendment. Yet when Mansfield attempted to bring to the floor a measure authorizing approval of the interim agreement, the Washington senator filibustered. In the resulting debate, Aiken commented, "the 'Hatfields and the McCoys' have been remanded to the discard, and the Jacksons and the Fulbrights have taken over."[282]

"I am just a country boy," remarked Jackson, consuming time by reading at around one-tenth of his normal speed, "but I think I know what is equality, and what is not, and the interim agreement is not equality."[283] Moreover, since the mid-1960s, Fulbright had spoken of the "Senate being more involved in policy matters"; his amendment simply applied the "Fulbright Doctrine" to a real-life problem.[284] Further taunting his rival, Jackson contended that if the Foreign Relations Committee had thoroughly vetted the interim agreement, there would be no need to explore the matter in detail on the floor; surely, the Washington Democrat mocked, no one wanted a repeat of the Tonkin Gulf Resolution, rushed through the Senate without exploring its implications. Fulbright shot back, charging that with his support for needless weapons systems, Jackson "has done more than any other Senator to

---

[277] Jackson quoted in William Miller to John Sherman Cooper, 5 Sept. 1972, Box 642, John Sherman Cooper Papers, University of Kentucky.

[278] William Miller to John Sherman Cooper, 9 Aug. 1972, Box 642, John Sherman Cooper Papers, University of Kentucky.

[279] William Miller to John Sherman Cooper, 15 Aug. 1972, Box 642, John Sherman Cooper Papers, University of Kentucky.

[280] Aiken, *A Senate Diary*, entry for week ending 19 Aug. 1972, p. 90.

[281] Gordon Allott press release, n.d. [1972], Box 56, FPD Series, Henry Jackson Papers.

[282] George Aiken, *Aiken: Senate Diary*, entry for week ending 19 Aug. 1972, p. 91.

[283] 118 *CR*, 92nd Congress, 2nd session, p. 27946 (11 Aug. 1972).

[284] 118 *CR*, 92nd Congress, 2nd session, p. 27942 (11 Aug. 1972).

destroy the fiscal responsibility of our country."[285] Indeed, it almost seemed that the Washington Democrat wanted to "keep the specter of superiority alive" so he could "frighten the Congress and the people into paying billions more for new weapons systems."[286]

Despite the rhetorical fireworks, Jackson had the votes: a Fulbright amendment to direct future U.S. negotiators to seek "overall equality, parity, and sufficiency" with the Soviet Union rather than strict numerical parity failed by a 48–38 margin. A six-week standoff ended when the Senate passed the Jackson amendment, 56–35, before approving the interim agreement. During a private meeting with the president after the White House signing ceremony, Jackson demanded that Nixon seek the resignation of the ACDA negotiators involved in the interim agreement and that he receive veto power over their replacements. The president, desirous of Jackson's neutrality in the fall election and without much interest in future arms control negotiations anyway, capitulated; between 1973 and 1977, the Jackson-influenced ACDA was almost as hard-line as the Pentagon on arms control matters.[287] Jackson had shown that an empowered Congress did not necessarily mean a more liberal one.

On the surface, Nixon's sweeping triumph in 1972 (the president carried every state except Massachusetts) seemed a crippling setback to the new internationalist vision of a demilitarized foreign policy that stressed economic cooperation, cultural exchange, and ideological issues such as human rights and support for democracy. Yet the president's coattails did not extend into races for Congress, especially the Senate. GOP candidates captured formerly Democratic open seats in New Mexico, North Carolina, and Oklahoma, and surprised a weak Democratic incumbent in Virginia. But the Democrats took six Republican-held seats, in Kentucky, Iowa, Delaware, Maine, South Dakota, and Colorado. Kentucky voters elected a moderate Democrat, Dee Huddleston, to replace Cooper, who retired. The other five states, however, chose the Senate's most radical freshman class in the twentieth century, an outcome that allowed the leftist National Coalition for an Effective Congress to proclaim, "The mandate to Congress is at least equal to the president's."[288]

In Colorado, Floyd Haskell, a former Republican leader of the state House of Representatives who defected to the Democratic Party because of his opposition to the Vietnam War, upset Gordon Allott, largely due to a brilliant commercial replaying some of Allott's more extreme statements on foreign policy.[289] In South Dakota, one-term congressman James Abourezk

---

[285] 118 *CR*, 92nd Congress, 2nd session, p. 27940 (11 Aug. 1972).

[286] *Washington Post*, 1 Sept. 1972.

[287] Bundy, *Tangled Web*, p. 346.

[288] Julian Zelizer, *On Capitol Hill: The Struggle to Reform Congress and Its Consequences* (New York: Cambridge University Press, 2004), p. 111.

[289] Michael Barone and Grant Ujifusa, *The Almanac of American Politics 1974* (Boston: Gambit, 1974), p. 111.

replaced the retiring Karl Mundt after a campaign that promised to bring Abourezk's anti-administration views to the Senate. In Maine, Representative William Hathaway, an early opponent of the Vietnam War, ousted Margaret Chase Smith despite polls showing him trailing for the entire contest.[290] In Delaware, Democrat Joseph Biden, who did not even reach the constitutionally minimum age for Senate service (30 years old) until after the election, retired incumbent Caleb Boggs. And, in the race with the greatest immediate importance, Dick Clark, a former professor and congressional staffer, scored an upset victory over Jack Miller (R-Iowa) by capitalizing on local reaction against Vietnam. Described by one observer as "a spirited and determined academic type, with a puritanical streak," Clark maintained that the aftermath of Vietnam provided "a good time for a thorough re-evaluation of American foreign policy" by casting aside that "the 'answers' of the past."[291]

These new senators entered office amidst an altered international climate. After the massive Christmas bombing of 1972, the United States and North Vietnam signed the Paris peace accords, in which the United States agreed to withdraw all of its troops, in exchange for a return of POWs. North Vietnam was permitted to maintain its forces in the south. Nixon, however, never envisioned a complete withdrawal from Southeast Asia. Congressional action ensured this outcome, with Cambodian affairs providing the first step. Developments confirmed Symington's belief that dissenters could maximize their effectiveness by achieving the technical expertise to intelligently critique national security policy.

In 1971, under prodding from Symington and Hughes, Pentagon officials provided the Armed Services Committee with classified information indicating that no B-52 bombing raids occurred in Cambodia until U.S. forces had invaded the country on April 30, 1970. In early 1972, "back channel" contacts from the Pentagon forwarded rumors to Hughes that, in fact, 3,630 unreported raids had occurred.[292] The Iowa senator had exposed a major scandal, discovering a two-track policy of reporting, with pilots instructed to list false coordinates of bombing runs that had crossed the Cambodian border. Seeking to control the damage, the Pentagon in April 1972 retired the commanding general in charge of the raids, James Lavalle, and reduced his rank from four to three stars.[293] After unsuccessfully pressing Stennis to supply the names of the servicemen who leaked the information to Hughes, the Defense Department then considered the matter closed.[294]

[290] *Wall Street Journal*, 9 October 1972.
[291] Dick Clark to Kristine Kanezi, 8 March 1973; Dick Clark to K. E. Weber, 2 May 1973; both in Box 28, Dick Clark Papers, University of Iowa.
[292] Harold Hughes to John Oswesler, 5 March 1974, Box S81, Harold Hughes Papers, University of Iowa.
[293] *New York Times*, 24 July 1973.
[294] Martin Jensen memorandum, 9 March 1972, Box S151, Harold Hughes Papers, University of Iowa.

Hughes instead demanded "full-scale" public hearings, which he envisioned as assembling evidence for use in courts martial of the relevant Air Force officials.[295] When the Air Force balked, the Iowa senator exercised his prerogative as an Armed Services Committee member and delayed all military promotions that came before the committee.[296] Goldwater threatened that "if this questioning continues along these lines, the Republicans are going to feel it their duty to answer"; Jackson complained that his Iowa colleague wanted to "impair the efficiency of the U.S. military."[297]

Hughes, however, was not easily intimidated. He eventually received public hearings on what he termed "the pattern of deception by U.S. combat air elements in Southeast Asia."[298] The hearings opened with testimony from Hughes' chief source, former Major Hal Knight, who revealed that when he asked his superior officer from whom the Air Force needed to conceal the bombing raids, the response was, "Well, I guess the Foreign Relations Committee."[299] Newly confirmed Air Force Chief of Staff George Brown defended the policy on the grounds that "for falsification to constitute an offense, there must be proof of 'intent to deceive'"; in this case, Brown stated, the reports were "submitted in conformity with orders from a higher authority."[300] While this argument exonerated the individual officers whose promotions Hughes had delayed, it did little good for the president.[301] The Pentagon's chief public affairs officer, Jerry Friedheim, had the thankless task of explaining why the Pentagon had briefed some senators (such as Tower, Russell, and Stennis) about the raids, but not Symington or Hughes. Such distinctions "very rarely" occurred, Friedheim assured the committee, but "the most senior military and civilian officials" decided to follow such a course in this case.[302]

The Hughes revelations helped bring about the termination of all U.S. military operations in Cambodia. In early June, the Senate voted 63–19 for an Eagleton amendment to prohibit using any U.S. funds in Cambodia. The House considered a similar amendment, sponsored by Joseph Addabbo

[295] Harold Hughes to John Stennis, 13 Oct. 1972; Harold Hughes press release, 25 Oct. 1972, both in Box S157, Harold Hughes Papers, University of Iowa.
[296] *Aerospace Daily*, 2 Nov. 1972.
[297] Barry Goldwater to John Stennis, 9 Jan. 1973, Series 43, Box 9, John Stennis Papers, Mississippi State University; Henry Jackson briefing book, 1973, Box 48, FPD Series, Henry Jackson Papers, University of Washington.
[298] Harold Hughes to Stuart Symington, 19 July 1973, Folder 1802, Stuart Symington Papers, University of Missouri.
[299] U.S. Senate, Armed Services Committee, *Hearings, Bombing in Cambodia*, 93rd Congress, 1st session, p. 9 (16 Aug. 1973).
[300] *New York Times*, 24 July 1973.
[301] Richard Moose to Stuart Symington, 24 July 1973, Folder 1802, Stuart Symington Papers, University of Missouri.
[302] U.S. Senate, Armed Services Committee, *Hearings, Bombing in Cambodia*, 93rd Congress, 1st session, p. 71 (23 Aug. 1973).

(D-New York), a Queens Democrat who hardly fit the profile of an anti-war congressman; neither did his chief ally in the effort, Robert Giaimo (D-Connecticut), who nonetheless framed the effort as "an important vote for the House of Representatives – and for the balance of power between the Congress and the President – as well as for its effect in cutting off bombing raids in Cambodia."[303] In its first vote to cut off funds for any Southeast Asian operation, the House adopted the Addabbo amendment.

When Nixon, as expected, vetoed the measure, Mansfield promised to attach the Eagleton amendment to every bill that came before the upper chamber until it became law.[304] After the Hughes hearings, the administration lacked the political strength to continue fighting the issue, and so focused on the fallout. Nixon issued a public letter laying the groundwork for GOP efforts to blame Congress for future U.S. reverses in Southeast Asia, promising that the Eagleton amendment would have "dangerous political consequences."[305]

The Nixon letter provided unintended commentary on how a more assertive Congress had become associated with the new internationalist foreign policy. While Vietnam and Watergate obviously weakened the presidency, the breadth of the congressional surge required figures such as Symington, who wanted Congress to exercise its powers over defense policy in ways that had not been seen since before the Cold War began. One other time in the Cold War – with the revisionists in the early 1950s – congressional power had become linked with a foreign policy viewpoint outside of the mainstream. Then, the revisionists had overstretched, producing a backlash against both their ideology and congressional power in general. It remained to be seen whether the new internationalists would commit the same error.

[303] Robert Giaimo to Curry First, 15 May 1973, Box 80, Robert Giaimo Papers, University of Connecticut.

[304] *Congressional Quarterly Weekly Report*, 30 June 1973.

[305] *Congressional Quarterly Weekly Report*, 11 Aug. 1973.

6

The New Internationalists' Congress

According to John Sherman Cooper, events in Southeast Asia prompted most members of Congress to reconsider "the scope of the respective congressional powers and the President's powers" in war-making.[1] Undoing 25 years of precedent through legislation, however, proved difficult. J. William Fulbright and Mike Mansfield initially championed a non-binding national commitments resolution urging the president to avoid entering foreign entanglements unilaterally. In the House, the second-ranking Democrat on the Foreign Affairs Committee, Clement Zablocki (D-Wisconsin), proposed a resolution asking the president to consult Congress whenever feasible before sending U.S. troops into combat.

Though Zablocki called his offering a "war powers" bill, the more sustained thought on this question occurred in the Senate. Debate centered on a measure sponsored by Jacob Javits holding that absent a declaration of war, the president could commit armed forces only to repel an armed attack, imminent threat of such an attack, or an attack on U.S. armed forces outside of the United States; protect and evacuate U.S. citizens; or pursuant to specific statutory authorization by Congress. When such an action occurred, the bill required the president to report the matter to Congress, after which the operation could continue only for 30 days without a congressional authorization. (In a concession to political realities, Javits exempted current hostilities from the bill's provisions.) Never one to downplay his significance, the New York senator described the measure as "one of the most important pieces of legislation in the national security field" in the twentieth century.[2]

The New York senator considered his approach the most effective way of enhancing congressional influence; he deemed using the appropriations

---

[1] U.S. Senate, Foreign Relations Committee, *Hearings, War Powers Legislation*, 92nd Congress, 1st session, p. 60 (8 March 1971).

[2] 118 CR, 92nd Congress, 2nd session, p. 11021 (29 March 1972).

power "unsatisfactory," since it was "applied after the fact."[3] This "serious imperfection," he contended, explained the difficulties of the Cooper-Church and McGovern-Hatfield amendments: both did not take account of the "natural reluctance of the Congress . . . to cut all supplies."[4] William Spong (D-Virginia), however, noted that his New York colleague's bill avoided a "broad area": reconciling the congressional war-making power with "the doctrine of anticipatory self-defense."[5] For guidance on resolving Spong's dilemma, many looked to the past. Constitutional lawyer Alexander Bickel almost wished "Senator Bricker were here," while in Clifford Case's opinion, "we could use more of the fighting spirit of Wayne Morse, Ernest Gruening, and the late Senator Taft."[6]

To have any chance of passage with a veto-proof majority, the bill required a conservative co-sponsor, and John Stennis, who "began to con-sider steps which we would not ever be placed in a similar position again" as Vietnam progressed, was interested.[7] But the Mississippi senator demanded excluding CIA operations from the bill's provisions and defining the mea-sure's vague prescriptions on presidential power in the broadest possi-ble fashion.[8] Still, with Zablocki publicly terming even this modest pro-posal "unwise and probably unconstitutional," the measure stalled in the House.[9]

The new internationalists played a marginal role in the war powers debates, largely because they considered Javits' approach insufficient. Case, for instance, favored clarifying the legislature's formal constitutional role – but also believed in affecting policy through the appropriations power. In 1972, the New Jersey senator, arguing that "access by the Congress to the terms of all international agreements is a Constitutional right," shepherded through the Senate a measure requiring the president to report all executive agreements within 60 days of their commencement.[10] The bill attracted only six negative votes; though it did not limit the president's ability to enter into executive agreements, Carl Marcy considered the measure the "appropriate

---

[3] U.S. Senate, Foreign Relations Committee, *Hearings, War Powers Legislation*, 92nd Congress, 1st session, p. 6 (8 March 1971).

[4] 118 *CR*, 92nd Congress, 2nd session, p. 11039 (29 March 1972).

[5] U.S. Senate, Foreign Relations Committee, *Hearings, War Powers Legislation*, 92nd Congress, 1st session, p. 324 (25 March 1971).

[6] U.S. Senate, Foreign Relations Committee, *Hearings, War Powers Legislation*, 92nd Congress, 1st session, pp. 457 (26 April 1971), 561 (26 July 1971).

[7] John Stennis to Charles Jacobs, 16 Nov. 1973, Series 33, Box 83, John Stennis Papers, Mis-sissippi State University; Thomas Eagleton oral history, Mississippi State University.

[8] John Stennis to Hooker Martin, 20 Nov. 1973, Series 33, Box 83, John Stennis Papers, Mississippi State University.

[9] *Congressional Quarterly Weekly Report*, 15 April 1972.

[10] U.S. Senate, Foreign Relations Committee, *Hearings, Transmittal of Executive Agreements to Congress*, 92nd Congress, 1st session, p. 4 (20 Oct. 1971).

follow-up on the Symington subcommittee" in that it addressed concerns about ensuring congressional information.[11]

Unlike Javits, Case deemed it insufficient simply to rectify a theoretical imbalance between Congress and the president. And so he introduced an amendment to bar funds to implement executive agreements with Portugal, for a military base on the Azores Islands, and for Bahrain, to assume the lease of a former British military base. (Case adopted this strategy "rather reluctantly because a fund cutoff is, admittedly, a drastic step."[12]) In an argument typical of those who employed procedural approaches to affect policy, the New Jersey senator claimed to have no opinion on the agreements themselves; instead, he affirmed an interest in resolving the "basic constitutional question" of whether the Senate's foreign policy power applied to matters other than "treaties on copyrights, extradition, stamp collections, and minor questions of protocol."[13] In fact, Case, a strong critic of Portuguese colonialism in Africa, hoped to defeat the Azores agreement, and colleagues recognized his motives.[14] John Sparkman considered the Case amendment "against the interests of the United States," while the State Department fumed that it would "dangerously curtail the President's ability to make rapid arrangements for United States use of a facility abroad in an emergency situation."[15] But when Case obtained the votes of seven strict constructionist Democrats who normally supported the administration's foreign policy, his amendment narrowly prevailed.

Congress revived war powers legislation in 1973: the Senate passed a slightly altered version of the Javits bill, while the House approved a weaker measure, giving the president a 120-day grace period for sending troops abroad. The 244–170 vote, however, fell well short of the margin necessary to override a veto. The intentions of many House backers seemed less than pristine: after the vote, one congressman commented, "I think we've made substantial headlines – I mean headway."[16] In a compromise, the conference report granted the president 90 days to send troops abroad before obtaining congressional approval.

As expected, Nixon vetoed the measure, which spokesman Ron Ziegler indicated "seriously undermines this nation's ability to act decisively and convincingly" in international affairs.[17] Just days before, however, in the

[11] Carl Marcy marginalia, in Morella Hansen to Carl Marcy, 28 Oct. 1970, Box 87, Clifford Case Papers, Rutgers University.

[12] Clifford Case newsletter, 28 June 1972, Box 132, Clifford Case Papers, Rutgers University.

[13] U.S. Senate, Foreign Relations Committee, *Hearings, Executive Agreements with Portugal and Bahrain*, 92nd Congress, 2nd session, p. 3 (1 Feb. 1972); 118 CR, 92nd Congress, 2nd session, p. 21356 (19 June 1972).

[14] Clifford Case press release, 5 March 1971, Box 132, Clifford Case Papers, Rutgers University.

[15] 118 CR, 92nd Congress, 2nd session, p. 21359 (19 June 1972).

[16] Elizabeth Drew, "Why Congress Won't Fight," *New York Times Magazine*, 20 Aug. 1973.

[17] *Congressional Quarterly Almanac 1973*, p. 905.

"Saturday Night Massacre," the president dismissed Special Prosecutor Archibald Cox and Attorney General Elliot Richardson, and so Congress approached the override vote in an unusually assertive mood. Ironically, the most vociferous advocate of sustaining the veto was Thomas Eagleton, who contended that the bill "opens Congress to wildly exaggerated claims of 'inherent' Presidential powers where none explicitly exist"; the Missouri senator particularly criticized the exclusion of CIA operations from the measure's scope.[18] But Eagleton's effort to persuade new internationalists to oppose the bill found few takers. "Tom," Gaylord Nelson told him, "I love the Constitution, but I hate Nixon more."[19] The Senate overrode the veto, 75–18.

The Senate's action left the measure's fate in the hands of 14 House liberals – Bella Abzug, John Culver, Robert Drinan, Bill Green, Bob Eckhardt, Ken Hechler, Liz Holtzman, John Moss, Lucien Nedzi, Edward Patten, Edward Roybal, William Clay, Paul McCloskey, and Louis Stokes – who had opposed both the original bill and the House-Senate conference report but whose votes were essential for a successful override. Democratic operatives and liberal organizations argued that the symbolic importance of overturning the veto outweighed any substantive objections to the measure. In the end, eight (Abzug, Drinan, Hechler, Holtzman, Patten, Clay, McCloskey, and Stokes) decided to override, making the tally 280 to 139, or one vote more than the required two-thirds. (Four administration supporters who had promised to side with the White House if necessary switched their votes once it became clear that the override would pass, producing a final margin of 284–135.) *Congressional Quarterly* termed the result a "stunning setback" for Nixon.[20]

Debate over the War Powers Act's effect persists: some argue that its mere existence has deterred presidential interventionism. As commentator Elizabeth Drew foresaw at the time, however, as "Congress tends to deal in indirection, to avoid substantive questions," the reform seemed unlikely to fulfill Javits' expectations.[21] As a result, tactics pioneered between 1957 and 1970 – foreign policy rider amendments, subcommittee government, framing issues for discussion – continued to provide the clearest path to influence foreign policy.

After the 1972 elections, F. Edward Hébert again failed to keep unwanted colleagues off his panel; the Democratic caucus expanded the Armed Services Committee's total membership and filled the slots with the committee's first African-American, Ron Dellums, and its first woman, Patricia Schroeder

---

18 Thomas Eagleton to Arthur Rymarson, 15 Oct. 1974, Folder 4538, Thomas Eagleton Papers, University of Missouri.
19 Thomas Eagleton oral history, Mississippi State University.
20 *Congressional Quarterly Weekly Report*, 10 Nov. 1973.
21 Elizabeth Drew, "Why Congress Won't Fight," *New York Times Magazine*, 20 Aug. 1973.

(D-Colorado). Abandoning the pretense of fairness that he had initially demonstrated as chairman, Hébert went out of his way to make the duo feel unwelcome. After telling Schroeder that he hoped she would not "be a skinny Bella Abzug," he added only one new chair to the committee table, which she and Dellums had to share.[22] (Rather than make a public fuss, the two shared the chair, which their future colleague, Barney Frank, described as "the only half-assed thing Ron and Pat ever did in their political lives."[23]) At one meeting, Hébert peered at the duo and remarked, "There are certain people who make me shudder every time they open their mouth"; at another, after Schroeder criticized the resumption of U.S. bombing raids in Cambodia, the chair urged her to "support our boys like you support the enemy."[24] Schroeder's passion attracted notice in the Senate: James Abourezk considered her "our primary (and most intelligent) supporter" on the committee, since she "gained a reputation among the defense press corps of knowing the business and is well-respected by her colleagues on defense matters."[25]

The committee's most effective critic of the Pentagon, however, was Les Aspin. With a flair for publicity and Pentagon contacts from his time on Robert McNamara's staff, Aspin's office regularly churned out press releases exposing defense cost overruns. (Steven Roberts of the *New York Times* believed that Aspin "had the quickest photocopying machine on Capitol Hill."[26]) More than most newcomers, the Wisconsin Democrat understood that "to most Congressmen, defense experts are people in uniform," handicapping critics' ability to debate individual weapons systems.[27] An amendment to place a ceiling on defense spending, on the other hand, provided an opportunity to cut the Pentagon budget while still allowing military officials to choose where to allocate funds. Moreover, Aspin noted, the approach tapped into skepticism that the Armed Services Committee sought "to find out what the military wants and then try to get it for them" rather than rigorously examining the Pentagon budget.[28]

Despite expectations that the U.S. withdrawal from Vietnam would yield a peace dividend, in 1973 the Pentagon requested a $5.6 billion increase in appropriations. The shift in public sentiment regarding defense issues

[22] Patricia Schroeder, *24 Years of House Work . . . And the Place Is Still a Mess: My Life in Politics* (Kansas City: Andrews McNeel Publishers, 1998), p. 40.

[23] Ron Dellums, *Lying Down with the Lions: A Public Life from the Streets of Oakland to the Halls of Power* (Boston: Beacon Press, 2001), p. 150.

[24] Schroeder, *24 Years of House Work*, p. 41.

[25] James Abourezk to Thomas Eagleton, 12 May 1975, Folder 4354, Thomas Eagleton Papers, University of Missouri.

[26] *New York Times*, 18 July 1983.

[27] James Dillon, "Congressman Aspin and Defense Budget Cuts," Kennedy School of Government Case C14-75-022, p. 3.

[28] *Congressional Quarterly Weekly Report*, 25 March 1972.

was stunning: according to one poll, 50 percent of the respondents believed that the defense budget could be cut without harming American security; 35 percent listed reducing Pentagon spending as the first priority for the new budget.[29] Aspin introduced an amendment to cap the defense authorization measure at $20.4 billion, $950 million below the level the committee requested. He individually lobbied between 35 and 40 congressmen every day in the three weeks before the final vote, discovering a surprisingly welcoming environment. Robert Giaimo spoke for many liberals in asserting, "We're going to cut that damned bill this year"; more surprising, Aspin won support from several cost-conscious conservatives.[30] Richard Nixon's former congressman (and a former John Birch Society member), John Rousselot, co-sponsored the amendment, believing that "Pentagon officials have got to wield a sharper pencil at budget time"; Steve Symms (R-Idaho) assisted Aspin in approaching right-wing congressmen.[31]

On the day of the vote, Hébert remained confident, asserting that "we've murdered ceiling amendments before."[32] The result, however, was not close: the amendment passed 243–176, the first time that the House had reduced an Armed Services authorization level. The two sides explained the outcome differently. Hébert blamed the late hour (slightly after 10 PM) of the vote, which did not give him the "time to explain the stupidity of the amendment."[33] Aspin, more realistically, noted that his colleagues "prefer to deal with issues indirectly and procedurally."[34]

The ceiling tactic represented one way in which procedural initiatives affected policy developments in the mid-1970s. Members of Congress also established new agencies – such as the State Department's Office of Human Rights – thereby creating additional participants in policymaking and expanding opportunities for behind-the-scenes influence. They installed legislative vetoes, which allowed Congress to rescind delegated authority with a resolution not subject to the presidential veto. They utilized conditional authorizations, an especially common tactic in foreign aid bills. And they increased reporting requirements, hoping to deter decisions that would be unpopular if they ever became public.[35]

By the early 1970s, a broader linkage had developed between the idea of altering congressional procedures and enacting a liberal policy agenda. Civil rights provided the connection on the domestic front: beginning in

[29] James Dillon, "Congressman Aspin and Defense Budget Cuts," Kennedy School of Government Case C14-75-022, p. 3.
[30] *National Journal*, 6 Oct. 1973.
[31] *National Journal*, 6 Oct. 1973.
[32] *National Journal*, 6 Oct. 1973.
[33] *National Journal*, 6 Oct. 1973.
[34] James Dillon, "Congressman Aspin and Defense Budget Cuts [sequel]," Kennedy School of Government Case C14-75-022S, p. 1.
[35] Lindsay, *Congress and the Politics of U.S. Defense*, p. 99.

the late 1950s, proponents of equality for African-Americans successfully demanded expansion of the House Rules Committee, which had bottled up civil rights legislation, and unsuccessfully pressed for changing Senate rules requiring a two-thirds majority vote to impose cloture. During the Nixon years, these procedural activists united behind calls for reforming campaign finance law.[36]

On the foreign policy front, the new internationalists also revived another institutional precedent – the role of subcommittee government. In the House, the Defense Appropriations Subcommittee grew far more suspicious of Pentagon authorization measures (even George Mahon privately dismissed Armed Services members as "yes men for the armed services") after Joseph Addabbo and Giaimo joined the subcommittee in 1973.[37] Giaimo focused on "curtailing the excessive spending that has been prevalent in the Armed Forces for many years"; Addabbo, fearful that "we have experienced a serious erosion of civilian control of the military forces," promised that if "new leadership is not forthcoming from the [Defense] Department, Congress will have no choice but to legislate a drastically curtailed program from the Department in the years ahead."[38]

In the Senate, after an early 1973 exposé by columnist Jack Anderson exploring the relationship between IT&T and U.S. hostility to Salvador Allende's democratically elected but Marxist government in Chile, the Foreign Relations Committee established a special subcommittee on multinational corporations, which Church chaired. The CIA tried but failed to shift the inquiry to the Armed Services Committee, where Henry Jackson, who "can be counted on not to comment further on what he learns about CIA or ITT actions in Chile," would chair any special subcommittee.[39] Instead, Frank Church, Clifford Case, and Stuart Symington grilled IT&T representatives, including former DCI John McCone, by this time on IT&T's board of directors, about the company's connections to the CIA.[40] Former DCI Richard Helms and former ambassador to Chile Edward Korry likewise received a frosty reception.[41]

---

[36] Zelizer, *On Capitol Hill*, pp. 47, 57, 100.

[37] George Mahon to Ralph Henry, 9 Oct. 1973; George Mahon memorandum, 19 Sept. 1973; both in Box 274, George Mahon Papers, Texas Tech University.

[38] Robert Giaimo to Robert Oliver, 19 June 1973, Box 80, Robert Giaimo Papers, University of Connecticut; U.S. House of Representatives, Defense Appropriations Subcommittee, *Report, Department of Defense Appropriations Bill, 1974*, 93rd Congress, 1st session, pp. 230, 232 (26 Nov. 1973).

[39] Theodore Shackley to Director of Central Intelligence, 21 Feb. 1973, Box 51, Henry Jackson Papers, University of Washington.

[40] Theodore Shackley, "Memorandum for the Record," 24 Feb. 1973, Box 51, Henry Jackson Papers, University of Washington.

[41] U.S. Senate, Subcommittee on Multinational Corporations, *Hearings, Multinational Corporations and U.S. Foreign Policy*, 93rd Congress, 1st session, p. 135 (21 March 1973).

Shortly thereafter, General Augusto Pinochet led a coup that toppled Allende's regime. In response, Ted Kennedy introduced a successful
amendment declaring the sense of the Senate that the United States should
deny all aid to Chile: "One cannot adhere to values of individual liberty
and then remain silent while those values are destroyed."[42] From Santiago,
Pinochet attributed Kennedy's sentiments to "the extremely active campaign that international Marxism has loosed abroad against Chile."[43] When
the Massachusetts senator protested that Chilean conditions fell "substantially short" of even minimal human rights standards, Pinochet retorted
that Kennedy's actions allowed him to "fully understand, as never before,
what those in my country have criticized as 'imperialism' of certain great
nations."[44]

Mocked Gale McGee, "All of us seem to be playing Secretary of
State on the floor of the Senate at the moment when these questions
are deeply involved in diplomacy."[45] Harboring no such inhibitions,
Abourezk believed that executive machinations had stretched "the del-
icate balance of power provided for by the Constitution...to a point
where it becomes virtually meaningless."[46] Arguing that "we cannot dis-
associate ourselves from the bloodshed in Chile," he sponsored an amendment to permit political émigrés from South America to enter the United
States.[47] Kennedy, meanwhile, convened hearings on the question before a
Judiciary subcommittee that he chaired, and successfully pressured the State
Department to liberalize its policies regarding accepting Chilean political
refugees.[48]

The following year, the South Dakota senator broadened the attack by
sponsoring amendments to prohibit assistance for internal security forces
and to any country with political prisoners. Piqued after learning that the
U.S.-funded International Police Academy (IPA) had trained several Chileans
involved in the Pinochet coup, Abourezk set his staff to investigate the program; when they discovered that some IPA classes featured course papers
on how best to use torture methods, he demanded an end to the program's

[42] 119 *CR*, 93rd Congress, 1st session, p. 32570 (2 Oct. 1973).

[43] Augusto Pinochet to Edward Kennedy, 27 March 1974, in U.S. Senate, Subcommittee on
   Refugees, *Hearings, Refugees and Humanitarian Problems in Chile, Part II*, 93rd Congress,
   2nd session, p. 92.

[44] Edward Kennedy to August Pinochet, 14 May 1974; Augusto Pinochet to Edward Kennedy, 5
   June 1974; both in U.S. Senate, Subcommittee on Refugees, *Hearings, Refugees and Humanitarian Problems in Chile, Part II*, 93rd Congress, 2nd session, pp. 96, 97.

[45] *Congressional Quarterly Weekly Report*, 5 Oct. 1974.

[46] U.S. Senate, Subcommittee on Separation of Powers, *Hearings, Congressional Oversight of
   Executive Agreements – 1975*, 94th Congress, 1st session, p. 3 (13 May 1975).

[47] James Abourezk, "Dear Colleague," 28 Sept. 1973, Box 209, Robert Taft, Jr. Papers, Library
   of Congress.

[48] "Brief Chronology re: Chilean Refugees," Box 314, James Abourezk Papers, University of
   South Dakota.

appropriations.[49] The South Dakota Democrat saw no reason to continue the "irresponsible policy of encouraging the abridgement of human rights in countries which receive our foreign aid."[50] The amendments barely failed, with each attracting 44 votes, and slightly narrower initiatives subsequently passed.

The new internationalists also infused their principles into law using the FMS program. With a firm Senate majority against expanding military aid and the administration's "Nixon Doctrine" calling for the United States to avoid excessive overseas involvement by training and equipping foreign militaries, the FMS program ballooned during the Nixon years. In 1974 alone, a $12.6 million armored personnel carrier went to Pakistan; two C-130 cargo planes (at nearly $12 million apiece) and 25 attack aircraft were sold to Argentina; the Chilean military purchased aircraft engines, aircraft parts, armored personnel carriers, radar sets, revolvers, rifles, and trucks; and a variety of military goods were transferred to Brazil.[51]

Searching for a way to allow "pressures from the public to prevent some of these sales," another member of the 1972 class, William Hathaway, sponsored an amendment to require the State Department to report all details of foreign military sales, after which the sale would be delayed for 30 days pending congressional action.[52] Though it fell short by a vote of 44 to 41, the Hathaway amendment set the stage for passage of a slightly less comprehensive offering from Nelson, which required a presidential report on any arms sale above $25 million and allowed either chamber to block the sale through a resolution of disapproval within 30 days.[53] Mimicking the approach of Case and Aspin, Nelson framed his offering as "a *procedural* step" that would merely "bring the issues out in the open."[54] He privately admitted, however, his policy aim: "Once Congress assumes more control over the arms sales program, hopefully the level of sales will be decreased."[55] After less than 30 minutes of debate, the amendment squeaked through by one vote, 44–43; the following year, the House passed a companion measure sponsored by Jonathan Bingham (D-New York), which modified the Nelson amendment to require a two-house legislative veto.

---

[49] James Abourezk to J. William Fulbright, 30 July 1974, Box 832, James Abourezk Papers, University of South Dakota.

[50] James Abourezk, "Dear Colleague," 27 June 1974, Box 832, James Abourezk Papers, University of South Dakota.

[51] Tom Daschle, "Selected U.S. Military and Police Exports, 1974," Box 657, James Abourezk Papers, University of South Dakota.

[52] 119 *CR*, 93rd Congress, 1st session, p. 21146 (25 June 1973).

[53] *Congressional Quarterly Weekly Report*, 10 April 1982.

[54] Gaylord Nelson article outline, 3 Feb. 1975, Box 590, Gaylord Nelson Papers, Wisconsin State Historical Society.

[55] Gaylord Nelson to Greg Moeller, 7 April 1975, Box 590, Gaylord Nelson Papers, Wisconsin State Historical Society.

Commentator Leslie Gelb astutely observed that the new internationalists' initiatives renewed the traditional debate between realism and idealism in American foreign policy.[56] The emerging congressional majority, however, struggled when human rights concerns and immediate U.S. strategic interests conflicted. Two of the most controversial – and least effective – foreign policy measures of the 1970s resulted.

The Jackson-Vanik amendment united human rights activists, hard-line Cold Warriors, and supporters of Israel in demanding a linkage between U.S.-Soviet economic relations and the emigration of Soviet Jews to Israel. The issue first emerged in 1972, when Jackson sought to use Soviet restrictions on emigration for all of its citizens to scuttle SALT. Gradually, he focused on Jewish emigration alone, after a quickly repudiated decision by Moscow to impose an "exit tax" requiring Jewish emigrants to repay the cost of their state-supplied education.[57] In 1973, Jackson easily obtained a majority to co-sponsor an amendment attached to a U.S.-Soviet trade agreement: as one senator noted, "There is no political advantage in not signing on. If you do sign, you don't offend anyone. If you don't sign, you might offend some Jews in your state."[58] By forcing the issue onto the agenda, the Washington Democrat applied pressure on the Israeli government and the powerful America Israeli Public Affairs Committee (AIPAC), which in turn endorsed his proposal, further increasing the chances of passage.

George Aiken, for one, sharply questioned Jackson's motives. "I don't believe that Scoop actually wants war with Russia," the Vermont senator confided, "but keeping alive the constant threat of war means good business for certain industries that manufacture materials needed in times of actual warfare," many of which were based in Washington state.[59] As the *Washington Post*'s Spencer Rich understood, however, Jackson possessed "an uncanny ability to smell out issues that galvanize the defense bloc into an unbeatable majority."[60] With the Soviets eager to save the trade deal and Kissinger viewing the agreement as a test of Nixon's policy of détente, both the administration and the Kremlin negotiated with Jackson, making the senator, in the words of the London *Times*, "the man who upped the price of détente."[61] One side did not bargain in good faith: as soon as the Soviets offered one concession, Jackson demanded another, and he eventually called for open emigration across the board, not just for Jews. When the Soviets refused, the Washington senator and his co-sponsor, Ohio

---

[56] *New York Times*, 10 Feb. 1976.
[57] Paula Stern, *Water's Edge: Domestic Politics and the Making of American Foreign Policy* (Westport: Greenwood Press, 1979), p. 20.
[58] *New York Times*, 6 April 1973.
[59] Aiken, *Senate Diary*, entry for week ending 8 June 1974, p. 299.
[60] *Washington Post*, 2 April 1973.
[61] *The Times* (London), 23 Oct. 1974; Stern, *Water's Edge*, p. 105.

congressman Charles Vanik, introduced their offering, which easily passed, and Moscow repudiated the trade agreement.[62]

The affair offered a lesson for foreign nations dealing with the new balance of power in Washington. Though the *International Herald Tribune* correctly termed it "one of the more extraordinary gaffes of diplomacy," Prime Minister John Malcolm Fraser of Australia was not off base when he informed the Chinese leadership that congressional influence made the United States erratic internationally.[63]

According to Flora Lewis of the *New York Times*, the "renewed interest of Congress in U.S. foreign policy has begun to trouble European leaders" as well.[64] This concern grew more intense during fall 1974 events in Cyprus. The Greek military regime, in its final days in power, orchestrated a coup in the ethnically divided nation, intending to stimulate a Greece-Cyprus union. In response, Turkish troops occupied the eastern third of the island, triggering a refugee crisis as Greek Cypriots fled to areas still controlled by the Cypriot government. The developments helped topple the colonels' regime, but Turkey refused to withdraw its forces.

In the operation, the Turks used weapons supplied by U.S. military aid, despite a requirement to employ such arms only in self-defense. That the Cypriot crisis occurred simultaneously with Nixon's resignation made urging respect for the law an unusually potent argument, and military aid critics took advantage. As "we have just experienced a period of American history when laws were considered mere 'technicalities' to be rationalized and circumvented to fit the concepts of policymakers," Eagleton introduced an amendment to end military assistance until the Turks withdrew their troops.[65] Addressing an almost full Senate chamber, the Missouri Democrat charged that the administration's refusal to suspend aid conveyed the impression that short-term strategic interests overrode the "tested maxim: 'When in doubt, follow the law.'"[66] The Ford White House, unsurprisingly, vehemently attacked Eagleton's measure, but more surprising was criticism from Mansfield, who, in passionate terms, worried that "we are looking for short answers, quick answers...to a problem which will take a long time to heal."[67] In the shadow of Watergate, the Majority Leader's words had little effect; the Senate approved the amendment 57–20.

[62] William Bundy, *Tangled Web*, p. 408.

[63] William Olson, "President, Congress, and American Foreign Policy: Confrontation or Collaboration?," *International Affairs* 52 (1976), p. 567.

[64] William Olson, "President, Congress, and American Foreign Policy: Confrontation or Collaboration?," *International Affairs* 52 (1976), p. 567.

[65] Tom Eagleton, "Dear Colleague," 9 Sept. 1974, Box 35, FPD Series, Henry Jackson Papers, University of Washington.

[66] *New York Times*, 1 Oct. 1974.

[67] *Congressional Quarterly Weekly Report*, 5 Oct. 1974.

The new president, as promised, vetoed the foreign aid bill that included Eagleton's offering. So, in an unprecedented move, supporters attached the amendment to a measure that Ford could not realistically veto – the continuing resolution, which funded governmental operations until Congress passed the final appropriations bill. With this tactic, wrote Arlen Large of the *Wall Street Journal*, "the Senate is making it plain that its revolt on foreign aid is serious and stubborn."[68] Speaking on behalf of the House establishment, Mahon, manager of the bill, asked colleagues to "withhold amendments until the time when the amendment can be offered on the proper legislative vehicle."[69] But the Texas Democrat, who almost never lost a roll-call vote, was overwhelmed on the floor, 307–90; Greek-American congressmen John Brademas (D-Indiana), Paul Sarbanes (D-Maryland), and Peter Kyros (D-Maine) led the charge, bolstered by strong pressure from Greek-American organizations.[70] The Senate quickly went along, and aid was suspended after a compromise that delayed implementation until spring 1975.

To commentator Robert Pastor, approval of the Eagleton amendment suggested that "the most serious foreign policy crisis" facing Secretary of State Henry Kissinger was not overseas but "in Washington with the Congress."[71] This new environment shaped the year's most significant congressional initiative, the fight over the planned expansion at Diego Garcia, which Richard Levine of the *Wall Street Journal* understood would "provide important clues to how serious Congress is about playing a larger, more forceful role in foreign policy."[72]

As with so many national security issues during the Nixon and Ford administrations, Symington changed the tenor of a defense debate, with an unintentional assist from Stennis. In 1969, the Mississippi senator designated himself chair of Armed Services' three most important subcommittees – the CIA subcommittee, the PIS, and the reprogramming subcommittee (which had authority over Pentagon requests to reassign previously appropriated funds). Jackson, despite ranking behind Symington in committee seniority, earned two crucial chairmanships: the arms control subcommittee (which oversaw SALT negotiations) and the subcommittee monitoring Soviet compliance with the Nuclear Test-Ban Treaty. Symington, meanwhile, received only one – insignificant – chairmanship, that of the Subcommittee on Military Construction.

---

[68] *Wall Street Journal*, 2 Oct. 1974.

[69] 120 *CR*, 94th Congress, 2nd session, p. 32425 (24 Sept. 1974).

[70] Unsigned memo, 2 Oct. 1974, Box 209, Robert Taft, Jr. Papers, Library of Congress; Henry Kissinger, *Years of Renewal* (New York: Simon & Schuster, 1999), p. 233.

[71] Robert Pastor, "Coping with Congress' Foreign Policy," *Foreign Service Journal* 52 (December 1975).

[72] *Wall Street Journal*, 10 April 1974.

As a pre-existing base, however, the Diego Garcia expansion plan fell under the purview of Symington's subcommittee. The Missouri Democrat opened hearings with tough questions to Pentagon officials, during which they explained the base's potential military capabilities far more ambitiously than the administration previously had offered.[73] (JCS chairman Thomas Moorer subsequently retracted his statement, claiming that he "had not quite understood the question" that Symington had asked.[74]) With his Pentagon contacts yielding rumors that William Colby questioned the scheme, the Missouri senator invited the DCI as the subcommittee's next witness. Colby downplayed the threat from Soviet bases in the Indian Ocean littoral, and even asserted, in response to a leading question from Symington, that the planned expansion might "trigger the escalation of the Soviet threat in the area."[75] Treating his appearance as an unauthorized leak, Colby agreed – ostensibly in the spirit of comity between the branches – to declassify his testimony before the House took up the military construction authorization measure. Commentator Warren Unna noted that Symington's "x-ray military vision" had derailed the administration's plans.[76]

The expected parties, on both sides, had already raised the issue in the lower chamber. Robert Leggett, contending that "the policy implications are momentous," cautioned his colleagues that "we risk seeing the name Diego Garcia linked in the future with Tonkin Gulf."[77] Sam Stratton, the House's most aggressive proponent of expansion, countered by dismissing the measure's opponents as "those who have traditionally resisted every attempt to maintain any kind of military balance with the Soviet armed forces."[78] Symington hoped to tip the balance by inserting the Colby material into the *Congressional Record* eight days before the scheduled House vote, only to see the issue overshadowed by Nixon's resignation.

In the Senate, however, after Symington refused Stennis' request to manage the portion of the bill dealing with expansion, immediate adoption of the administration's proposal had no chance.[79] Accordingly, the upper chamber postponed final action on the question for a year. For two months, Symington and Stratton confronted each other in the conference committee; the issue threatened to the derail the conference report on the military construction

[73] *Washington Star*, 12 March 1974.

[74] *Washington Post*, 13 March 1974.

[75] U.S. Senate, Subcommittee on Military Construction, *Hearings, Military Construction Authorization for Fiscal Year 1975*, 93rd Congress, 2nd session, pp. 193, 231 (22 July 1974).

[76] *Washington Post*, 3 Sept. 1974.

[77] Robert Leggett, "Dear Colleagues," 29 March 1974, Box 43, Samuel Stratton Papers, University of Rochester.

[78] Sam Stratton, "Dear Colleagues," 4 April 1974, Box 43, Samuel Stratton Papers, University of Rochester.

[79] Stuart Symington to John Stennis, 4 Sept. 1974, Series 43, Box 23, John Stennis Papers, Mississippi State University; *Wall Street Journal*, 10 April 1974.

bill.[80] With Diego Garcia joining the Eagleton amendment as a foreign policy rider threatening passage of a vital measure, the conferees established a hybrid structure in which the authorization would move forward in 1975 if the president certified that doing so was in the national interest, provided that neither chamber passed a resolution of disapproval within 60 days of the certification. Given the Senate's clearly expressed doubts about the plan, and expectations of a more liberal House following the 1974 midterm elections, this outcome seemed like a victory for Symington.

If so, the result was one of the few triumphs that Pentagon critics experienced in 1974. Uneasiness about the sustainability of détente, high-powered lobbying by the Pentagon, effective rallying of Republican support by former House minority leader Ford, a desire for firmness amidst the domestic turmoil associated with Watergate, the aftereffects of the 1973 Arab-Israeli war, and the usual legislative horse trading contributed to the outcome. Edmund Muskie, hopefully, pointed to this unusual combination to deny a "clear-cut swing in policy"; the liberal Americans for Democratic Action (ADA), reasoned that the "mood and atmospherics have to be just right to win an amendment in the Senate or in the House," since "too many politicians are afraid of appearing 'weak' on national defense."[81]

Serving his final year in the Senate after declining to stand for re-election, Harold Hughes best articulated the hope for how a more proactive congressional role would affect defense matters. In a letter to his Armed Services Committee colleagues, the Iowa senator contended that "we have been so obsessed by the threat of external attack that we have ignored or neglected the clear signs of our internal stagnation and decay." The military, unsurprisingly, recommended spending increases, and perhaps individual legislators never could challenge JCS expertise on technical matters. But Congress certainly could address the "broad assumptions on which our force levels are based." Examining the Pentagon budget through this perspective, the Iowa senator maintained, would reveal that too many of "these programs turn our 'defense' budget into an 'offense' budget," since the legislature had not redefined "America's military role in the world so that we will not jump blindly or recklessly into conflicts." In this respect, Hughes remained, as when he first entered the Senate in 1969, alarmed "at the complacency with which the Congress views this massive commitment of our reserves."[82]

With international events seeming to discourage the ideological reevaluation that Hughes desired, ceiling amendments became the tactic of choice,

---

[80] Ed Braswell to John Stennis, 2 Dec. 1974, Series 43, Box 99, John Stennis Papers, Mississippi State University.

[81] *ADA Legislative Newsletter*, 15 June 1974, Box 83, Robert Giaimo Papers, University of Connecticut; *New York Times*, 20 June 1974.

[82] Harold Hughes to Armed Services Committee, 22 May 1974, Box S175, Harold Hughes Papers, University of Iowa.

even though the strategy unintentionally reinforced the very national security state that figures such as Hughes and Symington sought to weaken. Kennedy, for instance, defended ceiling amendments on the grounds that "leaders in the Defense Department are the experts and can make the judgments."[83] The tactic also provided no guarantee of success: a 1974 Eagleton ceiling amendment failed by a 55–37 vote. Moreover, as Thomas McIntyre noted at the time, the approach limited legislative power: "If Congress is going to fulfill its constitutional responsibility in participating in basic decisions about defense policy," the New Hampshire Democrat cautioned, "it must be willing to dig into specific programs that have broad policy implications and challenge any unacceptable Pentagon programs."[84]

Beginning with his surprise decision to support the Cooper-Hart amendment, McIntyre had assumed an increasingly high-profile position on national security issues. In 1969, Stennis, no doubt expecting McIntyre to maintain the pro-Pentagon viewpoint of his first Senate term, named him chairman of the newly cleared Research and Development Subcommittee. The New Hampshire Democrat, who had come to believe that "the huge military establishment which has grown like Topsy since 1945 has long needed the counterbalance of a vigorous Congress," instead used the post to undertake what he termed "an unusually detailed examination of the enormous defense budget."[85]

The ADA considered McIntyre "one of the few moderate-to-liberal Senators who know how to build support for an amendment."[86] In 1974, implementing his theory that the Senate's anti-militarists needed to focus on individual weapons systems, he came out against developing the maneuverable reentry vehicle (MaRV), a counterforce weapon. For the first time in his career taking the lead in opposing the Pentagon, McIntyre argued that MaRV would place a "hair trigger on nuclear war" by making the threat to ICBMs so high as to motivate Moscow to launch a first strike during an international crisis.[87] Teaming with co-sponsor Edward Brooke, he brought the Senate into a secret session, aiming to overcome "the tremendous complexity of the issue" by persuading colleagues that, once authorized, the MaRV program could not be curtailed.[88]

[83] 120 *CR*, 93rd Congress, 2nd session, p. 29619 (21 Aug. 1974).
[84] Thomas McIntyre to Everett Sackett, 11 July 1974, Box 31, Series III, Thomas McIntyre Papers, University of New Hampshire.
[85] Thomas McIntyre to Lee Albushies, 7 May 1969; Thomas McIntyre to Charlotte Morrison, 7 Dec. 1970; both in Box 21, Series III, Thomas McIntyre Papers, University of New Hampshire.
[86] ADA Legislative Newsletter, 15 June 1974, Box 83, Robert Giaimo Papers, University of Connecticut.
[87] *Washington Post*, 4 June 1974.
[88] Thomas McIntyre to John Musberg, 30 Sept. 1974, Box 22, Series III, Thomas McIntyre Papers, University of New Hampshire.

McIntyre's effort triggered a showdown with the Senate's most enthusiastic supporter of counterforce weaponry, Henry Jackson. Behind the scenes, Jackson aide Richard Perle privately dismissed the New Hampshire senator's arguments as "sheer nonsense" and "simply childish."[89] Publicly, Jackson faulted McIntyre for exaggerating the threat that MaRV posed to deterrence. The Senate sided with Jackson, 48–37; McIntyre found it "awfully discouraging to know that 45 votes or so in the Senate are predictably reflexive to any request that both the Secretary of Defense and the majority of the Armed Services Committee in the Senate want."[90] After the experience, the New Hampshire senator concluded – in remarks that he designated "unusually strong criticism" of a colleague – that Jackson's doctrine would produce a "terrifying new strategic arms race."[91]

The counterforce debate occurred amidst the political turmoil associated with the Watergate investigation and Nixon's resignation, which came less than three months before the 1974 midterm elections. These contests, for good reason, are viewed as a turning point in postwar political history. A floundering economy and backlash against Ford's decision to pardon Nixon propelled the Democrats to a landslide victory: the party gained 49 House seats (even Ford's own, heavily Republican, district elected a Democrat) to assume a majority of 290–145. On foreign policy matters, the instincts of most Watergate freshmen favored more emphasis on human rights, less Pentagon spending, and a more powerful Congress. As one member of the class, New York's Richard Ottinger, recalled, "Everyone – whether they were liberal, moderate, or conservative – felt they were here to do congressional reform."[92] So, just as the new internationalist revolt seemed to be faltering, the turnover in the House provided it with new life.

The 1974 elections accelerated several patterns in the congressional handling of foreign policy issues, though often in unintended ways. First, while the year featured few significant Senate elections, it did have one race of enormous impact, when Arkansas Democrats denied renomination to Fulbright, making John Sparkman the Foreign Relations Committee's new chair. The Alabama Democrat, at the tail end of an undistinguished Senate career, seemed mostly interested in minutiae, such as how the committee arranged its furniture.[93] (When asked before the Arkansas primary to ponder the possibility of a Sparkman chairmanship, one veteran committee member replied,

---

[89] Richard Perle to Henry Jackson, 16 May 1974, Box 48, FPD Series, Henry Jackson Papers, University of Washington; Richard Perle to Henry Jackson, 4 May 1975, Box 35, FPD Series, Henry Jackson Papers, University of Washington.

[90] Thomas McIntyre to Addison Parker, 11 July 1974, Box 31, Series III, Thomas McIntyre Papers, University of New Hampshire.

[91] Thomas McIntyre press release, 5 May 1975, Box 48, FPD Series, Henry Jackson Papers, University of Washington; *Boston Globe*, 6 May 1975.

[92] *Congressional Quarterly Weekly Report*, 3 March 1984.

[93] Pat Holt oral history, U.S. Senate Historical Office; *Washington Post*, 14 June 1974.

"I'd rather not think about it."[94]) Meanwhile, the Watergate class pushed through a variety of reforms in the House, making it easier for individual members to bypass conservative committee chairs and influence foreign policy through action on the floor. A weakened Foreign Relations Committee and a House that allowed more individual initiative to affect policy set the stage for the lower chamber to emerge as the more powerful branch on international matters – a dramatic shift from the Cold War norm, and one that ultimately weakened the legislature's ability to influence foreign policy.

No figure better symbolized the Watergate class than Democrat Tom Downey, elected from New York's 2nd District, which included parts of Suffolk County, Long Island. Not quite 12 years old when John Kennedy was inaugurated president, Downey came from a politically active family – his parents took him to Washington during both the Kennedy and Johnson administrations to participate in foreign policy protests.[95] Shortly after graduating from Cornell (he recalled that he spent his "time in college protesting"), Downey was elected to the previously all-Republican county legislature, where he distinguished himself with his sharp mind and flair for publicity.[96] In 1974, having reached the minimum age (25) to run for the House, he challenged GOP incumbent James Grover, blanketing the district with calls from former Cornell classmates and veterans of the McGovern presidential campaign. Downey dominated the one debate to which Grover agreed, and on Election Day, in what the *Almanac of American Politics* termed one of the year's two biggest upsets, captured 55 percent of the vote.[97] The next day, a photo of him with his brother playing basketball outside their parents' home appeared on the *New York Times* front page.[98]

Described by one colleague as a "classic go-getter," Downey attacked senior members for "vagueness and lack of knowledge concerning important issues."[99] He requested, and received, a position on the Armed Services Committee, along with two other Watergate freshmen, Bob Carr (D-Michigan) and Jim Lloyd (D-California). News of Downey's assignment prompted Bob Sherman, an arms control expert who previously had worked for McGovern, to offer his services; in an unusual arrangement, Downey's office shared Sherman's salary with Bob Carr, and Sherman kept both freshmen up to speed on the latest strategic debates.[100] Less than two months after the congressional session started, one member admitted that the duo's "adversary position" had shifted the tenor of committee debate – although "it's

[94] *Washington Post*, 26 May 1974.
[95] *New York Times*, 12 July 1973.
[96] David Grann, "Beltway Boy," *The New Republic*, 9 Aug. 1999.
[97] Barone and Ujifusa, *The Almanac of American Politics 1976*, p. 258.
[98] *New York Times*, 7 Nov. 1974.
[99] *New York Times*, 10 Sept. 1975.
[100] Thomas Downey personal interview with author, 27 May 2004.

impossible to say what they'll do after they've been massaged by the Defense Department's persuasion."[101] Longtime Pentagon critic Lucien Nedzi considered Downey the most effective member of the Watergate class.[102]

Downey's presence affected Armed Services Committee affairs in a variety of ways. After the son of a constituent was charged in West Point's biggest cheating scandal in a generation, the New York Democrat pressed committee superiors to investigate; when they refused, he conducted an informal inquiry, exposing arbitrariness in the administration of the Academy's honor code and helping to mitigate the cadets' punishment.[103] On the policy front, Downey joined fellow Armed Services Committee dissenters Dellums and Schroeder in developing an "alternative defense bill" that recommended slashing more than $4 billion from the committee's level.[104] The New York Democrat argued that "our role in the world as a military force has got to be tempered," with the military reconfigured as "a tool of our foreign policy, not our foreign policy being a tool of our military policy."[105]

Two procedural developments maximized the influence of figures like Downey. The first came in a more aggressive enforcement of the Democratic caucus rule subjecting committee chairs to a vote of approval by the caucus. The freshmen targeted Hébert. They were joined by committee liberals such as Otis Pike, who complained that under the Louisiana Democrat, "the Pentagon controls the House Armed Services Committee."[106] Hébert did little to help his cause: in a meeting with freshmen before the caucus vote, he condescendingly addressed them as "boys and girls," responded to questions evasively, and blamed his difficulties on Common Cause, an "insidious organization" that had "conducted one of the most vicious and reprehensible campaigns that I've ever seen in my life."[107] Acting as if no threat to his position existed, the chairman informed Downey that a seat on his panel depended on the freshman backing the B-1 bomber; he also tried to name the members of Armed Services subcommittees before the formal election of a committee chair.[108] This arrogant attitude helped produce what Les Aspin described as an "earthquake," when the caucus unseated the Louisiana Democrat, 152–133.[109] Although the new chair, Mel Price, had

[101] *Congressional Quarterly Weekly Report*, 15 March 1975.
[102] *New York Times*, 10 Sept. 1975.
[103] Thomas Downey personal interview with the author, 27 May 2004; *New York Times*, 23 June 1976, 6 July 1977.
[104] *New York Times*, 15 May 1975.
[105] *Christian Science Monitor*, 28 May 1975.
[106] *Congressional Quarterly Weekly Report*, 18 Jan. 1975.
[107] Thomas Downey personal interview with author, 27 May 2004; *Congressional Quarterly Weekly Report*, 18 Jan. 1975; Zelizer, *On Capitol Hill*, p. 171.
[108] Les Aspin to F. Edward Hébert, 15 Jan. 1975, copy in Box 39, Samuel Stratton Papers, University of Rochester; Thomas Downey personal interview with author, 27 May 2004.
[109] *New York Times*, 16 Jan. 1975.

few ideological differences with his predecessor, he promised to pay attention to the views of the caucus; Pentagon sources conceded that the result left them "rattled" and "shaken."[110] Hébert complained that the freshmen had been "transformed into a mob of crusading knights."[111]

The second key institutional change came in passage of the Budget Control and Impoundment Act, which established committees to develop an overall congressional budget. (Prior to the measure's enactment, the president, in accordance with 1921 legislation, submitted his budget recommendations, which then went to 33 separate authorization committees in the House and Senate.[112]) The new body possessed the power to limit the individual committee totals at the start of the authorization process – something that Aspin, with his ceiling amendments, had tried to do at its conclusion. The first chairs of the two committees, Brock Adams (D-Washington) in the House and Edmund Muskie in the Senate, were both liberals; Adams' committee in particular was stacked with liberal Democrats, such as Liz Holtzman (D-New York), who saw the committee's task as a policy-related one of addressing "what is really necessary for the defense of this country and what is not."[113] When Adams named Pentagon critic Robert Giaimo to chair the Budget Committee's first defense task force, the Pentagon lost control of a defense-related committee for the first time since the start of the Cold War.

Abourezk expected these changes to make 1975 "a 'do-or-die' year if we are going to have an impact" on the defense budget. Thanks to a more sympathetic House, Senate dissenters could now offer their initiatives in both chambers, "using the same formula, thereby doubling our chances."[114] Contrary to Abourezk's hopes, for the first time since the ABM fight, Pentagon critics were on the defensive: consideration of the defense authorization measure coincided with the seizure of the *Mayaguez*, a U.S. merchant ship, by Cambodia's Khmer Rouge government. When the 40 seamen aboard were taken prisoner, U.S. naval vessels launched a rescue effort, which cost 18 American lives. In the aftermath, Sam Stratton detected a new recognition that "this is not the year in which to cut back our military strength."[115] The defense authorization bill passed the House 332–64, with every new internationalist amendment but one failing by at least 124 votes. Downey lamented that his colleagues seemed inclined to "forget that it is the Congress and not

---

[110] *Congressional Quarterly Weekly Report*, 15 Feb. 1975.

[111] Zelizer, *On Capitol* Hill, p. 167.

[112] Zelizer, *On Capitol* Hill, p. 152.

[113] U.S. House of Representatives, Budget Committee, *Hearings, Fiscal Year 1976 Budget and the Economy*, 94th Congress, 1st session, p. 425 (5 March 1975).

[114] James Abourezk to Thomas Eagleton, 12 May 1975, Folder 4354, Thomas Eagleton Papers, University of Missouri.

[115] 121 *CR*, 94th Congress, 1st session, pp. 15429, 15458 (20 May 1975).

the generals in the Pentagon who are charged under the Constitution with writing spending legislation."[116]

The 1975 session also featured the Cold War era's final full-scale Senate challenge to the defense budget, even as the Armed Services Committee contained an unprecedented number of Pentagon critics. In addition to Symington, Richard Schweiker, and McIntyre, three newly elected Democrats joined the panel: John Culver, who succeeded Hughes in Iowa; Gary Hart, who ousted conservative Peter Dominick in Colorado; and Patrick Leahy, the first Vermont Democrat ever elected to the Senate. All three requested Armed Services Committee slots, so they could, according to Hart, prove that "it is one thing to be antimilitarist and another to be antimilitary."[117] Culver especially distinguished himself, both for his willingness to defy conventional wisdom – early on, he commented that "the United States doesn't have to be first in every respect in defense" – and for the passion that he brought to national security questions.[118]

Symington praised the trio for creating "a new and pleasant atmosphere on that committee when it comes to any real objective analysis of various military requests," but the group scored no major victories.[119] In a more desultory debate than earlier in the 1970s, critics seemed to go through the motions, as if cognizant that their offerings would fail: a frustrated Symington chastised colleagues for their excessive deference to the professional military, whose recommendation for a weapons system, "to my mind, does not necessarily mean much."[120] The Senate ultimately considered 31 amendments, and in each case upheld the recommendations of the Armed Services Committee, mostly by margins of between 20 and 25 votes, despite an embarrassing admission from Sam Nunn (D-Georgia) that waste – or what he termed a need to "incentivize bureaucracy" – accounted for part of the desired defense spending increase.[121] Dick Clark astutely recognized that his colleagues "have somehow become so embarrassed or falsely humiliated by the experience of Southeast Asia" that most feared being portrayed as soft on defense.[122] The lessons of Vietnam did not match the new internationalists' anticipations.

With their defense agenda apparently losing popular support, the new internationalists faced two options: regrouping in time for the 1976 elections or achieving victory by using procedural means. The latter option proved irresistible, especially since a promising new procedure had just come into

---

[116] 121 *CR*, 94th Congress, 1st session, p. 15468 (20 May 1975).
[117] Gary Hart, *The Good Fight: The Education of an American Reformer* (New York: Random House, 1993), p. 163.
[118] *Congressional Quarterly Weekly Report*, 15 March 1975.
[119] 121 *CR*, 94th Congress, 1st session, p. 25351 (28 July 1975).
[120] 121 *CR*, 94th Congress, 1st session, p. 16406 (2 June 1975).
[121] 121 *CR*, 94th Congress, 1st session, p. 16409 (2 June 1975).
[122] 121 *CR*, 94th Congress, 1st session, pp. 16699–16700 (3 June 1975).

existence. Though by statute the Budget Committee acted only in an advisory capacity in 1975, Pentagon critics appealed to Muskie and Adams to intervene on defense spending bills. In a peculiar reading of events, Culver explained to Muskie that the authorization debate "demonstrated many senators believe that there is, and should be made clear, a direct relationship between U.S. foreign policy and military force structure."[123] The Maine Democrat had already lectured Defense Secretary James Schlesinger that, as the "examination by Congress of national security choices in this manner is new," the Budget Committee would oppose such "wedge" tactics as Pentagon requests that sought initial small outlays but that promised exploding long-term costs.[124] Even more aggressive action came from Adams, who implied that if the Appropriations Committee resisted his call for a $7 billion cut, he would fight the spending bill on the floor.[125] After the House acted, Muskie informed Senate Appropriations Committee chairman John McClellan that no leeway existed under budget guidelines to increase the lower chamber's defense total.[126] Pentagon critics thus used procedure to impose a de facto ceiling amendment.

The Budget Committee's intervention could not conceal the critics' weakness in 1975 defense debates. But one item, the B-1 bomber, went against the grain, previewing the type of weapon-specific military debate that Congress would feature for the remainder of the Cold War. Pike summarized the opposition's case: because of delays, cost overruns, and design flaws, "we are spending money we do not have for a project we do not need and we are not getting it."[127] Even its defenders presented a weak case: Price conceded that the B-1 was a "sick program," but doubted that "the financial euthanasia that puts it out of its misery will make us, as a nation, any healthier."[128] Like no weapons program since the ABM, the plane generated grassroots opposition, coordinated by the Campaign to Stop the B-1 Bomber, headed by a 30-year-old labor lawyer, Bob Brammer.[129] The coalition spent its $50,000 budget wisely, focusing on matters such as letter-writing to members of Congress, which Brammer termed the "bread and butter" of achieving influence for groups that lacked financial resources.[130]

In the House, Downey joined Aspin in co-sponsoring the major anti-B-1 amendment; for the other side, Hébert, in his swan song as an important

---

[123] John Culver to Edmund Muskie, 6 Oct. 1975, Box 172, John Culver Papers, University of Iowa.

[124] U.S. Senate, Budget Committee, *Hearings, First Concurrent Resolution on the Budget*, 94th Congress, 1st session, p. 1082 (21 March 1975).

[125] *New York Times*, 11 Sept. 1975.

[126] *New York Times*, 26 Oct. 1975.

[127] *CQ Almanac* 1974, p. 576.

[128] 120 *CR*, 93rd Congress, 2nd session, p. 15504 (20 May 1974).

[129] *New York Times*, 24 July 1977.

[130] *National Journal*, 31 Dec. 1977.

player on defense issues, charged that "the antics and the tactics" of House liberals had placed the United States "way behind" the Soviet Union.[131] (How this devolution of the U.S. strategic position had occurred during his tenure as Armed Services Committee chairman the Louisiana Democrat did not explain.) Hébert painted the vote as a Cold War milestone: Moscow, he informed his colleagues, was "depending on this Congress to kill" a weapon the Soviets could not match.[132] The House rejected the Downey-Aspin amendment, but only by a margin of 227–164, easily the new internationalists' best showing in the year's defense debates. A companion Senate amendment sponsored by McGovern fared less well, losing by a 57–32 tally. Downey later expressed his pleasure with the outcome, since it usually took several years for defense critics to build the momentum necessary to kill a program. The New York Democrat believed that a roll call, at least, forced members to give the issue enough attention to demand a staff briefing; only by educating colleagues could critics ultimately prevail, since wholly uninformed members would rely on guidance from the Pentagon.[133]

Pike believed that the system survived because "part of the B-1 bomber is made in everybody's district."[134] Economic motives certainly affected the positions of normal Pentagon critics such as California's Democratic senators John Tunney and Alan Cranston. In rhetoric that could have come from Goldwater, Tunney was "convinced that there is a point of diminishing returns, a point where indiscriminate cuts begin to serious damage our credibility."[135] Earlier, however, he admitted that he was "somewhat prejudiced" on the issue, since the B-1's primary contractor was California-based Rockwell.[136] Even more defensively, Cranston understood that some might explain his support for the plane "because it relates in part to jobs in California and to contracts in California."[137] (Senators from Ohio, the other state with the most to gain from the B-1, offered similar arguments: Robert Taft, Jr., claimed that with up to 43,000 jobs on the line for the Buckeye State, cutting the B-1 would be "penny wise, pound foolish."[138]) As was his wont, Roman Hruska (R-Nebraska) made the case a bit too bluntly: defunding the plane, he claimed, "would cause chaotic disruptions and waste due to abrupt employee layoffs, which would exceed 70,000 of our citizens."[139]

[131] 121 CR, 94th Congress, 1st session, p. 15063 (19 May 1975).
[132] 121 CR, 94th Congress, 1st session, p. 15063 (19 May 1975).
[133] Thomas Downey, "Can America Survive Trident II?," *Nuclear Times*, Feb. 1983.
[134] 119 CR, 93rd Congress, 1st session, p. 26941 (31 July 1973).
[135] 121 CR, 94th Congress, 1st session, p. 17435 (5 June 1975).
[136] 120 CR, 93rd Congress, 2nd session, p. 17797 (5 June 1974).
[137] 121 CR, 94th Congress, 1st session, p. 17439 (5 June 1975).
[138] Robert Taft, Jr. press release, 9 May 1975, Box 129, Robert Taft, Jr. Papers, Library of Congress.
[139] 120 CR, 93rd Congress, 2nd session, p. 17786 (5 June 1974). In 1970, Hruska, then ranking minority member of the Senate Judiciary Committee, had probably sealed the fate of Nixon's

The economic impact of defense spending played an even more important role for House members, especially those who represented constituencies with major Pentagon contracts. In Jim Lloyd's contractor-rich southern California district (parts of which were once represented by Richard Nixon), Rockwell promised that the bomber would create 192,000 new jobs. Even congressmen with less obvious connections to the military-industrial complex felt the economic pressures of voting against defense appropriations. Philip Hayes, for instance, was a typical Watergate-class Democrat, elected from a swing district in southern Indiana. Hayes discovered the difficulty of translating his anti-militarist principles into policy when the Pentagon threatened to close a naval munitions depot that employed 600 of his constituents. The freshman congressman confessed that he was "under strong pressure to maintain what is euphemistically called a 'strong national defense position' as are other members who have military bases and defense contractors in their areas."[140]

The tenor of the national security debates convinced John Culver that his colleagues had assumed "that the failure of policy in Southeast Asia should mute this year's debate," even though such a position "makes no sense whatsoever."[141] This altered intellectual climate directly affected the fate of the Diego Garcia base. As expected, Ford certified expansion as in the national interest, giving Congress its chance to kill the proposal under the terms of the 1974 compromise legislation. House votes on the year's defense bill suggested that the lower chamber would uphold the president, as indeed it did, placing the base's fate in the Senate's hands. In the Armed Services Committee, the trio of Democratic freshmen, McIntyre, and Symington all issued dissenting reports. On the Senate floor, Mansfield himself introduced the resolution of disapproval, opening a discussion that Claiborne Pell (D-Rhode Island) promised would "provide a general indication of the future direction of American foreign policy after the experience in Indochina."[142]

The six-hour debate over the Mansfield Resolution was the Senate's most passionate foreign policy discussion in several years. The Majority Leader set the tone, asserting that he had witnessed "too much hanky-panky in the field of foreign policy as far as the military is concerned" to ignore Vietnam's central lesson: that the United States "should have no design on

---

unsuccessful nominee for the Supreme Court, G. Harrold Carswell, who was under attack for unimpressive credentials and limited intellectual ability. "Even if he is mediocre," Hruska maintained, "there are a lot of mediocre judges and lawyers. They are entitled to a little representation, aren't they, and a little chance? We can't have all Brandeises, Cardozos, and Frankfurters, and stuff like that there."

[140] *New York Times*, 16 Oct. 1975.
[141] John Culver, "Talking Points for General Defense Debate," n.d. 1975, Box 182, John Culver Papers, University of Iowa.
[142] 121 *CR*, 94th Congress, 1st session, p. 25334 (28 July 1975).

maintaining a modern-day empire by replacing the autonomy of individual nations."[143] In a sign of the shifting nature of Senate dissent, Symington, the key figure in fighting the expansion in 1974, deferred to Culver in 1975. Like other Mansfield supporters, the Iowa senator ambitiously framed the issue as "the first major test of our ability and determination to chart a new, more constructive direction in foreign and defense policy that does not rely exclusively on automatic military escalation and gunboat diplomacy."[144] Indeed, Culver contended that "Diego Garcia has symbolic importance far outweighing its military significance," since it provided an opportunity to demonstrate that the United States had abandoned its "'policeman of the world' fantasy."[145]

Opponents of the resolution countered with their own historical analogies: Stennis termed Diego Garcia "just another case" of the Cold War's central lesson – that the United States needed "money for more missiles, more armaments, everything of that kind, on the belief that to show a weakness would lessen our negotiating chances."[146] Dewey Bartlett (R-Oklahoma) wondered how anyone could interpret the base expansion as provocative, since "the Navy by its very nature is a great ambassador for this country."[147] The wildest remarks came from John Tower, who claimed that resolution proponents believed that "if we will simply unilaterally disarm, that will bring great moral pressure to bear on the Soviet Union to do the same" – a viewpoint worthy of "fools," which proved that "the Senate cannot formulate and implement foreign policy in a fast-changing world."[148] To Symington, such rhetoric suggested "that there are people who would not object to a direct confrontation with the Soviet Union."[149]

As had occurred with the ABM six years before, the expansion's fate depended on a bipartisan bloc of moderates – in this case Democrats Lawton Chiles, John Glenn, Warren Magnuson, and John Pastore; and Republicans Bob Packwood, James Pearson, Richard Schweiker, Robert Stafford, and Lowell Weicker. The previous year, these senators had accepted the Symington compromise. But now, forced to choose, they confirmed the earlier interpretations offered by Clark and Culver: they feared weakening the U.S. defense posture after the humiliating final withdrawal from Vietnam. When all nine opposed the Mansfield Resolution, the measure lost 53–43.

The full effects of the ideological shift apparent in the resolution's rejection would not emerge for another two years, though the new internationalists'

---

[143] 121 *CR*, 94th Congress, 1st session, p. 25318 (28 July 1975).

[144] 121 *CR*, 94th Congress, 1st session, p. 25325 (28 July 1975).

[145] 121 *CR*, 94th Congress, 1st session, p. S12439 (11 July 1975).

[146] 121 *CR*, 94th Congress, 1st session, p. 25347 (28 July 1975).

[147] 121 *CR*, 94th Congress, 1st session, p. 25331 (28 July 1975).

[148] 121 *CR*, 94th Congress, 1st session, p. 25338 (28 July 1975).

[149] 121 *CR*, 94th Congress, 1st session, p. 25337 (28 July 1975).

assumption that the legislature deserved a more prominent foreign policy role increasingly came under attack. In reviewing the record of the previous five years, Bartlett contended that "Congress literally fiddled while Vietnam burned," the War Powers Act exemplified "overreaction and unconstitutionality," and the Jackson-Vanik and Eagleton amendments demonstrated that the results of congressional activism "have been dismal."[150] Commentator Marquis Childs claimed that "in instance after instance, Congress steps in and confuses or disrupts the lines of policy laid down by the executive," so that even "when all the well meaning and often helpful acts are added up on the credit side of the ledger, the confusion of authority between executive and legislature is clearly disastrous."[151] Tellingly, Childs cited the same two examples as did Bartlett: Jackson-Vanik and the Eagleton amendment.

As if to respond to such criticisms, in July 1975, the Senate voted 41–40 to resume cash and government-financed weapons sales to Turkey. Eagleton, however, forecast that attempts to weaken the embargo were "doomed" in the House.[152] Speaking for the majority, Robert Drinan dismissed the administration's proposal as little more than a "blank check for the continued support of Turkish aggression on Cyprus."[153] The Massachusetts congressman urged his colleagues to "uphold the law, to reassert our Nation's historic opposition to armed aggression, and to reject this attempt at foreign blackmail"; Watergate freshman Bob Edgar (D-Pennsylvania) believed that "if our defense agreements require that our Government bribe tyrants and appease aggressors, then we are as corrupt as those we are quick to condemn."[154] As Eagleton predicted, the House retained the embargo, 223–206. The next day, Turkey closed the 27 U.S. bases on its soil.

The congressional response to South Vietnam's collapse also demonstrated the difficulties of a legislative body responding to a fast-changing world. In the frantic days before the Thieu regime collapsed in South Vietnam, Ford attempted to redeem Nixon's promise to prevent a military victory by Hanoi. In late January 1975, the President requested a $522 million package of military aid for South Vietnam and Cambodia; the initiative, which could not even clear the Senate Armed Services Committee, prompted 21 House liberals, led by Drinan, to file suit in federal court to halt all military operations in Cambodia.[155]

Ford's request for humanitarian assistance for the South Vietnamese and blanket authority for evacuating U.S. nationals raised more complicated questions. Congressional conservatives viewed both initiatives as the

[150] 121 *CR*, 94th Congress, 1st session, p. 16685 (3 June 1975).
[151] *Washington Post*, 29 July 1975.
[152] *Congressional Quarterly Weekly Report*, 24 May 1975.
[153] 121 *CR*, 94th Congress, 1st session, p. 24502 (24 July 1975).
[154] 121 *CR*, 94th Congress, 1st session, pp. 24497, 24503 (24 July 1975).
[155] *Congressional Quarterly Weekly Report*, 15 Feb. 1975.

minimum the United States should do.[156] While few on the other side denied the genuine humanitarian needs in South Vietnam, Donald Fraser recognized that the "distrust of the executive branch runs so deep" that most of his colleagues feared granting any discretion to the president.[157] Convinced that "the American people are looking to Congress for creative leadership, not empty rhetoric," Bob Edgar introduced a substitute to maintain the president's evacuation authority but to funnel all humanitarian aid through international agencies – only to be denounced by Aspin and Harrington for proposing a second Tonkin Gulf Resolution.[158] Eventually, after 14 hours of debate, the House passed the bill at 2:40 AM, with a majority of Democrats opposed. Freshman Michael Blouin (D-Iowa), terming the day a "circus," remarked sarcastically, "If people think panic reigns in Saigon, they should have checked the tempo of this floor."[159]

In the Senate, Clark headed a group that advocated delaying aid until the president presented an evacuation plan respecting the congressional power to declare war, but given the fluid situation in South Vietnam, this approach was tantamount to denying all aid. When the South Vietnamese regime collapsed a few days later, Kissinger publicly blamed the outcome on Congress, an analysis Mike Mansfield termed "a distortion so immense that it borders on – I choose the word carefully – it borders on the irrational."[160]

Despite events in Vietnam and Turkey, on some issues – particularly those relating to the perceived excesses of Cold War liberalism, or where the gap between Cold War foreign policy and traditional American ideals was particularly jarring – the new internationalists continued to hold sway. The most significant amendment to the 1975 foreign aid bill (indeed, one of the most significant amendments of any point during the Cold War) came from a Watergate freshman, Tom Harkin (D-Iowa), who proposed severing aid to any nation with a persistent pattern of gross human rights violations. The president could waive the curb on national security grounds, but a motion from either chamber of Congress could override the action.[161]

On the House floor, Harkin argued that this "straightforward human rights amendment" would constitute "just exercising the proper oversight

[156] Dewey Bartlett to John Stennis, 25 March 1975, Series 43, Box 29, John Stennis Papers, Mississippi State University.

[157] 121 *CR*, 94th Congress, 1st session, pp. 11489–11490 (23 April 1975).

[158] Bob Edgar, "Dear Colleague," 22 April 1975; Michael Harrington, "Dear Colleague," 21 April 1975; both in Box 86, Robert Giaimo Papers, University of Connecticut; 121 *CR*, 94th Congress, 1st session, p. 11497 (23 April 1975).

[159] 121 *CR*, 94th Congress, 1st session, p. 11513 (23 April 1975); *Congressional Quarterly Weekly Report*, 26 April 1975.

[160] Oberdorfer, *Senator Mansfield*, p. 444.

[161] U.S. Senate, Subcommittee on Foreign Assistance, *Hearings, Foreign Assistance Authorization, Fiscal Year 1976*, 94th Congress, 1st session, pp. 656–657 (23 Sept. 1975).

that we ought to exercise in Congress."[162] It came as little surprise that leading figures on the Foreign Affairs Committee opposed it. Doc Morgan remarkably charged that the amendment would, for the first time(!), introduce political concerns into the foreign aid program; Dante Fascell (D-Florida), more realistically, wondered how to translate vague wording, such as "gross violations" of human rights, into actual policy. But positions on the amendment did not break down along clear-cut ideological lines. Continuing his quixotic crusade against Indira Gandhi, Wayne Hays hoped that Harkin's offering would force the administration to end aid to Ceylon, led by "that miserable Bandaranaike woman, who is only exceeded in her miserableness by the head of the Government of India, to whom we are also giving a handout."[163] In the end, most liberals sided with Harkin and enough conservatives agreed with Hays: the amendment passed, 238–164. Despite opposition from Humphrey, who asserted that "we must be careful not to punish needy people simply because it is their misfortune to be governed by an oppressive regime," and McGee, who claimed that the amendment would open a "Pandora's box," the Senate concurred.[164]

The reaction against the perceived excesses of the U.S. intelligence community also sustained the new internationalists' momentum. Nixon's June 1973 decision to send DCI Richard Helms to Iran and nominate William Colby in his stead offered the first glimpse of the new congressional attitude toward CIA activities. With Stennis hospitalized from a gunshot wound suffered in a robbery attempt, Symington became acting Armed Services Committee chair – "to the horror," the *Washington Post*'s Clayton Fitchey discovered, "of the military establishment."[165] The Missouri senator thus possessed the institutional power to force Colby to become the first DCI nominee to testify publicly; as the lead opposition witness, he invited none other than Robert Drinan. The "conscience" of the Massachusetts congressman compelled him to oppose Colby's confirmation, because of the nominee's close association with immoral covert operations in the Vietnam War, but he focused his testimony against past congressional oversight of the CIA.[166] Speaking "with all due respect" to his hosts, Drinan claimed that "it has been the Senate Armed Services Committee which, more than any other agency in Congress, has prevented the Congress and the people of this

---

[162] 121 *CR*, 94th Congress, 1st session, p. 28306 (10 Sept. 1975).

[163] 121 *CR*, 94th Congress, 1st session, p. 28308 (10 Sept. 1975).

[164] Hubert Humphrey to M. H. Eggleston, 5 Dec. 1975, Box 5, Legislation 1975 series, Hubert Humphrey Papers, Minnesota State Historical Society; U.S. Senate, Subcommittee on Foreign Assistance, *Hearings, Foreign Assistance Authorization, Fiscal Year 1976*, 94th Congress, 1st session, p. 660 (23 Sept. 1975).

[165] *Washington Post*, 14 April 1973.

[166] U.S. Senate, Armed Services Committee, *Hearings, Nomination of William E. Colby*, 93rd Congress, 1st session, p. 33 (20 July 1973).

country from knowing anything about the CIA."[167] From his perspective, "the senior members of the House and of the Senate have conspired to prevent the younger members of the House and of the Senate from knowing anything about the CIA."[168] The intensity of these remarks took even Symington aback (he thanked Drinan for his "frankness"); Sam Nunn, rapidly emerging as a conservative force on the committee, accused the Massachusetts Democrat of saying that "every Congressman and every Member of the Senate should have all the top secret information that relates to the CIA on demand."[169]

By 1974, advocates of enhanced congressional oversight increasingly admitted that their goal was, for all practical purposes, to prevent covert operations. Abourezk, for instance, sponsored an amendment requiring disclosure of CIA appropriations, prompting Stennis to scoff that the Senate "might as well abolish the agency"; Pastore demanded a secret session, lest there "be a newspaperman from Moscow" in the press gallery.[170] Despite the spirited defense of the existing informal oversight arrangement, the amendment garnered 33 votes, more than expected.

A few months later, attention shifted to the House. In April 1974, Michael Harrington requested from Lucien Nedzi, chair of the Intelligence Subcommittee, material from classified files regarding CIA involvement in the coup that toppled Salvador Allende's elected, but Marxist, regime in Chile. Nedzi, after consulting with Hébert, provided the information, on condition that Harrington reveal nothing about the file, even to other House members. The documents contained evidence of CIA attempts to destabilize the Allende regime, directly contradicting public claims made by the Nixon and Ford administrations. Ignoring the confidentiality requirement, Harrington circulated the information to other committee chairs, requesting that they investigate American involvement in the coup; the material eventually found its way to the press.

In what Harrington termed a "petty and unconscionable attempt to silence criticism and perpetuate the cover-up of CIA misdeeds," the Armed Services Committee conducted a special investigation of his actions.[171] The Massachusetts Democrat defiantly informed his colleagues that the committee itself "ought to have some twinge of conscience in being complicit by the

---

[167] U.S. Senate, Armed Services Committee, *Hearings, Nomination of William E. Colby*, 93rd Congress, 1st session, p. 4 (20 July 1973).

[168] U.S. Senate, Armed Services Committee, *Hearings, Nomination of William E. Colby*, 93rd Congress, 1st session, p. 39 (20 July 1973).

[169] U.S. Senate, Armed Services Committee, *Hearings, Nomination of William E. Colby*, 93rd Congress, 1st session, pp. 49, 49 (20 July 1973).

[170] 120 *CR*, 94th Congress, 2nd session, pp. 17487, 17489 (4 June 1974).

[171] 121 *CR*, 94th Congress, 1st session, p. 19853 (19 June 1975).

silence in what the executive branch is saying to the Congress."[172] After the
Armed Services Committee's senior Republican, Bob Wilson of California,
compared Harrington to Benedict Arnold – a comparison, Wilson suggested
in a collegial spirit, that he did not intend as "unkind" – the committee
denied the Massachusetts Democrat further access to classified files.[173]

The Harrington revelations emboldened Abourezk to offer an amendment
to remove the CIA's ability to engage in clandestine activity to destabilize
foreign governments, producing a debate that the *Washington Post* deemed
"the first time that either house of Congress had conducted an open debate
and openly voted on whether the United States should engage in secret foreign operations in peacetime."[174] To the South Dakota senator, the United
States needed to gather intelligence, but events in Chile suggested that the
CIA was "conducting a secret war without either the approval of Congress
or the knowledge of the American people."[175] Despite its extreme nature,
the amendment attracted support from some new internationalists. Terming
the Chilean episode a "direct contradiction of the traditional principles for
which this country has stood," Church voted for the amendment as a protest
against the status quo of congressional oversight, even though he considered
Abourezk's approach a bit extreme.[176]

The offering nonetheless failed, receiving only 17 votes; the *Washington
Post* noted that some could view its defeat as an "official affirmation of
'dirty tricks' of unprecedented scope and explicitness."[177] A more accurate
interpretation, however, centered on Abourezk's ability to frame the issue
in terms favorable to his ideological perspective, which in turn helped to
secure passage of other desirable legislation. The same day that the Senate rejected the Abourezk amendment, it approved Hughes' final legislative
offering, an amendment prohibiting covert operations unless deemed by the
president "important to the national security." (Abourezk's proposal contained no such waiver.) More important, the Hughes amendment required
the Foreign Affairs and Foreign Relations committees, for the first time, to
receive briefings on intelligence activities. A testy exchange with Stennis concluded with Hughes expressing his hope to eventually see his Mississippi

[172] U.S. House of Representatives, Armed Services Committee, *Hearings, Special Subcommittee
on Intelligence Inquiry into Matters Regarding Classified Testimony Taken on April 22,
1974 Concerning the CIA and Chile*, 93rd Congress, 2nd session, pp. 14, 18 (25 Sept.
1974).
[173] U.S. House of Representatives, Armed Services Committee, *Hearings, Special Subcommittee
on Intelligence Inquiry into Matters Regarding Classified Testimony Taken on April 22,
1974 Concerning the CIA and Chile*, 93rd Congress, 2nd session, p. 17 (25 Sept. 1974).
[174] *Washington Post*, 7 Oct. 1974.
[175] James Abourezk to Henry Jackson, 20 Sept. 1974, Box 35, FPD Series, Henry Jackson
Papers, University of Washington.
[176] 120 *CR*, 94th Congress, 2nd session, p. 33477 (2 Oct. 1974).
[177] *Washington Post*, 7 Oct. 1974.

colleague support legislation "that will require an absolute oversight by Congress of CIA and other intelligence operations."[178]

Hughes admitted the amendment would check "the wide-ranging power of the CIA" only if it were accompanied by a "greater congressional willingness to play its oversight role."[179] But after six years of studying the issue, the Iowa senator knew of no other way to address the problem "other than drawing public attention to it."[180] With memories of the Harrington affair still fresh, conditions in the House dictated adding a clause to prohibit members from publicizing any information received in an intelligence briefing. Liz Holtzman attempted to weaken the provision, but sponsor Leo Ryan (D-California) objected that the change would lose needed votes for the amendment from House moderates. Like Hughes, Ryan viewed the amendment as a first step toward bringing "the CIA under some kind of jurisdiction by the Foreign Affairs Committee."[181]

Less than two weeks after passage of the Hughes-Ryan amendment, Seymour Hersh of the *New York Times* revealed that the CIA had illegally conducted intelligence operations against thousands of Americans, including four former members of Congress.[182] On January 20, 1975, the Senate Democratic caucus considered a motion for an investigatory committee, modeled on the committee chaired by former senator Sam Ervin (D-North Carolina) that investigated the Watergate scandal. A few Southern Democrats opposed the idea: Mississippi's Jim Eastland wondered, "What's wrong with overthrowing the government of Chile? It was a commie government, wasn't it?"[183] The strongest remarks, however, came from Stennis, whose "booming voice" denouncing the proposal carried to reporters outside of the closed-door meeting.[184] The caucus nonetheless voted 45–7 in favor of an inquiry, in what one Democrat termed "really the first time that John Stennis has gone to the mat and gotten decisively trounced."[185] Status quo advocates unsuccessfully called for John Pastore rather than Church to head the special committee; shortly thereafter, the House voted to launch an inquiry of its own, with Nedzi as chair.

In early 1975, the administration finally launched a public relations counterattack. On February 20, Colby appeared before the Defense Appropriations Subcommittee for three hours of nationally televised testimony; Mahon

---

[178] 120 CR, 94th Congress, 2nd session, p. 33490 (2 Oct. 1974).
[179] Harold Hughes to Robert Hart, 31 October 1974, Box S83, Harold Hughes Papers, University of Iowa.
[180] Harold Hughes to Hubert Humphrey, 14 Feb. 1974, Box S83, Harold Hughes Papers, University of Iowa.
[181] 120 CR, 93rd Congress, 2nd session, p. 39166 (11 Dec. 1974).
[182] *New York Times*, 22 Dec. 1974.
[183] *Newsweek*, 27 Jan. 1975.
[184] *New York Times*, 21 Jan. 1975.
[185] *New York Times*, 21 Jan. 1975.

assured the DCI that "you are among people who believe in the intelligence mechanism."[186] In his April 10 State of the World message, Ford asserted that it would be "catastrophic" if an excessively rigorous congressional investigation "in effect" dismantled the CIA.[187] The next month, Stennis warned that "congressional and media clamor" had left foreign governments "aghast" at the activities of "well-organized and well-financed domestic ideological enemies of CIA."[188]

Ironically, defenders of the status quo then received assistance from the CIA's strongest critics. After the *New York Times* revealed that Nedzi, in his capacity as chair of Armed Services' CIA subcommittee, had known about covert operations in Chile but had not revealed the information to his colleagues, other Democrats on the House special committee, led by Harrington, Giaimo, and James Stanton (D-Ohio), demanded his removal as chair. Nedzi then resigned, after which Stratton – detecting an opportunity to embarrass his opponents – introduced a measure for the House to reject the resignation. (The New York congressman ridiculed Stanton, Harrington, and Ron Dellums for believing that they had a "higher duty to leak information to the newspapers."[189]) When the House overwhelmingly rejected Nedzi's resignation, Speaker Carl Albert had no choice but to abolish the special committee, which he reconstituted with new membership – dropping Harrington, Stanton, Giaimo, and Nedzi – under the chairmanship of another member of the Fearless Five, Otis Pike.

The contretemps over the Nedzi resignation diminished the ardor for attacking the CIA in the House, as Giaimo discovered when he introduced an amendment to reveal the agency's funding level. The Connecticut congressman had championed the issue even before the Harrington disclosures; in 1974, he asserted that he could no longer "in good conscience" vote for a defense budget "which includes concealed funds" for CIA "covert intelligence operations that work to overthrow governments philosophically different from ours."[190] Stratton claimed that the Giaimo amendment "would actually abolish the CIA"; Jack Kemp (R-New York), though not "trying to sound dramatic," indicated that "there are people's lives at stake" in the vote's outcome.[191] To Wisconsin Democrat David Obey, such remarks confirmed an old political adage: "If you can't dazzle them with brilliance, then baffle them with B.S."[192] If so, the tactics worked: the amendment lost

---

[186] *New York Times*, 21 Feb. 1975.

[187] *Washington Post*, 11 April 1975.

[188] John Stennis press release, May 1975, Series 43, Box 29, John Stennis Papers, Mississippi State University.

[189] Unidentified clipping, n.d. [1975], Box 39, Samuel Stratton Papers, University of Rochester.

[190] Robert Giaimo to Tae Hea Nahm, 18 Dec. 1974, Box 83, Robert Giaimo Papers, University of Connecticut.

[191] 121 *CR*, 94th Congress, 1st session, pp. 31045, 31048, 31049 (1 Oct. 1975).

[192] 121 *CR*, 94th Congress, 1st session, p. 31041 (1 Oct. 1975).

267–147. After the vote, in what his staffers conceded was a "terrible quote," a frustrated Giaimo asserted that "we need to divulge the whole CIA budget in public."[193]

Just as the House seemed inclined to rebuff any move against the intelligence community, however, events in Africa led Congress to reverse course. Beginning in the early 1960s, three independence movements – the Popular Movement for the Liberation of Angola (MPLA), the National Front for the Liberation of Angola (FNLA), and the National Union for the Total Independence of Angola (UNITA) – engaged in a complicated scramble for power in the Portuguese colony of Angola, in which each faction searched for outside patrons.[194] In light of Watergate and the withdrawal from Vietnam, Kissinger suggested that inaction would suggest "that the U.S. has abdicated in Southern Africa."[195] With a new government in Portugal committed to granting Angola independence by the summer of 1975, the African nation offered a timely opportunity, another Republican reasoned, "to find out if you could still have covert operations."[196] Accordingly, the administration authorized secret assistance to the FNLA and then later to UNITA.

As news of covert U.S. aid first emerged, one senator remarked, "Where the hell is Angola?"[197] Unfortunately for the administration, Dick Clark already knew the answer – the Hughes-Ryan amendment ensured that, as a Foreign Relations Committee member, he received briefings about the covert operation.[198] The recently named chair of the African Affairs Subcommittee had already aroused GOP concerns for what Republicans termed a tendency "to criticize the U.S. for not having contacted and assisted the 'liberation' movements in southern Africa."[199] Having learned from his former colleague, Harold Hughes, that "one of the best ways to curb illegal intelligence operations is to find out what's going on" and then to publicize the matter, in September 1975 Clark introduced

[193] Bob to Eileen Nixon, n.d. [1975], Box 86, Robert Giaimo Papers, University of Connecticut; *New Haven Journal-Courier*, 2 Oct. 1975.

[194] Thomas Noer, "International Credibility and Political Survival: The Ford Administration's Intervention in Angola," *presidential Studies Quarterly* 23 (1993), pp. 771–776; Daniel Spikes, *Angola and the Politics of Intervention* (Jefferson, NC, 1993), pp. 115–160.

[195] Roger Morris, "A Rare Resignation in Protest: Nat Davis and Angola," *Washington Monthly*, February 1976; Nathaniel Davis, "The Angola Decision of 1975: A Personal View," *Foreign Affairs* (fall 1978), pp. 123–124.

[196] Peter Lakeland to Jacob Javits, 5 February 1976, Box 63, Series 4, Subseries 2, Jacob Javits Papers, University of Stony Brook.

[197] Spikes, *Angola and the Politics of Intervention*, p. 155.

[198] Dick Clark personal interview with author.

[199] Bob Turner, "Africa: Witnesses and Weather," 16 June 1975; Robert Griffin handwritten memo, 16 June 1975; both in Africa subcommittee box, Senate Foreign Relations Committee series, Robert Griffin Papers, Central Michigan University.

an amendment to the foreign aid bill to bar appropriations for Angolan operations.[200]

In November, in a piece of bad luck for Ford's policy, funds for the covert operation expired, which required the administration to seek an emergency supplemental appropriation. With the entire Foreign Relations Committee on hand, CIA deputy director William Nelson continued the pattern of agency openness evident since Colby's performance in the Diego Garcia hearings, and admitted that covert assistance had ballooned to $32 million. Edward Mulcahy, the recently named assistant secretary of state for African affairs, appeared next. Late to the hearing and thus not privy to Nelson's disclosures, Mulcahy described the involvement as unchanged from 1974, compromising the administration's credibility to such an extent that the committee unanimously reported Clark's amendment, ensuring that it would win approval when the Senate considered the foreign aid bill the following January. Most members acted less from sympathy with Clark – who, as one staffer noted, continued to be viewed as "rather radical" – than from disgust with Mulcahy's duplicity.[201]

Clark relied on a traditional method of asserting congressional influence: a policy rider to the foreign aid bill. Seeking to maximize the pressure, John Tunney introduced an amendment to the defense appropriations bill to prohibit further assistance and to reduce the allocation by $33 million (the amount estimated already spent in Angola). Given the new internationalists' record on defense amendments in the 1975 session, Clark considered the tactic too risky, but Tunney countered that the Pentagon measure provided "exactly the right vehicle to take us where we wanted to go."[202] He gambled that Angola's superficial resemblance to the early stages of the involvement in Vietnam would generate sufficient support.

In a two-hour secret session on the morning of December 17, Tunney cited the dangers of excessive deference on national security matters to both the executive branch and senior senators. The Vietnam War and the Angolan involvement showed that "Congress, if it is to fulfill its responsibilities, must be informed about our foreign commitments and about financing covert operations."[203] Perceptively selecting his historical analogies, he chose to "paraphrase former Senator Taft"; despite their differing belief systems,

---

[200] Dick Clark to Pam Kringler, 26 November 1975, Box 44, Dick Clark Papers, University of Iowa.

[201] Dick Clark personal interview with author; Dick Moose personal interview with author; Robert Turner, "Yesterday's Angola Hearings," 17 June 1975, Africa subcommittee box, Senate Foreign Relations Committee series, Robert Griffin Papers, Central Michigan University.

[202] Dick Clark personal interview with author; Thomas Franck and Edward Weisband, *Foreign Policy by Congress* (New York: Oxford University Press, 1979), p. 52.

[203] John Tunney, "Dear Colleague," 16 December 1975, Box 6, John Tunney Papers, University of California, Berkeley.

Tunney praised Taft's warnings against giving "the military adventurists what they wanted," since the policy "has gotten us repressive right wing dictatorships as allies all over the world."[204]

To rebut Tunney, administration supporters called for upholding the Senate's institutional norms. By so doing, ironically, they helped make the amendment a referendum on the culture of the Cold War Congress. Using familiar arguments, they stressed the need to respect the committee process, the dangers of legislative haste, and the Senate's inability to address the details of international matters. James McClure (R-Idaho), for instance, denied that "a little limitation on an appropriation bill" could settle an issue of this importance, while Robert Griffin (R-Michigan) denounced "attempts to conduct foreign policy with intrinsically heavy-handed yanks on the federal purse strings."[205]

Tunney's tactic ensured a speedy debate in which the new internationalists did not have to spell out the full implications of their policy suggestions. After a last-ditch filibuster organized by Griffin collapsed, the amendment prevailed by a tally of 54–22.[206] Tunney had gambled and won: for the first time since the interwar era, a policy rider to a defense bill cleared the Senate without being watered down in any way. The Senate then passed the full Pentagon funding measure, and the House followed course. A month later, both chambers approved the Clark amendment, making permanent the ban on Angola covert aid.

Unfortunately for the new internationalists, African affairs, and the domestic lens through which they were interpreted, changed almost immediately thereafter. With the Tunney amendment eliminating any prospect for U.S. military intervention in Angola, the Vietnam analogy lost its relevance. Passage of the amendment also coincided with the pro-Soviet MPLA consolidating its power, assisted by Cuban "volunteers."[207] And so, as had occurred after the final debate about Vietnam aid, Kissinger turned the tables, suggesting that Angola proved the excesses of legislative activism. The first sign of the new strategy came when the Tunney amendment went before the House of Representatives. Administration critics mirrored the arguments of Tunney and Clark; Giaimo, charging that Ford's "Angolan policy conjures up horrifying memories of Vietnam," demanded that the administration present its

---

204 John Tunney, "Statement on Angola (closed sess.)," 17 December 1975, Box 2, John Tunney Papers, University of California, Berkeley.

205 James McClure to Cassandra Street, 4 May 1976, box 6-2, Foreign Relations Series, James McClure Papers, University of Idaho; Robert Griffin speech, "The Stakes in Angola," 18 December 1975, Angola folder, Africa box, Robert Griffin Papers, Central Michigan University.

206 Bob Wolthuis to Max Friedersdorf, 16 December 1975, Box 3, Robert Wolthuis Files, Congressional Relations Office Papers, Gerald Ford Presidential Library.

207 Piero Gleijeses, *Conflicting Missions: Havana, Washington, and Africa, 1959–1976* (Chapel Hill: University of North Carolina Press, 2003), pp. 200–217.

policy "publicly and defend it."[208] Convinced of "certain defeat," Mahon, floor leader of the anti-amendment forces, sought to " 'low key' the vote as much as possible to reduce the damage."[209] Instead, White House officials gave Giaimo what he wanted, launching a high-profile "presentation of the Administration's case," hoping the public would come to view Angola as a case of congressional recklessness.[210] Engaging in a bit of revisionist history, Kissinger described his Angolan policy as "effective so long as we maintained the leverage of a possible military balance"; blame for any subsequent deterioration fell on Congress, for depriving him of the "indispensable flexibility" necessary to conduct foreign affairs.[211]

Senate Republicans broadened the assault. Dewey Bartlett argued that the MPLA's victory "gave irrefutable proof that a committee of one hundred is unsuitable for day-to-day foreign policy decisions"; indeed, the "formulation of the issue through a rider on an appropriations bill" typified a "careless" process that "greatly reduced" the "odds in favor of correct decisions."[212] McClure hoped that the MPLA's triumph would cause "those members of Congress so anxious for the United States to sit back and allow events in the world to run their course" to "have second thoughts and reconsider our responsibility as leader of the free world."[213] Otherwise, the Idaho senator predicted, all southern Africa would fall under Soviet domination.

Although McClure's rhetoric was a bit overheated, it was Tunney and Clark, as one observer noted, who had "misjudged the public temper."[214] The progress of the intelligence inquiries only intensified the public reaction against the new internationalists' agenda. Previewing later conservative attacks, Stratton denounced Pike's committee almost from the start, claiming that his New York colleague secretly wanted to destroy the CIA.[215] The committee's report made a penetrating two-level critique, accusing the CIA of repeated intelligence failures – such as not predicting the Tet offensive, the Warsaw Pact invasion of Czechoslovakia, and the Yom Kippur War – while also bungling several high-profile covert operations. But when the administration balked at declassifying items in the document, Pike

---

[208] Robert Giaimo, "Dear Colleague," 19 Jan. 1976, Box 86, Robert Giaimo Papers, University of Connecticut.

[209] Cathie Bennett to Brent Scowcroft, 20 January 1976, Box 32, National Defense series, White House Central File, Gerald Ford Presidential Library.

[210] Max Friedersdorf, "Memorandum for the President," 22 January 1976, Box 32, National Defense series, White House Central File, Gerald Ford Presidential Library.

[211] U.S. Senate, Subcommittee on Africa, *Hearings, Angola*, 94th Congress, 2nd session, pp. 8–14, 34 (29 January 1976).

[212] 122 *CR*, 94th Congress, 2d session, pp. 608–610 (22 January 1976).

[213] James McClure to W. A. Shepherd, 9 April 1976; James McClure to Pat Carney, 26 April 1976; both in Box 6-2, Foreign Relations series, James McClure Papers, University of Idaho.

[214] *Newsweek*, 6 Feb. 1976.

[215] 121 *CR*, 94th Congress, 1st session, p. 32801 (29 Sept. 1975).

recommended releasing it without executive permission, claiming that a "secret" was only "some fact or opinion to which some bureaucrat has applied a stamp."[216] House conservatives, most of whom had not read the report, rebelled; by a vote of 246–124, the House repudiated its own committee's work. Two weeks later, excerpts appeared in a 24-page supplement published by the *Village Voice*; speculation centered on Les Aspin as the source for the leak.[217] Kissinger denounced the document as a "malicious lie" produced by a committee that had used material "in a tendentious, misleading, and totally irresponsible fashion."[218] The episode reinforced claims that Congress should refrain from involvement in intelligence matters.[219]

If Pike's efforts suffered from a perception that he wanted to "impale" the CIA, Church struggled with the opposite problem: eager, according to one staffer, "to prove that we were not Pike," the committee operated with excessive caution.[220] The chairman's attempt to accommodate conservatives, who entered the inquiry with a predetermined view, had no chance of success. The strongly pro-military Tower was the committee's ranking Republican, while the next senior GOP member, Goldwater, confided that Church "frightens the daylights out of me."[221] (To the Arizona senator, "the less we know about the CIA and what it is doing the better off the country is."[222]) In the end, Church erred by focusing on the agency's alleged involvement in assassination plots; when the committee finally produced its report, one staffer recalled, "we had lost three things – the public's attention, much of our own energy, and our leadership," since the Idaho Democrat was making a longshot presidential bid.[223]

All of a sudden, new internationalist foreign policy, in the words of *Newsweek*, had "become bad politics" – a development that also affected consideration of defense issues.[224] In early 1976, one administration official expected that the Pentagon "in the years ahead will have the toughest Congressional Liaison job in government outside of the White House."[225] By the end of the year, however, *Congressional Quarterly* described the result as a "rout" for Pentagon critics.[226] Jonathan Bingham conceded that the

[216] *New York Times*, 30 Jan. 1976.
[217] Thomas Downey personal interview with author, 27 May 2004.
[218] *Congressional Quarterly Weekly Report*, 21 Feb. 1976.
[219] *Wall Street Journal*, 20 Dec. 1975.
[220] Taylor Branch, "The Trial of the CIA," *New York Times Magazine*, 12 March 1976.
[221] Barry Goldwater to John Stennis, 19 Jan. 1976, Series 43, Box 29, John Stennis Papers, Mississippi State University.
[222] Barry Goldwater to John Stennis, 19 Jan. 1976, Series 43, Box 29, John Stennis Papers, Mississippi State University.
[223] Taylor Branch, "The Trial of the CIA," *New York Times Magazine*, 12 March 1976.
[224] *Newsweek*, 9 February 1976.
[225] Bob Worthuis to John Marsh, 15 Jan. 1976, Box 79, Counselors to the President – John Marsh Files, Gerald Ford President Library.
[226] *CQ Almanac 1976*, p. 127.

outcome suggested that most of his colleagues believed that "our own relative strength is declining, and that Angola demonstrates a new Soviet adven-
turism which must be countered."[227]

Important political and intellectual developments amplified the effect of
the shifting international environment. On the political front, the hard-line
presidential campaign of former California governor Ronald Reagan made
the administration even less willing than usual to compromise; Ford (a few
days before the important Texas primary) even threatened to veto the defense
appropriations bill if Congress made too many reductions.[228] Intellectually,
the mid-1970s featured the emergence of the neoconservatives. Mostly former Democrats, often Jewish intellectuals, and always admirers of Cold
War liberalism of the type practiced by Harry Truman, the neoconservatives argued that the new internationalists underestimated the Soviet threat
and that a lesser military role in U.S. foreign policy would encourage Soviet
expansionism. By linking a more robust overseas posture with a foreign policy supportive of traditional ideals such as democracy and self-determination,
the neoconservatives provided an increasingly powerful alternative to the
new internationalist agenda, especially as Soviet behavior in the mid-1970s
shifted toward a more aggressive course.[229]

As Downey discovered, "Everybody is walking on eggs when you talk
about cutting defense spending."[230] The House's most interesting defense
debate came over an amendment that the New York Democrat sponsored
to suspend MaRV construction. The discussion revealed that, as had been
the case in the 1950s, confronting the Pentagon was again politically risky.
Downey defended his offering as the best way to encourage negotiations on
a weapons system that was "uniquely provocative," indeed "nothing short
of insane."[231] The United States had to act fast, the New York Democrat
noted, since while MaRV testing was verifiable, its deployment was not. He
conceded that "the pros and cons of this amendment are somewhat more
technical and involved than the usual money issues" – though he considered
it "more significant in terms of the nation's ultimate security."[232]

Most colleagues disagreed: the amendment attracted only 95 votes after
a round of denunciations of its sponsor. Joe Waggoner (D-Louisiana) stated
that he had "no reluctance" to oppose an amendment offered by Downey,
since "once again he is wrong, dead wrong, he is completely wrong."[233]

---

[227] 122 CR, 94th Congress, 2nd session, p. 10245 (9 April 1976).
[228] *Wall Street Journal*, 1 April 1976.
[229] John Ehrman, *The Rise of Neoconservatism: Intellectuals and Foreign Affairs*, 1945–1994
(New Haven: Yale University Press, 1995).
[230] *Wall Street Journal*, 10 April 1976.
[231] 122 CR, 94th Congress, 2nd session, p. 10216 (9 April 1976).
[232] Thomas Downey, "Dear Colleague," 7 April 1976, Box 43, Samuel Stratton Papers,
University of Rochester.
[233] 122 CR, 94th Congress, 2nd session, p. 10219 (9 April 1976).

(Downey sarcastically expressed his appreciation for Waggoner's "feeling that we can discuss this as though we were charging San Juan Hill."[234]) Given "the various program terminations and prescriptions he has urged upon Congress," Jack Kemp concluded that his New York colleague favored "a definite position of unilateral disarmament."[235] And Stratton condescendingly praised Downey for displaying a "great deal of conscientiousness" in trying to master information that came before the Armed Services Committee; unfortunately, Stratton continued, his colleague must have missed the meeting that explained counterforce doctrine.[236]

The politics of procedure remained the last hope for defense critics in 1976; Stratton, recognizing the threat, complained that the Armed Services Committee was "getting murdered by the Budget Committee."[237] The new committee defined its prerogatives broadly: the chief staffer for its National Security Task Force described its goal as clarifying "some of the myths and misconceptions about the nature and extent of the increased emphasis on defense spending in the Soviet Union."[238] The task force's top two Democrats, Giaimo and Leggett, expected the Budget Committee to develop "coherent national priorities without being stampeded into accepting every Pentagon proposal as a result of election-year hysteria."[239] The duo's hopes, however, were misplaced: neither chamber's committee substantially reduced the administration's proposed defense hike of 14 percent. The Senate committee, after heavy lobbying from Stennis, even reported that "prudence and world conditions require some real growth in strategic and tactical forces."[240]

Critics did score one victory, owing to a combination of domestic politics and shrewd parliamentary tactics. In early 1976, prompted by grassroots activists, presidential candidate Jimmy Carter, campaigning in dovish Iowa, came out against the B-1. Carter's move pressured wavering Democrats to support their party's leader, and Culver sponsored an amendment to defer consideration of the plane for a year.[241] (The Iowa senator correctly anticipated that a massive lobbying campaign organized by Rockwell – what Mary McGrory termed the "current scramble to convert the country into

[234] 122 *CR*, 94th Congress, 2nd session, p. 10219 (9 April 1976).
[235] 122 *CR*, 94th Congress, 2nd session, p. 10221 (9 April 1976).
[236] 122 *CR*, 94th Congress, 2nd session, p. 10218 (9 April 1976).
[237] *Congressional Quarterly Weekly Report*, 27 March 1976.
[238] Jack Cove to Robert Giaimo, 29 June 1976, Box 104, Robert Giaimo Papers, University of Connecticut.
[239] Robert Giaimo and Robert Leggett, "Dear Colleague," 12 March 1976, Box 104, Robert Giaimo Papers, University of Connecticut.
[240] John Stennis to Edmund Muskie, 15 March 1976, Box 26, Gary Hart Papers, University of Colorado; *New York Times*, 21 March 1976.
[241] William Rockwell, Jr., "Dear Shareholder," 13 Aug. 1976, unprocessed box, William Proxmire Papers, Wisconsin State Historical Society.

a monster munitions factory" – would prevent Congress from killing the
B-1 outright.[242]) As commentator Elizabeth Drew noted, "this procedural
approach to a substantive issue – making something seem a matter of process, and therefore more reasonable than a frontal attack – is characteristic of
Culver's legislative style," and also characteristic, Drew could have noted, of
the congressional movement with which the Iowa senator affiliated.[243] The
Air Force, assured by Goldwater that he had the votes to prevail, was caught
unprepared.[244] The Iowan's procedural approach won just enough swing
votes – those of Democrats John Glenn, Herman Talmadge, and Dick Stone;
and Republicans Lowell Weicker and William Brock – for the amendment
to squeak through by one vote.[245] Explaining his rationale for choosing to
resist the B-1, Culver noted, "I have to decide which issues to hit hard on
and how to pick my shots, how to remain credible, not to be irrelevant. You
can't posture and fight in a knee-jerk way."[246]

The Iowa senator also understood that despite the victory, the session had
gone poorly for Pentagon critics. In a reverse from the previous few years,
the Pentagon had gotten the best of the lobbying effort. "Genuine concern,"
he noted, existed in Congress over Soviet activities in Angola; mainstream
figures in both parties were uncertain over the future of détente and the
SALT process; and the residual trauma over the defeat in Vietnam produced
a need to demonstrate "machismo."[247] Culver wished that his colleagues
would understand that "we will weaken America, not strengthen it, if we
overreact to Soviet defense spending by just dumping carloads of money on
the Pentagon."[248]

While the Iowa senator's views were increasingly falling out of favor, at
least on defense matters, the new internationalists still maintained the initiative on human rights; in February 1976, Leslie Gelb accurately predicted that
"liberals have at least an even chance of legislating their will into the new
aid bill."[249] A Kennedy amendment to terminate all military aid and sales
to Pinochet's regime in Chile best demonstrated the starkly different foreign
policy principles at play in mid-1970s Washington. The Massachusetts senator termed continued military aid to Chile an outcome that reflected the
"failure of American foreign policy in recent times," caused by "the fact

[242] *Washington Star*, 24 May 1976.
[243] Elizabeth Drew, *Senator* (New York: Simon & Schuster, 1979), p. 24.
[244] *Aviation Week and Space Technology*, 31 May 1976.
[245] William Proxmire to Henry Jackson, 29 July 1976, unprocessed box, William Proxmire
     Papers, Wisconsin State Historical Society.
[246] Drew, *Senator*, p. 25.
[247] John Culver, "Why Is the Pentagon Winning This Year?," notes, April 1976, Box 182, John
     Culver Papers, University of Iowa.
[248] "Culver Comments on Armed Services Committee Action," 14 April 1976, Box 182, John
     Culver Papers, University of Iowa.
[249] *New York Times*, 10 Feb. 1976.

that we have not put the issue of human rights in the forefront."[250] From the other side, Tower theorized that nations such as Chile lacked the "sophisticated political systems and social values associated with the major Western powers," and therefore "do not share, at this point in history, the degree of concern prevalent in the United States for what we consider to be 'human rights.'"[251] The debate changed few minds: Kennedy's amendment passed 48–39, obtaining support from several Democratic moderates. The measure's path through the House was more difficult. Harrington impetuously offered an amendment barring all aid to Chile, which failed by more than 100 votes; continuing his habit of rationalizing his opinions with curious arguments, Doc Morgan contended that other, unspecified, nations receiving U.S. assistance "may be more in violation of human rights than Chile."[252] The large margin of defeat fortified House conferees against the Kennedy amendment, ultimately producing a watered-down version of the Senate offering.[253]

The House, however, did target assistance to another former South American democracy, Uruguay, whose president, Juan Bordaberry, acquiesced in a coup that produced military rule in 1973. Even in the violent atmosphere of 1970s South America, Uruguayan human rights violations stood out; in 1976, Amnesty International estimated that 60,000 people – 2 percent of the country's population – had been arrested or detained since the coup. Contrary to his later image as mayor, Ed Koch (D-New York) affiliated with the new internationalists in the House, and after Amnesty International provided him with background information on Uruguay, Koch introduced an amendment to suspend military aid. The New York congressman hoped that passage would symbolize "intolerance for gross violation of human rights and military repression in countries which desire our friendship and assistance."[254] The administration countered that the amendment constituted interference in Uruguayan internal affairs, since the Montevideo government denied allegations of torture. (Donald Fraser incredulously asked State Department witnesses if they knew of "a single government in the world that admits that it actually engages in torture."[255]) After the committee approved the amendment, one Koch aide recalled, "Everybody and his brother trooped into our office and said, 'Hey, this guy can get something accomplished.'"[256]

[250] 122 *CR*, 94th Congress, 2nd session, p. 3614 (18 Feb. 1976).
[251] *Congressional Quarterly Weekly Report*, 21 Feb. 1976.
[252] *CQ Almanac 1976*, p. 221.
[253] Hubert Humphrey to Edward M. Kennedy, 2 April 1976, Box 6, Legislation 1976 file, Hubert Humphrey Papers, Minnesota State Historical Society.
[254] 122 *CR*, 94th Congress, 2nd session, p. 20511 (25 June 1976).
[255] U.S. House of Representatives, Subcommittee on International Organizations, *Hearings, Human Rights in Uruguay*, 94th Congress, 2nd session, pp. 121, 128 (4 Aug. 1976).
[256] Cynthia Arnson, *Crossroads: Congress, the President, and Central America, 1976–1992* (State College: Penn State University Press, 1993), p. 26.

House approval all but ensured passage of the offering; with Carter raising the human rights issue in the fall campaign, Senate Republicans shied
away from identifying themselves with the Uruguayan military dictatorship.
New internationalists therefore used the debate to champion their broader
agenda. Clark celebrated the amendment for understanding that "America
has developed a uniquely American idea, a set of values, with a concern for
human rights at its very core"; Abourezk described severing aid as a "symbolic act on our part and an actual act that will prevent them from continuing
the abuses of their own people with the use of American money."[257] Kennedy
summed up the principle, arguing that "we must stand with the oppressed,
not the oppressors," demonstrating "a commitment to democratic principles" and a "determination to adhere to principles of law."[258]

A test of how much popular support existed for Kennedy's thesis would
come in the 1976 elections. One positive sign came from Louisiana's August
primary, which decided the fate of Otto Passman. Shortly after the *Wall Street
Journal* reported that the congressman had improperly used House office
funds to purchase personal furniture, syndicated columnist Jack Anderson
revealed that the FBI was investigating allegations of Passman using his position to extort foreign aid shipping contracts for a business crony from foreign
governments. Passman's refusal to comment publicly on the charges – "I'm
not," he said, "going to put a noose around my neck" – sealed his political
fate; he lost to first-time candidate Jerry Huckaby, barely prevailing even in
his home parish of Ouachita.[259]

The fall election went down to the wire; Carter's overwhelming lead dwin-
dled as the public developed second thoughts about the untested former governor. Ultimately, Ford's gaffe in one of the presidential debates (he asserted
that Poland was not a satellite nation of the Soviet Union) and continued
revulsion at the president's pardon of Nixon allowed the Democrat to prevail.
But Carter's narrow victory denied him any clear mandate, while congressional elections yielded a superficially status quo result. In the House, only
two Watergate Democrats failed to win re-election, one from an overwhelmingly Republican district in Illinois, the other a Utah freshman defeated after
being arrested for soliciting a prostitute. The party breakdown in the Senate
remained the same, with 62 Democrats balanced against 38 Republicans.

On closer inspection, a noticeable shift to the right occurred in the Senate,
where an unusually large number (14) of seats changed hands. Several
Republicans were replaced by Democrats with conservative foreign policy credentials. In Nebraska, for instance, the victorious candidate, former

[257] 124 CR, 94th Congress, 2nd session, pp. 33230, 33233 (29 Sept. 1976).
[258] 124 CR, 94th Congress, 2nd session, pp. 33231–33232 (29 Sept. 1976).
[259] *Congressional Quarterly Weekly Report*, 21 Aug. 1976. After his defeat, revelations also
    surfaced that Passman had accepted a $100,000 bribe from South Korean lobbyist Tongsun
    Park. Zelizer, *On Capitol Hill*, pp. 195–196.

Omaha mayor Edward Zorinsky, was a lifelong Republican who switched to the Democrats only after GOP leaders selected another Senate candidate; in New York, a leading neoconservative, Daniel Patrick Moynihan, narrowly defeated Bella Abzug for the Democratic nomination before ousting incumbent James Buckley. While such Democratic gains barely altered the Senate's ideological tenor on foreign affairs, GOP pickups sent considerably more conservative figures to the upper chamber. Hard-line anti-Communists Malcolm Wallop, Orrin Hatch, and Harrison Schmidt defeated Democratic incumbents in Wyoming, Utah, and New Mexico. In Indiana, Indianapolis mayor Richard Lugar retired Vance Hartke, among the most liberal of Senate Democrats after his break from Johnson. Missouri's 1976 outcome undid the 1970 results: Stuart Symington retired, his son (then a Democratic congressman) lost in the primary, and Republican John Danforth captured the seat. Finally, and most dramatically, in California, Tunney fell to S. I. Hayakawa, the former San Francisco State University president who attracted national fame with his crackdown against student protesters and whose campaign sharply criticized the senator's African position and defense record.

A newly conservative congressional atmosphere was on display in the new administration's initial days in office. The change in administration ended Henry Jackson's veto power over the ACDA, and Armed Services Committee conservatives responded by targeting Paul Warnke, whom Carter nominated to serve simultaneously as director of the agency and as chief negotiator for SALT II talks. A former assistant secretary of defense, Warnke worked with opponents of the ABM, and thereafter vociferously opposed Nixon and Ford defense policies: between 1970 and 1974, he urged canceling the Airborne Warning and Control System (AWACS) and F-14 airplanes, counterforce weapons, and the Trident missile.[260] Even though his committee had no formal role regarding the nomination, Stennis convened Armed Services Committee hearings, during which Jackson implied that Warnke had lied about his past positions.[261] Committee Republicans presented a united negative front; a typical GOP attack came from Jake Garn (R-Utah), who simplistically contended that "we have created a monster. At the end of World War II, [the Soviets] were simply not a worldwide power; we were."[262]

In an almost mirror image of the early 1970s, these conservative critiques set the tone for debates on Warnke, which one senator correctly predicted would be a "hullabaloo."[263] Freshman Orrin Hatch (R-Utah), citing Warnke's record of opposing major weapons systems, compared naming

---

[260] "Warnke Recommendations on Specific Defense programs," n.d. [1977], Box 130, Clifford Case Papers, Rutgers University.

[261] *Congressional Quarterly Weekly Report*, 5 March 1977.

[262] *Washington Post*, 27 Feb. 1977.

[263] *New York Times*, 26 Feb. 1977.

him arms control negotiator "to giving Idi Amin the Nobel Peace Prize."[264] Five other GOP freshmen – Garn, Jesse Helms, Harrison Schmitt, Malcolm Wallop, and Dewey Bartlett – assumed prominent roles in what Bartlett described as a fight against the philosophy of relying "on the good will of the Soviet Union to justify the abandonment of our superiority."[265] The altered climate influenced Senate centrists: heretofore a strong arms control supporter, Brooke conceded that "changed strategic circumstances" were forcing him "as well as others to review previous positions advocated in the late 1960s and early 1970s."[266] Privately, the Massachusetts Republican concluded that the United States "can no longer afford to show unilateral restraint as it has for the past decade."[267] Ultimately, only the power of the presidency salvaged Warnke's nomination. After lobbying more than a dozen moderate and conservative Democrats, including the new majority leader, Robert Byrd, Carter obtained enough lukewarm endorsements to ensure confirmation. Sam Stratton, who testified against Warnke, reasoned that the closeness of the vote "signals that any treaty resulting from the talks must ensure absolute equality between the two parties," as mandated by the 1972 Jackson amendment.[268]

In this period of ideological transition, economic concerns, never far from the surface on Pentagon matters, emerged as an unusually public justification for increased defense spending. Tower criticized the administration for reducing funding for the A-7E attack plane, which forced the Vaught Corporation to close its Dallas plant.[269] House Majority Leader Jim Wright (D-Texas) considered it "natural, perhaps," to "support the FB-111, since it was developed in Fort Worth."[270] Stratton complained that "one of the burning problems in New York State, and in the Northeast, is our feeling that to some extent the military services have abandoned the Snow Belt for the Sun Belt."[271] David Emery (R-Maine) chastised the Pentagon for transferring too many jobs overseas, harming areas "of chronic unemployment and low income."[272] Garn touted the Minuteman missile, which was

---

[264] 123 *CR*, 95th Congress, 1st session, p. 6701 (8 March 1977).
[265] 123 *CR*, 95th Congress, 1st session, p. 6863 (9 March 1977).
[266] 123 *CR*, 95th Congress, 1st session, p. 6890 (9 March 1977).
[267] David Rossiter to Edward Brooke, 21 April 1978, Box 77, Edward Brooke Papers, Library of Congress.
[268] Samuel Stratton to Francis Quinlan, 15 March 1977, Box 91, Samuel Stratton Papers, University of Rochester.
[269] *New York Times*, 25 Feb. 1977.
[270] Jim Wright to Robert Giaimo, 26 Sept. 1977, Box 92, Robert Giaimo Papers, University of Connecticut.
[271] U.S. House of Representatives, Armed Services Committee, *Hearings, Military Posture and H.R. 5068*, 95th Congress, 1st session, p. 352 (4 March 1977).
[272] U.S. House of Representatives, Armed Services Committee, *Hearings, Military Posture and H.R. 5068*, 95th Congress, 1st session, pp. 250 (2 Feb. 1977), 847 (8 March 1977).

manufactured partly in Utah.[273] Bob Carr conceded that, for him, the "essential questions" regarding the 1977 defense bill "relate to Michigan."[274]

Downey, among the few not to succumb entirely to the pork barrel tide – his opposition to the B-1 came despite its promised economic benefits for Long Island – admitted that putting his "parochial interest aside" was "always difficult" and something that he did only partially.[275] He joined the Armed Services Committee primarily to protect his defense-industry rich district, and the congressman's staff carefully tracked his assistance for Grumman Aircraft, whose weapons systems he regularly supported.[276] (Downey later characterized some of his Grumman-related positions as "complete hypocrisy," given his overall approach to defense issues.[277]) Job-related concerns, of course, long had sustained what Dwight Eisenhower labeled the military-industrial complex. But the decline of anti-militarist sentiment allowed these matters to play a more prominent role, laying the groundwork for the dramatic expansion of Pentagon spending that began in 1980.

Ironically, the year's only major weapons system battle came through a procedure favorable to the new internationalists. In early 1977, Carter abandoned his campaign pledge and requested additional B-1 funding, producing a debate that Downey termed "difficult to characterize," in which B-1 supporters compared the B-52 bomber to obsolete rifles; contended that Congress should not discuss the issue because Soviet agents might be in the House gallery; fretted that the Warsaw Pact nations independently controlled their ICBMs (an assertion that undoubtedly startled any Soviet observers in attendance); and demanded that the House defer to members with experience as military pilots (an argument that Pat Schroeder and Tom Harkin, both licensed pilots, strongly challenged).[278] Shortly after the House sustained the program, however, the president used the authority provided by Culver's efforts in 1976 and cancelled the B-1, citing continued progress in developing the cruise missile. Carter's decision to terminate the bomber only after a messy House debate previewed the indecision that would mar his presidency.

The most striking aspect of the B-1 debate came less in its outcome than in its illustration of the changing institutional culture of the Senate. Most

[273] *New York Times*, 25 Feb. 1977.

[274] U.S. House of Representatives, Armed Services Committee, *Hearings, Military Posture and H.R. 5068*, 95th Congress, 1st session, p. 255 (2 Feb. 1977).

[275] Thomas Downey, "Dear Colleague," 29 July 1977, Box 92, Robert Giaimo Papers, University of Connecticut; U.S. House of Representatives, Armed Services Committee, *Hearings, Military Posture and H.R. 5068*, 95th Congress, 1st session, p. 336 (3 March 1977).

[276] Carolyn to Tom, 31 May 1984, Box 92, Thomas Downey Papers, Cornell University; Thomas Downey personal interview with author, 27 May 2004.

[277] Thomas Downey personal interview with author, 27 May 2004.

[278] 123 *CR*, 95th Congress, 1st session, p. 21144 (28 June 1977).

speeches occurred before an almost empty chamber; senators walked in, delivered prepared remarks, and then departed. Muskie, opposing the B-1 on behalf of the Budget Committee's majority, spoke before only four senators.[279] In the late 1970s, the Senate started piping speeches into members' offices, freeing senators from the obligation to come to the floor but also minimizing debate on most issues. Addressing the effects of this new environment, Minority Leader Howard Baker (R-Tennessee) was distressed to see "the Senate change gradually and inexorably," losing "some of its character as a deliberative body and a forum for meaningful debate."[280] Baker envisioned debates that "our citizens and the scholars of the present and the future will not see the burnished work product of capable staff, but instead will see something of a contribution of our talent as senators"; unfortunately, he concluded, it did not seem as if "this is the world's greatest deliberative body any more."[281]

These different norms in turn affected the Senate's foreign policy role, since dissenters in general and the new internationalists in particular had relied upon the intellectual give and take of debate to build public support for their positions. A few House members attempted to compensate for the Senate's lost standing. "Sooner or later," Watergate freshman Toby Moffett (D-Connecticut) lamented in early 1978, "this place gets the best of you. You get tired. You get cynical ... worn down, sidetracked, compromised to death."[282] Downey, however, continued to exhibit what he described as a "reasonably aggressive" style on defense matters, and he proved particularly creative in finding ways to maximize his influence.[283] He regularly wrote op-eds and letters to the editor (to local papers like *Newsday* and to national publications such as the *Washington Post* and *New York Times*), seeking to woo colleagues by circulating his viewpoints. Working through aide Bob Sherman, he scheduled informal briefings with top thinkers on strategic issues, to stay on top of the latest ideas of defense intellectuals.[284] Bernard Weinraub of the *New York Times* termed this "controversial, if somewhat iconoclastic figure" the Armed Services Committee's "most articulate liberal voice."[285]

While Downey led a band of House dissenters who challenged Pentagon strategic theory, key Senate liberals, such as Culver and Hart, started searching for a middle ground.[286] In so doing, they contributed to the Senate's

---

[279] *New York Times*, 2 Feb. 1978.

[280] 121 *CR*, 94th Congress, 1st session, p. 16700 (3 June 1975).

[281] 121 *CR*, 94th Congress, 1st session, p. 16700 (3 June 1975).

[282] *New York Times*, 12 April 1978.

[283] *New York Times*, 12 March 1978.

[284] Thomas Downey personal interview with author, 27 May 2004.

[285] *New York Times*, 12 March 1978, 16 March 1978.

[286] Gary Hart, "Dear Colleague," 5 July 1978, Box 25, Gary Hart Papers, University of Colorado; Gary Hart to Harry Byrd, Jr., 6 Feb. 1978, Box 26, Gary Hart Papers, University of Colorado; *Wall Street Journal*, 12 July 1978

rightward shift on defense issues. In the early 1970s, Hughes and Symington had offered intellectually coherent arguments against virtually all significant new weapons systems. Although their efforts rarely succeeded, they created an environment that yielded an overall cut in defense spending, which persisted through 1975: in 1974, Congress slashed 6.2 percent from the Pentagon's budget request; in 1975, the reduction was 10 percent.[287] By 1978, however, the debate was no longer on whether the budget should be cut, but instead only on how to spend the increased funds allocated to defense. In March, speaking as "political realists," three longtime Pentagon critics – Eagleton, Proxmire, and Hatfield – conceded that "the general sentiment" of the Senate was "not supportive of reductions."[288] Clark likewise admitted to "pessimism and skepticism about the proposals of keeping down defense spending," but promised "to keep trying" in the effort.[289]

The shifting nature of defense debate occurred amidst a broader reconsideration of many new internationalist achievements. The *Washington Post*, for instance, observed that "many congressmen have come to perceive that vaguely worded riders on foreign economic legislation are a bad way to protect anybody's human rights."[290] Reflecting this new mindset, the 1978 session featured the ultimate repeal of the Eagleton amendment: even Eagleton's staff saw the United States "at a dead end on the Cyprus issue," with the only question how Congress could "reverse a moral stand like that."[291] As it had twice before, the Senate approved repeal; in the House, Jim Wright urged colleagues to recognize that withdrawing the Eagleton amendment would give the Turks incentive to bargain in good faith. Though Paul Tsongas (D-Massachusetts) condemned Wright's argument for embodying "the quid-pro-quo approach that Texas is so famous for in politics," advocates of repeal prevailed, 208–205.[292]

Even policy successes unintentionally weakened the new internationalists' political position. The major debate of 1978 came over the Panama Canal Treaties, which guaranteed the neutrality of the canal and outlined its transfer to Panama in 2000. Few foreign policy issues in U.S. history have presented so stark a choice between serving the national interest and reflecting constituency wishes.[293] Polls showed overwhelming opposition to restoring Panamanian sovereignty, with opponents far more passionate about the issue than supporters; in early 1978, the office of Missouri freshman John

---

[287] "Notes for Budget Markup," 13 March 1978, Box 193, John Culver Papers, University of Iowa.

[288] Thomas Eagleton, William Proxmire, and Mark Hatfield to John Stennis, 10 March 1968, copy in Box 193, John Culver Papers, University of Iowa.

[289] Dick Clark to Donald Typer, 29 Sept. 1978, Box 69, Dick Clark Papers, University of Iowa.

[290] *Washington Post*, 9 Aug. 1978.

[291] Ann to Thomas Eagleton, 5 Dec. 1977, Folder 4381, Thomas Eagleton Papers, University of Missouri.

[292] 124 *CR*, 95th Congress, 2nd session, pp. 23697–23698 (1 Aug. 1978).

[293] *New York Times*, 10 Feb. 1978.

Danforth had received 12,384 letters condemning the treaties – and just 241 urging an aye vote.[294] Several months into the fight, White House chief of staff Hamilton Jordan conceded, "There's no basic constituency in support of a treaty. The only people who give a damn are the ones who oppose it."[295] Nonetheless, the treaties undeniably served the national interest; Charles Percy estimated that a secret ballot would have yielded passage by a margin of 85–15.[296] In this sense, Sam Nunn accurately described the battle as "a case of most senators struggling to make what they knew was the best policy compatible with their own political survival."[297]

Ronald Reagan's opposition to canal negotiations had jumpstarted his 1976 presidential campaign, and in 1977, he and other conservatives dominated discussion about Panama.[298] Richard Viguerie, the New Right tactician whose use of direct mail revolutionized American politics, considered the canal question "an issue the conservatives can't lose on."[299] The administration, meanwhile, seemed unconcerned with senators' political needs; in early 1978, a White House spokesman reasoned, "If it's a tough issue, well, then senators will have to be senators for a change."[300] The turning point came when Howard Baker not only endorsed the treaties, but also agreed to co-sponsor leadership amendments that clarified U.S. security rights regarding the canal. Byrd then exercised his prerogative as majority leader to consider the neutrality treaty first, hoping that amendments to it could satisfy colleagues' security-related concerns and thereby allow the more important transfer treaty to pass unscathed.[301] By early February 1978, even the *Wall Street Journal* editorial board was recommending passage, lest the treaties distract from more significant battles over strategic arms policy.[302]

When the treaties reached the floor on February 8, a Senate debate was broadcast (by National Public Radio) for the first time in American history.[303] Before an almost empty chamber, with at least one senator asleep, Byrd recalled Edmund Burke's famous words to his British constituents: "Your representative owes you, not his industry only, but his judgment; and he betrays, instead of serving you, if he sacrifices it to your opinion."[304] (The majority leader neglected to mention that voters had not returned Burke to

[294] *The New Republic*, 14 Jan. 1978.
[295] *Newsweek*, 13 Feb. 1978.
[296] *New York Times*, 20 April 1978; *Washington Post*, 12 April 1978.
[297] *Wall Street Journal*, 19 April 1979.
[298] *Newsweek*, 27 March 1978.
[299] *National Journal*, 8 Oct. 1977.
[300] *The New Republic*, 14 Jan. 1978.
[301] *New York Times*, 2 Feb. 1978.
[302] *Wall Street Journal*, 3 Feb. 1978.
[303] *New York Times*, 9 Feb. 1978.
[304] *Newsweek*, 20 Feb. 1978.

Parliament in the following election.[305]) As Robert Kaiser of the *Washington Post* noticed, the formal debate provided "a symbolic substitute for deeper issues that have rarely been addressed directly: the true lessons of the Vietnam War and the proper role for the United States in the post-Vietnam War era."[306] Hatch, for instance, wondered if the United States was "going the way of Rome," with the treaties culminating "that pattern of surrender and appeasement that has cost us so much all over the world."[307] After the Utah senator half-heartedly denied reports that he had personally insulted Panamanian president Omar Torrijos ("I have never called him a tinhorn dictator, but he may be exactly that"), Church, the treaties' floor manager, commented privately, "One more day with him and I'll be ready for a padded cell."[308]

Pat Leahy compared the affair to a soap opera: "You could listen to the debate for several days, leave for a week or two, and come back to it having missed very little."[309] Treaty critics expected this extended discussion to intensify public pressure on undecided senators, but momentum swung in the other direction when Nunn announced his support, lest rejection produce a "dangerous erosion of Executive Branch effectiveness in foreign affairs."[310] The administration secured the clinching votes by backing a reservation sponsored by Dennis DeConcini (D-Arizona) asserting the right to station troops in Panama after 2000. In an unintended commentary on the administration's performance to date, a White House aide remarked after the neutrality treaty passed in a 68–32 vote, "They'll never be able to say again that we can't do anything right."[311]

Although Byrd claimed to have three votes in reserve, the neutrality treaty's narrow margin gave critics heart about derailing the transfer treaty. And so the dilatory tactics continued: commentator Marquis Childs wondered if he could survive any more of Virginia's Harry Byrd's "droning on with all the vibrancy and dynamism of a sleepy night watchman in a marshmallow factory."[312] This frustration boiled over after Malcolm Wallop (R-Wyoming) introduced an amendment stating that Panama's failing to fulfill the terms of the 1978 treaties would restore the 1903 and 1936 treaties – even though a provision of the neutrality treaty had already nullified the two earlier documents. After the Senate tabled the motion, Moynihan blasted the Wyoming senator for wasting his colleagues' time, noting that "we

305 *New York Times*, 10 Feb. 1978.
306 *Washington Post*, 12 April 1978.
307 *Washington Post*, 12 April 1978.
308 *New York Times*, 20 April 1978; Ashby and Gramer, *Fighting the Odds*, p. 543.
309 *Washington Post*, 12 April 1978.
310 "Sam Nunn Report to Georgia," 14 March 1978, Box 2, Record Group II, Subgroup 5, Sam Nunn Papers, Emory University.
311 *Newsweek*, 27 March 1978.
312 *Washington Post*, 14 March 1978.

are all at least supposed to have learned to read before we come into this chamber."[313] The former Harvard professor dismissed Wallop's offering as "inane, so devoid of intellectual competence, or even rhetorical merit, as literally to silence the supporters of these treaties. Are we to reduce the U.S. Senate to a playground, a playpen of juvenilia, to the fantasies of pubescent youth?"[314]

"Pity the historians," the *Washington Post* editorialized at the time, "who, looking back at the climactic moment of the Senate's consideration of the Panama Canal treaties, find themselves peering at Dennis DeConcini."[315] The Arizona senator became a major player in early April, when the Panamanians announced that Torrijos considered the DeConcini reservation unacceptable. The *New York Times* tartly noted that, unlike foreign policy players of previous generations, the freshman Democrat, who won in 1976 only after a vicious primary rendered the GOP nominee unelectable, demonstrated neither "ideological ardor nor intellectual fervor" about international affairs.[316] Now, clearly enjoying the spotlight, he gave little indication of backing down; citing findings from a one-time personal inspection of Panama, the Arizona senator even considered offering a second reservation, to grant the United States the right to send troops anywhere in Panama until the transfer occurred.[317]

Church, despondent, summed up the general sentiment among treaty supporters: "My version of hell is having to listen to DeConcini drone on about the Panama Canal for eternity."[318]

DeConcini's activities stimulated a reevaluation of a central new internationalist assumption: that an empowered Congress would produce a more moral foreign policy. The *Washington Post* lamented an institutional structure in which the fate of a critical international initiative could "hinge on the ill-informed whims on a 40-year-old freshman senator of no previous renown, of no known international awareness, of little experience of any kind," a "lightweight whom serious senators should regard as an institutional embarrassment."[319] *Newsweek* more bluntly labeled the Arizona senator "Dennis the Menace."[320] The dean of Washington correspondents, Scotty Reston, feared that DeConcini's conduct highlighted the increasingly "unpredictable" congressional role in foreign and defense policy.[321] The new internationalists had shattered the Cold War institutional culture, which

---

[313] *New York Times*, 20 March 1978.
[314] *New York Times*, 20 March 1978.
[315] *Washington Post*, 13 April 1978.
[316] *New York Times*, 13 April 1978.
[317] *Washington Post*, 11 April 1978; *New York Times*, 13 April 1978.
[318] Ashby and Gramer, *Fighting the Odds*, p. 548.
[319] *Washington Post*, 13 April 1978.
[320] *Newsweek*, 24 April 1978.
[321] *New York Times*, 14 April 1978.

demanded deference to senior, mostly conservative members. This change, however, had a leveling effect, increasing the influence of all senators, even those, like DeConcini, who possessed minimal credentials on foreign policy matters.

Under enormous political and editorial pressure, DeConcini agreed to a watered-down reservation that paved the way for the transfer treaty's approval, 68–32. The outcome, however, offered no political victory for supporters, as at least one treaty supporter fully understood. Facing re-election in 1978, Thomas McIntyre came under fierce pressure on Panama from William Loeb, the ultra-conservative publisher of the *Manchester Union-Leader*, and the state's equally conservative Republican governor, Meldrim Thomson.[322] Not only did the Democrat refuse to back down, but he coupled his endorsement of the treaty with a public attack on the radical right, whose emergence he deemed "an ominous change...in the very character and direction of American politics."[323] The day after announcing his decision, appearing on *Good Morning America*, McIntyre cited the issue's complexity to account for public sentiment, noting that he could not explain the reasons for the treaty's necessity in a brief conversation with a constituent – a remark widely interpreted as implying that Granite State voters lacked the intelligence to understand the question.[324] Letters denouncing McIntyre's decision flooded his office, their sentiments best captured by a pithy telegram: "You damn fink, you sold us out."[325]

Even though he mishandled the canal matter politically, the New Hampshire senator discerned how a new conservative movement would make the treaties a key issue in the 1978 midterm elections. Frustrated at the slow pace of events in the Senate and facing opposition from Representative Larry Pressler, Abourezk declined to stand for a second term. Republicans recruited strong challengers for Floyd Haskell and William Hathaway, Representative William Armstrong in Colorado and Representative William Cohen in Maine. Biden, the lowest-profile member of the 1972 freshmen, avoided a first-tier opponent, as did Clark, who faced Iowa's conservative former lieutenant governor, Roger Jepsen. After Thomson, surprisingly, declined to make the race, McIntyre likewise attracted a weak foe – Gordon Humphrey, a little-known New Right activist and state coordinator of the Conservative Caucus, a grassroots organization that opposed the Panama Canal Treaties.

The new internationalists' foreign policy came under attack in each of these Senate contests. In Colorado, Haskell refused to backtrack, criticizing

---

[322] *Manchester Union-Leader*, 25 Feb. 1978, 1 March 1978.
[323] *Washington Post*, 3 March 1978.
[324] Thomas McIntyre to Ralph Worcester, 27 April 1978, Box 104, Series III, Thomas McIntyre Papers, University of New Hampshire.
[325] Anne Marvel to Thomas McIntyre, 18 April 1978, Box 104, Series III, Thomas McIntyre Papers, University of New Hampshire.

Carter only for displaying insufficient attention to human rights violations in friendly states such as Pakistan, the Philippines, and South Africa.[326] In New Hampshire, Humphrey flooded the expensive Boston airwaves with commercials advocating a more aggressive defense posture and terming the Panama Canal Treaties "another engraved invitation to the Soviets to expand their influence."[327] In Burkean language, Clark justified his treaty vote by citing his "responsibility not only to reflect the popular mood, but to make intelligent judgments on his own personal initiatives"; in any case, he believed that nationalistic appeals would fall short, since "Iowans are not hicks."[328] His opponent certainly was no intellectual heavyweight: Jepsen variously claimed that the Clark amendment imposed sanctions against South Africa, "one of our best friends"; responded "no comment" when asked what policy the United States should adopt in Angola; and wildly asserted that Clark favored military aid to African Communists as part of a foreign policy of "encouraging and supporting terrorists."[329] But the MPLA's consolidation of power in Angola bolstered the Republican's theme that Clark's international approach, bent toward "appeasement and not supporting our friends and allies," reflected "the exact thoughts of Russia."[330]

In June, in an ominous sign for the new internationalists, New Jersey Republicans refused to renominate Clifford Case, a key player in the group's activism dating from 1972, when he sponsored the Case Act on executive agreements and the Case-Church amendment to cut off funds for military operations in Vietnam. Case's defeat previewed a broader pattern for November: the *Washington Post*'s Robert Kaiser recognized that "the big losers in . . . Senate voting were liberals, whose rank and morale were both depleted."[331] In South Dakota, Pressler won by more than 40 points; Cohen and Armstrong ousted Hathaway and Haskell by almost identical 20-point margins. Pressler had run ahead in polls, and the Maine and Colorado races had been rated as toss-ups – but the overwhelming margins of defeat for Democrats suggested a transformation of public opinion.

The evening's most stunning results, however, came in Iowa and New Hampshire. In the Hawkeye State, with Clark's base among Catholic

326 Floyd Haskell robo letter, n.d. [1977], Series II, Box 45, Floyd Haskell Papers, University of Colorado; *Rocky Mountain News*, 10 May 1977.
327 Unidentified clipping, n.d. [1978], Box 104, Series III, Thomas McIntyre Papers, University of New Hampshire; *Washington Post*, 9 Nov. 1978.
328 Dick Clark to Carl Schmidt, 15 Sept. 1978, Box 69, Dick Clark Papers, University of Iowa.
329 *Des Moines Register*, 16 May 1978; *Fort Dodge* Messenger, 10 May 1978. One Clark staffer snidely but probably accurately remarked that he "doubted that Jepsen could even begin to describe" the politics of the region. Staff memo, n.d. [1978], Box 72, Dick Clark Papers, University of Iowa.
330 *Des Moines Register*, 21 May 1978; *Daily Iowan*, 30 Aug. 1978.
331 *Washington Post*, 9 Nov. 1978.

Democrats weakened by his pro-choice view on abortion and Jepsen unusually well-funded from national conservatives (and, rumors went, from
a South African government seeking retribution for Clark's activism),
the incumbent lost by just over 25,000 votes, 52–48 percent.[332] In New
Hampshire, the percentage breakdown was almost identical in Humphrey's
upset over McIntyre. In neither state had the challenger led in even one
pre-election poll. A few months later, according to *Newsweek*, national
Democrats still considered the McIntyre and Clark defeats "especially
chilling."[333]

Beginning with the ABM fight in 1969, a sizeable bloc of Senate liberals,
eventually joined by ideological comrades from the House, attempted to use
congressional power to remake American foreign policy, abandoning what
they saw as the rigid, military-centered anti-Communism of the Cold War
era and adopting instead an approach focused on promoting human rights
and democracy overseas. As the revisionists discovered two decades before,
however, a congressionally sponsored foreign policy could backfire on its
proponents, causing not only policy difficulties but also political problems.
It remained unclear, however, how the myriad institutional changes implemented by the new internationalists would affect foreign policy now that the
most ardent advocates of those reforms were on the political and ideological
decline.

[332] *Newsweek*, 11 June 1979.
[333] *Newsweek*, 11 June 1979.

7

The Triumph of the Armed Services Committee

Politically, the 1978 Senate races previewed the 1980 election, which concluded with the GOP capturing control of the Senate for the first time since 1955. Ideologically, they revealed a change in public opinion that had profound institutional effects. Since the early 1960s, the new internationalists had attempted to use the institutional powers of the upper chamber to alter foreign policy – quite successfully so in the early and mid-1970s. Voters rejected this approach in 1978, producing a less active and less ideologically consistent Senate, which in turn accelerated the upper chamber's decline vis-à-vis the House.

With John Sparkman's retirement, Frank Church inherited the Foreign Relations Committee chairmanship. The Idaho senator appointed William Bader, a Carl Marcy protégé, as chief of staff; he looked to reverse the decline of both the Senate and the new internationalists by reinvigorating the committee.[1] The task was impossible: the bipartisan Foreign Relations Committee that Arthur Vandenberg and Henry Cabot Lodge had dominated during the Truman administration and that J. William Fulbright and Stuart Symington had used so effectively to challenge Nixon's foreign policy no longer existed. Clifford Case's defeat removed him as the committee's ranking member; though the similarly inclined Jacob Javits took his place, three conservative Republicans – Jesse Helms, S. I. Hayakawa, and Richard Lugar – joined the committee. For the first time in the Cold War, conservatives formed the majority of the committee's GOP contingent; invoking its authority under the 1970 Legislative Reorganization Act, the minority hired its own staff, abandoning the committee's tradition of nonpartisan personnel policy. Bader's aggressiveness alienated much of the remaining staff, while Church's preference for centralized control encountered resistance from the subcommittee chairs; within a matter of months, the Idaho senator and John

---

[1] *New York Times*, 9 Jan. 1979.

Glenn (D-Ohio), who chaired the Asian affairs subcommittee, were barely on speaking terms.[2]

This committee turmoil formed the backdrop to Senate consideration of the SALT II treaty. While the treaty mostly benefited the United States, it contained a variety of points upon which arms control critics could seize. SALT II prevented both sides from building very large ICBMs, but it allowed the Soviets to keep the 326 SS-18 missiles they already possessed. The treaty did not count as an intercontinental weapon the Backfire bomber, although it had the capability for such use, since the Soviets primarily targeted the PRC with the plane. The treaty placed no limitations on Soviet SS-20 missiles, which had a 3,000-mile range and thus threatened Europe but not the United States. Finally, questions existed about the U.S. ability to verify Soviet compliance in light of the loss of Iranian intelligence posts after the Shah's regime fell in late 1978.[3]

It quickly became clear that on SALT Carter would not receive the bipartisan support that played such a critical role in passing the Panama treaty. Six days after the 1978 midterm elections, Howard Baker announced his opposition to the treaty; one colleague described the Tennessee senator as "tired" of paying a political price for "doing the right thing."[4] Baker's decision left the hard-line, knowledgeable Jack Garn and John Tower as the most prominent GOP voices on SALT. Tower had been the Republicans' most passionate critic of arms control since the 1960s, while Garn focused on SALT to such an extent that his wife claimed that the Utah senator talked about the treaty in his sleep. According to one staffer, the freshman understood "that in the Senate knowledge is power, because so many senators are spread so thin on so many issues."[5]

In sharp contrast to consideration of past arms control treaties, as the *Wall Street Journal*'s Al Hunt noticed, it was the Armed Services Committee and not the Foreign Relations Committee that possessed the "Senate heavyweights."[6] Bitterly hostile questions from the committee's newly elected Republicans – William Cohen, Gordon Humphrey, Roger Jepsen, and Virginia's John Warner – illustrated the significance of the 1978 elections. Humphrey, the most conservative of the quartet, privately described Bob Dole as a socialist; in public, he demanded "military superiority over those Russian bastards."[7]

---

[2] John Holum to George McGovern, 8 Nov. 1979, Box 58, Staff Files, John Glenn Papers, Ohio State University; Ashby and Gramer, *Fighting the Odds*, p. 563.

[3] *Congressional Quarterly Weekly Report*, 12 May 1979.

[4] *Washington Post*, 19 Jan. 1979.

[5] *New York Times*, 28 May 1979.

[6] *Wall Street Journal*, 19 April 1979.

[7] *Wall Street Journal*, 22 Jan. 1979; *Washington Post*, 3 March 1979; *New York Times*, 24 July 1979.

With unanimous opposition from committee Republicans, all focus fell on Sam Nunn; Hunt argued that the Georgia Democrat wielded "as much power as anyone in the Senate on military issues, and his influence is widening."[8] (One White House strategist confessed, "I can envision winning SALT without Jackson and possibly even without Baker, but without Nunn, we're dead."[9]) On July 25, in what Charles Mohr of the *New York Times* termed the debate's "most dramatic development," the Georgia senator announced the price for his backing the treaty: that the president personally mobilize support for a 5 percent real increase in future defense spending.[10] "All Sam is asking," complained one Senate staffer, "is that Carter alienate the liberal wing of the Democratic Party with an election year coming up."[11]

Nunn wanted to devote this money to a variety of new weapons systems, the most controversial of which was the MX missile.[12] The 71-foot-tall missile contained ten 5.5-foot-long nuclear warheads, each of which was 17 times more powerful than the atomic bomb that destroyed Hiroshima.[13] The MX evolved from a confused rationale: the Air Force's Strategic Air Command wanted it as a more powerful offensive weapon; the Pentagon desired the MX to close an alleged window of vulnerability, in which Soviet missile technology could develop sufficient accuracy to decimate U.S. ICBMs in their silos; and neoconservative thinkers around Henry Jackson envisioned the missile as a tit-for-tat response to the deployment of Soviet heavy missiles.[14] The version of the MX offered in the late 1970s combined evolutionary strategic capabilities (it was similar in design but slightly more powerful than the Minuteman II and Minuteman III missiles) with a revolutionary launching strategy dubbed the "racetrack," which consisted of 4,600 missile shelters in remote areas of the Rocky Mountain West, connected by underground ditches and railways through which the missiles could be moved randomly.

If fully funded, the MX promised to create up to 130,000 defense-related jobs, but the missile aroused furious resistance, across party lines, in states where it would be based.[15] Regional opposition spread as far east as western Nebraska, whose congresswoman, Republican Virginia Smith, attacked

---

[8] U.S. Senate, Armed Services Committee, *Hearings, Department of Defense Authorization for Fiscal Year 1980*, 96th Congress, 1st session, p. 62 (25 Jan. 1979); *Wall Street Journal*, 10 April 1979.

[9] *Wall Street Journal*, 10 April 1979.

[10] *New York Times*, 26 July 1979.

[11] *New York Times*, 26 July 1979.

[12] Sam Nunn, Henry Jackson, and John Tower to Jimmy Carter, 2 Aug. 1979, Box 989, John Tower Papers, Southwestern University.

[13] *Time*, 6 Dec. 1982.

[14] Elizabeth Drew, "A Political Journal," *The New Yorker*, 20 June 1983.

[15] David Kennedy, "Les Aspin and MX," Kennedy School of Government case study C14-83-568.0, pp. 1–2.

MX for taking "prime agricultural land" from her district's "loyal, hard-working, and dedicated Americans"; Nevada's at-large congressman, Jim Santini, asked colleagues how they would feel if the government placed mobile nuclear missiles in the heart of their district, "much of it undisturbed and potentially valuable federal land."[16] An amendment co-sponsored by Tom Downey and Pat Schroeder to stop the MX attracted 100 votes; indicative of the declining strength of Pentagon critics in the upper chamber, a comparable Senate offering failed 77–11.

Tower's staff worried that Nunn's conditional endorsement of SALT II could create a "consensus for increased defense spending" that "deflected attention away from the flaws in the treaty."[17] Instead, SALT supporters lost the momentum after the Georgia senator issued his demands. Trying to put a positive spin on developments, Gary Hart detected in the Nunn position a "new consensus," linking "limits on strategic arms with over-all modernization of our forces," thus ending an era of "severe polarization of defense spending."[18] Liberals, in any case, had little power to stop Nunn. When Paul Tsongas, who had ousted Edward Brooke in 1978, put together a letter co-signed by 10 like-minded colleagues and (oddly) Larry Pressler expressing concern that the debate had "recast SALT as a vehicle for sharply increased military expenditures," expected signatories such as Thomas Eagleton passed.[19] The Missouri Democrat, up for re-election in 1980, said that he would "keep a 'low profile' on SALT for the present."[20]

Democrats' tailoring their positions to the new political realities had a disastrous impact. During a campaign swing back in Idaho, Church announced that U.S. surveillance had detected a Soviet combat brigade in Cuba. A few days later, the Foreign Relations Committee chair pronounced SALT II doomed if the soldiers remained.[21] The Idaho senator's overreaction – the Soviet troops hardly constituted a threat – was widely pilloried by treaty supporters: "It's called survival as he perceives it," one Democratic colleague scoffed.[22]

In the event, the treaty had little chance of approval by this time. In late November, Republican figures indicated that 40 senators, including 9 Democrats, would vote no; the seizure of hostages at the American

[16] Jim Santini, "Dear Colleagues," 11 Sept. 1979, Box 98, Robert Giaimo Papers, University of Connecticut; 124 *CR*, 95th Congress, 2nd session, p. 32678 (29 Sept. 1978).

[17] Rhett Dawson, "Memorandum to Senator Tower," 14 Aug. 1979, Box 970, John Tower Papers, Southwestern University.

[18] Gary Hart press release, 2 Aug. 1979, Box 16, Gary Hart Papers, University of Colorado.

[19] Paul Tsongas, et al., to Jimmy Carter, 3 August 1979, Folder 4507, Thomas Eagleton Papers, University of Missouri.

[20] Thomas Eagleton marginalia, in Skipp Hayes to Thomas Eagleton, 3 Aug. 1979, Folder 4507, Thomas Eagleton Papers, University of Missouri.

[21] *Washington Post*, 6 Sept. 1979.

[22] *Washington Post*, 11 Sept. 1979.

embassy in Iran solidified this opposition.[23] The penultimate act came on December 20, when the Armed Services Committee, ignoring its lack of formal jurisdiction on the question, voted 10–0, with 7 abstentions, to issue a report against the treaty. The move symbolized the Foreign Relations Committee's decline: while it would make headlines on occasional issues during Ronald Reagan's first term, never again would the committee exercise a decisive impact on Cold War foreign policy. When Soviet forces subsequently invaded Afghanistan, President Carter asked the Senate to defer action on the treaty indefinitely.

The SALT debate recalled the battle over the ABM; in both cases, a congressional bloc skeptical of the executive's national security philosophy used a lengthy discussion of a specific issue to explore broad policy concerns. The congressional right also targeted the foreign aid program, its intellectual case fortified by Jeane Kirkpatrick's 1979 *Commentary* article, which posited a distinction between totalitarian (Communist) regimes and authoritarian (undemocratic right-wing) governments. Kirkpatrick reasoned that authoritarian regimes often evolved into free ones – and in any case were friendly to the United States. From this framework, she argued that human rights diplomacy had retarded the cause it claimed to promote by making authoritarian regimes more vulnerable to takeover by totalitarian left-wing or religious movements.[24]

While a variety of riders to the 1979 foreign aid bill drew upon Kirkpatrick's thinking, the most obvious was a Helms amendment to make "our Nation's human rights policy more responsive to other policy needs" by providing aid to any country that "demonstrates any significant improvement in its human rights record."[25] To Helms, it seemed that "we have had a great deal of bombast from time to time in the Senate about Chile and Argentina from those who are, apparently, blind to the conduct of other Marxist nations. Maybe the trouble is that Argentina and Chile are both anti-Communist nations."[26] With senators increasingly afraid of appearing soft on Communism, Javits, floor leader for this section of the committee's bill, agreed to compromise. The North Carolina senator rejoiced that at last public opinion recognized that Allende was "a moral bum. He ruined the country, its economy. He kept a mistress out at a country place."[27]

Political developments strengthened this right-wing activism: in contrast to the 1960s, when the new internationalists (correctly) believed that their

[23] "Senate checklist," 21 Dec. 1979, Box 91, Legislative Assistant Series, Strom Thurmond Papers, Clemson University.

[24] Jeane Kirkpatrick, "Dictatorships and Double Standards," *Commentary*, Nov. 1979.

[25] 125 *CR*, 96th Congress, 1st session, p. 15405 (19 June 1979).

[26] 125 *CR*, 96th Congress, 1st session, p. 15406 (19 June 1979).

[27] Peter Ross Range, "Thunder from the Right," *New York Times Magazine*, 8 Feb. 1981.

foreign aid offerings would benefit them politically, by the late 1970s, the conservative worldview enjoyed more popular support. In Samuel Stratton's opinion, "recent events have changed the views of most Americans, and even some members of Congress who generally lag behind the public when it comes to defense."[28] House Majority Whip John Brademas admitted as much in his efforts to beat back another conservative amendment, this one to bar indirect aid to Cambodia, Laos, Vietnam, or Uganda. If "you've got a safe district," Brademas told Democratic colleagues, "you can give us a vote."[29] Enough did: the amendment failed, 203–198. Yet the uncertain political climate of the late 1970s made it difficult to determine what constituted a safe district: Brademas, for one, would lose his seat in the next election.

The clearest example of the intersection between the continued congressional assertiveness and the altered ideological environment came in a region largely ignored by U.S. diplomacy for the previous quarter century, Central America. On May 19, 1977, the Foreign Operations Subcommittee, chaired after Passman's defeat by the erratic liberal Clarence Long (D-Maryland), voted to suspend assistance to Nicaragua's Anastasio Somoza. From the Senate, Ted Kennedy confidentially asked the new House Speaker, Tip O'Neill, to do "everything possible" to pass anti-Somoza legislation, given the "increasing violence and military repression" in Nicaragua.[30] In the House, seeking to build off his success of the previous year regarding Uruguay and citing Somoza's pattern of gross human rights violations, Ed Koch reasoned, "If there ever was an occasion to cut off military aid, this is it."[31] When asked what would be lost to U.S. security by such a move, Undersecretary of State for Security Assistance Lucy Benson remarked, "I cannot think of a single thing."[32]

More so than any other Latin American regime, however, the Somozas had cultivated allies among the American political elite. (As a Koch aide remarked, "You could tell [Somoza] knew how to bullshit well."[33]) The dictator's West Point classmate, Staten Island congressman John Murphy, headed the "Somoza Lobby," which also included Foreign Operations Committee member Charles Wilson (D-Texas) – who denied that any human rights violations occurred in Nicaragua, whose "main sin seems to me to be

[28] Samuel Stratton to J. F. Inness, 17 June 1980, Box 97, Samuel Stratton Papers, University of Rochester.

[29] *New York Times*, 4 Aug. 1979.

[30] Ted Kennedy to Tip O'Neill, 11 Dec. 1978, Series II, Box 19, Thomas P. O'Neill Papers, Boston College.

[31] 123 *CR*, 95th Congress, 1st session, p. 20580 (23 June 1977).

[32] U.S. House of Representatives, Subcommittee on Foreign Operations, *Hearings, Foreign Assistance and Related Agencies Appropriations for 1978*, 95th Congress, 1st session, pp. 746–747 (5 May 1977).

[33] Arnson, *Crossroads*, p. 26.

that it is friendly to the United States" – and DuPage County Republican Edward Derwinski, who urged the House, if it wanted to discuss oppressive regimes, not to "forget the Democratic machine of Chicago."[34] The bloc gained invaluable assistance from Clement Zablocki, the new chair of the Foreign Affairs Committee, who opposed Congress singling "out countries that are friendly to us in trying to get them to live up to our mores."[35] The full House overturned the subcommittee, voting 225–180 to keep aid flowing to Nicaragua.

Recognizing the shifting balance in Congress, White House officials subsequently rebuffed requests from congressional liberals to apply discretionary authority to bar assistance – acting, a George McGovern staffer realized, "because of their fear of Congressman Charlie Wilson."[36] The Texas Democrat, in effect, blackmailed the administration: he would round up the votes of "fellow rednecks" for the foreign aid bill provided that Carter did not isolate Somoza.[37] The dictator showed his gratitude by inviting Wilson to Managua, where Somoza toasted the Texas congressman as "the only thing preserving freedom in the hemisphere" and offered a $50,000 campaign contribution.[38] While the lobby could prevent a severance of aid, however, it lacked the strength to obtain increased assistance for the beleaguered government, despite consistent demands as the anti-Somoza Sandinista rebellion intensified.

The lobby's most effective opposition came from the unlikeliest of sources – Senator Edward Zorinsky (D-Nebraska), who assumed the chairmanship of the Inter-American Affairs Subcommittee in January 1979. The Nebraska Republican-turned-Democrat, who conceded that many considered him "to the right of Attila the Hun," joined the Foreign Relations Committee for purely parochial reasons: he sought a forum from which to promote Nebraskan grain exports.[39] As the committee's junior member, he received the vacant Inter-American chairmanship, even though he had no interest in Latin America, spoke no Spanish, and had never traveled south of Acapulco. To nearly everyone's surprise, Zorinsky took his new assignment seriously, researched Nicaraguan history, and concluded that Somoza's corruption justified the rebellion. By June 1979, he supported diplomatic recognition and military aid for the provisional Sandinista government; he

---

[34] 123 *CR*, 95th Congress, 1st session, p. 20579 (23 June 1977).

[35] 123 *CR*, 95th Congress, 1st session, p. 20580 (23 June 1977).

[36] John Holum to George McGovern, 9 Aug. 1978, Box 1003, George McGovern Papers, Princeton University.

[37] John Holum to George McGovern, 9 Aug. 1978, Box 1003, George McGovern Papers, Princeton University.

[38] George Crile, *Charlie Wilson's War: The Extraordinary Story of the Largest Covert Operation in History* (New York: Atlantic Monthly Press, 2003), pp. 34–36.

[39] *St. Louis Post-Dispatch*, 29 Oct. 1979.

then traveled to Managua, where former guerrilla leaders welcomed him as he pronounced himself "tired of the old communist-under-every-bush approach."[40]

After the Sandinistas assumed power in July 1979, Carter reached out to the new government, proposing a $75 million package of emergency economic assistance. Zorinsky outmaneuvered Helms and shepherded the aid package through the Senate. In the House, however, administration critics proved better organized; Robert Bauman (R-Maryland) claimed that "dedicated leftists" in the State Department intended to "overthrow the established governments of Central America one by one."[41] The Maryland Republican introduced an amendment to defund Nicaraguan aid; citing the Sandinistas' leftist tendencies and the American electorate's drift to the right, Zablocki, the bill's floor manager, compared arguing against the offering to "throwing peas against the wall."[42] The amendment overwhelmingly passed, 267–105.

Only an extraordinary intervention by the leadership saved the "emergency" aid package, whose fate was decided in May 1980, nine months after its introduction. Majority Leader Jim Wright delivered an impassioned address urging his colleagues to "think about something that is a lot more serious than the next election" and to avoid a "revisitation of McCarthyism" tarring those who supported aid as anti-American.[43] Speaker O'Neill then concluded debate by addressing the House personally – the first time in his career that he had spoken on a foreign aid measure – after which the lower chamber overturned the Bauman amendment. Such leadership intervention was effective, of course, because of its exceptional nature; it did not present a model for sustained assistance to Nicaragua.

The 1980 congressional session also featured a variety of initiatives explicitly designed to undo the reforms pushed through by the new internationalists. Jim Lloyd, facing a difficult (and ultimately unsuccessful) re-election contest in his defense contractor-rich southern California district, sponsored an amendment to remove "dual use" items (defense goods with both military and non-military applications) as restricted exports to countries with human rights violations. "For goodness sakes, folks," Lloyd complained, the time had come "to help business in the United States."[44] In any case, he reasoned, "strict control of the sale of these items *to our allies* is not necessary."[45] Understanding that the California congressman was "trying to

---

[40] *Omaha World-Herald*, 29 June 1979; *St. Louis Post-Dispatch*, 29 Oct. 1979.

[41] 126 CR, 96th Congress, 2nd session, p. 12549 (28 May 1980).

[42] *Congressional Quarterly Weekly Report*, 19 April 1980.

[43] 126 CR, 96th Congress, 2nd session, p. 12553 (28 May 1980).

[44] 126 CR, 96th Congress, 2nd session, p. 12555 (28 May 1980).

[45] Jim Lloyd, "Dear Colleagues," 16 May 1980, Box 101, Robert Giaimo Papers, University of Connecticut.

do a job for companies in his area," Jonathan Bingham correctly noted that the amendment's "very broad" wording would subvert the arms embargo against Chile and Argentina.[46] With unemployment on the rise, however, Lloyd's jobs-related argument carried the day. So too did an amendment to allow military aid to counties prohibited by previous legislation, provided that the president certified that the aid would serve the national interest. Carter argued that he needed flexibility in light of the Soviet invasion of Afghanistan.

The most significant revision targeted a vital reform of the new internationalists, the Hughes-Ryan amendment. Zablocki termed Hughes-Ryan, which required eight congressional committees to receive reports on covert intelligence operations, a remnant from a "period when certain emotions prevailed in our country"; he called for the CIA to report only to the Intelligence committees.[47] In the end, just 50 congressmen voted to retain Hughes-Ryan; in the Senate, only Proxmire opposed the change. House Republicans not incorrectly interpreted the vote, according to John Ashbrook (R-Ohio), as eliminating the perception "that the U.S. Congress is trying to make it so difficult that we cannot engage in covert operations."[48] In this sense, Edward Derwinski asserted, repealing Hughes-Ryan reflected public opinion, since most voters would respond favorably if asked the question, "Do you think God should bless the CIA?"[49]

This defense-oriented environment also affected the House and Senate Budget Committees, which had sustained the new internationalists' national security agenda even after the movement lost its ideological and political potency. In late 1977, in what the House committee's new chairman, Robert Giaimo, conceded were "serious charges," Mel Price criticized Budget's "propensity to get into program details which are more appropriately the province of the Armed Services Committee."[50] But Giaimo held his ground, arguing that defense oversight constituted an essential part of the Budget Committee's activities.[51] In 1977 and 1978, committee liberals aggressively attempted, in Robert Leggett's words, to defend congressional "responsibility to provide for the national defense."[52] By 1980, however, such procedural

---

[46] 126 CR, 96th Congress, 2nd session, p. 12556 (28 May 1980).

[47] 126 CR, 96th Congress, 2nd session, p. 12539 (28 May 1980).

[48] 126 CR, 96th Congress, 2nd session, pp. 12540–12542 (28 May 1980).

[49] 126 CR, 96th Congress, 2nd session, p. 12543 (28 May 1980).

[50] Melvin Price to Robert Giaimo, 31 Oct. 1977; Robert Giaimo handwritten memo, 3 Nov. 1977; both in Box 104, Robert Giaimo Papers, University of Connecticut.

[51] Robert Giaimo and Robert Leggett to Melvin Price, 11 Nov. 1977, Box 104, Robert Giaimo Papers, University of Connecticut.

[52] U.S. House of Representatives, Task Force on National Security and International Affairs, *Hearings, Alternative DOD Budgets*, 95th Congress, 2nd session, pp. 9 (22 Feb. 1978), 324 (1 March 1978); Thomas Dine, "Politics of the Purse," in Alan Platt and Lawrence Weller, eds., *Congress and Arms Control* (Boulder: Westview Press, 1978), p. 72.

gimmickry could not trump the House's new ideological orientation. Despite the House Committee's disproportionately liberal membership, amendments to reduce defense spending lost by overwhelming margins. "Let's face the realities," Giaimo lectured his colleagues. "There is overwhelming support in this Congress for defense, and you're kidding yourself if you think you can cut it substantially here."[53]

In the Senate, Tower told the Senate Budget Committee's ranking Republican, Oklahoma's Henry Bellmon, that "alarming deficiencies" caused by "the low priority defense has been accorded in the United States in the past quarter century will not be addressed – let alone corrected – unless substantial additional funds are provided."[54] (Ridiculing Tower's "B.S.," Gary Hart's staff marveled that anyone could claim that Congress had underfunded the post-NSC 68 military.[55]) Tower's efforts had the desired effect: with unanimous GOP support, the Budget Committee set an authorization level $5 billion higher than the administration's request, increasing an executive branch defense submission for the first time since the committee's creation.

For many new internationalists, the political climate of 1980 demanded such revisionist history. Citing the Iranian hostage crisis, the Soviet invasion of Afghanistan, the oil price shock, the Sandinista triumph in Nicaragua, and conservative complaints against SALT II, GOP presidential nominee Ronald Reagan relentlessly attacked the Carter administration for allowing American security to deteriorate. Tower believed that the Republicans "surely represent majority views on the Soviet threat and national defense," while the National Conservative Political Action Committee (NCPAC) targeted senators such as Church with television ads accusing the incumbent of voting against needed defense funds.[56] In response, an Eagleton press release boasted that he had voted for over $1 trillion in defense spending, and noted that, unlike many liberal colleagues, he had never opposed a final defense appropriations bill: "Like Harry S. Truman... Tom Eagleton believes that the strongest national defense is a defense which gets top value out of every last taxpayer dollar."[57] Culver incredibly cited a "remarkable...consensus" between Nunn and him on defense issues.[58] Hart's staff stressed the senator's record of initiating "substantial

---

[53] *Congressional Quarterly Weekly Report*, 22 March 1980.

[54] John Tower to Henry Bellmon, 25 March 1980, Box 26, Gary Hart Papers, University of Colorado.

[55] Bill Shore marginalia, on John Tower to Henry Bellmon 25 March 1980, Box 26, Gary Hart Papers, University of Colorado.

[56] John Tower, "A Time of Peril, a Time for Action," Sept. 1979, Box 969, John Tower Papers, Southwestern University; *Wall Street Journal*, 11 Sept. 1980.

[57] "Senator Tom Eagleton on Defense," press release, 10 June 1980, Folder 4384, Thomas Eagleton Papers, University of Missouri.

[58] 126 CR, 96th Congress, 2nd session, p. 18423 (2 July 1980).

increases in defense spending" to overcome "questionable votes," such as his opposing the Diego Garcia base expansion.[59]

Hart, Eagleton, and Pat Leahy barely survived the Reagan landslide, but the Democratic majority in the Senate did not. McGovern fell by 20 points, John Culver by 8, and Church was defeated despite running 23 points ahead of Carter in Idaho. In a stunning result, Gaylord Nelson, among the first senators to come out against the Vietnam War, lost to a weak opponent; in Alaska, Ernest Gruening's grandson, Clark Gruening, was upset by Republican Frank Murkowski after ousting Mike Gravel in the Democratic primary. "Being swept out of Washington with these senators," commentator Michael Getler understood, "are many of the notions and attitudes about American policy that have come to be accepted around the world for the past decade."[60] All told, the Republicans assumed a 53–47 Senate advantage, while in the House, GOP gains provided conservatives with an ideological majority. Surveying the election results, John Glenn argued, "There certainly is some redefinition of party and party goals that must be done in the near future."[61] Drawing upon an example from the past, the Ohio senator urged resurrecting Hubert Humphrey's idea, forwarded after the 1956 elections, of a party study of foreign policy.

In international affairs, Reagan promised higher defense spending, more aggressive challenging of Soviet expansionism, and replacement of Carter's emphasis on human rights by working with authoritarian regimes that were anti-Communist. The new president not only confronted a Congress realigned on partisan and ideological lines, but also a legislature in the midst of fundamental institutional change. In the Senate, the 1980 elections hastened the demise of the Foreign Relations Committee, which one administration official characterized as having "died on the vine."[62] Javits' 1980 defeat left at the panel's helm Charles Percy, the one-time "boy wonder" of GOP politics whose erratic voting record and transparent ambition erased much of his promise.[63] Church's defeat, meanwhile, elevated Claiborne Pell to the position of ranking minority member. A senator correctly described by *Congressional Quarterly* as "a mild-mannered idealist with an evident distaste for confrontation," Pell was once labeled "one of the most accomplished fence-sitters in Senate history."[64] Percy and Pell were the only two of the Foreign Relations Committee's 17 members who had served on the

[59] Bill Shore to Peter, 28 May 1980; "Hart Key Defense Votes," n.d. 1980; both in Box 51, Gary Hart Papers, University of Colorado.

[60] *Washington Post*, 5 Nov. 1980.

[61] John Glenn to John Peer Nugent, 16 Dec. 1980, Andrews–JHG correspondence – defense box, John Glenn Papers, Ohio State University.

[62] Lindsay, *Congress and the Politics of U.S. Defense Policy*, p. 55.

[63] *New York Times*, 5 May 1981; Carl Marcy oral history, U.S. Senate Historical Office.

[64] Marvin Kalb, "Hawks, Doves, and Flutterers in the Foreign Relations Committee," *New York Times Magazine*, 19 Dec. 1967; *Congressional Quarterly Weekly Report*, 14 March 1981.

committee when Fulbright left the Senate in January 1975, a dizzying rate of turnover that left the new chair, as one White House aide put it, "personally isolated"; indeed, "most of his friends in the Senate have died off or been defeated."[65]

Describing the Foreign Relations Committee's standing in the new Senate, Paul Tsongas publicly conceded the obvious: "We are not known among our colleagues apparently for being a very strong committee."[66]

Though Percy spoke of reestablishing the committee's preeminence by fostering a bipartisan consensus, Judith Miller of the *New York Times* discovered "ideological divisions, legislative disarray, and political floundering" afflicting the "historically prestigious panel."[67] Of the ideologues, Helms was the most important: as one Senate aide understood, his staking "out an ultraconservative position ... draws the whole spectrum to the right."[68] The North Carolina senator focused on issues relating to human rights. He visited dictatorships such as Argentina, Uruguay, and Chile to express his support for the local government, placed aides in mid-level positions within the State Department, and undermined Percy to such an extent that the *Washington Post* described Helms as the committee's real chairman.[69]

Limits, however, existed to the extent of Helms' power. In early 1981, the president nominated Ernest Lefever as assistant secretary of state for human rights. A former pacifist who held a Ph.D. in ethics from Yale's Divinity School, Lefever's denunciations of human rights policies made him a favorite of conservative groups.[70] (In 1974, for instance, Lefever dismissed reports of torture by Pinochet's government as the "normal level of police abuse" in a nation "of the Iberian tradition"; in 1979, he urged Congress to "remove from the statute books all clauses that establish a human rights standard or conditions that must be met by another government before our government transacts normal business."[71]) What one Democratic staffer termed "two very full and acrimonious days of hearings" featured the nominee faulting Carter for having failed to "recognize that there are moral and political limits to what the United States government can and should do to modify the internal behavior of another sovereign state" and calling for limiting sanctions to "unfriendly totalitarianisms" such as the Soviet Union, Vietnam, Cuba, Angola, Ethiopia, and Afghanistan.[72] When pressed by Pell and Tsongas

---

[65] *New York Times*, 5 May 1981.

[66] 127 CR, 97th Congress, 1st session, p. 25222 (30 Sept. 1981).

[67] *New York Times*, 5 May 1981.

[68] Peter Ross Range, "Thunder from the Right," *New York Times Magazine*, 8 Feb. 1981.

[69] *Washington Post*, 10 May 1981.

[70] *Chicago Sun-Times*, 5 March 1981.

[71] Victoria Cordova to Gary Hart, 10 May 1981, Box 41, Gary Hart Papers, University of Colorado; *New York Times*, 13 Feb. 1981.

[72] Unsigned memorandum, "Lefever Hearings," n.d. [1981], Box 69A, Senate Series, Paul Tsongas Papers, Center for Lowell History; Victoria Cordova to Gary Hart, 10 May 1981, Box 41, Gary Hart Papers, University of Colorado.

about how the United States should respond to right-wing human rights violators such as Guatemala, Argentina, and Chile, Lefever repeatedly declined to answer or claimed not to understand the question; Pell, exasperated, wondered if he were "misexpressing myself."[73]

Tower claimed that Lefever's views "represent those of mainstream America," but the nominee proved too extreme for four committee Republicans and all the committee's Democrats.[74] In a 13–4 negative vote, the committee for the first time in its history rejected a nomination, and Lefever shortly thereafter withdrew his candidacy.[75] Despite its symbolism, the rejection only marginally affected policy. The administration ended restrictions on aid to Argentina and Chile, noting the "immense improvement" in both nations' human rights records.[76] In the Senate, Democrats declined to challenge the president's agenda, having learned, two high-placed staffers observed, the lessons from "past Republican efforts and the efforts of right-wing organizations such as NCPAC to use foreign aid votes against incumbent Democrats during elections."[77]

The Foreign Relations Committee's collapse most clearly affected two disputes that recalled earlier battles in the Cold War Congress. During the 1980 campaign, Reagan advocated repealing the Clark amendment, which the new secretary of state, Alexander Haig, termed a "self-defeating and unnecessary restriction."[78] By 1981, the issue's symbolism was more important than its substance. Representative Stephen Solarz (D-New York) spoke for liberals in describing repeal as "a frontal assault on the whole fabric of Congressional adopted restraints on foreign policy prerogatives of the executive"; from the conservative camp, the *Wall Street Journal* denounced the amendment as "one of those limp products of post-Vietnam fear and guilt," the "relic of a bygone era, deserving to join its author in the dustbin of American political history."[79] Bowing to political realities in April, Senate Democrats agreed to a Percy-Tsongas compromise to repeal the amendment as of March 1, 1983, but with provisos denying an endorsement of military aid to UNITA and urging independence for the South African colony of Namibia.[80]

---

[73] U.S. Senate, Foreign Relations Committee, *Hearings, Nomination of Ernest W. Lefever*, 97th Congress, 1st session, p. 108 (18 May 1981).

[74] John Tower press release, 19 May 1981, Box 75C, Senate Series, Paul Tsongas Papers, Center for Lowell History.

[75] *New York Times*, 21 May 1981.

[76] U.S. House of Representatives, Inter-American Affairs Subcommittee, *Hearings, U.S. Economic Sanctions against Chile*, 97th Congress, 1st session, p. 43 (10 March 1981).

[77] Gerry Connell and Dick McColl to Democratic foreign policy LAs [legislative assistants], 14 Sept. 1981, Box 40, Gary Hart Papers, University of Colorado.

[78] *Washington Post*, 11 Jan. 1981.

[79] *New York Times*, 22 March 1981; *Wall Street Journal*, 16 Dec. 1981.

[80] Foreign Relations Committee notes, n.d. [1981], Box 87B, Senate Series, Paul Tsongas Papers, Center for Lowell History; *New York Times*, 14 May 1981.

In mid-September, a head count by Tsongas showed a 44 to 36 margin in favor of the compromise, with 12 more senators leaning in favor of the committee's position.[81] But with Percy subjected to what one Democratic staffer termed "continuing administration pressure," in late September, the Illinois senator reneged, fantastically claiming that he had not understood the compromise's "rigid" nature.[82] This move, according to *Congressional Quarterly*, "bared tensions" between the chairman and committee Democrats, and Tsongas brought the original committee amendment to the floor.[83] Even then, the Massachusetts senator seemed mostly interested in making a point with Percy and placing the United States on record in favor of Namibian self-rule; he described the Clark amendment itself as "kind of an anachronism."[84] With Republicans championing presidential flexibility and Tsongas' rhetoric making the debate – as Richard Lugar later noted – "not between repeal or retention of the Clark amendment [but] between two proposals with regard to repeal," the Senate voted 66–29 in favor of the administration's proposal.[85] The result left the fate of what the *Wall Street Journal* labeled "Dick Clark's ghost" to the House.[86]

Foreign Relations Committee squabbling also prevented the committee from playing a significant role in what the administration euphemistically termed the "Royal Saudi Air Force enhancement package." As a foreign military sale in excess of $25 million (the five AWACS planes offered by the administration alone cost $5.8 billion), the Saudi arms purchase was subject to a two-house veto under the terms of the Nelson-Bingham amendment. Even though Congress never had blocked an arms sale, AIPAC – unquestionably the most powerful national lobby in Washington – immediately came out in opposition, after which even the administration conceded defeat in the House. Initially, the sale's chances seemed bleak in the Senate; freshman Mark Andrews (R-North Dakota) envisioned AWACS becoming Reagan's "diplomatic Bay of Pigs."[87]

In early October, however, the administration reversed the tide. On October 4, Chief of Staff James Baker and White House counsel Edwin Meese joined Glenn and Nunn at the Georgetown residence of Virginia senator John Warner to plot strategy.[88] Seeking to rescue the sale, the politically savvy

[81] "Senate Head Count on Percy-Tsongas Compromise on Clark Amendment," 16 Sept. 1981, Box 87B, Senate Series, Paul Tsongas Papers, Center for Lowell History.

[82] Victoria Cordova to Gary Hart, 22 Sept. 1981, Box 40, Gary Hart Papers, University of Colorado; 127 *CR*, 97th Congress, 1st session, p. 22522 (30 Sept. 1981).

[83] *Congressional Quarterly Weekly Report*, 3 Oct. 1981.

[84] 127 *CR*, 97th Congress, 1st session, p. 22522 (30 Sept. 1981).

[85] 131 *CR*, 99th Congress, 1st session, p. S7835 (10 June 1985).

[86] *Wall Street Journal*, 16 Dec. 1981.

[87] John Tower and John Stennis, "Dear Colleagues," 11 Sept. 1981, Box 23, Gary Hart Papers, University of Colorado; *Wall Street Journal*, 2 Oct. 1981.

[88] *Wall Street Journal*, 29 Oct. 1981.

Baker assumed control of the lobbying effort, Nunn and Glenn agreed to solicit Democratic support, and the White House engaged in old-fashioned horse trading.[89] The administration obtained Dennis DeConcini's vote by promising that Reagan would not campaign against the Arizona Democrat in 1982; Slade Gorton (R-Washington) and John Melcher (D-Montana) secured approval for pet public works projects; and Charles Grassley received a commitment for the dismissal of Iowa's U.S. attorney, who was investigating allegations that South Africa illegally funneled money into Jepsen's 1978 campaign.[90] Though Glenn complained that these tactics undermined senators "who conscientiously weigh matters not in terms of '*what's in it for me?*' but what's best for the country," the lobbying effort inched the administration to around 40 votes.[91]

By a closer margin than expected (9–8), the Foreign Relations Committee recommended disapproving the sale.[92] A few hours later, even though it possessed no formal jurisdiction on the question, the Armed Services Committee voted 10-5 the other way, with Tower saying that he wanted to balance Foreign Relations' action.[93] Still, one day before the scheduled vote, it appeared as if opponents of the sale would narrowly prevail. In response, the administration focused its efforts on Roger Jepsen. "We just beat his brains out," remarked White House aide Ed Rollins. "We stood him up in front of an open grave and told him he could jump in if he wanted to."[94] Jepsen was, in almost every way, the opposite of the man he ousted. Whereas Dick Clark positioned himself at the liberal end of the spectrum, Jepsen was a reliable conservative. Whereas Clark had ranked among the Senate's most intellectually astute members, Jepsen was, as the *Washington Post* delicately observed, "not known for his foreign policy expertise."[95] And whereas Clark had maintained his beliefs passionately, even under political pressure, administration sources sensed that "Roger couldn't stand a lot of heat."[96]

In May, declaring that the sale "undermines the security of Israel," Jepsen promised to do everything in his power to block it.[97] As the issue became controversial, however, one lobbyist found the Iowa Republican "casting around for a fig leaf" to justify abandoning his position; at a meeting with

[89] John Glenn, "Press Talking Points," n.d. [Oct. 1981], Box 56, Staff notes series, John Glenn Papers, Ohio State University.
[90] *Washington Post*, 24 Dec. 1981.
[91] "JG Review," n.d. [Oct. 1981], Box 56, Staff files series, John Glenn Papers, Ohio State University.
[92] *CQ Almanac 1981*, p. 136.
[93] *Congressional Quarterly Weekly Report*, 17 Oct. 1981.
[94] Michael Barone and Grant Ujifusa, *The Almanac of American Politics 1984* (Washington, DC: National Journal, 1983), p. 411.
[95] *Washington Post*, 28 Oct. 1981.
[96] *Wall Street Journal*, 29 Oct. 1981.
[97] *Congressional Quarterly Weekly Report*, 31 May 1981.

Senate Republicans in late October, he broke down into tears when discussing the conflicting pressures on his loyalty.[98] The White House provided the fig leaf by incredibly promising that Jepsen would function as the administration's "point man" in developing a U.S.-Israeli "strategic alliance."[99] A more astute politician might have quietly voted to uphold the sale and hoped that few noticed. Jepsen, however, citing a need to refute "wild allegations" in the press, went before the Senate to list the reasons for his decision: "classified information" lessened his concerns that the sale would harm U.S. security; the matter had become a test of presidential credibility; and "large numbers of Iowans" had urged him to support the administration.[100] He added that he had realized these points only after "hours and hours" of "prayerful and careful deliberation," filled with "anguish."[101]

Few involved in the debate, on either side, could stomach such hypocrisy. When Democrats demanded that Jepsen take the Senate into closed session to share his "highly classified information," the Iowan conceded that he possessed no such intelligence.[102] One White House aide commented that, based on his pathetic negotiating technique, it was surprising that the senator had not traded his vote for an agreement to place the MX missile in Iowa; when Jepsen claimed that he voted as he did after his wife discerned that a fundamentalist reading of the Bible justified the arms sale, another aide quipped that "the Lord smiled" on the administration.[103] On the day of the Senate vote, the *Des Moines Register* presented a front-page summary of the major arguments for and against the sale – leading both columns with a quote from Jepsen.[104] Much like DeConcini in the Panama Canal debate, Jepsen provided an extreme example of how a Senate in which most members involved themselves in foreign policy matters, regardless of their expertise or even level of interest, produced a leveling mediocrity and diminished the institution's standing on international questions.

Despite the buffoonish nature of Jepsen's behavior, his switch carried enormous psychological impact; one Democratic aide remarked that the defection "made it easier for others to squirm out of uncomfortable positions."[105] Eight senators who were either uncommitted or leaning against the sale quickly indicated their support for the administration; the critics' last chance vanished when Maine's William Cohen announced that he, too, had changed his mind. When the motion of disapproval failed on a 52–48

[98] *Wall Street Journal*, 29 Oct. 1981.
[99] *Wall Street Journal*, 29 Oct. 1981.
[100] 127 *CR*, 97th Congress, 1st session, p. 25861 (28 Oct. 1981).
[101] 127 *CR*, 97th Congress, 1st session, p. 25861 (28 Oct. 1981).
[102] *Congressional Quarterly Weekly Report*, 3 Nov. 1981.
[103] *Washington Post*, 28 Oct. 1981.
[104] *Des Moines Register*, 29 Oct. 1981.
[105] *Wall Street Journal*, 28 Oct. 1981; *Newsweek*, 9 Nov. 1981.

vote, the London *Times* described the result as "the most dramatic example yet of the persuasive powers of President Reagan."[106]

"I don't know if we can reach a consensus on some of the pending foreign issues," one GOP committee member remarked in April, "but Chuck sure hasn't been able to find it."[107] Percy's weakness especially contrasted with the performance of Armed Services chairman John Tower. As a longtime GOP operative noted, the Texas senator was hardly "a candidate for the Senate's Mr. Congeniality": once, when asked to explain a colleague's vote against a defense amendment, the chairman remarked, "He abuses the right to be stupid."[108] Tower nonetheless emerged as the Senate's most powerful member on national security issues in the early 1980s. Behind the scenes, he advised Defense Secretary Caspar Weinberger; in public, he defined his role as focusing "Congress' attention on the military requirements, requirements that are driven by the threat to our national security and our vital interests abroad."[109] Tower's relentlessness served him well in an upper chamber increasingly filled with more timid figures. As Tsongas noted, "a super-aggressive type like John Tower" enjoyed an advantage, especially with Percy as a "very accommodating" Foreign Relations chair.[110]

Percy's inability to prevent the Armed Services Committee from weighing in on the AWACS sale illustrated the one-sided nature of the contest between the two committees. Four years earlier, in hearings before the Rules Committee, the Armed Services Committee lost a claim to partial jurisdiction over arms sales when Dick Clark maneuvered Tower into admitting that he had "no objection to policy matters relating to military sales being exclusive jurisdiction of Foreign Relations."[111] In May 1981, the Texas senator returned to the issue – in the process reviving the early Cold War dispute between Millard Tydings and Henry Cabot Lodge – by demanding his committee's formal participation in the military aid authorization bill. Tower also wanted joint authority on resolutions of disapproval of arms sales. Without these jurisdictional changes, he claimed, "the Armed Services Committee will be unable to fulfill its legislative responsibilities."[112]

Percy's initial inclination to compromise generated a revolt in his own committee. Joseph Biden demanded "no deal with Tex Tower"; Rudy Boschwitz (R-Minnesota) expressed "deep concern" that Percy had opened "the door to the erosion of this committee's jurisdiction without any

[106] *The Times* (London), 30 Oct. 1981.
[107] *Wall Street Journal*, 29 April 1981.
[108] *New York Times*, 29 April 1982; *Washington Post*, 26 April 1983.
[109] *New York Times*, 29 April 1982.
[110] *New York Times*, 29 Sept. 1981.
[111] U.S. Senate, Rules Committee, *Hearings, Committee System Reorganization Amendments of 1977*, 95th Congress, 1st session, p. 182 (19 Jan. 1977).
[112] John Tower to Charles Percy, 20 May 1981, Box 58, Staff series, John Glenn Papers, Ohio State University.

assurance of gains on our part."[113] After further discussion in two executive sessions, Percy reversed himself and promised to "vigorously oppose" any change; the intercession of Majority Leader Baker produced a cease-fire in which Tower agreed to drop his request for referring military aid to the Armed Services Committee.[114] The more significant question of arms sales jurisdiction, however, remained unresolved.

In the words of the *New York Times*' Judith Miller, the increasing number of "Armed Services forays on Foreign Relations' terrain" had produced a "classic dispute that, by Senate standards, is no longer gentlemanly."[115] The Foreign Relations Committee looked to turn the tables in summer 1981, after the General Accounting Office issued a report charging the Pentagon with misusing its authority to lease excess military supplies. A program designed to help domestic businesses had become a way to bypass congressional restrictions on military aid and arms sales: between 1977 and 1981, countries to which Congress had restricted or barred military assistance, such as Saudi Arabia, Argentina, and Chile, received leased equipment, which, in each case, was never returned.

To rectify the problem, Zorinsky sponsored an amendment to transfer oversight from Armed Services to Foreign Relations, while also establishing a two-house legislative veto provision for the program. Typically, Percy envisioned a "possible compromise" with the Armed Services Committee, but the Nebraska senator wanted the issue decided by an up-or-down vote.[116] Tower responded as expected. Privately, he labeled the amendment "an unwarranted and harmful jurisdictional raid"; publicly, he charged Zorinsky with accusing Armed Services Committee colleagues of dereliction and incompetence.[117] The Texas senator's concerns extended beyond protecting turf: he detected in the Nebraska senator's offering a revival of "the syndrome of the 1970s," characterized by initiatives such as the Eagleton and Clark amendments.[118] When a Tower motion to uphold Armed Services' jurisdiction prevailed by 10 votes, Charles Mathias astutely interpreted the result as "extremely significant" and "far-reaching"; given the committee's attitude, the Maryland Republican realized, the Pentagon would have a blank check.[119]

[113] Joseph Biden to Charles Percy, 18 June 1981; Rudy Boschwitz to Charles Percy, 23 June 1981; both in Box 77C, Senate Series, Paul Tsongas Papers, Center for Lowell History.

[114] Charles Percy to John Tower, 4 June 1981; Charles Percy to Foreign Relations Committee members, 16 June 1981; both in Box 58, Staff series, John Glenn Papers, Ohio State University.

[115] *New York Times*, 29 Sept. 1981.

[116] Charles Percy to Foreign Relations Committee members, 16 June 1981, Box 77C, Senate Series, Paul Tsongas Papers, Center for Lowell History.

[117] John Tower to "Committee Colleague," 23 Sept. 1981, Box 40, Gary Hart Papers, University of Colorado; 127 CR, 97th Congress, 1st session, p. 25053 (22 Oct. 1981).

[118] 127 CR, 97th Congress, 1st session, p. 25057 (22 Oct. 1981).

[119] 127 CR, 97th Congress, 1st session, p. 25057 (22 Oct. 1981).

The outcome typified the Armed Services Committee's dominance of Senate proceedings in the early 1980s, and captured the Senate atmosphere at the time when Reagan announced the result of the strategic review initiated when he took office in January 1981. On October 2, 1981, the president issued a report that advocated constructing 100 B-1 bombers, to be combat-ready by 1987; deploying 100 MX missiles, through a method other than the racetrack basing scheme; and ending "years of neglect" about strategic defense, a term the administration did not define precisely. This agenda, the White House promised, would "increase Soviet incentives to negotiate genuine arms reductions" and allow the United States to respond "to unconstrained growth in Soviet weapons."[120]

The call for reviving the B-1 attracted the most immediate attention. While Tower rallied GOP support, the pro-B-1 Glenn and Alan Cranston sponsored informal "members only" briefings for Democrats.[121] Senate consideration of the issue continued the trend of former military pilots – in this case Garn and Glenn – using their experience to place Pentagon critics on the defensive; Garn ridiculed "all these other experts, who may not have even been buck privates," suddenly coming "out with all these facts and figures, pulling them out of the sky."[122] That B-1 opponents hoped to achieve victory by wooing such figures as Bob Dole suggested how little chance they had of prevailing.[123] A Fritz Hollings (D-South Carolina) amendment to delete funding for the plane failed, 68–26; five years before, the vote on a similar offering from Culver yielded an evenly divided Senate.

Senate Democrats struggled to adjust to this altered institutional environment. "Heartened that we have at last begun the long process of rebuilding our military forces after years of neglect," Glenn organized a study group of like-minded colleagues.[124] Eagleton, less enthusiastic about the direction of affairs, conceded, "We all know that defense spending is going to rise sharply in the coming years," and "politically, our party probably bears a special burden in this area because of the perception (fair or not) that we have been weak on defense."[125] In the end, with Democrats badly divided and most Republicans disinclined to challenge the Armed Services Committee, the Senate ceded initiative on defense matters to the House.

[120] *New York Times*, 3 Oct. 1981.

[121] John Glenn, "Dear Colleague," 1 Nov. 1981, Andrews–JHG correspondence box, John Glenn Papers, Ohio State University.

[122] 127 *CR*, 97th Congress, 1st session, pp. 29488, 29491 (3 Dec. 1981).

[123] Council for a Livable World memorandum, "A Sampling of B-1 Views of Moderate Senators," 30 Oct. 1981, unprocessed box, William Proxmire Papers, Wisconsin State Historical Society.

[124] John Glenn to Maxwell Taylor, 2 April 1981, Defense box, Andrews-JHG correspondence series, John Glenn Papers, Ohio State University.

[125] Thomas Eagleton to Robert Byrd, personal, 5 May 1981, Folder 4384, Thomas Eagleton Papers, University of Missouri.

Even Tower conceded that he spent a "large portion" of his time "trying to fend off competition from other committees."[126] With his House counterpart, the aged and ineffectual Mel Price, concentrating on such minutiae as defending appropriations for the irradiation of food, such challenges were far more potent in the lower chamber.[127] The Defense Appropriations Subcommittee, for instance, increasingly engaged in general policy oversight and funded programs not authorized by the Armed Services Committee.[128] The subcommittee, which had played an assertive role from time to time under George Mahon, returned to its roots after Mahon's retirement, when Joseph Addabbo assumed the chairmanship in January 1979.

Correspondent Martin Tolchin described Addabbo as "something of an anomaly," a military subcommittee chair openly skeptical of the Pentagon. Personally, the Queens congressman was "an old-fashioned politician who has relied less on oratorical skills than on backroom dealings, and the quiet application of his acknowledged expertise on military matters."[129] As Defense Appropriations chairman, Addabbo made his intentions clear: since "Members of Congress always talk cut, cut, cut where the Pentagon is concerned, but in the end they always support spending," they needed a politically acceptable way to vote their consciences.[130] Though (in a dig at Downey and Addabbo) Samuel Stratton complained that "perhaps one of the reasons why New York State doesn't get more defense dollars channeled in our direction is that a substantial percentage of the New York delegation consistently votes against all defense legislation," Addabbo successfully tended to his own pork-barrel needs: Alfonse D'Amato, an expert in the matter, once remarked, "Joe Addabbo enables us to bring home the bacon" on defense contracts.[131]

Despite earlier predictions that the Pentagon would "deal with him at arm's length," Addabbo built considerable influence – but limits existed to his ability.[132] Though Toby Moffett gushed that the New York congressman was "perhaps the foremost defense authority in the Congress," Addabbo was no defense intellectual; he approached the issue more from an abstract

[126] Lindsay, "Congress and Defense Policy," in James Lindsay and Randall Ripley, eds., *Congress Resurgent: Foreign and Defense Policy on Capital Hill* (An Arbor: University of Michigan Press, 1993), p. 390.

[127] Thomas Downey personal interview with author, 27 May 2004; Robert Art, "Congress and the Defense Budget: Enhancing Policy Oversight," *Political Science Quarterly* 100 (1985), p. 234.

[128] Lindsay, "Congress and Defense Policy," in Lindsay and Ripley, eds., *Congress Resurgent*, p. 387.

[129] *New York Times*, 9 Aug. 1982.

[130] *New York Times*, 9 Aug. 1982.

[131] Samuel Stratton to editor, *Plattsburgh Press-Republican*, 24 March 1983, Box 103, Samuel Stratton Papers, University of Rochester; *New York Times*, 9 Aug. 1982.

[132] *Army Magazine*, Jan. 1979.

hostility to a big defense budget.[133] In 1981, the New York congressman tried and failed to block the B-1, though he did assemble a subcommittee majority to delete funding for the MX. On the floor, however, he ran up against Stratton, who, as Bernard Weinraub of the *New York Times* noted, had "emerged as a dominant force" on Armed Services.[134] Indeed, by 1981, Stratton was the committee's de facto chair, and he ridiculed the "lot of amateur strategists" opposing the MX.[135] (That Oregon Democrat James Weaver openly speculated that "bows and arrows" might better protect U.S. security than nuclear weapons did little to weaken Stratton's position.[136]) The MX amendment, as expected, fell short, but the margin of defeat was a respectable 100 votes, giving the Queens congressman a base upon which to build in 1982.

Addabbo was more effective when targeting minor areas of waste; he believed that "we could cut $30 to $50 billion without affecting much."[137] Legislators who focused on Pentagon cost overruns, such as Willaim Proxmire and Les Aspin, once were the exceptions; by the 1980s, this approach was standard fare.[138] With budget deficits rapidly expanding and reports of contractor overcharges proliferating, this line of attack resonated: John Glenn privately informed Rockwell's chairman of the board that "we must pay attention to the various complicated and somewhat arcane cost estimating procedures and ensure that differences in techniques…cannot be turned into sensational diatribes against a program that is fundamentally sound."[139]

A stress on waste had political appeal, and Addabbo's institutional approach demonstrated mastery of the art of subcommittee government. Neither tactic, however, was conducive to presenting an alternative defense philosophy, as figures such as Symington or Harold Hughes had done in the early 1970s. With Senate Democrats unwilling or unable to challenge Tower's preeminence and most other House critics constrained for institutional, tactical, or political reasons, the most powerful congressional case against Reagan's national security agenda came from Tom Downey. Ignoring advice from key contributors in his district, the New York congressman believed that the administration's approach to strategic matters was "wholly wrong," and he resisted it aggressively.[140] He possessed the knowledge base

---

[133] 127 CR, 97th Congress, 1st session, pp. 28019, 28059 (18 Nov. 1981); Les AuCoin personal interview with author, 13 May 2004.

[134] *New York Times*, 8 Feb. 1979.

[135] 127 CR, 97th Congress, 1st session, p. 15199, 15202 (9 July 1981).

[136] 127 CR, 97th Congress, 1st session, p. 15190 (9 July 1981).

[137] *Wall Street Journal*, 27 April 1983; Les AuCoin personal interview with author, 13 May 2004.

[138] James Lindsay, "Congress and Defense Policy," p. 382.

[139] John Glenn to Robert Anderson, 2 June 1982, Andrews–JHG correspondence box, John Glenn Papers, Ohio State University.

[140] Thomas Downey personal interview with author, 27 May 2004.

for the task: Mike Wallace of *60 Minutes* termed Downey "one of the leading military experts in Congress," while reporter Tom Goldstein considered the congressman "as well informed on arms control and weaponry as about any non-military figure could be."[141] In a caustic response to the 1981 strategic review (which he termed an act of "monumental" incompetence), the New York Democrat ridiculed Reagan for having "achieved the stunning feat of simultaneously spending tens of billions of dollars while decreasing military effectiveness."[142] The administration responded by threatening to deny White House passes to Downey's constituents.[143]

Future majority whip Tony Coelho (D-California) estimated that Downey's reputation allowed his position on national security matters to carry with it between 12 and 15 votes, an astonishing total for a congressman barely over 30 who lacked a major committee assignment dealing with international affairs.[144] (Caucus rules had required him to switch off the Armed Services Committee when he joined the Ways and Means Committee in 1979.) Armed Services Democrats recognized the threat. The committee's second ranking Democrat, Charles Bennett of Florida, complained that Downey "generally comes here to do in some program," but conceded that "when you are as bright as the gentleman from New York is," it was easy to obscure the real issue by coming "to the well of the House and impress people with your brilliance."[145]

Downey's biting wit made him something of a polarizing figure: as Michael Barone noted, "There is something in Downey that infuriates many conservative politicians, a combination perhaps of self-assuredness and self-righteousness, compounded with political skills."[146] The New York congressman ridiculed Stratton's "marvelous" description of MX as exclusively designed for defensive purposes; in Stratton's mind, apparently, "our missiles are for defense; their missiles are for offense."[147] (Stratton countered that Downey had "been on the Ways and Means Committee perhaps so long that he has not been able to keep up with some of the latest developments that are happening in our nation's defense."[148]) Downey dismissed the fulminations of Tennessee Republican Robin Beard as "more useful before the American Legion as opposed to the Congress of the United States."[149]

---

[141] Tom Goldstein, "Coming Up Downey," *Rolling Stone*, 14 April 1983; *Congressional Quarterly Weekly Report*, 26 Sept. 1981.

[142] Thomas Downey press release, 2 Oct. 1981, Box 220, Thomas Downey Papers, Cornell University.

[143] Thomas Downey personal interview with author, 27 May 2004.

[144] Myron Waldman, "The Growing Influence of Tom Downey," *LI*, 25 Oct. 1981.

[145] 128 *CR*, 97th Congress, 2nd session, p. 18580 (29 July 1982).

[146] Michael Barone and Grant Ujifusa, *The Almanac of American Politics 1986* (Washington, D.C.: National Journal, 1985), p. 385.

[147] 127 *CR*, 97th Congress, 1st session, p. 15206 (9 July 1981).

[148] 127 *CR*, 97th Congress, 1st session, p. 15207 (9 July 1981).

[149] 127 *CR*, 97th Congress, 1st session, p. 15222 (9 July 1981).

His sarcasm generated GOP rage – Bob Dornan, who had taken to calling himself "B-1 Bob," once grabbed Downey's tie and called him a "draft-dodging wimp."[150] But Downey's approach also rallied the base: he earned kudos from Democrats such as Ohio's John Seiberling for his "brilliant expositions" on defense policy at a time when most Pentagon skeptics refrained from taking on the administration.[151]

On non-military matters, more congressmen challenged Reagan's policies, employing a previously all but inert venue – the Foreign Affairs Committee. In 1981, the determined stance of its Subcommittee on Africa, chaired by Harold Wolpe (D-Michigan), blocked the administration's efforts to repeal the Clark amendment. Meanwhile, for the first time in 30 years, the full committee violated the seniority rule, ousting Pennsylvania Democrat Gus Yatron from the chairmanship of the Inter-American Subcommittee.[152] Committee Democrats then bypassed the subcommittee's next ranking member, Dan Mica (D-Florida), giving the chairmanship instead to Maryland's Michael Barnes, a wiry, articulate liberal first elected in 1978. (Mica denounced the move as a "radical-liberal revolt."[153]) Jonathan Bingham spoke for the majority in expressing the "widespread feeling" that Yatron "didn't have all that much interest" in the job and would be an ineffective media spokesman; a committee insider added that "some doubts [existed] about how vigorous Dan Mica would be."[154] Evans and Novak fumed that Foreign Affairs Democrats wanted "repeal the 1980 election and preserve Jimmy Carter's human rights policies."[155]

The *Washington Post* described Barnes as the "bland star" for his ability to make headlines without engaging in histrionics.[156] He was immediately thrust into the spotlight, since the Reagan administration inherited a highly unstable situation in Central America. Focus initially centered on El Salvador, which experienced more than 9,000 political killings in 1980 alone and where a weak military regime teetered near collapse. The deaths with the most international impact came in December 1980, when the bodies of three U.S. nuns and a Catholic layperson were discovered in a shallow roadside grave. Amidst widespread suspicion blaming the assassinations on right-wing paramilitary groups, Carter immediately suspended all assistance.[157]

Though Reagan wanted to restore military aid, administration officials stumbled in responding to the nuns' deaths. In late December 1980, shortly

---

[150] *Washington Post*, 31 March 1985.
[151] 127 *CR*, 97th Congress, 1st session, p. 15208 (9 July 1981); Les AuCoin personal interview with author, 13 May 2004.
[152] *Washington Post*, 12 March 1981.
[153] *Washington Post*, 2 Feb. 1981.
[154] *Congressional Quarterly Weekly Report*, 7 Feb. 1981.
[155] *Washington Post*, 2 Feb. 1981.
[156] *Washington Post*, 12 March 1982.
[157] *Washington Post*, 5 Dec. 1980.

after her nomination as UN ambassador, Jeane Kirkpatrick asserted, "The nuns were not just nuns. The nuns were also political activists...on behalf of the [opposition] Frente."[158] A few months later, Haig oddly claimed that "the vehicle that the nuns were riding in may have tried to run a roadblock," prompting an exchange of fire.[159] Families of the sisters accused the Secretary of State of conducting a "smear campaign," while Kirkpatrick's comments provoked widespread ridicule.[160]

In the Senate, Kennedy and Tsongas urged a legislative veto of military aid to El Salvador, or, as a fallback position, restrictive conditions on any assistance that did occur. Most Democrats, however, shied away from the traditional tactic of attaching policy riders to foreign aid bills – conscious, as one staffer privately asserted, of the "chilling...examples of Senators Clark and Church."[161] According to Tsongas, "The last election changed things," since "not only did we lose Democrats and liberals, but those who are left are so weary. Everyone is running for cover from Reagan and the conservative trend."[162]

House liberals displayed more energy. A June 1982 State Department briefing paper termed obtaining House support "our principal difficulty" regarding Central American policy, given "human rights concerns, diminished but still present fears of a Vietnam-style escalation, and other competing concerns."[163] The efforts of Barnes, Wolpe, and Washington's Don Bonker, chair of the Human Rights and International Organizations Subcommittee, symbolized a remarkable development of the early Reagan years, in which the Foreign Affairs Committee emerged as a more powerful force than its Senate counterpart.[164]

House Democrats also targeted the administration's apparently casual attitude toward nuclear war. The most politically potent arms control issue, a verifiable U.S.-USSR nuclear freeze, grew out of a powerful grassroots movement (around 500,000 people rallied in New York City June 1982).[165] In Congress, as had become the norm on strategic questions, Downey provided the most cogent intellectual defense of the concept, arguing that the freeze would restore "arms control as a national security tool."[166] Deterrence could

---

[158] Arnson, *Crossroads*, p. 63.

[159] *New York Times*, 19 March 1981.

[160] *Washington Post*, 20 March 1981.

[161] James McCormick, "Decision Making in the Foreign Affairs and Foreign Relations Committees," in Ripley and Lindsay, eds., *Congress Resurgent*, pp. 118–148.

[162] *New York Times*, 1 March 1981.

[163] *New York Times*, 16 Aug. 1982.

[164] James McCormick, "Decision Making in the Foreign Affairs and Foreign Relations Committees," in Ripley and Lindsay, eds., *Congress Resurgent*, pp. 118–148.

[165] *New York Times*, 30 May 1982; *Washington Post*, 1 Aug. 1982.

[166] Thomas Downey to editor, *Los Angeles Times*, 19 Feb. 1982, Box 239, Thomas Downey Papers, Cornell University.

succeed, the New York Democrat understood, only if both sides believed that the other could not launch a successful first strike, but technological advancements associated with weapons systems such as the Trident II missile and anti-satellite, space-based lasers threatened to destabilize the strategic balance. By preventing force modernization, the freeze would maintain deterrence until both sides committed to building down their forces – which, Downey admitted, could take some time, since "this administration has no shortage of people in very high places who have built careers out of opposition to arms control."[167]

As expected, the Senate rejected the freeze, but the Foreign Affairs Committee reported the measure favorably, 26–9, with 7 of the committee's 16 Republicans in support. (Solarz described his GOP colleagues as motivated by "fear not of the bomb but of their voters."[168]) Administration officials charged that the resolution would undermine START talks occurring in Geneva; behind the scenes, according to one Hill Republican, the president launched a "full-court press with the A-squad."[169] To offer a positive alternative, Stratton and William Broomfield (R-Michigan) co-sponsored a resolution advocating what they called a freeze, but only at "equal and substantially reduced levels" in which the Soviets would accept the blatantly one-sided START proposals.[170] Downey denounced the proposal, which resembled the 1972 Jackson amendment to the SALT agreement, as a "Hollywood freeze" that would produce "a nuclear furnace."[171]

The dueling resolutions reached the floor in what one reporter described as a "dramatic late-night session" on August 5, 1982.[172] Rhetoric on both sides became heated: after Floyd Spence (R-South Carolina) denounced freeze proponents for supporting "a position which favors our adversary" and "taking the Russian side in this controversy," Barney Frank sarcastically promised "to refrain from giving aid and comfort to the enemy so as not to further disarrange the gentleman from South Carolina."[173] The debate concluded with high drama: Minority Leader Robert Michel (R-Illinois) recalled Neville Chamberlain to chastise Democrats for "crying 'freeze in our time' "; Speaker Tip O'Neill delivered an emotional floor speech recalling his having witnessed nuclear tests three decades before and lamenting the world's subsequent failure to end the arms race.[174]

---

[167] Thomas Downey speech, "Arms Control and Nuclear War," Syracuse University, 22 April 1982, Box 239, Thomas Downey Papers, Cornell University.
[168] *New York Times*, 24 June 1982.
[169] *Washington Post*, 10 Aug. 1982.
[170] *CQ Almanac 1982*, p. 113.
[171] Thomas Downey, "Dear Colleague," 29 July 1982, Box 239, Thomas Downey Papers, Cornell University; *Newsday*, 27 May 1982.
[172] *Washington Post*, 6 Aug. 1982.
[173] 128 *CR*, 97th Congress, 2nd session, p. 19776 (5 Aug. 1982).
[174] 128 *CR*, 97th Congress, 2nd session, pp. 19788, 19791 (5 Aug. 1982).

Four Pennsylvania Republicans – Bill Goodling, Lawrence Coughlin, William Clingler, and James Coyne – decided the freeze's fate. Early in the roll call to substitute Broomfield-Stratton for the freeze resolution, Goodling, despite having backed the freeze in committee, voted himself "present," saying that he did not want to oppose the president. The morning of the vote, Coyne boasted to a Philadelphia radio station of having co-sponsored the committee's freeze resolution, and he initially voted against the Broomfield-Stratton substitute. Several minutes into the roll call, however, he switched his vote, which tied the ballot at 202. Coughlin then changed his vote from nay to aye, giving Broomfield-Stratton a 203–201 lead. Although, as Speaker, he rarely voted, O'Neill did so in this instance, making the tally 203–202. Clingler cast his vote as time expired; with a tie constituting a rejection of the substitute, he would decide the outcome. When Clingler voted for Bloomfield, yielding a final result of 204–202, the Republican side of the aisle erupted in shouts and cheers.[175]

Judith Miller termed the vote a "major symbolic victory" for the White House.[176] The outcome, however, came at considerable cost for the administration. Befitting the institution's emerging importance, the 1982 midterm elections focused on House races. The day after the vote, Coyne's opponent, former congressman Peter Kostmayer, denounced the incumbent for having "crumbled under political pressure"; a few days before the election, correspondent Al Hunt termed the Kostmayer-Coyne race "a test of sentiment on the nuclear-weapons freeze."[177] In November, Coyne lost his seat, as did John LeBoutillier (R-New York), another original freeze backer who changed his mind after explaining that "in times of need, you help the party."[178] Overall, Democrats gained 26 seats, though the GOP retained its Senate majority, which had grown to 54–46 after the expulsion of Harrison Williams following the Abscam scandal.

House Democrats interpreted the election results as a mandate for their foreign policy agenda. In early December, Tom Harkin introduced an amendment to prevent both the CIA and Defense Department from furnishing military equipment to anti-Communist forces in Nicaragua. Conservatives dismissed the effort – in Bob Dornan's opinion, "What is Mr. Harkin's terrorist is my freedom fighter, and what is his freedom fighter is my terrorist" – but the House leadership negotiated a compromise.[179] Harkin agreed to withdraw his offering, and in exchange Intelligence Committee Chairman Edward Boland (D-Massachusetts) introduced an amendment, which the House unanimously passed, to limit the covert operation's scope to

---

[175] *Washington Post*, 6 Aug. 1982, 10 Aug. 1982.
[176] *New York Times*, 6 Aug. 1982.
[177] *Wall Street Journal*, 29 Oct. 1982.
[178] *Washington Post*, 7 Aug. 1982.
[179] 128 CR, 97th Congress, 2nd session, p. 29465 (8 Dec. 1982).

interdicting arms from Nicaragua to the Salvadoran leftists.[180] By prohibiting aid for the purpose of overthrowing the Sandinista regime, the Boland
amendment set the stage for three years of battles between the White House
and Congress over Latin American policy.

The lame-duck session also delivered a stinging setback to the MX.
With political and technological difficulties having doomed previous basing
schemes, the president proposed the "Dense Pack," which called for placing 100 MX missiles in close proximity to each other at Wyoming's Warren
Air Force Base. In theory, this approach would frustrate a Soviet first strike,
since the first few Soviet ICBMs to explode would disable the other incoming
missiles. In reality, Dense Pack never had a chance. Vocal attacks on the missile by Downey and critical hearings before the Addabbo subcommittee had
sustained anti-MX sentiment throughout the summer of 1982, and in the
post-election period, Democrats openly ridiculed the system.[181] Ed Markey
(D-Massachusetts) joked that "Dense Pack is six generals sitting around the
Pentagon trying to figure out what the window of vulnerability is"; Frank
accused the president of suffering from "Brezhnev envy."[182] Seizing upon a
statement by National Security Adviser William Clark that the MX was "too
important to allow the risk of technical debates to delay the introduction of
the missile," Downey sent a mocking "Dear Colleague" letter describing the
missile as "the lead weapon in the new NNW force"; for "those unfamil-
iar with Pentagon acronyms," the New York Democrat quipped, "NNW,
pronounced 'new,' stands for No Need to Work."[183]

Administration supporters – except for South Carolina's Thomas Hart-
nett, who expressed no concern with basing the MX in "barns in South
Carolina and haylofts" – steered clear of the basing issue. Having run out of
intellectually defensible arguments, Stratton based his position for approving
the missile on complaints that Addabbo's staff had behaved in an uncollegial
fashion when dealing with their Armed Services Committee counterparts.[184]
An Addabbo amendment to block Dense Pack funding passed by what *Time*
termed a "surprisingly decisive" 245–176 margin; the New York congressman (who covered his office door with anti-MX cartoons) hoped to send a
message that "defense spending must be curtailed."[185] In what would prove

[180] 128 *CR*, 97th Congress, 2nd session, p. 29466 (8 Dec. 1982).
[181] U.S. House of Representatives, Defense Appropriations Subcommittee, *Hearings, Department of Defense Appropriations for 1983, part 9*, 97th Congress, 2nd session, p. 723
(17 Aug. 1982).
[182] 128 *CR*, 97th Congress, 2nd session, p. 29062 (7 Dec. 1982); Thomas Downey personal
interview with author, 27 May 2004.
[183] Thomas Downey, "Dear Colleague," 6 Dec. 1982, Box 239, Thomas Downey Papers, Cornell University.
[184] 128 *CR*, 97th Congress, 2nd session, pp. 29070, 29075 (7 Dec. 1982).
[185] 128 *CR*, 97th Congress, 2nd session, p. 29456 (8 Dec. 1982); *Wall Street Journal*, 27 April
1983; *Time*, 20 Dec. 1982.

a critical concession, however, Les Aspin persuaded House Democrats to allow MX research and development funds to continue, subject to a vote of approval in the next Congress.[186]

Nuclear issues dominated the first session of the new Congress. In early March 1983, with 4,000 activists demonstrating in the rain outside the Capitol, the Foreign Affairs Committee overwhelmingly approved a freeze resolution.[187] Zablocki brought the measure to the floor quickly, expecting an easy triumph; Tip O'Neill predicted passage by at least 60 votes. But when debate started, as Margot Hornblower of the *Washington Post* noticed, the Foreign Affairs Committe chairman "appeared bewildered and unable to answer pointed questions about how a nuclear freeze would work"; at various times in the debate, under withering cross-examination from Stratton, he claimed that the freeze would and would not allow force modernization, and would and would not allow construction of the B-1 bomber.[188]

Zablocki, in the words of Mary McGrory, never had been considered "one of the intellectual giants of the House, nor one of its keener parliamentarians," but the weakness of this particular performance left Democrats "embarrassed and humiliated."[189] Les AuCoin (D-Oregon), a key freeze supporter, termed the debate "a disaster. Once the blood was in the water, it was like sharks on a feeding frenzy."[190] (After one of Zablocki's many reinterpretations of the freeze, Georgia Republican Newt Gingrich mockingly declared, "This resolution looks better with each passing hour."[191]) When an amendment to cripple the freeze lost by only six votes, the House leadership postponed additional action for two weeks.

The two weeks became a month; when debate resumed, Zablocki read a speech prepared by arms control staffers, accepted no questions, and allowed AuCoin, Downey, and Ed Markey to carry the burden of the debate.[192] The damage from the Wisconsin Democrat's earlier poor performance, however, could not be undone: Stratton, displaying his usual parliamentary cleverness, headed a conservative coalition that delayed the final vote – in the spirit, he sarcastically claimed, of assisting "the Foreign Affairs Committee in developing the best possible resolution" – by offering a battery of unprinted amendments that further bewildered Zablocki.[193] (Privately, Stratton expressed a preference for a "more of everything" nuclear strategy, since "we find

---

[186] Les AuCoin personal interview with author, 13 March 2004.
[187] *New York Times*, 9 March 1983; *Washington Post*, 9 March 1983.
[188] *Washington Post*, 18 March 1983.
[189] *Washington Post*, 20 March 1983.
[190] *Washington Post*, 18 March 1983.
[191] 129 CR, 94th Congress, 1st session, p. 9257 (20 April 1983).
[192] Les AuCoin personal interview with author, 13 March 2004; 129 CR, 94th Congress, 1st session, p. 9234 (20 April 1983).
[193] 129 CR, 94th Congress, 1st session, p. 9261 (20 April 1983).

ourselves outnumbered by the massive Soviet buildups in almost every category of military capability."[194]) Leon Panetta (D-California) lamented that "one of the most distorted debates" he ever had witnessed concluded with legislators losing "sight of what this basic resolution is all about."[195] Though the House eventually approved the measure, Tony Coelho conceded that opponents' skill had "gutted the resolution."[196]

Shortly after the vote, David Shribman of the *New York Times* described the resolution as "more symbolic than real," in that the measure tested the House's attitude on arms control.[197] If so, advocates of the freeze paid a heavy price for a victory of limited value. By creating a political climate in which moderates sought a counterbalancing issue to reassure voters that they were not anti-defense, the freeze strengthened the MX. As Aspin reasoned, "the usual pattern of this place is that people begin to get a little uncomfortable if they've gone too far one way and start looking to pop back the other way."[198] These events formed the background, in the words of commentator Elizabeth Drew, of "a story of well-intentioned people acting out of a combination of their own sense of what it means to be 'responsible'; their own sense of what they needed to 'position' themselves politically or lay the groundwork for political advancement; and political fear."[199]

In early 1983, Reagan appointed a panel of experts headed by Ford's national security adviser, General Brent Scowcroft, to recommend yet another basing system for the MX. Since its agenda, Scowcroft admitted, included "political practicality elements" of developing a plan that would clear Congress, the commission informally involved Aspin in deliberations from the start.[200] The Wisconsin congressman had long since abandoned the mindset that made him one of the House's most quoted Pentagon critics in the early 1970s. With a reputation for untrustworthiness – someone whose primary goal was "to look after Les" – Aspin seemed willing to compromise ideological consistency.[201] In approaching the MX, Aspin had two goals: politically, he wanted to fortify his position after a close re-election bid in 1980; personally, he looked to further his ambition to become Armed Services chairman or secretary of defense.[202]

---

[194] Samuel Stratton to editor, *New York Times*, 1 Feb. 1983, Box 103, Samuel Stratton Papers, University of Rochester.
[195] 129 *CR*, 94th Congress, 1st session, p. 9360 (21 April 1983).
[196] *Washington Post*, 5 May 1983.
[197] *New York Times*, 6 May 1983.
[198] Elizabeth Drew, "A Political Journal," *New Yorker*, 20 June 1983.
[199] Elizabeth Drew, "A Political Journal," *New Yorker*, 20 June 1983.
[200] *New York Times*, 19 April 1983.
[201] Thomas Downey personal interview with author, 27 May 2004; Les AuCoin personal interview with author, 13 May 2004.
[202] Elizabeth Drew, "A Political Journal," *New Yorker*, 20 June 1983.

In April, the Scowcroft Commission issued its report, which Mc-George Bundy described as "good and bad arguments...mixed together with remarkable inattention to their intrinsic incompatibility."[203] First, the commission endorsed construction of 100 MX missiles, initially to be placed in hardened Minuteman silos, thereby symbolizing a commitment to strategic modernization. Second, the commission endorsed the Midgetman, a single-warhead missile that was popular with moderate House Democrats, especially Albert Gore, Jr. (D-Tennessee). Finally, the commission endorsed continued arms control negotiations. The package offered Democrats a trade – the MX for the Midgetman and a more serious commitment to arms control.[204] Aspin, Gore, and several like-minded Democratic colleagues, dubbing themselves the Working Group, also expected the Scowcroft proposal to weaken administration hard-liners like Caspar Weinberger, William Casey, and Richard Perle.

MX critics interpreted what AuCoin termed "the Treaty of Pennsylvania Avenue" much differently.[205] The Oregon Democrat, who in 1983 secured a seat on the Defense Appropriations Subcommittee "for very specific reasons" – he wanted a post from which to challenge the administration's defense philosophy – termed the MX vote "the first test of whether Congress will respond to clear public feeling that they want less defense spending."[206] In the subcommittee, Addabbo and AuCoin confronted Working Group leader Norm Dicks (D-Washington), a former Jackson staffer who was worried about "getting identified as a freezie."[207] Along with Aspin, Gore, and allies within the administration, Dicks arranged for Reagan to issue a letter promising a commitment to arms control. Though the missive's vagueness generated ridicule from liberals, Dicks rejoiced that "we're beginning to see a bipartisan approach to some of these issues."[208] The subcommittee then voted 9–3 for the MX appropriation.

At the start of the session, Addabbo asserted that the MX would lose by 50 votes; after the subcommittee tally, he scaled back his predicted margin of victory to five.[209] Downey explained the critics' position a few days later in a *Washington Post* op-ed. "The deal," noted the New York congressman, "trades a very explicit missile for some very vague promises," leaving the Working Group members saying that "MX is a dumb idea...but we need

---

[203] Kennedy, "Les Aspin and MX," p. 9.

[204] *New York Times*, 12 April 1983; *Washington Post*, 12 April 1983.

[205] Les AuCoin personal interview with author, 13 May 2004.

[206] 129 CR, 94th Congress, 1st session, p. 29235 (25 Oct. 1983); *New York Times*, 13 April 1983.

[207] Elizabeth Drew, "A Political Journal," *New Yorker*, 20 June 1983.

[208] Elizabeth Drew, "A Political Journal," *New Yorker*, 20 June 1983; *Washington Post*, 13 May 1983.

[209] *New York Times*, 15 May 1983.

it anyway, to support the smart idea of arms control."[210] A successful arms control treaty, Downey reminded his colleagues, required a dedication to the concept, but the White House was "convinced in its bones that real men don't control weapons, they build them."[211] AuCoin followed up with a "Dear Colleague" letter listing 14 failures in the Aspin/Scowcroft reasoning, all derived from one central flaw: an administration "determined to achieve arms control does not need to be pushed into it. An administration hostile to arms control cannot be pushed into it."[212]

The Working Group, however, influenced far more votes (55 Democrats, 11 Republicans) than Addabbo had anticipated; with MX opponents recognizing the looming defeat, floor debate – characterized, as Barney Frank noted, by scarcely "any good words being said about the weapons system in question" – proved unusually contentious.[213] Downey expressed amazement that "of the 35 or so homes that it had in the past, we have managed to find in our own infinite wisdom the most dangerous and the most destabilizing"; privately, he expressed disappointment with "these good and decent men who are making decisions that are in my opinion a tragedy of the largest order."[214] AuCoin, speaking "for a lot of mainstream Democrats who are very bitter," ridiculed assertions by Gore, Dicks, and Aspin that they had obtained a commitment from the administration to move forward with arms control.[215] "If that is a bargain," the Oregon Democrat asserted, "all I can say is, to my colleagues on this side of the aisle who have entered into it, I am just pleased they are not negotiating with the Soviet Union."[216] (Journalists revived the quote in 2000, when the Democrats nominated Gore as their presidential candidate.[217]) In a crushing defeat for MX opponents, the alliance between Working Group and pro-administration members gave the MX a 53-vote margin of victory.

Since the Armed Services Committee appointed only pro-MX members to the conference committee, O'Neill designated Downey, AuCoin, and Markey as special conferees on the bill. The committee's de facto chairman, Stratton, resented the move, and – mimicking a tactic of former chairman F. Edward Hébert – provided no chairs for the trio when they arrived for the conference. Senate Democrats such as Ted Kennedy and Carl Levin (D-Michigan), both

---

[210] *Washington Post*, 20 May 1983.
[211] *Washington Post*, 20 May 1983.
[212] Les AuCoin, "Dear Colleague," 21 May 1983, in Kennedy, "Les Aspin and MX," p. 23.
[213] 129 CR, 94th Congress, 1st session, p. 13383 (23 May 1983); Kennedy, "Les Aspin and MX," p. 21.
[214] 129 CR, 94th Congress, 1st session, pp. 13372–13373 (23 May 1983); Elizabeth Drew, "A Political Journal," *New Yorker*, 20 June 1983.
[215] Elizabeth Drew, "A Political Journal," *New Yorker*, 20 June 1983.
[216] 129 CR, 94th Congress, 1st session, p. 13542 (24 May 1983); Elizabeth Drew, "A Political Journal," *New Yorker*, 20 June 1983.
[217] Les AuCoin personal interview with author, 13 May 2004.

of whom opposed the MX, could do little to assist: new rules in the upper chamber required conferees to support the Senate version of the bill, regardless of their personal inclinations. Nonetheless, the willingness of House dissenters to fight helped MX critics regain some momentum.[218] Votes later in 1983 progressively narrowed the gap; by mid-1984, the MX cleared the House by only two votes, 199–197, in what Downey termed "one of the most hard-fought battles in the history of Congress."[219]

In the late 1960s, the Senate explored national security policy in detail while Pentagon supporters in the House manipulated the rules to stifle debate. By the mid-1980s, the situation was reversed. Though Tower described the MX as "a textbook case of how not to manage an important national security issue," he nearly rammed through the missile's authorization without debate; only the necessities of Democratic presidential politics prevented such an outcome.[220] Hart's staffers, looking to preempt others "from taking the lead on the MX" and predicting that opposing the MX would allow the Colorado Democrat to woo liberals for his longshot presidential bid "with an issue that also has broad appeal to the centrist supporters of John Glenn," who also was vying for the nomination, recommended that the senator filibuster against the system.[221] Partisanship, of course, affected both sides: Tower considered the "success of MX inextricably linked to Reagan/Republican Party defense program."[222]

Hart got some mileage out of resuscitating earlier quotes by Tower, Jackson, and Weinberger against the Minuteman silo basing mode, but otherwise, discussion in the upper chamber was desultory; even the notoriously thin-skinned Tower ignored Hart's criticisms.[223] As in the House, few senators offered a positive defense of the MX (although Wyoming's Alan Simpson did claim divine endorsement, since God's position could not be served if His servants "fail to defend themselves and are then sponged from the face of the Earth by a wholly godless ideology who do not believe in Him"), while most critics, as Glenn recognized, seemed "much more eager to stop that missile than to decide on any positive alternative."[224] Despite multiple references to the 1969 ABM fight – the closeness of which, Stennis recalled,

---

[218] Les AuCoin personal interview with author, 13 May 2004.

[219] Thomas Downey, "Report from Washington," summer 1984, Box 187, Thomas Downey Papers, Cornell University.

[220] U.S. Senate, Armed Services Committee, *Hearings, MX Missile Basing System and Related Issues*, 98th Congress, 1st session, p. 96 (20 April 1983).

[221] Kent to Gary Hart, 9 May 1983; Kent to Gary Hart, 5 July 1983; both in Box 29, Gary Hart Papers, University of Colorado.

[222] John Tower, "Chairman's Talking Points for Republican Policy Committee Luncheon," 5 June 1984, Box 967, John Tower Papers, Southwestern University.

[223] 129 *CR*, 94th Congress, 1st session, p. 31233 (7 November 1983).

[224] John Glenn, "Dear Colleague," 12 May 1983, Box 59, Senate files, John Glenn Papers, Ohio State University; 129 *CR*, 94th Congress, 1st session, p. 13711 (25 May 1983).

"scared me out of my senses" – the Senate MX debate matched neither the technical complexity nor the suspense of its late 1960s predecessor.[225] And it certainly did not stimulate a broader exploration of the assumptions behind U.S. national security policy.

In April 1983, Downey commented that regarding strategic issues, "congressional involvement is wholesome"; Tower, on the other hand, believed that "every time Congress tries to second-guess the President on national security and foreign affairs...we're wrong."[226] The disparity between the viewpoints of the two chambers' key figures on defense issues explained why the House seized the initiative on national security policy in the early 1980s, a pattern reinforced by the departure of many of the Senate's leading defense specialists. In August 1983, Tower attributed his surprise decision to not stand for re-election to discontent with serving in a Senate that had "lost its corporate memory" – 63 of its members had served fewer than 10 years, and 43 were in their first term.[227] (The Texas senator's announcement prompted a plunge in the stock prices of defense contractors Lockheed, General Dynamics, and Northrop.[228]) Nine days later, Henry Jackson suffered a massive coronary; the *Wall Street Journal* correctly noted that the death of an "undisputed giant of the Senate" symbolized "the fading of the World War II political generation."[229]

The House's more prominent role on defense matters, however, highlighted the difficulty of framing issues for national discussion from the lower chamber. In June 1983, Downey privately informed MX critics that Reagan's talent for molding public opinion meant that "we're currently running behind in our efforts."[230] After a strategy session in his office, Downey, AuCoin, and Markey scheduled a joint press conference and rally on the Capitol steps with former national security adviser McGeorge Bundy. The event received some coverage – from CBS, PBS, the *New York Times*, *Newsday*, UPI, the *Boston Globe* – but neither the *Washington Post* nor the *Wall Street Journal* sent a reporter; nor did ABC, CBS, or political journals such as *Congressional Quarterly*, *National Journal*, and *Roll Call*.[231] Limits existed to the degree of press attention any House member could attract, even one with the media and intellectual savvy of Downey.

In any case, illustrating the difference between the two chambers, opposition House members had to surpass institutional hurdles before they could focus on framing their case before the public. In the more freewheeling

---

[225] 129 *CR*, 94th Congress, 1st session, p. 20765 (26 July 1983).

[226] 129 *CR*, 94th Congress, 1st session, p. 9350 (21 April 1983); *New York Times*, 9 April 1983.

[227] *Wall Street Journal*, 28 Aug. 1983.

[228] *Wall Street Journal*, 11 Sept. 1983.

[229] *Wall Street Journal*, 6 Sept. 1983.

[230] Thomas Downey, "Dear Colleagues," (MX opponents only), 6 June 1983, Box 239, Thomas Downey Papers, Cornell University.

[231] "Press sign-in," n.d. [1983], Box 234, Thomas Downey Papers, Cornell University.

Senate, figures outside of the ideological mainstream – such as Hughes and Gruening on the left or Helms and McCarran on the right – could exert influence disproportionate to their numbers. The House, however, was a majoritarian institution, whose rules frustrated attempts by renegade ideological blocs to seize control of the agenda. Those intent on challenging an administration's national security doctrine therefore needed to build a majority, and had to concentrate on educating their colleagues rather than shaping public opinion.[232]

Internal institutional changes increased the importance of this strategy. After Hébert's ouster, Pentagon authorization bills had come with open rules, under which amendments could be offered from the floor. In the late 1970s, however, Stratton started introducing substitutes to all liberal offerings, thereby creating parliamentary disarray whenever Pentagon critics sponsored defense-related amendments. Lucien Nedzi, just before he retired from the House in 1980, complained, "Things were better under Rivers. At least things got done."[233] As a result of such sentiments, the lower chamber returned to modified closed rules on defense bills – exactly what the New York Democrat had hoped his tactics would accomplish – making it harder to amend committee offerings.[234]

Gradual changes in congressional norms further weakened the position of House members seeking to develop an alternative to Reagan's international approach. The strong partisanship of younger Republicans polarized the House, while new congressional schedules, which allowed members to return to their districts for four days a week, prevented the personal bonding common in Congress after World War II. C-SPAN, which began televising House proceedings in 1979, subtly encouraged soundbite-oriented speeches and discouraged debate.[235] Subcommittee government, while still useful, could not overcome the breakdown of the legislative process, as occurred with increasing frequency in the 1980s. Only twice during Reagan's administration (1981 and 1985) did Congress authorize a foreign aid bill, thus minimizing opportunities for policy riders. House liberals explored policy-related amendments to the Pentagon appropriations bill, cognizant that, in Aspin's words, "to gain leverage over the executive, we needed something which the president wanted to sign, a bill which he considered essential."[236] Pro-Pentagon members, however, shied away from a tactic most associated with the new internationalists, while liberals had little chance of seeing their riders survive conference with the Senate. In addition, defense contractors

---

[232] Thomas Downey personal interview with author, 27 May 2004.
[233] Charles Whalen, *The House and Foreign Policy: The Irony of Congressional Reform* (Chapel Hill: University of North Carolina Press, 1982), p. 150.
[234] Les AuCoin personal interview with author, 13 May 2004.
[235] Les AuCoin personal interview with author, 13 May 2004.
[236] Aspin quoted in Blechman, *The Politics of National Security*, p. 106.

bitterly opposed this tactic, and had the capacity to reward their supporters (in perhaps the most egregious example of this behavior, a non-profit group funded by the munitions industry conferred a "Defense Industry Award" of $10,000 upon William Dickinson, citing his "outspoken and sustained support of defense preparedness").[237] As partisanship grew more poisonous, even Pentagon appropriations started to come under continuing resolutions, catch-alls passed at the end of a session that funded government agencies at the previous year's level.[238] By definition, continuing resolutions did not include policy-related riders attached to specific spending bills.

House members suffered from one other significant handicap in mobilizing congressional power: facing the electorate every two years minimized their political leeway to adopt controversial foreign policy positions. This obstacle especially affected Democrats elected between 1972 and 1976, many of whom had captured previously Republican seats and therefore did not represent safe districts.

House members' politically inspired reticence manifested itself most clearly as Reagan's Central American policy entered its most controversial stage, between 1983 and 1985. With the regime of José Napoleon Duarte in El Salvador stabilizing – at least in part due to U.S. policies – attention shifted to the Nicaraguan contras. Front-page exposés in *Time* and the *New York Times* suggested that the administration was flouting the spirit and probably the letter of the Boland amendment, which prohibited U.S. support for toppling the Sandinista government.[239] The president again used the bully pulpit to improve his political standing. In what *Time* termed "one of the best [speeches] of his presidency," Reagan informed a joint session of Congress that if Communism triumphed in Central America, "our credibility would collapse, our alliances would crumble, and the safety of our homeland would be put in jeopardy."[240] Traditional Democratic opponents were not persuaded. Barnes, opening hearings on the matter, criticized the "alarming escalation of our military commitment"; in Boland's Intelligence Committee, DCI William Casey advanced the dubious argument that since the United States aimed solely to "harass" the Sandinistas, the administration had not violated the Boland amendment, even if, as everyone conceded, the contras themselves wanted to overthrow the Sandinistas.[241] Both committees passed, by nearly straight party-line votes, bills to terminate contra aid.

---

[237] *Wall Street Journal*, 28 July 1983. Defending the propriety of the action, a spokesman noted, "Mr. Dickinson is not a wealthy man."

[238] Lance Lehoys, "The Fiscal Straightjacket: Budgetary Constraints on Congressional Foreign and Defense Policymaking," in Ripley and Lindsay, eds., *Congress Resurgent*, p. 45.

[239] *Time*, 4 April 1983; *New York Times*, 3 April 1983.

[240] *Time*, 9 May 1983.

[241] U.S. House of Representatives, Subcommittees on Human Rights and International Organizations, Western Hemisphere Affairs, *Hearing, U.S. Policy in Central America*, 98th Congress, 1st session, pp. 1–2 (3 Aug. 1983).

This tactical aggressiveness recalled confrontations such as the Diego Garcia fight between Congress and the president during the first half of the 1970s. A few members, as had occurred in these previous crises, framed the matter as broadly as possible. Downey, for instance, felt as if some colleagues "have transited the last 30 years without learning very much about American diplomatic history"; the United States seemed to be preparing a "land version of the Bay of Pigs, with the 10,000 thugs, brigands, and thieves" of the contra army.[242] The New York congressman – echoing arguments offered by the new internationalists in the 1970s – deemed such a policy not only morally indefensible, but also doomed to fail, since "it remains our adherence to ideals, and not our abandonment of them, that offers our most successful strategy for competing with our adversaries."[243] Newt Gingrich, then just developing a reputation for his sharp partisan attacks, mocked Downey for having "articulated brilliantly the radical doctrine of his wing of his party."[244]

In fact, Downey and a few others notwithstanding, the administration's critics actively avoided a showdown with the White House, lest they, as one staffer observed, be backed into "a position that could be interpreted later as helping to create a 'new Cuba' in Central America."[245] But when Reagan spurned all attempts at compromise, two key Democratic moderates, Jim Wright and Dave McCurdy (D-Oklahoma), reluctantly endorsed the aid cutoff, which then passed the House 228–195.[246] In the Senate, however, liberals could not obtain a majority; the resulting conference committee provided $24 million in assistance through 1984. Tom Eagleton lamented that, in the new Senate climate, he felt "so goddamned powerless."[247]

Through early 1984, Reagan seemed well positioned to consolidate his Central American victory, as administration supporters focused on what they termed a double standard on human rights. Lloyd Bentsen (D-Texas) chastised fellow Senate Democrats for their criticism of Reagan's El Salvador policy, despite signs that the Duarte government was achieving some meaningful reform. From the tenor of his colleagues' comments, the Texas senator lamented, "you would think there had been a coup – not an election – in El Salvador."[248] Along the same lines, House Republicans highlighted an amendment to terminate aid to Zimbabwe sponsored by Jerry Lewis. The

---

[242] 129 *CR*, 98th Congress, 1st session, p. 21442 (28 July 1983).

[243] Thomas Downey to Sylvan Fox, Box 239, Thomas Downey Papers, Cornell University.

[244] 129 *CR*, 98th Congress, 1st session, p. 21444 (28 July 1983).

[245] Steve to Gary Hart, 10 March 1983, Box 25, Gary Hart Papers, University of Colorado; for statements of Democratic reticence, see *Los Angeles Times*, 16 May 1983; *Congressional Quarterly Weekly Report*, 30 April 1983.

[246] *New York Times*, 27 July 1983.

[247] Thomas Eagleton to Christopher Dodd, 29 Nov. 1983, Folder 4390, Thomas Eagleton Papers, University of Missouri.

[248] 130 *CR*, 98th Congress, 2nd session, p. 7456 (3 April 1984).

California Republican cited human rights violations by Robert Mugabe's regime, including the politically inspired arrest of the nation's first black ruler, Bishop Abel Muzorewa. With some in Congress demanding democracy for El Salvador and Chile, Lewis noted, "the least we should do is to have a uniform standard."[249] Democrats blocked the amendment, employing arguments that bolstered GOP charges: Harold Wolpe celebrated Zimbabwe's relatively advanced judicial system, asserted Muzorewa was simply detained and had not disappeared like 1970s political prisoners in South America, and described U.S. aid as "appropriate to the progress that is being made" in the African nation.[250] With House human rights activists appearing to defend politically oriented detentions by leftist governments while criticizing similar behavior by right-wing regimes, the White House was winning the war of ideas.

Then the administration committed a series of blunders. In a March 1984 interview, Reagan implied that, contrary to his stated policies, the covert operation would end only with the Sandinistas' ouster, drawing condemnation from two moderates on the heretofore tame Senate Intelligence Committee, Daniel Patrick Moynihan and David Durenberger (R-Minnesota).[251] The next month, the *New York Times* revealed that contra commandoes, supervised by the CIA, had mined Nicaraguan ports, in violation of international law; both houses of Congress overwhelmingly passed symbolic resolutions of condemnation.[252] Most important, a dispute arose over whether William Casey had, as legally required, informed the Intelligence Committees of the operation. Casey, who believed that "the business of Congress is to stay out of my business," clearly had not gone out of his way to keep the legislature in the loop: early in his tenure, the two committees installed a microphone at the witness table, since the DCI's mumbling made him almost inaudible.[253] Summarizing the general sentiment among House Democrats, Norman Mineta (D-California) remarked, "If you were talking to Casey, and your coat caught fire, he wouldn't tell you about it unless you asked."[254] The mining gave critics of contra aid momentum, and a 1984 House-Senate conference report terminated assistance, but allowed the administration to request new contra aid on or after February 28, 1985.

The status of contra aid and the MX missile thus remained unresolved heading into the 1984 elections. A contested Democratic presidential primary season yielded a weak nominee, former Vice President Walter Mondale,

[249] 130 *CR*, 98th Congress, 2nd session, p. 11646 (9 May 1984).
[250] 130 *CR*, 98th Congress, 2nd session, pp. 11647–11648 (9 May 1984).
[251] *Washington Post*, 30 March 1984.
[252] *New York Times*, 10 April 1984.
[253] Barbara Hinckley, *Less Than Meets the Eye: Foreign Policy Making and the Myth of the Assertive Congress* (Chicago: University of Chicago Press, 1994), p. 4.
[254] Mineta quoted in Blechman, *Politics of National Security*, p. 156.

who overwhelmingly lost to Reagan. Nonetheless, Democrats captured GOP-held Senate seats in Illinois, Iowa, and Tennessee. In Iowa, Jepsen's re-election chances – never strong anyway – plunged after he voided a traffic ticket by invoking an obscure constitutional provision protecting members of Congress traveling to their official duties. Shortly thereafter, the incumbent, who campaigned on a family values theme, admitted that he had previously visited a massage parlor. Tom Harkin, author of the most significant human rights amendment of the 1970s, carried all six of the state's congressional districts en route to a 55 percent victory. In Illinois, Percy had understood that the Foreign Relations chairmanship might impair his re-election; in 1984, he faced a primary challenge from a right-wing congressman and opposition from pro-Israel groups.[255] The Democrats also nominated a particularly strong candidate, downstate congressman Paul Simon, a former MCPL treasurer and sponsor of an early amendment to cut off funding for the MX (in 1980). As did Harkin, Simon scored a solid victory after running as the slight favorite throughout the campaign. Finally, in Tennessee, MX Working Group member Al Gore coasted to victory after Majority Leader Baker declined to stand for re-election. In high-profile Senate races in New Hampshire and North Carolina, however, New Right incumbents Jesse Helms and Gordon Humphrey prevailed, and the GOP gained 14 seats in the House, confirming the institution's greater vulnerability to presidential coattails.

Shortly after the election, looking to create a procedural venue from which to promote his defense goals, Downey in vain urged the leadership to establish a select committee on arms control, to monitor disarmament talks and thereby enable a "larger proportion of the House to have direct exposure" to strategic issues without "interfering with or distorting the legislative operation of the House."[256] The New York Democrat also assumed the chairmanship of the Budget Committee's Task Force on Defense and International Affairs, where he operated under the premise that "the idea that the simple expenditure of money will guarantee that we will be strong is not true."[257] In the event, however, the ideological and procedural agenda that Downey personified suffered a series of crippling blows in the new congressional session. By early 1986, a variety of initiatives had all but shattered the framework through which Congress responded to the Cold War.

The process began, ironically, with an unprecedented rebellion in the Armed Services Committee, where Mel Price's personal and intellectual

---

255 Chris Chamberlain to Paul Tsongas, 6 Nov. 1980, Box 78B, Senate Series, Paul Tsongas Papers, Center for Lowell History.
256 Thomas Downey press release, 5 Dec. 1984, Box 191, Thomas Downey Papers, Cornell University.
257 U.S. House of Representatives, Task Force on Defense and International Affairs, *Hearings, Defense and the Deficit: A Review of Defense Spending and Its Relationship to National Security*, 99th Congress, 1st session, p. 72 (28 March 1985).

frailty was obvious by late 1984. Most House liberals recoiled from the prospect of a Stratton chairmanship; capturing the consensus, Richard Ottinger labeled his New York colleague a "militarist at heart" who was "off his rocker" with regard to military spending.[258] Stratton, the committee's third-ranking member, certainly could not rely on personal ties with fellow members; in the early 1980s, when he indicated his interest in a minor honorific post, he received only one vote (his own) from the state delegation.[259] Nonetheless, he retained a following within the committee; in a 1983 tussle widely viewed as a proxy battle for the next chair, he prevented the more moderate Charles Bennett, the committee's second-ranking member, from assuming the chairmanship of the Seapower Subcommittee.[260]

With Price's political position weakened, Aspin, the panel's seventh-ranking Democrat, urged the party caucus to reject Price and install him as the committee's new head. Described by *Congressional Quarterly* as "one of the handful of members who appear to find personal, as well as political, satisfaction in the game of legislative strategy," the Wisconsin congressman's tactics were brilliant: Bennett and Stratton recoiled from challenging the seniority system and therefore supported Price until it was too late.[261] With younger Democrats convinced that the party needed a figure who could articulate Democratic positions to the media and liberals eager to preempt a Stratton chairmanship, the caucus ousted Price by a 118–112 vote, and then elected Aspin over Bennett, who jumped into the race after Price's defeat.

Liberals whose votes gave Aspin the chairmanship, however, would regret their decision. For the first time since Mendel Rivers' death in 1970, the Armed Services Committee had effective leadership, thus enabling the committee to play a more decisive role in House affairs. Moreover, the Wisconsin congressman quickly demonstrated his unreliability. Several high-profile Democrats, such as Howard Wolpe and Bob Edgar, voted for him only after Aspin promised to oppose further funding for the MX.[262] When, after his election, the Wisconsin Democrat announced that he would favor the MX, AuCoin detected a "deep disillusionment, a very real anger" toward the new chair.[263] At an emotional meeting of the Democratic caucus described by Mary McGrory as a "tribunal on the character of Representative Les Aspin," AuCoin denounced his colleague as a "private contractor" of the White House.[264] Aspin held firm, however, in his support for the MX,

---

[258] *Congressional Quarterly Weekly Report*, 31 March 1984.
[259] Thomas Downey personal interview with author, 27 May 2004.
[260] *Congressional Quarterly Weekly Report*, 12 January 1983.
[261] *Congressional Quarterly Weekly Report*, 5 Jan. 1985.
[262] *Washington Post*, 26 May 1985.
[263] *Congressional Quarterly Weekly Report*, 30 March 1985.
[264] *Washington Post*, 24 March 1985; *Congressional Quarterly Weekly Report*, 2 March 1985, 30 March 1985.

convinced that the Democrats needed to stop being "the Doctor No of the defense debate."[265]

When the MX came to the floor, the 10 hours of debate featured members talking past each other; the time constraints of a closed rule prevented much questioning. Stratton opened for MX supporters, blaming the Soviets for destabilizing the international order and arguing that building the MX would fulfill the spirit of the 1972 Jackson amendment demanding strategic equality; he also pointed to the 3,200 jobs that the appropriation would create.[266] The debate's most controversial moment, however, came when Aspin charged that rejecting the MX would "be giving some help to the Soviet Union," drawing jeers from Democrats and a standing ovation from Republicans.[267] As had become customary, AuCoin and Downey presented the strongest arguments against the MX, the Oregon Democrat stressing the weapon's destabilizing effects, the New York congressman urging colleagues to focus on preserving deterrence. Other anti-MX speakers focused on their desire to reallocate MX funds for domestic programs; the most bizarre speech came from James Weaver, who contended that Reagan, "obsessed with building more nuclear weapons," was "presiding over the liquidation of our own farms" comparable to Stalin's purge of the kulaks in the 1930s.[268]

Some Democrats searched for the middle ground, in this case seeking to trade their votes for something concrete for themselves or for their districts: White House political director Ed Rollins noticed, "The wish list came out early this year."[269] After the phase-out of the Titan missile program cost his district 1,100 jobs, Arkansas Democrat Tommy Robinson obtained their transfer to civilian work in a federal communications center in exchange for backing the MX. Vulnerable Democrats from North Carolina, Tennessee, and Texas demanded that the White House terminate a $5 million advertising effort by the Republican Congressional Campaign Committee; Rollins gave his assurance.[270] To pressure wavering Democrats, the White House recalled its chief arms negotiator, Max Kampelman, a former adviser to Hubert Humphrey and prominent neoconservative theorist; six Democrats changed their minds in the final 72 hours, enough to give the administration a 219–213 victory. By the end of the year, the administration and Senate moderates worked out a deal for a cap of 50 missiles – half of what the administration desired, but nonetheless a key victory for the president, since opponents claimed that deploying even one MX would destabilize the

[265] New York Times, 7 June 1985.
[266] 131 CR, 99th Congress, 1st session, pp. H1391–1392 (25 March 1985).
[267] New York Times, 27 March 1985.
[268] 131 CR, 99th Congress, 1st session, p. H1413 (25 March 1985).
[269] Wall Street Journal, 23 March 1985.
[270] Wall Street Journal, 23 March 1985.

arms race. Reflecting on the outcome, Pat Schroeder lamented, "We have all become afraid of being called a wimp."[271]

Reagan also scored an impressive triumph on contra aid. As in the MX battle, the administration framed its proposal as a necessary bargaining chip, in this instance to encourage the Sandinistas to agree to a U.S.-backed peace deal. (The president even sent Bob Dole to the Vatican in a vain attempt to win the Pope's endorsement for his program.[272]) The character of Senate debate differed from that of the early 1980s, due to the election of the upper chamber's first three Vietnam veterans (Harkin, Gore, and John Kerry), each of whom compared Central American events to the early stages of the U.S. involvement in Vietnam.[273] In the end, however, Senate moderates, assuming that the House would reject aid, took the politically safe course and sided with the administration.[274] The House, meanwhile, considered several competing measures: the *Wall Street Journal* complained that a "preoccupation with the *procedure* of the aid is merely designed to hide the fact that what's at issue is the *substantive* imperative of getting help to the contras."[275] On the key question of covert assistance, head counts suggested that critics held an advantage of 20 or 30 votes, but the final tally required the Speaker to hold open the roll call for several minutes until two party loyalists, Edward Roybal (D-California) and Henry Gonzalez (D-Texas), sunk the administration's request, 215–213.[276] Reagan, enraged by the result, announced that he would "return to the Congress again and again to seek a policy that supports peace and democracy in Nicaragua."[277]

The day after the vote, Nicaraguan president Daniel Ortega made a state visit to Moscow, a move that an O'Neill aide conceded "enormously undercut the position" of the Speaker.[278] Moderates led by McCurdy immediately opened negotiations with the administration to reconsider the vote. The Oklahoma Democrat received a public letter from Reagan affirming the administration's commitment to settling the crisis through negotiations; House Republicans such as William Broomfield, in a less conciliatory mood, contended that "a vote against the contras is a vote in support of the spread of communism."[279] On June 12, after voting 232–196 against extending the Boland amendment, the House approved by 64 votes a $27 million aid package. "Faced with C-SPAN cameras," the *Wall Street*

---

[271] 131 *CR*, 99th Congress, 1st session, p. H1513 (25 March 1985); *Congressional Quarterly Weekly Report*, 30 March 1985.

[272] *Washington Post*, 6 April 1985.

[273] *Washington Post*, 23 April 1985.

[274] *Washington Post*, 26 April 1985.

[275] *Wall Street Journal*, 11 Feb. 1985.

[276] *Washington Post*, 15 April 1985.

[277] *Time*, 6 May 1985.

[278] *Time*, 17 June 1985; Arnson, *Crossroads*, p. 199.

[279] 131 *CR*, 99th Congress, 1st session, p. H4126 (12 June 1985); *Time*, 24 June 1985.

Journal noted, "even many liberals were wary of an outright vote against contra aid."[280]

The contra aid and MX battles bequeathed a House leadership increasingly embittered at Reagan's approach to national security affairs. Regarding Central America, Speaker O'Neill declared that Reagan would not "be happy until he has the Marines and the Rangers there and has a complete victory."[281] Majority Leader Wright, meanwhile, privately stated that he placed greater trust in the ability to secure world peace of the new Soviet leader, Mikhail Gorbachev, than he did of Reagan.[282]

The administration's triumphs continued when Congress considered policy toward Angola. For nine years, in the face of withering conservative assaults, the Clark amendment survived, the last significant tribute to the new internationalists' assertion of congressional authority. Shortly after his second inauguration, Reagan again called for repealing the amendment, citing the need to resist a joint Cuban-MPLA offensive against Jonas Savimbi's UNITA forces. As it had in 1981, the Senate followed the president's lead, by a 63–34 margin.[283] The House Subcommittee on Africa, as expected, voted to retain the amendment. House conservatives, as expected, demanded repeal: Stratton urged colleagues to "recognize that the overall strategy for that amendment is no longer current in the United States."[284] When the Foreign Affairs Committee sustained its subcommittee's action, it appeared as if the House would repeat its 1981 performance, when it frustrated the administration's efforts at repeal.

Then a figure from the past intervened. After his defeat in 1950, Claude Pepper returned to Miami to practice law; when redistricting gave Dade County a new House seat in 1962, the former senator easily prevailed. In contrast to his previously rebellious nature, Pepper developed a close relationship with the House leadership, even earning a seat on the Rules Committee. In the early 1980s, moreover, he emerged as one of the party's most potent campaigners, an octogenarian congressman who fought Reagan's attempts to curb the growth of Social Security.

Pepper's congressional district changed demographically during his time in office. By 1980, Cuban-Americans formed nearly 30 percent of the population, and Reagan carried the district in the year's presidential contest. Like all Southern Florida politicians, the Miami Democrat supported a hard line toward Fidel Castro, and after Cuban-American groups lobbied him about the Clark amendment, he joined Stratton in sponsoring the repeal

---

[280] *Wall Street Journal*, 11 Feb. 1985.
[281] *Time*, 24 June 1985.
[282] Thomas Downey personal interview with author, 27 May 2004.
[283] 131 *CR*, 99th Congress, 1st session, p. S7836 (11 June 1985); *Washington Post*, 12 June 1985.
[284] 131 *CR*, 99th Congress, 1st session, pp. H5418, H5422 (10 July 1985).

initiative. But though his postwar demands for a peaceful response to Communism had long passed, Pepper nonetheless sought to reconcile his position on Angola with his earlier embrace of Atlantic Charter internationalism.[285] To the Florida congressman, the issue was "not a complex matter at all" – the House needed "to allow the world to perceive the United States as still interested in freedom and democracy for this tragic part of the world."[286] The Clark amendment, he contended, created the impression that Americans had "washed our hands" of southern Africa, contrary to the traditional U.S. support for self-determination abroad.[287] "The people of Angola," the congressman concluded, "have a right to be free."[288]

Shortly after Pepper's speech, 60 House Democrats joined 176 Republicans in voting to repeal the Clark amendment; Stratton rejoiced that "a unique and controversial decade of U.S. foreign policy came to an abrupt end."[289] (Downey, on the other hand, denounced the House for embracing the "bizarre" approach of "attempting to assert its machismo through the foreign aid bill."[290]) Despite earlier assurances to the contrary, Pepper and Stratton quickly called for extending military aid to Savimbi's UNITA forces. Claiming a congressional consensus in favor of a more aggressive response to Angola, Stratton complained that the State Department and the media seemed to believe that "a few wackos got up and somehow mesmerized the House of Representatives and the great Clark amendment suddenly was flushed down the drain."[291] As Stratton had hoped, in early 1986, the administration granted $15 million in assistance to UNITA.

In 1999, David Grann of *The New Republic* traced the post-congressional career of Tom Downey, who lost his House seat in 1992, in the fallout from the House Bank scandal. Downey, who established his own lobbying firm, "has become Mr. Washington," said one official close to then-vice president Al Gore. "He knows everyone and is connected to everyone." Grann contended that the "erstwhile antiwar radical who always fought the system" had, in fact, passed from the scene by 1988, when Downey focused on the intricacies of the Ways and Means Committee, developing close relationships with corporate interests over which the committee had

[285] U.S. House of Representatives, Subcommittee on Africa, *Hearings, Angola: Intervention or Negotiation*, 99th Congress, 1st session, p. 70 (12 Nov. 1985).
[286] 131 *CR*, 99th Congress, 1st session, p. H5425 (10 July 1985).
[287] 131 *CR*, 99th Congress, 1st session, p. H5425 (10 July 1985).
[288] *New York Times*, 11 July 1985.
[289] Samuel Stratton press release, 1 July 1985, Box 103, Samuel Stratton Papers, University of Rochester.
[290] *New York Times*, 14 July 1985.
[291] U.S. House of Representatives, Subcommittee on Africa, *Hearings, Angola: Intervention or Negotiation*, 99th Congress, 1st session, p. 96 (12 Nov. 1985).

jurisdiction while rarely involving himself in the national security debates just beginning to emerge from the post-Cold War world.[292]

Downey's metamorphosis from activist congressman to well-placed lobbyist testified, in many ways, to the altered nature of Washington political culture: Congress no longer seemed capable of launching effective challenges, either intellectually or politically, to the executive position in foreign policy. By the mid-1990s, most of the key players from the late Cold War period were no longer in public service: in addition to Downey, AuCoin, McCurdy, Barnes, and Wolpe lost their last election campaigns. Stratton, Price, Pepper, Boland, and O'Neill had died; Tower, Tsongas, Hart, Goldwater, and Garn all voluntarily left the Senate. Addabbo died in office, ethics allegations forced Wright to resign, and Gore and Aspin left Congress to serve in the Clinton administration. With the sole exception of John McCain, who succeeded Goldwater as an Arizona senator, the replacements for each of these figures made little or no impact on international matters.

In the Congress that these legislators left behind, many of the patterns that decreased congressional influence – and functionality – in the latter stages of the Cold War intensified: poisonous partisanship; the House seizing the initiative from the Senate; leveling tendencies that diminished the significance of intellectual achievement; a political culture that exalted style over substance; the role of C-SPAN and floor rules in discouraging genuine debate on the floor. In short, the institution seemed no more capable than in 1985 of effectively reviving the role that it retained in most of the Cold War of exercising influence through varied, often subtle and creative, ways.

Two abortive replacements for the new internationalist structural and ideological approach emerged after Congress repealed the Clark amendment in 1985. The first sought to use the legislature as a base for launching country-specific anti-Communist crusades in the Third World. In addition to resuming funding for the Nicaraguan contras, Congress extended assistance to anti-Communist forces in Angola, Cambodia, and, most spectacularly, Afghanistan, where much of the credit (or blame) for the U.S. decision to aid the mujahideen forces lies with Charles Wilson, who ferociously embraced the Afghan anti-Communist cause after his efforts for Somoza came to naught.[293] While the Afghan operation persisted, this overall vision of the congressional role in world affairs was undone by the Reagan administration – first by the president's decision to open serious arms control negotiations with Mikhail Gorbachev, which previewed the looming end to Cold War tensions, and then with the revelation of the Iran-contra affair, which rendered unlikely additional legislative attempts to arm irregular armies in the Third World.

---

[292] David Grann, "Beltway Boy," *The New Republic*, 9 Aug. 1999.
[293] Crile, *Charlie Wilson's War.*

The anti-Communists' setback seemed to benefit a bipartisan bloc, mostly in the Senate, that sought to use the end of the Cold War to revive Wilsonianism, through a search for alternatives to power politics, based on international law and economic sanctions. This group, most prominently Mark Hatfield and the new Senate majority leader, George Mitchell (D-Maine), made its most determined stand in opposing the resolution authorizing the first Gulf War. In the end, few if any Democrats suffered political fallout from their decision to vote against this quick and popular war – though more because of the Bush administration's political ineptness rather than any strong public support for a Wilsonian worldview.

Most congressional Democrats, interpreting the outcome as good fortune, did not take political risks on international matters again. With the exception of calls by the Congressional Black Caucus for intervention to restore Jean-Bertrand Aristide's government in Haiti and sporadic efforts to block most favored nation trading status for China, in the 1990s congressional Democrats deferred to the Clinton administration, excluding international questions involving very different sorts of issues than those common in the Cold War, such as economic globalization and its effects. Legislative Republicans, especially after the 1994 elections brought a new group of GOP activists to both chambers, most often approached foreign policy through an overtly partisan lens, with perhaps the best example coming in the decision of the House, in 1999, to simultaneously fund and condemn, in separate resolutions, the unauthorized military intervention in Kosovo.[294]

This record bequeaths a fundamental irony. At the time, the Cold War often was considered a period of diminished congressional influence in the international arena. Not only was this impression untrue, however, but the legislature played a much more substantial role on foreign policy questions between the end of World War II and the repeal of the Clark amendment than it does today. It remains unclear when, or even if, Congress will resume the degree of influence over international matters that it attained during most periods after World War II; it seems likely, however, that at some point, legislators will realize that the Cold War experience provides insight on how the institution's most talented members can affect the course of foreign policy. In the meantime, scholars of U.S. foreign relations could do worse than to apply Downey's dictum: that for understanding the U.S. response to the Cold War international environment, experience suggests that "congressional involvement is wholesome."[295]

[294] *Washington Post*, 17 April 1999.
[295] 129 CR, 94th Congress, 1st session, p. 9350 (21 April 1983).

Appendix A

The Foreign Aid Revolt of 1963

1. **HR 7885. The Foreign Assistance Act of 1963.** Morse amendment to recommit the bill to the Foreign Relations Committee for one week. Rejected 29–46 (R 8–17, D 21–29). November 1, 1963.
2. **HR 7885. The Foreign Assistance Act of 1963.** Ellender amendment to lower the amount for development loans in FY 1964 to $900 million instead of $975 million. Rejected 40–43 (R 12–14, D 28–29). November 5, 1963.
3. **HR 7885. The Foreign Assistance Act of 1963.** Morse amendment to reduce the amount for development loans in FY 1964 to $950 million and repeal the standing authorizations for FY 1965 and 1966. Accepted 42–40 (R 13–11, D 29–29). November 5, 1963.
4. **HR 7885. The Foreign Assistance Act of 1963.** Kuchel amendment prohibiting aid to any country that extends its territorial limits on the high seas beyond the limits recognized by the United States, and penalizes U.S. vessels for fishing within those limits. Accepted 57–29 (R 23–4, D 34–25). November 7, 1963.
5. **HR 7885. The Foreign Assistance Act of 1963.** Fulbright amendment to Gruening amendment to give the president more discretion in cutting off aid to aggressor nations and to limit the amendment to foreign aid, and not all forms of U.S. assistance. Rejected 32–46 (R 4–23, D 28–23). November 7, 1963.
6. **HR 7885. The Foreign Assistance Act of 1963.** Morse amendment to cut funds for supporting assistance from $400 million to $380 million. Accepted 51–41 (R 17–13, D 34–28). November 13, 1963.
7. **HR 7885. The Foreign Assistance Act of 1963.** Morse amendment to allow the President to aid a Latin American military junta only if he declares it in the national interest and Congress does not adopt a disapproving resolution within 30 days. Rejected 11–178 (R 2–29, D 9–49). November 14, 1963.

8. **HR 7885. The Foreign Assistance Act of 1963.** Morse amendment to end foreign aid after June 30, 1965 unless recipient countries have adopted several self-help measures and reforms, the aid is being given under an irrevocable prior contract, and the number of aid recipients has been reduced to 50. Rejected 29–56 (R 11–19, D 18–37). November 14, 1963.

9. **HR 7885. The Foreign Assistance Act of 1963.** Morse amendment substituting the House-passed bill, authorizing $3.502 million (as opposed to the Senate's $3.7 billion) and making a number of restrictions on the administration of the program. Rejected 15–68 (R 3–27, D 12–41). November 14, 1963.

Vote Key
Democrats in solid
Republicans in italics
Y – yes
N – no
(+) – paired for
(−) – paired against
ay – announced yes
an – announced no
(?) – did not vote or otherwise make position known

	1	2	3	4	5	6	7	8	9
ALABAMA									
Hill	N	Y	N	Y	N	Y	N	N	N
Sparkman	N	N	N	N	Y	N	N	N	N
ALASKA									
Bartlett	–	N	N	Y	N	Y	N	N	N
Gruening	Y	Y	Y	Y	N	Y	Y	Y	+
ARIZONA									
Hayden	N	N	an	Y	Y	N	N	N	N
Goldwater	+	ay	ay	ay	an	Y	N	Y	N
ARKANSAS									
Fulbright	N	N	N	N	Y	N	N	N	N
McClellan	ay	Y	Y	Y	Y	Y	N	Y	N
CALIFORNIA									
Engle	an	an	an	+	+	–	–	–	–
Kuchel	N	N	N	Y	N	N	N	N	N
COLORADO									
Allott	N	Y	Y	Y	N	Y	N	Y	N
Dominick	N	Y	+	Y	N	Y	N	N	N

	1	2	3	4	5	6	7	8	9
CONNECTICUT									
Dodd	N	N	N	Y	N	Y	Y	Y	N
Ribicoff	Y	+	Y	Y	N	Y	N	N	N
DELAWARE									
Boggs	N	N	N	Y	N	N	N	N	N
Williams	Y	Y	Y	Y	N	Y	N	Y	Y
FLORIDA									
Holland	N	N	N	N	N	Y	N	N	N
Smathers	an	N	N	N	an	N	an	–	–
GEORGIA									
Russell	Y	Y	Y	Y	an	Y	N	Y	Y
Talmadge	Y	Y	Y	Y	N	Y	N	Y	Y
HAWAII									
Inouye	N	N	N	Y	Y	N	N	N	N
Fong	N	Y	Y	Y	N	N	N	N	N
IDAHO									
Church	Y	Y	Y	N	Y	Y	N	N	N
Jordan	Y	ay	ay	Y	N	Y	N	Y	N
ILLINOIS									
Douglas	N	N	N	Y	N	N	N	N	N
Dirksen	N	N	N	Y	?	N	N	N	N
INDIANA									
Bayh	–	N	N	N	Y	N	Y	N	N
Hartke	–	N	N	N	N	N	N	N	N
IOWA									
Hickenlooper	N	N	N	+	Y	N	N	N	N
Miller	–	Y	Y	Y	N	Y	N	Y	N
KANSAS									
Carlson	N	N	N	Y	Y	Y	N	N	N
Pearson	N	Y	Y	Y	an	Y	N	N	N
KENTUCKY									
Cooper	–	N	N	N	?	–	N	N	N
Morton	–	N	N	N	N	N	an	–	–
LOUISIANA									
Ellender	Y	Y	Y	Y	N	Y	+	+	+
Long	+	Y	N	N	–	ay	an	+	+

	1	2	3	4	5	6	7	8	9
MAINE									
Muskie	N	N	N	Y	Y	N	N	N	N
Smith	N	N	N	Y	N	N	N	N	N
MARYLAND									
Brewster	N	Y	Y	Y	N	N	N	N	N
Beall	+	N	Y	Y	N	Y	N	Y	N
MASSACHUSETTS									
Kennedy	N	N	N	N	Y	N	N	N	N
Saltonstall	N	N	N	Y	Y	N	N	N	N
MICHIGAN									
Hart	N	N	N	N	N	N	N	N	N
McNamara	N	–	–	ay	+	N	N	N	N
MINNESOTA									
Humphrey	N	N	N	N	Y	N	N	N	N
McCarthy	N	N	N	N	Y	N	N	N	N
MISSISSIPPI									
Eastland	+	ay	+	Y	–	Y	N	N	N
Stennis	?	ay	+	+	an	ay	an	+	+
MISSOURI									
Long	N	Y	Y	N	–	Y	N	N	N
Symington	Y	Y	Y	ay	N	Y	N	Y	N
MONTANA									
Mansfield	N	N	N	N	Y	N	N	N	N
Metcalf	an	N	N	Y	Y	N	N	N	N
NEBRASKA									
Curtis	Y	Y	Y	Y	N	+	an	+	+
Hruska	+	Y	Y	Y	N	Y	N	ay	ay
NEVADA									
Bible	+	Y	Y	Y	N	Y	N	Y	Y
Cannon	Y	Y	Y	Y	N	Y	N	N	N
NEW HAMPSHIRE									
McIntyre	N	N	N	Y	Y	Y	N	N	N
Cotton	Y	?	?	Y	N	Y	Y	Y	Y
NEW JERSEY									
Williams	N	N	N	N	+	N	N	N	–
Case	N	N	N	N	N	N	N	N	N
NEW MEXICO									
Anderson	?	N	Y	Y	Y	N	an	an	an
Mechem	+	Y	Y	Y	N	Y	N	N	N

	1	2	3	4	5	6	7	8	9
NEW YORK									
Javits	N	an	an	N	N	N	N	N	N
Keating	N	N	N	Y	N	N	N	N	N
NORTH CAROLINA									
Ervin	Y	Y	Y	?	–	Y	Y	Y	Y
Jordan	Y	Y	Y	Y	N	ay	N	Y	Y
NORTH DAKOTA									
Burdick	N	Y	Y	Y	Y	Y	N	Y	N
Young	N	Y	Y	Y	Y	ay	N	N	N
OHIO									
Lausche	N	Y	Y	N	Y	N	N	N	N
Young	Y	Y	Y	Y	N	Y	Y	ay	N
OKLAHOMA									
Edmonson	N	+	+	Y	N	Y	N	Y	Y
Monroney	N	N	N	N	Y	N	N	N	N
OREGON									
Morse	Y	Y	Y	Y	N	Y	Y	Y	Y
Neuberger	N	N	N	Y	Y	N	N	N	N
PENNSYLVANIA									
Clark	Y	N	N	N	Y	N	N	N	an
Scott	+	N	Y	ay	N	N	N	N	N
RHODE ISLAND									
Pastore	N	–	–	–	+	N	N	N	N
Pell	N	N	N	N	Y	Y	N	N	N
SOUTH CAROLINA									
Johnston	Y	Y	Y	Y	N	Y	Y	Y	Y
Thurmond	Y	Y	Y	ay	–	Y	N	Y	Y
SOUTH DAKOTA									
McGovern	Y	N	N	N	Y	Y	N	an	an
Mundt	Y	Y	Y	Y	N	Y	N	Y	N
TENNESSEE									
Gore	Y	N	N	N	Y	N	N	an	an
Walters	Y	an	an	N	Y	an	an	an	+
TEXAS									
Yarborough	an	Y	Y	Y	N	Y	N	Y	N
Tower	Y	ay	ay	Y	N	Y	N	Y	N
UTAH									
Moss	–	N	N	Y	Y	N	N	N	N
Bennett	Y	ay	ay	ay	an	Y	N	Y	N

	1	2	3	4	5	6	7	8	9
VERMONT									
Aiken	N	N	–	an	an	N	N	N	N
Prouty	N	an	ay	ay	N	Y	N	N	N
VIRGINIA									
Byrd	Y	Y	Y	Y	Y	Y	N	Y	Y
Robertson	Y	Y	Y	Y	–	Y	Y	Y	Y
WASHINGTON									
Jackson	+	Y	Y	Y	Y	Y	an	–	–
Magnuson	N	+	Y	Y	+	Y	an	an	–
WEST VIRGINIA									
Byrd	–	Y	Y	N	Y	N	N	N	N
Randolph	N	Y	Y	N	N	Y	N	N	N
WISCONSIN									
Nelson	Y	N	N	Y	Y	Y	Y	N	N
Proxmire	N	Y	Y	N	N	Y	Y	Y	Y
WYOMING									
McGee	–	–	–	–	+	N	N	N	N
Simpson	Y	Y	Y	Y	N	Y	Y	Y	Y

Appendix B

The Senate and U.S. Involvement in Southeast Asia, 1970–1974

1. **HR 15628. Foreign Military Sales Act.** Byrd (West Virginia) amendment stating that provisions limiting U.S. military involvement in Cambodia would not preclude the President from taking such actions as might be necessary to protect U.S. forces in South Vietnam. Rejected 47–52 (R 29–13, D 18–39). June 11, 1970.

2. **HR 15628. Foreign Military Sales Act.** Cooper-Church amendment barring funds for U.S. military operations in Cambodia after July 1, 1970, unless specifically authorized by Congress, including the retention of U.S. combat forces, advisers, and air activities in direct support of Cambodian forces. Adopted 58–37 (R 16–26, D 42–11). June 30, 1970.

3. **HR 17123. Military Procurement Authorization.** McGovern-Hatfield amendment limiting to 280,000 the maximum number of U.S. troops in Vietnam after April 30, 1971, and providing for complete withdrawal of troops by December 31, 1971, but authorizing the president to delay the withdrawal for a period of up to 60 days if he found the withdrawal would subject U.S. troops to clear and present danger. Rejected 39–55 (R 7–34, D 32–21). September 1, 1970.

4. **HR 17123. Military Procurement Authorization.** Proxmire amendment barring use of funds to send draftees to Vietnam unless they volunteered for such duty. Rejected 22–68 (R 3–35, D 19–33). September 1, 1970.

5. **HR 6531. Military Draft.** Chiles amendment to McGovern-Hatfield amendment cutting off funds for support of U.S. military activities in Indochina as of June 1, 1972, if all American POWs had been released by 60 days before the cutoff date. Rejected 44–52. (R 10–33, D 34–19). June 16, 1971.

6. **HR 17123. Military Procurement Authorization.** McGovern-Hatfield amendment cutting off funds for U.S. military activities in Indochina

as of December 31, 1971, with a 60-day extension of that deadline if American POWs had not been released by that date. Rejected 42–55 (R 8–36, D 34–19). June 16, 1971.

7. **HR 6531. Military Draft.** Mansfield substitute amendment declaring it U.S. policy to terminate at earliest practicable date all U.S. military activities in Indochina and providing for the phased withdrawal of all troops and the accompanying phased release of American POWs not later than nine months of enactment, subject to the release of all POWs. Adopted 57–42. (R 12–32, D 45–10). June 22, 1971.

8. **S 3390. Foreign Military Aid Authorizations.** Cooper amendment forbidding use of funds for U.S. participation in the Indochina war except for withdrawal of the remaining troops from South Vietnam, Laos, and Cambodia four months after enactment, contingent only on the release of all American POWs. Adopted 50–45 (R 11–33, D 39–12). July 24, 1972.

9. **HR 15495. Defense Procurement Authorization.** Brooke amendment requiring cutoff of funds for support of U.S. air, naval, and grounds troops in Vietnam, Laos, and Cambodia within four months of enactment of bill, pending the release of U.S. POWs. Adopted 49–47 (R 11–33, D 38–14). August 2, 1972.

10. **HR 7447. Second Supplemental Appropriations, Fiscal 1973.** Eagleton amendment to prohibit any funds in the bill and any funds previously appropriated by Congress from being used to support combat activities in or over Cambodia and Laos. Adopted 63–19 (R 20–16, D 43–3). May 31, 1973.

11. **S 1443. Foreign Military Aid, Fiscal 1974.** Tower amendment to strike a section placing a $150 million ceiling on military grant assistance to Cambodia. Rejected 33–59 (R 27–14, D 6–45). June 26, 1973.

12. **HR 9286. Defense Procurement.** Fulbright amendment to delete the provision of the bill authorizing funds for military assistance for South Vietnam and Laos. Rejected 43–51 (R 9–31, D 34–20). September 27, 1973.

13. **S 2999. Fiscal 1974 Defense Supplemental Authorization.** Kennedy amendment to bar use of funds authorized by S 2999, or funds appropriated for the Defense Department by any other act which remain unobligated on the date of that bill's enactment, from being spent in, for, or on behalf of any country in Southeast Asia. Adopted 43–38 (R 11–25, D 32–13). May 6, 1974.

Vote Key

Democrats in solid
Republicans in italics
Y   – yes
N   – no
(+) – paired for
(−) – paired against
ay – announced yes
an – announced no
(?) – did not vote or otherwise make position known

	1	2	3	4	5	6	7	8	9	10	11	12	13
ALABAMA													
Allen	Y	N	N	N	N	N	N	N	?	an	Y	N	N
Sparkman	Y	N	N	N	N	N	N	N	N	−	Y	N	an
ALASKA													
Gravel	N	Y	Y	Y	Y	Y	Y	Y	Y	Y	an	Y	ay
Stevens	Y	Y	N	N	Y	N	Y	Y	Y	Y	Y	N	N
ARIZONA													
Fannin	Y	N	N	N	N	N	N	N	N	N	Y	N	?
Goldwater	Y	N	N	N	N	N	N	N	N	−	Y	N	N
ARKANSAS													
Fulbright	N	Y	Y	Y	+	+	Y	Y	Y	Y	N	Y	?
McClellan	Y	N	N	N	N	N	Y	N	N	Y	N	N	N
CALIFORNIA													
Cranston	N	Y	Y	Y	Y	Y	Y	Y	Y	Y	N	Y	Y
Murphy	Y	N	N	N	(defeated 1970)								
Tunney	(elected 1970)			Y	Y	Y	Y	Y	Y	N	Y	Y
COLORADO													
Haskell	(elected 1972)									ay	N	Y	Y
Allott	Y	N	N	N	N	N	N	N	N	(defeated 1972)			
Dominick	Y	N	N	N	N	N	N	N	N	ay	Y	N	N
CONNECTICUT													
Dodd	Y	an	N	N	(defeated 1970)								
Ribicoff	N	Y	Y	Y	Y	Y	Y	Y	Y	Y	N	Y	Y
Weicker	(elected 1970)			N	N	N	N	N	+	N	N	Y
DELAWARE													
Biden	(elected 1972)									Y	?	Y	Y
Boggs	Y	N	N	N	N	N	N	N	N	(defeated 1972)			
Williams	Y	N	N	N	(retired 1970)								
Roth	(elected 1970)			N	N	N	N	N	N	N	N	N

	1	2	3	4	5	6	7	8	9	10	11	12	13
FLORIDA													
Holland	Y	N	N	N	(retired in 1970)								
Chiles	(elected 1970)				Y	Y	Y	Y	Y	Y	N	N	?
Gurney	Y	N	N	N	N	N	N	N	N	Y	Y	N	N
GEORGIA													
Russell	Y	an	N	?	(died 1971)								
Gambrell					N	N	Y	ay	ay	(defeated 1972)			
Nunn	(elected 1972)									Y	N	N	N
Talmadge	Y	N	N	N	N	N	Y	Y	N	+	N	N	N
HAWAII													
Inouye	N	Y	Y	Y	Y	Y	Y	Y	Y	Y	N	Y	Y
Fong	Y	N	N	N	N	N	N	N	N	ay	Y	N	N
IDAHO													
Church	N	Y	Y	Y	Y	Y	Y	Y	Y	ay	N	Y	ay
Jordan	Y	N	N	N	N	Y	Y	N	N	(retired 1972)			
McClure	(elected 1972)									Y	N	N	N
ILLINOIS													
Stevenson	(elected 1970)				Y	Y	Y	Y	Y	Y	N	Y	Y
Percy	N	Y	N	Y	Y	Y	Y	Y	Y	Y	N	Y	Y
Smith	Y	Y	N	N	(defeated 1970)								
INDIANA													
Bayh	N	Y	Y	N	Y	Y	Y	Y	Y	Y	N	Y	ay
Hartke	N	Y	Y	Y	Y	Y	Y	Y	Y	Y	N	Y	?
IOWA													
Clark	(elected 1972)									Y	an	ay	Y
Hughes	N	Y	Y	Y	Y	Y	Y	Y	Y	Y	N	Y	Y
Miller	Y	N	N	N	N	N	N	N	N	(defeated 1972)			
KANSAS													
Dole	Y	Y	N	N	N	N	N	N	N	N	Y	N	N
Pearson	Y	Y	N	N	N	N	Y	Y	Y	Y	N	an	Y
KENTUCKY													
Huddleston	(elected 1972)									Y	N	Y	Y
Cook	Y	N	N	N	N	N	N	Y	Y	Y	N	N	Y
Cooper	N	Y	N	N	N	N	N	N	N	(retired 1972)			
LOUISIANA													
Ellender	Y	N	N	N	N	N	N	?	(died 1972)				
Johnston	(elected 1972)									Y	Y	N	N
Long	Y	–	–	N	N	N	N	N	N	N	N	?	?

	1	2	3	4	5	6	7	8	9	10	11	12	13
MAINE													
Hathaway	(elected 1972)									Y	N	Y	ay
Muskie	N	Y	Y	N	Y	Y	Y	Y	Y	?	N	Y	Y
Smith	N	N	N	N	N	N	N	N	N	(defeated 1972)			
MARYLAND													
Tydings	N	Y	Y	an	(defeated 1970)								
Beall	(elected 1970)				N	N	N	N	N	N	Y	N	N
Mathias	N	Y	Y	N	Y	Y	Y	Y	Y	Y	an	Y	Y
MASSACHUSETTS													
Kennedy	N	Y	Y	N	Y	Y	Y	Y	Y	Y	N	Y	Y
Brooke	N	Y	Y	N	Y	Y	Y	Y	Y	Y	N	Y	Y
MICHIGAN													
Hart	N	Y	Y	Y	Y	Y	Y	Y	Y	Y	an	Y	Y
Griffin	Y	N	N	N	N	N	N	N	N	N	Y	N	N
MINNESOTA													
McCarthy	N	Y	Y	Y	(retired 1970)								
Humphrey	(elected 1970)				Y	Y	Y	Y	Y	Y	N	Y	Y
Mondale	N	Y	Y	Y	Y	Y	Y	Y	Y	Y	N	?	Y
MISSISSIPPI													
Eastland	Y	N	N	N	N	N	N	N	N	N	N	N	N
Stennis	Y	N	N	N	N	N	N	N	N	?	?	N	N
MISSOURI													
Eagleton	N	Y	Y	N	Y	Y	Y	Y	Y	Y	N	Y	Y
Symington	N	Y	Y	N	Y	Y	Y	Y	Y	Y	N	Y	Y
MONTANA													
Mansfield	N	Y	Y	Y	Y	Y	Y	Y	Y	Y	N	Y	Y
Metcalf	N	Y	Y	N	Y	Y	Y	Y	Y	Y	N	Y	?
NEBRASKA													
Curtis	Y	N	N	N	N	N	N	N	N	N	Y	N	N
Hruska	Y	N	N	N	N	N	N	N	N	N	Y	N	N
NEVADA													
Bible	Y	Y	N	N	N	N	Y	Y	Y	ay	N	N	Y
Cannon	Y	Y	an	an	N	N	Y	Y	N	ay	N	N	N
NEW HAMPSHIRE													
McIntyre	N	Y	Y	N	Y	Y	Y	N	N	Y	N	N	N
Cotton	Y	N	N	N	N	N	N	N	N	ay	Y	N	N
NEW JERSEY													
Williams	N	Y	Y	N	Y	Y	Y	Y	Y	Y	?	Y	Y
Case	N	Y	Y	N	Y	Y	Y	Y	Y	Y	N	Y	Y

	1	2	3	4	5	6	7	8	9	10	11	12	13
NEW MEXICO													
Anderson	N	Y	?	?	Y	Y	Y	Y	Y	(retired 1972)			
Montoya	N	Y	Y	N	Y	Y	Y	Y	Y	Y	N	Y	Y
Domenici	(elected 1972)									Y	Y	N	N
NEW YORK													
Goodell	N	Y	Y	Y	(defeated 1970)								
Buckley	(elected 1970)			N	N	N	N	N	N	Y	N	N
Javits	N	Y	Y	N	Y	Y	Y	Y	Y	Y	N	an	Y
NORTH CAROLINA													
Ervin	Y	N	N	N	N	N	N	N	N	ay	Y	N	an
Jordan	N	Y	N	N	Y	Y	Y	?	N	(defeated 1972)			
Helms	(elected 1972)									N	Y	N	N
NORTH DAKOTA													
Burdick	N	Y	Y	N	Y	Y	Y	Y	Y	Y	N	Y	Y
Young	Y	N	N	N	Y	Y	Y	N	N	Y	Y	Y	N
OHIO													
Young	N	Y	Y	Y	(retired 1970)								
Saxbe	N	Y	N	N	N	N	N	N	N	Y	Y	Y	
Taft	(elected 1970)		an	N	N	N	N	N	Y	?	an
OKLAHOMA													
Harris	N	Y	Y	Y	Y	Y	Y	Y	Y	(retired 1972)			
Bartlett	(elected 1972)									Y	Y	N	N
Bellmon	Y	N	N	N	N	N	N	N	N	Y	Y	N	N
OREGON													
Hatfield	N	Y	Y	Y	Y	Y	Y	Y	Y	Y	N	Y	Y
Packwood	N	Y	an	?	Y	N	N	N	N	Y	Y	N	?
PENNSYLVANIA													
Schweiker	N	Y	Y	N	Y	Y	Y	Y	Y	Y	N	Y	Y
Scott	W	N	N	N	N	N	N	N	N	N	Y	N	an
RHODE ISLAND													
Pastore	N	Y	Y	Y	Y	Y	Y	Y	Y	Y	N	Y	Y
Pell	N	Y	Y	N	Y	Y	Y	Y	Y	Y	N	Y	Y
SOUTH CAROLINA													
Hollings	Y	Y	N	N	N	N	Y	Y	Y	Y	N	N	N
Thurmond	Y	N	N	N	N	N	N	N	N	N	Y	N	N
SOUTH DAKOTA													
Abourezk	(elected 1972)									Y	N	Y	Y
McGovern	N	Y	Y	Y	Y	Y	Y	ay	Y	Y	N	Y	Y
Mundt	ay	an	an	an	an	an	an	?	?	(retired 1972)			

	1	2	3	4	5	6	7	8	9	10	11	12	13
TENNESSEE													
Gore	N	Y	N	N	(defeated 1970)								
Baker	Y	N	N	N	N	N	N	N	N	?	Y	N	N
Brock	(elected 1970)				N	N	N	N	N	N	Y	N	N
TEXAS													
Yarborough	N	Y	Y	Y	(defeated 1970)								
Bentsen	(elected 1970)				N	N	Y	Y	Y	Y	N	N	?
Tower	Y	N	N	N	N	N	N	N	N	N	Y	N	N
UTAH													
Moss	N	Y	+	an	Y	Y	Y	Y	Y	Y	N	Y	Y
Bennett	?	N	N	N	N	N	N	N	N	an	ay	N	an
VERMONT													
Aiken	N	Y	N	N	N	N	Y	N	N	Y	N	Y	N
Prouty	Y	N	N	N	N	N	N	(died 1971)					
Stafford	(appointed 1971)							Y	Y	Y	N	N	Y
VIRGINIA													
Byrd, Jr.	Y	N	N	N	N	N	N	N	N	Y	N	N	N
Spong	N	Y	N	N	−	−	Y	Y	Y	(defeated 1972)			
Scott	(elected 1972)									N	N	N	N
WASHINGTON													
Jackson	N	Y	N	N	N	N	N	N	N	N	Y	N	N
Magnuson	N	Y	Y	N	Y	Y	Y	Y	Y	Y	N	N	Y
WEST VIRGINIA													
Byrd	Y	Y	N	N	N	N	Y	N	N	Y	N	Y	Y
Randolph	N	Y	N	N	N	N	Y	N	N	Y	N	N	Y
WISCONSIN													
Nelson	N	+	Y	Y	Y	Y	Y	Y	Y	Y	N	Y	Y
Proxmire	N	Y	Y	Y	Y	Y	Y	Y	Y	Y	N	Y	Y
WYOMING													
McGee	Y	N	N	N	N	N	N	N	N	?	Y	N	N
Hansen	Y	N	N	N	N	N	N	N	N	N	Y	N	an

Appendix C

The Senate of the New Internationalists, 1973–1976

1. **S 1443. Foreign Military Aid, Fiscal 1974.** Hathaway amendment to require, at least 30 days prior to the approval or issuance of an export license for certain commercial arms sales, publication in the *Federal Register* of the items to be exported. Rejected 41–44 (R 6–31, D 35–13). June 25, 1973.

2. **S 1443. Foreign Military Aid, Fiscal 1974.** Pell amendment to provide for military assistance or sales to Greece only after the president had conducted a comprehensive review and has reported to Congress that Greece is complying with its political and military obligations under NATO. Adopted 46–41 (R 4–34, D 42–7). June 25, 1973.

3. **S 1443. Foreign Military Aid, Fiscal 1974.** Nelson amendment to require the president to report to Congress any proposed arms sale exceeding $25 million to a country prior to undertaking the transaction; and to provide for a procedure by which either the House or Senate could disapprove the transaction within 30 days. Adopted 44–43 (R 9–29, D 35–14). June 25, 1973.

4. **HR 9286 Defense Procurement.** Hughes amendment to require annual congressional authorization of troop levels by major geographical areas overseas during peacetime. Rejected 22–62 (R 2–30, D 20–32). September 21, 1973.

5. **HR 9286 Defense Procurement.** McIntyre amendment to reduce by $885 million the authorization for development and procurement of the Trident submarine. Rejected 47–49 (R 10–30, D 37–19). September 27, 1963.

6. **S 2335. Foreign Economic Aid.** Abourezk amendment to bar the use of any funds to support an internal security force or programs of domestic surveillance of any foreign government. Rejected 44–51 (R 8–33, D 36–18). October 1, 1973.

7. **S 2335. Foreign Economic Aid.** Abourezk amendment to bar foreign aid to any country which the president determines to be interning

or imprisoning its citizens for political purposes; and to require the president to certify annually to Congress that recipient countries are not holding political prisoners. Rejected 23–67 (R 0–40, D 23–27). October 1, 1973.

8. **S 3000. Defense Procurement Authorization.** Proxmire amendment to require the CIA to submit a public report on or before March 1 of each year disclosing the overall amount of funds requested in the budget for U.S. intelligence activities for the next succeeding fiscal year. Rejected 33–55 (R 9–31, D 24–24). June 4, 1974.

9. **S 3000. Defense Procurement Authorization.** McIntyre amendment to halt the funding of counterforce research until the President reported that the SALT talks had failed to achieve a controls agreement for MIRVs. Rejected 37–49 (R 6–31, D 31–18). June 10, 1974.

10. **HR 16243. Defense Appropriations, Fiscal 1975.** Eagleton amendment to limit defense spending for FY 1975 to $81 billion. Rejected 37–55 (R 7–32, D 30–23). August 21, 1974.

11. **HJ Res. 1131. Continuing Appropriations, Fiscal 1975.** Kennedy amendment to bar any funds in the bill from being used to provide military assistance to Chile. Adopted 47–41 (R 6–29, D 41–12). October 1, 1974.

12. **S 3394. Foreign Aid Authorization.** Abourezk amendment to make the bill's prohibition on training of foreign police applicable to all government agencies except for intelligence-gathering activities necessary to U.S. security. Rejected 24–56 (R 4–25, D 20–31). October 2, 1974.

13. **S 3394. Foreign Aid Authorization.** Abourezk amendment to prohibit activities abroad by U.S. agencies, including the CIA, that would be illegal under U.S. or foreign laws, except covert actions employed solely to gather intelligence. Rejected 17–68 (R 3–30, D 14–38). October 2, 1974.

14. **S 3394. Foreign Aid Authorization.** Humphrey motion to table, and thus kill, the Cranston amendment to terminate by the end of FY 1976 all military assistance to military dictatorships or authoritarian governments. Motion to table agreed to 56–25 (R 29–2, D 27–23). October 2, 1974.

15. **Defense Department Procurement Authorization.** McGovern amendment to eliminate $840.5 million in the bill for continued development of the B-1 bomber. Rejected 32–57 (R 6–31, D 26–26). June 5, 1975.

16. **S. Res. 160.** Adoption of the resolution to prohibit the Defense Department from constructing naval and air support facilities on Diego Garcia. Rejected 43–53 (R 4–32, D 39–21). July 28, 1975.

17. **S 2230. Aid to Turkey.** Passage of the bill to provide a partial lifting of the embargo on arms shipments to Turkey. Passed 47–46 (R 27–9, D 20–37). July 31, 1975.

18. **HR 9861. Defense Department Appropriations, Fiscal 1976.** Eagleton amendment to provide for an overall reduction of $500 million. Rejected 38–55 (R 6–31, D 32–24). November 18, 1975.
19. **HR 9861. Defense Department Appropriations, Fiscal 1976.** Tunney amendment to eliminate all funds in the bill for the covert operation in Angola. Accepted 54–22 (R 16–15, D 38–7). December 19, 1975.
20. **HR 12438 Defense Department Authorization.** Culver amendment to bar obligation before February 1, 1977 of funds authorized in the bill for production of the B-1 bomber. Adopted 44–37 (R 7–22, D 37–15). May 20, 1976.

Vote Key
Democrats in solid
Republicans in italics
Y – yes
N – no
(+) – paired for
(−) – paired against
ay – announced yes
an – announced no
(?) – did not vote or otherwise make position known

	1	2	3	4	5	6	7	8	9	10	11	12	13	14	15	16	17	18	19	20
ALABAMA																				
Allen	N	N	N	N	N	N	N	N	N	N	Y	N	N	Y	?	N	N	N	N	N
Sparkman	an	ay	ay	N	N	N	N	an	ay	?	?	?	?	Y	−	N	Y	N	N	?
ALASKA																				
Gravel	ay	ay	ay	Y	Y	Y	Y	Y	Y	ay	ay	ay	?	?	Y	Y	N	Y	Y	N
Stevens	N	N	Y	N	N	N	N	N	N	N	N	N	N	Y	N	N	Y	N	Y	an
ARIZONA																				
Fannin	N	N	N	N	N	N	N	N	?	N	N	N	N	Y	N	N	Y	N	?	N
Goldwater	?	N	N	?	N	N	N	N	N	N	N	N	N	?	N	?	ay	N	an	N
ARKANSAS																				
Bumpers	(elected 1974)														Y	Y	Y	N	Y	Y
Fulbright	Y	Y	Y	N	Y	?	?	?	Y	Y	Y	?	?	?	(defeated 1974)			N	N	N
McClellan	Y	Y	N	N	N	N	N	N	N	N	N	N	N	Y	N	N	N	N	N	N
CALIFORNIA																				
Cranston	Y	Y	Y	Y	Y	Y	Y	?	Y	Y	Y	Y	N	N	N	Y	N	Y	Y	N
Tunney	Y	Y	Y	Y	Y	Y	Y	?	Y	Y	Y	Y	?	?	N	N	N	Y	Y	−

303

	1	2	3	4	5	6	7	8	9	10	11	12	13	14	15	16	17	18	19	20
COLORADO																				
Hart	(elected 1974)														Y	Y	N	Y	Y	Y
Haskell	ay	ay	ay	Y	Y	Y	Y	Y	Y	Y	Y	Y	N	N	Y	Y	Y	Y	Y	Y
Dominick	N	N	N	?	Y	N	N	N	N	N	?	?	?	?	(defeated 1974)					
CONNETCICUT																				
Ribicoff	Y	Y	Y	Y	N	Y	Y	Y	?	Y	Y	Y	Y	N	Y	Y	N	Y	Y	Y
Weicker	N	?	Y	Y	N	N	N	Y	N	N	Y	an	ay	?	N	N	N	Y	Y	N
DELAWARE																				
Biden	?	?	?	Y	Y	Y	Y	N	Y	Y	Y	N	Y	N	+	Y	N	Y	Y	Y
Roth	N	N	N	N	Y	Y	N	N	N	Y	N	N	N	Y	N	N	N	Y	Y	?
FLORIDA																				
Chiles	Y	Y	Y	N	Y	N	N	N	N	N	Y	N	N	Y	N	N	Y	N	?	N
Stone	(elected 1974)														N	N	N	N	ay	N
Gurney	N	N	N	N	N	N	N	N	N	N	N	N	N	Y	(defeated 1974)					
GEORGIA																				
Nunn	–	N	N	N	N	N	N	N	N	N	N	N	N	Y	N	N	Y	N	N	Y
Talmadge	N	N	N	N	N	N	N	N	N	N	N	N	N	Y	N	?	N	N	?	N
HAWAII																				
Inouye	Y	Y	Y	N	Y	N	N	ay	ay	N	an	N	N	N	N	Y	Y	N	Y	Y
Fong	N	N	N	N	N	N	N	N	N	N	N	an	N	Y	Y	N	Y	N	?	N
IDAHO																				
Church	Y	Y	Y	Y	Y	Y	Y	Y	ay	Y	Y	N	Y	N	N	Y	N	Y	ay	ay
McClure	N	?	?	N	N	N	N	N	N	N	?	N	N	Y	N	N	N	N	N	N

ILLINOIS																		
Stevenson	Y	Y	an	Y	Y	Y	Y	Y	Y	Y	N	N	Y	N	N	Y	?	Y
Percy	Y	N	N	Y	Y	N	Y	an	N	?	N	N	N	Y	N	N	N	?
INDIANA																		
Bayh	Y	Y	?	Y	Y	an	Y	ay	?	ay	ay	Y	ay	N	Y	Y	ay	Y
Hartke	Y	Y	Y	Y	?	Y	?	Y	N	N	N	N	Y	N	Y	Y	Y	Y
IOWA																		
Clark	+	ay	ay	Y	Y	Y	Y	Y	Y	Y	Y	N	Y	Y	Y	Y	Y	Y
Culver	(elected 1974)			Y	Y	Y	N	Y	Y	Y		Y	N	Y	Y	Y	Y	Y
Hughes	ay	ay	Y	Y	N	Y	Y	Y	Y	N	(retired 1974)							
KANSAS																		
Dole	N	N	N	N	N	N	Y	?	?	N	N	N	N	Y	N	?	N	N
Pearson	N	Y	an	an	N	N	N	ay	N	Y	Y	Y	Y	Y	Y	Y	Y	Y
KENTUCKY																		
Ford	(elected 1974)			N	Y	Y	N	Y	?	Y		N	Y	?	Y	Y	Y	Y
Huddleston	Y	Y	N	Y	?	Y	N	N	Y	+	N	Y	Y	N	Y	Y	Y	Y
Cook	N	N	N	Y	Y	N	?	?	?	(defeated 1974)								
LOUISIANA																		
Johnston	N	Y	N	N	N	N	N	N	Y	N	Y	N	Y	N	Y	N	?	?
Long	N	N	N	N	N	N	N	N	N	N	Y	Y	Y	N	Y	Y	?	N
MAINE																		
Hathaway	Y	Y	Y	Y	Y	Y	Y	N	Y	N	Y	Y	Y	Y	Y	Y	Y	Y
Muskie	Y	Y	Y	Y	?	Y	Y	Y	Y	?	N	Y	Y	Y	Y	Y	Y	Y

	1	2	3	4	5	6	7	8	9	10	11	12	13	14	15	16	17	18	19	20
MARYLAND																				
Beall	N	N	N	N	N	N	N	N	N	N	N	N	N	Y	N	N	N	N	N	N
Mathias	ay	ay	ay	N	Y	Y	N	Y	ay	Y	ay	Y	N	Y	Y	Y	Y	Y	?	Y
MASSACHUSETTS																				
Kennedy	Y	Y	Y	ay	Y	Y	N	?	Y	Y	Y	?	N	N	Y	Y	N	Y	Y	Y
Brooke	Y	Y	Y	N	Y	Y	N	N	Y	N	?	Y	Y	Y	Y	Y	N	N	Y	Y
MICHIGAN																				
Hart	Y	Y	Y	Y	Y	ay	Y	Y	Y	Y	Y	Y	N	N	Y	Y	Y	Y	Y	?
Griffin	N	N	N	N	N	N	N	N	N	N	N	N	N	Y	N	N	Y	N	N	N
MINNESOTA																				
Humphrey	Y	Y	Y	N	Y	Y	N	N	Y	Y	Y	N	N	N	Y	Y	N	Y	Y	Y
Mondale	Y	Y	Y	Y	Y	Y	N	Y	Y	Y	Y	N	Y	N	N	Y	N	?	Y	Y
MISSISSIPPI																				
Eastland	N	N	N	N	N	N	N	N	N	N	N	N	N	Y	N	?	?	N	?	N
Stennis	?	?	?	N	N	N	?	N	N	N	N	N	N	Y	N	N	Y	N	N	N
MISSOURI																				
Eagleton	N	Y	Y	N	N	Y	N	Y	Y	Y	Y	Y	N	N	?	Y	N	Y	?	Y
Symington	N	Y	Y	N	Y	Y	?	?	?	Y	Y	N	N	N	N	Y	Y	Y	Y	Y
MONTANA																				
Mansfield	Y	Y	Y	Y	Y	Y	Y	Y	Y	Y	Y	Y	Y	N	Y	Y	Y	Y	Y	Y
Metcalf	Y	Y	Y	Y	N	Y	Y	Y	?	Y	Y	N	Y	N	+	Y	Y	Y	Y	Y

NEBRASKA																	
Curtis	N	N	N	N	N	N	N	N	?	an	ay	N	N	Y	N	N
Hruska	N	N	an	N	N	N	N	N	N	N	Y	N	N	Y	N	N
NEVADA																	
Bible	Y	Y	N	Y	N	N	N	N	Y	N	Y	(retired 1974)				
Cannon	N	Y	N	Y	N	N	N	Y	N	N	N	?	N	N	?	N
Laxalt	(elected 1974)								N	N	?	N	N	N	?	N
NEW HAMPSHIRE																	
Durkin	(elected 1975)								Y	Y	Y	Y	Y	N	Y	Y
McIntyre	Y	Y	N	Y	N	N	N	N	N	Y	Y	N	–	Y	N	Y
Cotton	?	N	N	?	N	N	N	N	?	N	Y	(retired 1974)				
NEW JERSEY																	
Williams	?	?	N	Y	Y	Y	Y	Y	Y	Y	Y	Y	Y	N	Y	Y
Case	Y	N	Y	Y	N	Y	?	Y	N	Y	Y	N	Y	N	Y	Y
NEW MEXICO																	
Montoya	Y	N	N	N	Y	N	N	N	N	Y	Y	N	N	N	ay	?
Domenici	N	N	N	N	N	N	N	N	N	Y	N	N	N	Y	N	N
NEW YORK																	
Buckley	N	N	N	N	N	N	N	N	Y	?	N	N	?	N	N	an
Javits	N	Y	ay	+	N	Y	Y	Y	Y	Y	Y	Y	Y	N	Y	Y

	1	2	3	4	5	6	7	8	9	10	11	12	13	14	15	16	17	18	19	20
NORTH CAROLINA																				
Ervin	N	N	N	N	N	ay	ay	N	N	N	N	N	N	Y	(retired 1974)					
Morgan	(elected 1974)														N	N	N	an	N	N
Helms	an	an	N	N	N	N	N	N	N	N	N	N	N	Y	N	Y	an	N	Y	N
NORTH DAKOTA																				
Burdick	Y	Y	Y	N	Y	Y	Y	N	Y	Y	Y	Y	N	N	Y	Y	Y	Y	Y	Y
Young	N	N	N	N	N	N	N	N	N	N	N	N	N	Y	N	N	N	N	N	?
OHIO																				
Glenn	(elected 1974)														N	N	?	Y	Y	N
Metzenbaum	(appointed 1974)							Y	Y	Y	N	N	Y	N	(defeated 1974)					
Saxbe	N	N	?	?	Y	N	N	(resigned 1974)												
Taft	?	?	?	?	ay	N	N	N	N	N	N	N	N	?	N	N	N	N	Y	−
OKLAHOMA																				
Bartlett	N	N	N	N	N	N	N	N	N	N	N	N	N	Y	N	N	N	N	N	N
Bellmon	N	N	?	?	N	N	N	?	N	?	?	?	?	?	?	?	Y	N	N	N
OREGON																				
Hatfield	Y	Y	Y	ay	Y	Y	N	?	Y	Y	Y	Y	Y	N	Y	Y	Y	Y	Y	+
Packwood	Y	N	Y	N	Y	N	N	?	Y	Y	?	?	?	?	Y	N	Y	N	Y	Y
PENNSYLVANIA																				
Schweiker	Y	Y	Y	N	N	Y	N	Y	Y	Y	Y	Y	Y	N	?	N	Y	N	Y	Y
Scott	N	N	N	N	N	N	N	N	N	N	N	N	N	N	N	N	Y	N	N	N
RHODE ISLAND																				
Pastore	Y	Y	N	N	N	Y	Y	N	Y	N	Y	N	Y	Y	Y	N	N	N	ay	+
Pell	Y	Y	Y	N	N	Y	?	Y	Y	Y	Y	Y	N	Y	Y	Y	N	Y	Y	Y

SOUTH CAROLINA																		
Hollings	N	?	N	N	N	N	N	Y	N	N	N	N	N	N	N	Y	N	N
Thurmond	N	N	N	N	N	N	N	?	N	N	N	Y	N	N	N	N	N	N
SOUTH DAKOTA																		
Abourezk	Y	Y	Y	Y	N	N	Y	Y	Y	N	Y	N	N	Y	Y	N	Y	Y
McGovern	Y	Y	Y	Y	N	N	Y	Y	Y	N	Y	N	N	Y	Y	Y	Y	Y
TENNESSEE																		
Baker	?	N	N	N	?	Y	N	N	Y	N	N	Y	Y	N	N	Y	N	?
Brock	N	N	an	N	N	N	N	N	N	N	N	Y	N	N	N	Y	?	?
TEXAS																		
Bentsen	N	Y	?	Y	N	?	Y	N	Y	N	N	Y	?	N	N	?	?	?
Tower	N	N	N	N	N	N	N	?	N	N	ay	N	N	Y	N	N	N	N
UTAH																		
Moss	Y	Y	ay	Y	Y	an	N	N	ay	?	an	Y	N	N	N	Y	Y	?
Bennett	N	N	N	N	N	N	N	N	?	?	?		(retired 1974)					
Garn	(elected 1974)								N	N	Y	?	Y	N			Y	N
VERMONT																		
Leahy	(elected 1974)								Y	Y	N	Y	N	Y			Y	Y
Aiken	N	N	N	N	N	N	N	N	N	N	?	Y	(retired 1974)					
Stafford	N	N	N	Y	N	N	Y	N	N	N	Y	Y	N	Y			Y	N

	1	2	3	4	5	6	7	8	9	10	11	12	13	14	15	16	17	18	19	20
VIRGINIA																				
Byrd, Jr.	N	N	Y	N	Y	N	N	N	N	N	N	N	N	N	N	N	N	N	N	N
Scott	N	N	N	N	N	N	N	N	N	Y	N	N	Y	Y	Y	Y	N	N	Y	N
WASHINGTON																				
Jackson	N	Y	N	N	N	N	N	N	N	Y	Y	N	N	Y	N	N	N	N	–	Y
Magnuson	Y	Y	Y	N	N	Y	N	Y	N	Y	Y	Y	Y	Y	Y	N	N	N	Y	Y
WEST VIRGINIA																				
Byrd	Y	Y	Y	N	Y	Y	N	N	N	?	Y	N	N	Y	N	Y	Y	N	Y	Y
Randolph	Y	Y	Y	N	N	Y	an	Y	Y	N	Y	Y	N	Y	Y	Y	Y	Y	Y	Y
WISCONSIN																				
Nelson	Y	Y	Y	Y	Y	Y	Y	Y	Y	N	Y	Y	Y	N	Y	Y	N	Y	Y	Y
Proxmire	Y	Y	Y	Y	Y	Y	Y	Y	N	N	Y	Y	Y	N	N	Y	Y	Y	Y	Y
WYOMING																				
McGee	N	Y	N	N	–	N	an	N	?	Y	N	?	an	ay	?	N	ay	N	+	?
Hansen	N	N	N	N	N	N	N	N	?	Y	N	N	N	Y	N	N	Y	N	N	N

Appendix D

The House and the End of the Cold War, 1980–1985

(Only the votes of members who served in each Congress from 1980 through 1985 are compiled in this table.)

1. **HR 6974. Defense Department Authorization.** Simon amendment to delete $500 million of the $1.6 billion in the bill for continued development of the MX Missile. Rejected 152–250 (R 29–120, D 123–130). May 15, 1980.

2. **HR 6942 Foreign Aid.** Weiss amendment to delete a provision in the bill to reduce the number of congressional committees receiving advance notice of covert operations by federal agencies, thereby restoring the Hughes-Ryan amendment. Rejected 50–325 (R 2–130, D 48–195). May 28, 1980.

3. **HR 6942. Foreign Aid.** Bauman amendment to delete $5.5 million in military aid for Nicaragua. Adopted 267–105. (R 132–2, D 135–103). May 28, 1980.

4. **HR 6942. Foreign Aid.** Wright substitute for the Bauman amendment, to allow the bill's $25 million in Econcomic Support Fund aid to Nicaragua, and to require the president to report to Congress every 90 days on the internal situation in Nicaragua, including the government's observance of human rights. Adopted 243–144 (R 31–116, D 212–28). June 5, 1980.

5. **HR 4995. Defense Department Appropriations, Fiscal 1982.** Addabbo amendment to delete $1.801 billion from Air Force procurement intended for the B-1 bomber. Rejected 142–263. (R 21-157, D 121–106). November 18, 1981.

6. **HR 4995. Defense Department Appropriations, Fiscal 1982.** Addabbo amendment to delete $1.913 in Air Force research and development funds for the MX missile and basing system. Rejected 139–264 (R 27–151, D 112–113). November 18, 1981.

7. **HR 6030. Defense Department Authorization, Fiscal 1983.** Downey amendment to delete $336.7 million for development of the Trident II missile and add $26 million for development of the Axe non-nuclear missile. Rejected 89–312 (R 5–178, D 84–134). July 29, 1982.

8. **HJ Res. 521. Nuclear Arms Freeze.** Broomfield-Stratton substitute to call for a nuclear freeze by the United States and the Soviet Union at equal and substantially reduced levels. Adopted 204–202 (R 151–27, D 53–175). August 5, 1982.

9. **HR 7335. Department of Defense Appropriations, Fiscal 1983.** Addabbo amendment to delete $988 million for procurement of five MX missiles. Adopted 245–176 (R 50–138, D 195–38). December 7, 1982.

10. **H Con. Res. 113. MX Missile Development.** Adoption of the concurrent resolution to permit use of funds appropriated in fiscal 1983 to develop a basing method for the MX missile and to conduct MX test flights. Adopted 239–186. (R 148–18, D 91–168).

11. **HR 2969. Department of Defense Authorization.** Bennett amendment to delete $2.6 billion for procurement of 27 MX missiles. Rejected 207–220 (R 18–147, D 189–73). July 20, 1983.

12. **HR 2969. Department of Defense Authorization.** Markey amendment to bar the deployment of U.S. combat troops to El Salvador, Nicaragua, Honduras, Guatemala, or Costa Rica unless authorized by joint resolution, intended to evacuate U.S. citizens, or to respond to a clear and present danger of military attack on the United States. Rejected 165–259 (R 9–155, D 156–104). July 26, 1983.

13. **HR 2760. Prohibition on Covert Action in Nicaragua.** Hyde amendment to the Wright amendment to delay the prohibition on U.S. covert action in Nicaragua until the House Armed Services, Foreign Affairs, and Intelligence committees had held hearings on the feasibility of section 802 of the bill, which authorized overt aid to countries in Central America for the interdiction of cross-border arms shipments. Rejected 194–229 (R 155–7, D 39–222). July 28, 1983.

14. **HR 2760. Prohibition on Covert Action in Nicaragua.** Passage of the bill to prohibit support by U.S. intelligence agencies for military or paramilitary operations in Nicaragua and to authorize $30 million in fiscal 1983 and $50 million in fiscal 1984 to help friendly countries in Central America for the interdiction of cross-border shipments of arms to anti-government forces in the region. Passed 228–195 (R 18–145, D 210–50). July 28, 1983.

15. **HJ Res. 247. Aid to Nicaragua.** Michel amendment in the nature of a substitute to provide $14 million for humanitarian assistance for the Nicaraguan anti-government rebels to be distributed by the Agency

for International Development. Rejected 213–215 (R 167–14, D 46–201). April 24, 1985.

16. **HR 2577. Supplemental Appropriations, Fiscal 1985.** McDade amendment to provide $27 million in humanitarian assistance to the Nicaraguan rebels, to be allocated in three equal installments, to coincide with the president's submission of reports every 90 days until March 31, 1986, by a U.S. agency other than the CIA or Department of Defense. Adopted 248–184 (R 175–7, D 73–177). June 12, 1985.

17. **HR 1872. Department of Defense Authorization, Fiscal 1986.** Bennett amendment to the Mavroules substitute for the Dickinson amendment, to deny all funds for production of MX missiles. Rejected 185–230 (R 21–154, D 164–76). June 18, 1985.

18. **HR 1555. Foreign Assistance Authorization, Fiscal 1986.** Stratton-Pepper amendment to repeal the so-called "Clark amendment to the International Security and Development Act of 1980, prohibiting assistance for military or paramilitary operations in Angola. Adopted 236–185 (R 176–6, D 60–179). July 10, 1985.

	1	2	3	4	5	6	7	8	9	10	11	12	13	14	15	16	17	18
ALABAMA																		
Dickinson	N	?	?	N	N	N	N	Y	N	Y	N	N	Y	N	Y	Y	N	Y
Nichols	N	N	Y	N	N	N	N	Y	N	Y	N	N	Y	N	Y	Y	N	Y
Bevill	N	N	Y	Y	N	N	N	Y	N	Y	N	N	N	N	Y	Y	N	Y
Flippo	N	N	Y	Y	N	N	N	Y	N	Y	N	N	N	N	Y	Y	?	?
Shelby	N	N	Y	N	N	N	N	Y	N	Y	N	N	Y	N	Y	Y	N	Y
ALASKA																		
Young	N	?	?	–	N	N	N	Y	N	Y	N	N	N	N	Y	Y	N	Y
ARIZONA																		
Udall	?	N	Y	Y	N	N	N	N	Y	N	Y	Y	Y	Y	N	N	Y	N
Stump	N	N	Y	N	N	N	N	Y	N	Y	N	N	Y	N	Y	Y	N	Y
Rudd	?	N	Y	N	N	N	N	N	Y	Y	N	N	Y	N	Y	Y	N	Y
ARKANSAS																		
Alexander	N	N	N	Y	N	N	N	N	?	Y	N	Y	N	Y	N	N	N	N
Hammerschmidt	N	N	Y	N	N	N	N	Y	Y	Y	N	Y	N	Y	Y	Y	N	Y
Anthony	N	N	Y	Y	N	N	?	N	Y	N	Y	N	N	Y	N	N	Y	Y

CALIFORNIA

Matsui	Y	N	N	Y	N	N	Y	N	Y	Y	N	N	Y	N	Y	Y	N	N	N	Y	N	N
Fazio	N	N	N	Y	N	N	Y	N	N	Y	N	N	Y	N	N	Y	N	Y	N	Y	N	N
Miller	Y	N	Y	Y	N	Y	Y	N	Y	Y	N	N	Y	N	Y	Y	N	Y	N	Y	Y	N
Dellums	Y	N	Y	Y	Y	Y	Y	N	Y	Y	N	N	Y	N	Y	Y	N	Y	N	Y	Y	N
Stark	Y	N	Y	Y	Y	Y	Y	N	Y	Y	N	N	Y	N	Y	Y	N	Y	N	Y	Y	?
Edwards	Y	N	Y	Y	Y	Y	Y	N	Y	Y	N	N	Y	N	Y	Y	N	Y	N	Y	Y	N
Mineta	Y	N	Y	Y	N	Y	Y	N	Y	Y	N	N	Y	N	Y	Y	N	Y	N	Y	Y	N
Shumway	N	N	N	N	N	N	N	Y	N	N	Y	Y	Y	N	N	N	Y	N	Y	N	N	Y
Coelho	Y	N	Y	Y	N	Y	Y	N	Y	Y	N	N	Y	N	Y	Y	N	Y	N	Y	Y	N
Panetta	Y	N	Y	Y	N	Y	Y	N	Y	Y	N	N	Y	N	Y	Y	N	Y	N	Y	Y	N
Pashayan	N	N	N	N	N	N	N	Y	N	N	Y	Y	Y	N	N	N	Y	N	Y	N	N	Y
Lagomarsino	N	N	N	Y	N	N	Y	Y	N	N	Y	Y	Y	N	N	Y	Y	N	Y	N	N	Y
Moorhead	N	N	N	Y	N	N	Y	Y	N	N	Y	Y	Y	N	N	N	Y	N	Y	N	N	Y
Beilenson	Y	N	N	Y	?	N	Y	N	Y	Y	N	N	Y	N	N	Y	N	Y	N	Y	Y	?
Waxman	Y	Y	Y	Y	Y	Y	Y	N	Y	Y	N	N	Y	N	Y	Y	N	Y	N	Y	Y	N
Roybal	Y	Y	Y	Y	Y	Y	Y	N	Y	Y	N	N	Y	N	Y	Y	N	Y	N	Y	Y	N
Dixon	Y	Y	Y	+	+	Y	Y	N	Y	Y	N	N	Y	N	Y	Y	N	Y	N	Y	Y	N
Hawkins	Y	?	N	?	?	?	Y	N	?	Y	N	N	Y	N	?	Y	N	Y	N	Y	Y	N
Brown	Y	N	N	Y	?	N	Y	N	Y	Y	N	N	Y	N	Y	Y	N	Y	N	Y	N	?

315

	1	2	3	4	5	6	7	8	9	10	11	12	13	14	15	16	17	18
COLORADO																		
Schroeder	Y	Y	Y	Y	Y	Y	Y	N	Y	N	Y	Y	N	Y	N	N	Y	N
Wirth	Y	N	N	Y	Y	N	Y	N	Y	N	Y	Y	N	Y	N	N	Y	N
Kramer	N	N	Y	N	N	N	N	Y	N	Y	N	N	Y	N	Y	Y	N	Y
CONNECTICUT																		
McKinney	Y	?	?	?	Y	Y	N	N	Y	N	Y	Y	Y	Y	N	Y	Y	N
FLORIDA																		
Hutto	N	N	Y	N	N	N	N	Y	N	Y	N	N	Y	N	Y	Y	N	Y
Fuqua	N	N	Y	N	N	N	N	?	Y	Y	N	N	N	N	Y	Y	N	Y
Bennett	N	N	Y	Y	N	N	N	Y	Y	N	Y	N	N	Y	Y	Y	Y	N
Chappell	N	N	Y	N	N	N	N	Y	N	Y	N	N	Y	N	Y	Y	N	Y
Gibbons	N	?	Y	Y	N	N	N	N	Y	N	Y	Y	N	Y	Y	Y	Y	N
Nelson	N	N	Y	Y	N	N	N	Y	N	Y	N	N	N	N	Y	Y	N	+
Mica	N	N	Y	N	Y	N	N	N	Y	Y	Y	N	N	N	Y	Y	Y	Y
Lehman	Y	N	N	Y	Y	Y	Y	N	Y	N	Y	Y	N	Y	N	N	N	N
Pepper	N	N	N	Y	–	–	–	N	Y	Y	N	Y	N	Y	Y	Y	–	Y
Fascell	N	N	Y	Y	N	N	N	N	Y	N	Y	N	N	N	N	Y	N	Y
GEORGIA																		
Fowler	Y	N	Y	Y	Y	N	?	N	N	N	Y	N	Y	Y	N	N	Y	Y
Gingrich	N	N	Y	N	N	N	N	Y	N	Y	N	N	Y	N	Y	Y	N	Y
Jenkins	N	N	Y	N	N	N	N	Y	Y	Y	N	N	N	N	Y	Y	Y	Y
Barnard	N	N	Y	N	N	N	N	Y	Y	Y	N	N	Y	N	Y	Y	N	Y

HAWAII																
Heftel	N	?	?	Y	Y	Y	N	Y	?	+	?	?	?	Y	Y	?
Akaka	N	–	–	Y	N	N	N	Y	N	Y	N	N	Y	N	N	N
ILLINOIS																
Russo	Y	N	Y	Y	Y	N	N	Y	N	Y	N	N	Y	N	Y	N
Hyde	N	N	N	N	N	Y	Y	N	Y	N	N	Y	Y	Y	Y	Y
Collins	Y	Y	Y	Y	Y	N	N	Y	N	Y	Y	N	Y	N	Y	N
Rostenkowski	N	N	N	Y	Y	N	N	Y	N	Y	N	Y	Y	N	Y	N
Yates	Y	?	Y	Y	?	N	N	Y	N	Y	Y	N	Y	N	Y	N
Porter	Y	N	N	Y	N	N	Y	Y	Y	N	N	Y	Y	Y	Y	Y
Annunzio	N	N	?	Y	N	N	N	Y	N	Y	N	N	Y	N	Y	N
Crane	N	N	N	N	N	Y	Y	Y	Y	N	N	Y	Y	Y	N	Y
Michel	N	N	N	N	N	Y	Y	N	Y	N	N	Y	Y	Y	N	Y
Price	N	Y	N	N	N	N	Y	N	Y	N	N	Y	Y	N	N	N
INDIANA																
Sharp	Y	N	Y	N	N	N	N	Y	N	Y	N	Y	Y	N	Y	Y
Hillis	N	N	N	N	N	Y	Y	Y	Y	N	N	Y	Y	Y	N	Y
Myers	N	N	N	N	N	Y	Y	Y	Y	N	N	Y	Y	Y	N	Y
Hamilton	N	N	N	Y	N	N	N	Y	N	Y	N	N	Y	N	Y	Y
Jacobs	Y	N	Y	Y	Y	N	N	Y	N	Y	N	Y	Y	N	Y	N

	1	2	3	4	5	6	7	8	9	10	11	12	13	14	15	16	17	18
IOWA																		
Leach	Y	?	?	Y	Y	Y	N	N	Y	N	Y	Y	N	Y	N	N	N	N
Tauke	N	N	Y	N	Y	N	N	N	Y	N	N	N	Y	N	Y	Y	Y	Y
Smith	Y	N	Y	Y	Y	N	N	N	Y	N	Y	Y	N	Y	N	N	N	N
Bedell	Y	N	Y	Y	?	?	Y	N	Y	N	Y	Y	N	Y	N	N	N	N
KANSAS																		
Glickman	Y	N	Y	Y	Y	N	N	N	Y	Y	Y	N	N	Y	N	N	N	Y
Whittaker	N	N	Y	N	N	N	N	Y	Y	Y	N	N	Y	N	Y	Y	N	Y
KENTUCKY																		
Hubbard	N	N	Y	Y	N	N	N	Y	Y	Y	N	N	Y	N	Y	Y	N	Y
Natcher	N	N	Y	N	N	N	N	N	Y	N	Y	N	N	Y	N	N	Y	Y
Mazzoli	Y	N	Y	Y	Y	Y	N	N	Y	Y	Y	N	N	Y	Y	Y	N	N
Snyder	N	N	Y	N	N	Y	N	Y	Y	Y	Y	N	N	N	Y	Y	N	Y
Hopkins	N	N	Y	N	N	N	N	Y	Y	Y	N	Y	Y	N	Y	N	Y	Y
Perkins	N	N	Y	N	N	Y	N	N	Y	N	Y	N	N	Y	N	N	N	N
LOUISIANA																		
Livingston	N	N	Y	N	N	N	N	Y	N	Y	N	N	Y	N	Y	Y	N	Y
Boggs	N	–	–	Y	N	N	N	N	Y	Y	N	Y	N	Y	N	N	Y	Y
Huckaby	N	N	Y	Y	N	N	N	Y	Y	Y	N	N	Y	N	Y	Y	N	Y
Moore	N	N	Y	N	N	N	N	Y	N	Y	N	N	Y	N	Y	Y	N	Y
Breaux	?	N	Y	Y	–	–	N	Y	N	Y	N	N	Y	N	Y	Y	N	Y
Long	N	N	N	N	N	N	N	?	Y	Y	Y	Y	N	Y	N	Y	Y	Y

MAINE														
Snowe	N	N	Y	N	N	N	Y	N	Y	N	N	Y	N	Y
MARYLAND														
Mikulski	Y	N	Y	N	Y	N	N	Y	N	N	Y	Y	Y	N
Holt	N	N	Y	Y	N	N	N	Y	Y	Y	N	Y	Y	N
Byron	N	N	Y	Y	N	N	Y	Y	N	N	N	Y	Y	Y
Mitchell	Y	Y	Y	N	Y	N	N	Y	N	N	Y	N	Y	N
Barnes	Y	N	Y	N	N	Y	N	N	N	N	N	Y	Y	N
MASSACHUSETTS														
Conte	?	N	Y	N	N	Y	N	Y	N	N	N	N	Y	N
Boland	Y	N	Y	Y	Y	Y	N	Y	N	N	N	Y	+	N
Early	Y	N	Y	Y	Y	Y	N	Y	?	N	N	Y	Y	N
Mavroules	Y	N	Y	Y	Y	Y	N	Y	N	N	N	Y	Y	N
Markey	Y	Y	Y	Y	Y	Y	N	Y	Y	Y	N	Y	Y	N
O'Neill							N							
Moakley	Y	N	Y	+	Y	Y	N	Y	N	N	N	Y	Y	N
Donnelly	Y	Y	Y	?	Y	Y	N	Y	Y	Y	N	Y	Y	N
Studds	Y	Y	Y	Y	Y	Y	N	Y	N	N	N	Y	Y	N

319

	1	2	3	4	5	6	7	8	9	10	11	12	13	14	15	16	17	18
MICHIGAN																		
Conyers	Y	Y	N	Y	Y	Y	Y	N	Y	N	?	?	N	Y	N	N	Y	N
Pursell	Y	?	?	Y	Y	Y	N	N	Y	Y	N	N	Y	N	Y	Y	N	Y
Wolpe	?	Y	N	Y	Y	Y	Y	N	Y	N	Y	Y	N	Y	N	N	Y	N
Kildee	Y	Y	N	Y	Y	Y	Y	N	Y	N	Y	Y	N	Y	N	N	Y	N
Traxler	N	Y	Y	Y	Y	Y	N	N	Y	N	Y	Y	N	Y	N	N	Y	Y
Vander Jagt	N	N	Y	N	N	N	N	Y	N	Y	?	N	Y	N	Y	Y	N	Y
Davis	N	N	Y	N	N	N	N	Y	N	N	N	N	Y	N	Y	Y	N	N
Bonior	Y	Y	N	Y	Y	N	+	N	Y	N	Y	Y	N	Y	N	N	Y	N
Ford	Y	N	N	Y	Y	Y	Y	N	Y	N	Y	N	N	Y	N	N	Y	N
Dingell	Y	N	Y	Y	Y	Y	N	N	Y	N	Y	N	N	Y	N	Y	N	N
Broomfield	N	N	Y	N	N	N	N	Y	N	Y	N	N	Y	N	Y	Y	N	Y
MINNESOTA																		
Frenzel	N	?	+	Y	N	N	N	Y	Y	Y	Y	N	Y	N	Y	Y	N	Y
Vento	Y	+	−	+	N	Y	Y	N	N	N	Y	Y	N	Y	N	N	Y	N
Sabo	Y	N	N	Y	Y	Y	Y	N	Y	N	Y	Y	N	Y	N	N	Y	N
Oberstar	Y	?	N	Y	Y	Y	Y	N	Y	N	Y	Y	N	Y	N	N	Y	N
MISSISSIPPI																		
Whitten	N	N	Y	N	N	N	N	?	Y	N	Y	N	N	Y	N	Y	Y	Y
Montgomery	N	N	Y	N	N	N	N	Y	N	N	N	N	Y	N	Y	Y	N	Y
Lott	N	N	Y	N	N	N	N	Y	N	Y	N	N	Y	N	Y	Y	N	Y

	1	2	3	4	5	6	7	8	9	10	11	12	13	14	15	16	17	18	19	20	21
MISSOURI																					
Clay	Y	Y	Y	N	?	N	N	N	Y	Y	N	Y	N	N	Y	?	N	Y	Y	Y	N
Young	Y	N	N	N	N	N	?	N	Y	N	Y	N	Y	N	Y	Y	N	N	Y	Y	N
Gephardt	Y	N	Y	Y	N	Y	Y	Y	N	Y	Y	N	Y	Y	N	Y	N	Y	N	N	N
Skelton	N	N	Y	N	N	N	Y	?	?	N	Y	Y	Y	Y	N	Y	Y	N	Y	N	Y
Coleman	?	N	Y	N	N	N	N	N	Y	Y	N	Y	N	Y	Y	Y	Y	Y	Y	N	Y
Taylor	N	N	Y	N	N	N	N	N	Y	Y	N	Y	N	Y	Y	Y	Y	Y	Y	N	Y
Volkmer	N	N	N	Y	N	Y	N	Y	Y	Y	Y	N	Y	N	Y	N	Y	N	Y	Y	Y
MONTANA																					
Williams	Y	N	Y	Y	Y	Y	Y	N	N	Y	Y	Y	N	Y	N	N	Y	N	Y	Y	N
Marlenee	N	N	Y	?	N	?	N	Y	Y	N	N	N	Y	N	Y	Y	Y	?	N	N	Y
NEBRASKA																					
Bereuter	N	N	Y	N	N	N	N	N	Y	N	Y	Y	N	Y	Y	N	Y	Y	Y	Y	Y
Smith	N	N	Y	Y	Y	Y	Y	Y	N	N	Y	Y	N	Y	Y	Y	Y	Y	N	Y	Y
NEW JERSEY																					
Florio	Y	N	Y	Y	?	N	N	N	Y	Y	N	Y	N	Y	Y	N	N	N	Y	N	N
Hughes	Y	N	Y	Y	Y	Y	N	N	Y	Y	N	Y	N	Y	Y	N	N	Y	Y	N	N
Howard	?	N	Y	Y	N	N	N	?	Y	Y	Y	Y	N	Y	Y	N	N	Y	Y	N	N
Roe	Y	N	Y	Y	N	N	N	N	Y	Y	Y	Y	N	Y	Y	N	N	Y	Y	Y	?
Rodino	?	–	–	Y	Y	Y	Y	N	Y	+	N	Y	Y	N	N	N	Y	–	Y	N	N
Courter	N	N	+	N	N	N	N	Y	N	Y	N	Y	Y	Y	Y	Y	Y	Y	N	Y	Y
NEW MEXICO																					
Lujan	Y	?	+	N	N	N	+	Y	Y	N	N	N	Y	N	Y	Y	Y	Y	Y	N	Y

	1	2	3	4	5	6	7	8	9	10	11	12	13	14	15	16	17	18
NEW YORK																		
Carney	N	?	?	N	N	N	N	Y	N	Y	N	N	Y	N	Y	Y	N	Y
Downey	Y	Y	N	Y	Y	Y	Y	N	Y	N	Y	Y	N	Y	N	N	Y	N
Lent	?	N	Y	N	N	N	N	Y	Y	Y	N	N	Y	N	Y	Y	N	Y
Addabbo	Y	N	N	Y	Y	Y	N	N	Y	N	Y	Y	–	+	N	N	+	N
Solarz	?	N	N	Y	Y	Y	Y	N	Y	N	Y	N	N	Y	N	N	Y	N
Green	Y	N	N	Y	Y	Y	N	N	Y	N	Y	N	N	Y	N	N	+	Y
Rangel	Y	Y	N	Y	Y	Y	Y	N	Y	N	Y	Y	N	Y	N	N	Y	N
Weiss	Y	Y	N	Y	Y	+	Y	N	Y	N	Y	Y	N	Y	N	N	Y	N
Garcia	?	+	–	Y	?	+	N	N	N	N	Y	Y	N	Y	N	Y	Y	N
Fish	N	N	Y	Y	N	N	N	Y	N	Y	N	N	Y	Y	N	Y	N	Y
Gilman	N	N	Y	N	N	N	N	Y	N	Y	N	N	Y	N	Y	Y	N	Y
Stratton	?	N	Y	N	N	N	N	Y	N	Y	N	N	Y	N	Y	Y	N	Y
Solomon	N	N	Y	?	N	N	N	Y	Y	Y	N	N	Y	N	Y	Y	–	Y
Horton	Y	N	Y	N	Y	Y	N	N	Y	Y	N	N	Y	Y	Y	Y	Y	N
Kemp	N	N	?	N	N	N	N	Y	N	Y	N	N	N	Y	Y	Y	N	N
LaFalce	Y	N	N	Y	Y	N	N	N	Y	N	Y	N	N	N	N	N	Y	N
Lundine	Y	N	?	Y	Y	N	Y	N	N	N	Y	Y	N	Y	Y	Y	Y	N
NORTH CAROLINA																		
Jones	N	N	Y	Y	?	?	N	Y	Y	Y	Y	N	N	Y	N	N	Y	N
Whitley	N	N	Y	Y	N	N	N	Y	N	Y	N	N	N	Y	N	Y	N	Y
Neal	N	N	Y	Y	N	N	N	N	Y	Y	N	N	N	Y	N	N	N	N
Rose	?	N	Y	?	N	N	N	Y	?	Y	N	Y	N	Y	N	N	N	?
Hefner	N	N	Y	Y	N	N	N	Y	Y	Y	N	N	Y	Y	N	Y	Y	?
Broyhill	N	N	Y	N	N	N	Y	Y	N	Y	N	N	Y	N	Y	Y	N	Y

State / Member																			
OHIO																			
Luken	N	N	Y	N	N	N	N	N	Y	N	N	N	N	Y	Y	N	N	N	N
Gradison	N	N	Y	N	Y	N	Y	N	Y	N	Y	N	Y	Y	Y	N	N	Y	Y
Hall	Y	N	N	N	N	N	Y	N	Y	N	N	Y	N	N	N	N	Y	Y	?
Latta	N	N	Y	N	Y	N	N	Y	N	N	Y	Y	Y	Y	N	Y	N	Y	Y
Miller	Y	N	N	N	N	N	Y	Y	N	Y	N	N	N	N	Y	N	Y	N	Y
Pease	Y	N	Y	N	N	N	Y	N	Y	Y	Y	Y	N	N	Y	Y	Y	Y	Y
Seiberling	Y	Y	Y	N	Y	N	Y	Y	Y	Y	N	Y	N	N	Y	N	Y	Y	N
Oakar	N	Y	Y	N	N	?	N	Y	Y	N	Y	Y	N	N	N	N	Y	N	N
Stokes	Y	Y	?	+	Y	Y	N	Y	Y	N	Y	Y	N	Y	Y	N	N	Y	N
OKLAHOMA																			
Jones	N	N	Y	N	N	N	N	?	N	N	N	N	Y	N	Y	N	Y	N	Y
Synar	Y	N	Y	Y	Y	–	Y	N	Y	N	Y	N	N	N	N	N	Y	N	N
Watkins	N	N	Y	N	N	N	N	Y	Y	N	N	N	N	Y	N	N	Y	N	Y
Edwards	N	N	Y	N	N	Y	N	Y	N	N	Y	N	N	Y	N	Y	N	N	Y
OREGON																			
AuCoin	Y	Y	Y	Y	Y	N	N	Y	Y	N	N	Y	N	N	Y	N	N	Y	N
Weaver	?	Y	Y	Y	Y	N	N	N	N	Y	N	Y	N	Y	Y	N	N	Y	N

	1	2	3	4	5	6	7	8	9	10	11	12	13	14	15	16	17	18
PENNSYLVANIA																		
Gray	Y	Y	N	Y	Y	Y	Y	N	Y	N	Y	Y	N	Y	N	N	Y	N
Yatron	Y	N	N	Y	N	N	N	N	Y	Y	N	Y	N	Y	N	N	N	N
Edgar	Y	N	N	?	Y	Y	Y	N	Y	N	Y	Y	N	Y	N	N	Y	N
Shuster	N	N	Y	–	N	N	N	Y	?	Y	N	N	Y	N	Y	Y	N	Y
McDade	N	?	?	Y	N	N	N	+	Y	Y	N	N	+	?	Y	Y	N	Y
Murtha	N	N	Y	Y	N	N	Y	Y	N	Y	N	N	N	N	Y	N	N	Y
Coughlin	N	?	?	Y	Y	N	N	N	N	Y	N	Y	Y	Y	Y	Y	Y	Y
Ritter	N	N	Y	N	N	N	N	Y	N	Y	N	N	N	N	Y	N	N	Y
Walker	N	N	Y	N	N	N	N	N	Y	Y	N	N	N	N	N	N	N	N
Walgren	Y	Y	Y	Y	Y	Y	Y	N	Y	N	Y	Y	Y	Y	Y	Y	Y	N
Goodling	Y	N	Y	Y	Y	Y	N	P	Y	N	Y	N	Y	N	Y	Y	Y	Y
Clingler	N	N	Y	N	N	N	N	Y	Y	Y	N	N	N	N	Y	Y	N	Y
RHODE ISLAND																		
St. Germain	Y	N	N	Y	Y	Y	N	N	Y	N	Y	Y	N	Y	N	N	Y	N
SOUTH CAROLINA																		
Spence	N	N	Y	N	N	N	N	N	N	Y	N	N	N	Y	Y	Y	N	Y
Derrick	N	?	?	Y	N	N	N	N	Y	Y	Y	N	Y	N	Y	Y	N	N
Campbell	N	N	Y	N	N	N	N	Y	N	N	N	N	Y	N	Y	Y	N	Y
SOUTH DAKOTA																		
Daschle	Y	?	?	Y	N	Y	N	N	Y	N	Y	Y	N	Y	N	N	Y	N

TENNESSEE																		
Quillen	N	N	Y	N	N	Y	N	Y	N	N	N	N	N	N	Y	Y	N	Y
Duncan	N	N	Y	N	N	Y	N	Y	N	N	N	N	N	N	Y	Y	N	Y
Jones	N	N	Y	N	N	N	Y	N	?	?	N	N	Y	?	Y	Y	N	N
Ford	Y	Y	N	Y	+	Y	+	−	Y	Y	Y	Y	N	Y	−	N	Y	N
TEXAS																		
Wilson	N	?	?	N	N	Y	N	Y	?	N	N	Y	Y	Y	?	N	N	Y
Archer	N	N	N	N	N	Y	N	Y	N	N	N	N	N	N	Y	N	N	Y
Brooks	Y	Y	N	Y	Y	N	Y	N	?	N	Y	Y	Y	Y	N	Y	N	N
Pickle	N	N	Y	N	N	Y	N	Y	N	N	N	N	N	N	Y	Y	N	Y
Leath	N	N	Y	N	N	Y	N	Y	N	N	N	N	N	N	Y	Y	N	Y
Wright	?	?	Y	N	N	Y	N	Y	N	N	N	N	N	Y	Y	N	N	?
de la Garza	N	?	Y	N	N	Y	N	Y	N	N	N	N	N	N	Y	Y	N	Y
Stenholm	N	N	Y	N	N	Y	N	Y	N	N	N	N	N	N	Y	Y	N	Y
Leland	Y	Y	N	+	Y	N	Y	N	Y	Y	Y	Y	Y	Y	N	N	Y	N
Gonzalez	N	N	Y	N	N	Y	N	Y	N	N	Y	Y	N	Y	N	N	Y	N
Loeffler	N	N	Y	N	N	Y	N	Y	N	N	N	N	N	N	Y	Y	−	Y
Frost	N	N	Y	N	Y	Y	N	N	Y	Y	Y	Y	N	Y	N	N	N	N
VERMONT																		
Jeffords	Y	N	Y	Y	Y	N	N	N	Y	Y	N	N	N	N	Y	N	+	N

325

	1	2	3	4	5	6	7	8	9	10	11	12	13	14	15	16	17	18
VIRGINIA																		
Whitehurst	N	N	Y	N	N	N	N	Y	N	Y	N	Y	Y	N	Y	Y	N	Y
Daniel	N	N	Y	N	N	N	N	Y	N	Y	N	Y	Y	N	Y	Y	N	Y
WASHINGTON																		
Swift	Y	N	Y	Y	N	Y	N	N	Y	N	Y	N	N	Y	N	N	Y	N
Bonker	Y	N	Y	Y	Y	Y	Y	N	Y	N	Y	Y	N	Y	N	N	Y	N
Foley	N	N	Y	Y	N	N	N	N	Y	Y	N	?	N	Y	N	N	N	N
Dicks	N	N	Y	Y	N	N	N	N	Y	Y	N	N	N	Y	N	N	N	N
Lowry	Y	N	Y	Y	Y	Y	Y	N	Y	N	Y	Y	N	Y	N	N	Y	N
WEST VIRGINIA																		
Rahall	Y	N	Y	Y	Y	Y	?	N	Y	N	Y	Y	N	N	N	N	N	N
WISCONSIN																		
Aspin	Y	N	N	Y	N	Y	?	N	Y	Y	N	N	Y	Y	N	Y	N	N
Kastenmeier	Y	Y	N	Y	Y	Y	Y	N	Y	N	Y	Y	Y	Y	Y	N	Y	N
Petri	N	N	Y	Y	Y	N	N	Y	Y	N	N	Y	N	N	Y	N	Y	Y
Obey	Y	N	N	Y	N	Y	Y	N	Y	N	Y	Y	Y	Y	N	N	Y	N
Roth	N	N	N	N	N	N	N	N	N	Y	N	N	Y	N	Y	Y	Y	Y
Sensenbrenner	N	Y	Y	N	N	Y	N	Y	Y	Y	N	Y	Y	N	Y	Y	Y	Y
WYOMING																		
Cheney	N	N	Y	N	N	N	N	N	N	Y	N	Y	Y	N	Y	Y	N	Y

326

Index